ASHKENAZ (?)   MAGOG (?)

Caspian Sea

RARAT

Garden of Eden (?)

ASSYRIA   MINNI (?)

Tigris River

River

Babylon   Chebar (?)

CHALDEA   ELAM

PERSIA

Persian Gulf

N

LANDS ASSOCIATED
WITH BABYLON
In Ezekiel's Day

"The Nations Shall Know THAT I AM JEHOVAH" —How?

"And the nations shall know that I am Jehovah."
—Ezekiel 36:23; 39:7, AS.

Dedicated
to the Sanctifying of
the Divine Name
Among God's "Men of Goodwill"
of All the Nations

Symbols of Scripture translations quoted from or cited herein:

AS – American Standard Version Bible, by the American Committee of Revision, of 1901 C.E.

AV – Authorized or King James Version Bible, of 1611 C.E.

Dy – Roman Catholic English translation of the Latin Vulgate, made at Douay and Rheims, as of 1610 C.E.

LXX– The Greek Septuagint Version of the inspired Hebrew Scriptures, of the first three centuries B.C.E., as translated into English

NEB– The New English Bible, by the Delegates of the Oxford University Press and the Syndics of the Cambridge University Press, 1961, 1970 (England)

Yg – Young's Literal Translation of the Holy Bible, by Robert Young, as of 1862 C.E.

Any Bible quotation or citation not followed by any special abbreviations is made from the *New World Translation of the Holy Scriptures* (*NW*) in its revised edition of 1971 C.E.

DATING: In dating events the abbreviation B.C.E. means "Before Our Common Era," and the abbreviation C.E. means "Of Our Common Era," thus designating the number of the year before or after the year 1 C.E.

CONTENTS

CHAPTER AND SUBJECT   PAGE

1 Nations Long Ago Had to Know Who He Is . . .   7
2 His Own People Had to Know Who He Is   21
3 God's Chariot Is on the Move!   35
4 Commissioned to Speak in the Divine Name . . .   54
5 Appointed as a Watchman to Christendom . . .   72
6 The Days of Christendom Are Numbered   92
7 Christendom Will Know—at Her End   114
8 Detestable Religious Things
      over Which to Sigh   142
9 Marking Foreheads of Those to Be Spared . . .   162
10 Christendom's Fiery Destruction
      from the Celestial Chariot   182
11 Disappointment in Store
      for Overconfident Ones   194
12 "Until He Comes Who Has the Legal Right" . . .   213
13 Christendom's Associates Turn upon Her! . . .   237
14 Hypocritical Religionists Stunned at the News . .   264
15 The Watchman Lives to Get the Report   278
16 A Shepherd-King for All Mankind   293
17 A "Garden of Eden" for the Sake of His Name . .   312
18 Resurrection to Unity in a "Garden of Eden" . . .   335
19 Defeat Awaits Attack by Nations under Gog . . .   349
20 Land of Magog No More to Threaten Mankind . .   368
21 Life in Security under Messiah's Reign   382
22 Human Happiness in Paradise
      under Divine Government   399

Subject Index   408

Chapter 1

Nations Long Ago Had to Know Who He Is

JUST as nations of long ago did not like him, the nations of today do not like him. Neither do they like his name. By not mentioning his name they seek to ignore his existence, to let him become a person unknown, to let his name fade from memory. Strangely, though, the nations have proved unable to blot his name out of human history. They have not kept his name from being heralded far and wide throughout the earth, in our twentieth century. Obviously the Bearer of that name must be greater than all the nations. His is the greatest name in all the universe. It is the oldest name on record. It is immortal! It adorns the greatest One in all heaven and earth. It is just as imperishable as its Bearer is. Nations of the past got to know it. Present-day nations, as political organizations, will likewise get to know that incomparable Name. Shortly they will perish, but not the Name! Before they perish they shall know the superiority of the One bearing that Name.

[2] In this regard history will have to repeat itself, but on a far grander scale. Recorded history of the past justifies us in expecting that name to be put in its rightful place among all who dwell on earth. The vindication of it as the name of the One who really lives, who is almighty and supreme, will strike the

---

1. What has been the attitude of the nations toward the greatest name in the universe, and what will they have to know about its Bearer?
2. What will vindication of that name mean, and to whom is this of highest concern now?

7

nations with awe. Even though unwillingly, they will have to recognize the One whose name has been unjustly reproached and downgraded among men. They will know that he is and that he has spoken and that what he has spoken never fails to occur. The significance of this to all nations is of the highest concern to every member of this present generation of mankind right now.

³ To us of today any event that occurred in the year 1513 before our Common Era occurred a long time ago. Nearly three thousand five hundred years ago! But to the Eternal One whose name must be vindicated such a time period is not calculated according to the earth's daily spinning on its axis and its yearly movement around the sun. Those three and a half millenniums are viewed as but three and a half of our days. And what is a mere half a week of time to Him? To Him it was just half a week ago that he confronted the first-class political power of the sixteenth century before our Common Era. So it was no mere poetic outburst when an inspired songwriter of that day said to Him: "A thousand years are in your eyes but as yesterday when it is past, and as a watch during the night."*

⁴ To Him it did not matter that that first world power had the latest military equipment in great quantity and could dominate the then inhabited earth. Its highly prized wisdom and its high degree of civilization made no difference to Him. The great number of its religious gods and goddesses did not overawe Him but showed how ignorant and misguided that highly civilized world power was in a religious way. What counted with Him then was that this world power had got into difficulty with him. How?

---

* Quoted from the words of the prophet Moses, in Psalm 90:4. See also 2 Peter 3:8.

3. To that Name Bearer, why is what happened in 1513 B.C.E. as if it happened just half a week ago?
4. What counted with Him as regards that first world power?

[5] Have we ever seen an inoffensive people being oppressed by a powerful, militarized, nationalistic political government in this twentieth century? Such a question turns our minds to a number of oppressed peoples and racial groups. So, then, we can appreciate the tyrannical oppression that had gone on for scores of years upon an innocent people in a land in which they were alien residents. According to the three great branches into which our human family is divided, these alien residents were of the Semitic branch and were dwelling in a Hamitic land. The oppression upon them finally became so extreme that it attempted what is called "genocide" nowadays, to bring about the disappearance of that particular family of Shemites that had now grown to the size of an outstanding people, a nation populous indeed but having no active part in the government of that Hamitic land.

[6] Seemingly it was a racial issue that troubled the Hamitic land, for that large body of alien residents of another race might even furnish a military threat to this first-rate world power. But if we study the situation more deeply, we can discern that there was an issue of importance even greater than that of the racial issue. It was a religious issue. The records of ancient history prove beyond denial by our irreligious scientifically educated modernists that religion played a dominant part in the life of the nations, even of the rulers. A remarkably different religion was identified with that alien people residing in that world-famous Hamitic land. That was why the hard core of that people refused to join in worshiping the many gods of the land. So the wiping out of this people of Shemitic stock would mean the wiping out of this religion. This was, according to the priests of the gods of the land, the more desirable thing.

---

5. In the matter of oppression, with what were innocent people of one branch of the human family threatened while residing as aliens in the land of another race?
6. Then, the troublesome issue was of what kind, and how so?

⁷ Just like with hundreds of millions of East Indians of this twentieth century, it seemed strange to those ancient worshipers of the many Hamitic gods that this alien people in their midst should worship but one God, who was believed to be the One Creator of all heaven and earth. But to those worshipers of many ancient gods and goddesses this One God of that alien resident people could not be a true, living, all-powerful God. Otherwise, why would he let them be oppressed as mere slaves for more than a hundred years? Why would he let their oppressors proceed with the nationalistic plan of wiping out his worshipers and his religion from the earth? Why had he not before now delivered his worshipers from their polytheistic oppressors and slave masters? Those were good questions. If he were the God that these oppressed people worshiped him as being, then he ought to answer those questions. He ought to make himself known to that Hamitic nation! By doing this, too, he could make himself known to all nations!

⁸ For that matter, what about making himself known to His own worshipers? Even to many of these He may have appeared as an unknown God.* Under the distressing circumstances of that sixteenth century before our Common Era, did they have to know that He is, that he has a name different from the names of all the gods and goddesses of their oppressors, and that he is their God who recognizes them as his people? Yes! He had been no unknown God to their forefathers of earlier centuries. These had even known his personal name, but had especially come to appreciate him as "God Almighty" because of what he did in their favor. Why, then, should they not worship this God of their forefathers?

---

* See the prophecy of Ezekiel, chapter twenty, verses 6-10.

7. What questions did the Hamitic oppressors raise about the God of the alien residents, and for what action did such questions call?
8. Was it fitting for this God to make himself known also to his own oppressed worshipers, and on what basis?

[9] He had made wonderful promises to their fore-fathers, promises not only of interest and importance to them as descendants but of greatest interest and importance to all mankind. He had foretold the affliction such as came upon them in this Hamitic land. Could he be unaware of the affliction when it actually came upon them? Not consistently so! For a fact, he was clocking the time of this affliction, because he had predetermined and foretold when that affliction would end and should end.* They had the records of the time lengths of the lives of their forefathers in succession and of the generations involved. If they had consulted these and had made correct calculations, they would have known that now was the time for their deliverance. It was the time marked by their God to make himself known to them as their Deliverer and to crown his name with never-fading glory. It was the time for Him to prove with deeds that he makes no sworn declaration that is impossible for him to carry out. He is still God Almighty despite the passing of centuries. As his time had come, he could be expected to give to his name a place in human history above all other names.

HOW WILL HE DO IT?

[10] The question before those who still had faith in the unbreakable promises of God was, How will he do it? How will he prove himself to be no mythical god? How will he vindicate his very existence? How will he make his name to be respected, indeed, to be feared by all the nations of the earth? Not by some ordinary means that could be explained by our modern-day scientists. No, but by something that even twentieth-century scientists cannot account for despite all their laboratory experiments, by things so humanly unbe-

* See the first book of Moses, Genesis, chapter fifteen, verses 12-14.

9. Why was this God clocking the time of their affliction, and what was it timely for him to do respecting his name?
10. So what questions did worshipers with faith in Him ask, and what would be the proper way for Him to act as God in answer?

lievable that doubters would call them merely mythical
and legendary. But how else than by such a demon-
stration of his superior power and scientific intelli-
gence could it be proved to even this generation of
mankind that he is the one God Almighty? One who
is a God should be able to do things that ordinary men
of any century of time could not do. Otherwise, how
can he rank as God? Reasonably, he should be expected
to do things that the magic-practicing priests of all
the false gods could never do. He should distinguish
himself by doing inexplainable things, *miracles!*

¹¹ How, though, would these miraculous feats of
power be identified with this one living and true God,
so as to be unmistakably attributed to him as the
true Source? Especially so, when he is invisible and
has no visible, material idol or image to represent him
to the eyes and touch of men? Simply by having these
miraculous performances announced beforehand and
having them performed in his name, and this by means
of a living human representative, spokesman or prophet, whom he sent to speak and perform in His name.
It was not necessary for this invisible, almighty God
to present himself in person to fleshly human creatures who were too frail in eyesight and bodily makeup to endure a direct confrontation with the heavenly Maker of the sun and all the billions of galaxies
of stars and sources of cosmic rays. In fulfillment
of the predictions made by human spokesmen in his
name, he could perform the specified miracles by remote control, and this would be safest for puny human
creatures with their limited abilities to endure only
so much without being destroyed. All this would show
divine consideration for mere human creatures of our
tiny earth!

¹² The idol gods of that ancient Hamitic land had
their magic-practicing priests and other official rep-

---

11. How would the Source of these miracles be identified, and what
consideration would that Source show for humans on earth?
12. Whom did this non-idolatrous God use to speak and act in His
name, and how did this one get his personal name?

resentatives, among whom were the notable men Jan'nes and Jam'bres.* Who, then, was the historic figure whom the non-idolatrous God sent to speak and act in his personal name? He was no stranger to the land. In fact, he had been born in that southern Hamitic land eighty years previously. Thus he was now an old man, likely too old to be recognized as a fugitive from the land for forty years, a man whom they might have felt justified in killing as a manslayer. They had wanted to have him killed even as a newborn baby by having him hurled into their sacred river, which they worshiped as a god. But as he was floating in a handmade bulrush ark on the waters near the shore, he was rescued by the compassionate daughter of the then ruler of the land. She was moved to adopt this beautiful baby boy, and fittingly she gave him the name meaning "Drawn Out," or, "Saved out of Water," that is to say, Mo·sheh', or, as we would pronounce the name today, Moses. This meant a defeat for the river god that had not been permitted to swallow him down.†

¹³ Seemingly without knowing that she was being maneuvered, the ruler's daughter gave over the suckling baby to his own mother, Joch'e·bed, to nurse and rear until the child should be old enough to be brought into the ruler's palace. With greatness of heart she was acting contrary to her father's cruel policy of genocide against the enslaved alien residents of her land. In this way the endangered child was shielded against death at the hands of the oppressors of his people and he received instruction in the worship, not of the many false gods of the land, but of the God of his father Amram.‡ Strong family and religious attachment to his people remained deep-seated in this

---

* See the Second Letter to Timothy, chapter three, verse eight.
† See the book of Exodus, chapter one, verse twenty-two, through chapter two, verse ten.
‡ See the book of Exodus, chapter six, verse twenty.

13. So how had Moses been reared, and what caused him to flee from the land?

child, who was evidently marked out for an important role in history, until he was forty years old, even in spite of spending most of those years at the king's court and being instructed in all its worldly wisdom. Then, because of being so indignant at the harsh treatment meted out to his enslaved people, he attempted to lead a liberation movement. There was bloodshed, and he had to flee for his life.*

¹⁴ What or who could have induced him now as an aged man of eighty years to leave the land of his fugitive existence and to return to the land of the oppressors of his people, who had sought his life? Had he not already failed once as a liberator? Yes! But now it would be his God who would act as the Liberator of those who worshiped Him notwithstanding their longtime affliction. By now he was almost a stranger to his own people, but his older sister, Miriam, and brother, Aaron, were still alive down there in the land of enslavement. To a large extent he would have to identify himself to them. "What brings you back? Who sent you?" they would ask him. To present himself to them as their liberator in his own name would not work with them now any more than it had worked in the first place. Only if he came in the name of their God as Liberator would they be inclined to accept him as their visible leader. Yet, what was the name of this God who had sent him? How could he prove that this God had sent him to lead them to freedom? Had this God changed his name?

¹⁵ The divine Sender of Moses knew that his doubting people were wondering why the God of their forefathers had permitted for so long this wickedness practiced upon them, and he knew that they would ask Moses these questions. By means of a miraculous manifestation, not in some mythical land, but at the foot

---

* Exodus, chapter two, verses 11-22.

---

14. On his return to be a leader of his oppressed people, what questions would they be inclined to ask him to assure themselves?
15. Where and in what manner did God give orders to Moses to return to the land of the oppressive slave drivers?

of Mount Horeb in the wilderness of Sinai of the Arabian Peninsula, God gave orders verbally to Moses to return to the land of the oppressive slave drivers. What was he to say when he presented himself first to his own people? By means of an invisible angel at a miraculously burning thornbush of the wilderness God told him what to say. According to *The New English Bible* published in a land far westward from the Sinaitic Peninsula, 3,482 years later (in 1970 C.E.), Moses was to say in explaining his mission:

[16] "You must tell the Israelites this, that it is JEHOVAH the God of their forefathers, the God of Abraham, the God of Isaac, the God of Jacob, who has sent you to them. This is my name for ever; this is my title in every generation. Go and assemble the elders of Israel and tell them that JEHOVAH the God of their forefathers, the God of Abraham, Isaac and Jacob, has appeared to you and has said, 'I have indeed turned my eyes towards you; I have marked all that has been done to you in Egypt, and I am resolved to bring you up out of your misery in Egypt, into the country of the Canaanites, Hittites, Amorites, Perizzites, Hivites, and Jebusites, a land flowing with milk and honey.' They will listen to you, and then you and the elders of Israel must go to the king of Egypt."—Exodus 3:15-18.

[17] Courageously Moses obeyed this God of his forefathers, Jehovah. By miraculous signs that Jehovah instructed Moses to perform, Moses proved that Jehovah the God of liberation had indeed sent him to be their leader into liberty. Their liberation could have come in an easy way for the Egyptians, if these, on demand of Jehovah, would lift their oppression upon the Israelites and let them go free to their Promised Land of milk and honey. But what is there to be done when the king Pharaoh of Egypt scorns the demand

---

16. What was Moses told to say to his people in explanation of his return?
17. What was Pharaoh's reaction to the demand for release of the Israelites, and so what only was left for God to do to him?

made upon him in the name of the living and true
God and gives the challenging answer: "Who is Jehovah, so that I should obey his voice to send Israel
away?" To back up his defiance of Jehovah as if he were
a mere Nobody, the idol-worshiping Pharaoh of Egypt
added: "I do not know Jehovah at all and, what is
more, I am not going to send Israel away." And when
Pharaoh, the commander of the finest military forces
in that ancient world, sticks to his decision, what else
is there to do but to make him know Jehovah, to
force him to know that the God making the demand upon him for the releasing of His people is
Jehovah? Pharaoh asked for it!

[18] Do any of the political rulers of this twentieth
century take the attitude of that Pharaoh of 1514/-
1513 B.C.E., as recorded in Exodus 5:1, 2? The national situation that developed away back there called
forth for the first time the divine declaration that
served notice upon the political nations of Bible times
concerning God's purpose to make them know who
he is. But the nations of this modern world need to
heed this ancient declaration of God's purpose as also
applying to them. They might well consider very seriously whether they are typified or prefigured by
the ancient land of the Pharaohs, when Jehovah said
to Moses: "The Egyptians will certainly know that I
am Jehovah when I stretch out my hand against
Egypt, and I shall indeed bring the sons of Israel out
from their midst."—Exodus 7:1-5.

[19] Also, to the disobedient Pharaoh of Egypt Moses
was ordered to say: "By this you will know that I am
Jehovah. Here I am striking with the rod that is in
my hand upon the water that is in the Nile River, and
it will certainly turn into blood." It did so. This proved
to be the first of the ten plagues by means of which

18. What declaration of divine purpose was called forth by the national
situation that developed back there, and what, with reference to themselves, might nations of today well consider?
19. By what as the first of ten plagues was Pharaoh obliged to know
that God is Jehovah?

the tough, resisting Egyptians learned to know in a way disastrous to them that the true God is Jehovah. —Exodus 7:17-25.

[20] That first plague, that of turning the Nile River and its canals into blood, was not directly aimed at Moses' people, who dwelt separate in the northeastern part of Egypt known as Goshen. But they felt the effects of this plague that afflicted the whole land of Egypt for seven days. However, they knew that Jehovah was not meaning to punish them by this plague, and by suffering with the Egyptians they were enabled to feel how real a blow it was to the oppressive Egyptians. The same thing was true of the second plague, that of frogs overrunning the land of Egypt, not even the land of Goshen being spared. (Exodus 7:19 to 8:15) Pharaoh may have drawn some comfort from the fact that Moses' own people were obliged to suffer from those plagues the same as did the Egyptians. He may have doubted that Jehovah was able to protect his own people, the Israelites, from those plagues which Egypt's magic-practicing priests seemed to imitate. So the situation was a challenging one for Jehovah. Was he able to meet it?

[21] The first two plagues did not soften Pharaoh's heart sufficiently. In fact, Jehovah's yielding to Pharaoh's cries for relief really hardened the defiant ruler. A third plague upon Egypt was now in order. It produced swarms of gnats all over Egypt. The magic-practicing priests were unable to duplicate it. They could not credit the plague to any of their demon gods. So to Pharaoh they were obliged to say: "It is the finger of God!" Notably, they did not say: 'It is the finger of Jehovah!' Did they deliberately sidestep saying God's true name? At any rate, their ignoring of the true God's name did not hide the facts, nor did it save them.—Exodus 8:16-19.

---

20. How did Moses' people fare during the first two plagues, and what doubt therefore may Pharaoh have had concerning Jehovah?
21. What did the third plague force Egypt's priests to admit, and why?

PROTECTION THROUGH WORSHIPING THE TRUE GOD

²² Is there any protection possible through worshiping the true God, even this God with the unliked name? The way in which the fourth plague upon Egypt was maneuvered answered this question in a positive way. Listen to the historic record, in Exodus 8:20-24:

²³ "Then Jehovah said to Moses: 'Get up early in the morning and take a position in front of Pharaoh. Look! He is coming out to the water! And you must say to him, "This is what Jehovah has said: 'Send my people away that they may serve me. But if you are not sending my people away, here I am sending upon you and your servants and your people and into your houses the gadfly; and the houses of Egypt will simply be full of the gadfly, and also the ground upon which they are. And on that day I shall certainly make the land of Goshen upon which my people are standing distinct, that no gadfly may exist there; in order that you may know that I am Jehovah in the midst of the earth. And I shall indeed set a demarcation between my people and your people. Tomorrow this sign will take place.' "' And Jehovah proceeded to do so; and heavy swarms of gadflies began to invade the house of Pharaoh and the houses of his servants and all the land of Egypt. The land came to ruin as a result of the gadflies."

²⁴ Thus hardhearted Pharaoh was further made to know that the true God is Jehovah on two counts, by the plague of gadflies itself, which also could be said to be "the finger of God," and by the miraculous separating of Jehovah's people, the Israelites, and protecting them from the plague of gadflies. If Pharaoh had sent to the land of Goshen, he would have found this to be so, just as he did in connection with the very next plague, which struck all sorts of livestock of the Egyptians

22. What question on ability of the true God to protect his worshipers arises, and how did the handling of the fourth plague answer this?
23. What was Moses told to say in announcing the fourth plague, and with what outworking?
24. From then on, on what two counts was Pharaoh made to know that God is Jehovah, and after what experience did Pharaoh let Jehovah's people go?

with pestilence so that they died. Concerning Pharaoh's checkup as to whether Jehovah had really made a distinction between the livestock of the Israelites and the livestock of the Egyptians, we read: "Then Pharaoh sent, and, look! not so much as one of Israel's livestock had died." (Exodus 9:7) But even this was not enough knowledge of Jehovah for unteachable Pharaoh. It was only after the tenth and last plague had killed off his firstborn son and the firstborn sons of all his Egyptian subjects that he relented enough to let Jehovah's people go. It was his own fault that he learned to know Jehovah in only the hard way for Egypt.

²⁵ Despite all of this, the God of miracles was not through with forcing Pharaoh and his subjects to know that he is Jehovah. Some days after the departure of the Israelites with all their firstborn of man and livestock with them, they encamped by the Red Sea, on its western bank, near the head of the Gulf of Suez, and "in view of Baal-zephon ("Lord of the North, or, of the Watchtower")." Near this geographical spot Jehovah purposed to make himself known still more to his enemies. It was just as Jehovah said to Moses: "Then Pharaoh will certainly say respecting the sons of Israel, 'They are wandering in confusion in the land. The wilderness has closed in upon them.' So I shall indeed let Pharaoh's heart become obstinate, and he will certainly chase after them and I shall get glory for myself by means of Pharaoh and all his military forces; and the Egyptians will certainly know that I am Jehovah."—Exodus 14:1-4.

²⁶ Really, then, it was not the Israelites that were trapped at the Red Sea with the Egyptian military forces fast bearing down upon them, but it was the Egyptians themselves that fell into a trap for their destruction. By this there was one final lesson that

25. Thereafter God declared to Moses that he would get further glory for himself by means of Pharaoh how, and so the Egyptians would certainly know what?
26. How had Jehovah now determined to settle accounts with the Egyptians, and what did he tell Moses was the purpose of this?

was to be given to the Egyptians in knowing Jehovah. This would settle his accounts with them. When Jehovah now told Moses that he would open up a corridor through the bed of the Red Sea for the Israelites to go foward to the eastern bank and to deliverance, he disclosed to Moses the purpose of this, saying: "As for me, here I am letting the hearts of the Egyptians become obstinate, that they may go in after them and that I may get glory for myself by means of Pharaoh and all his military forces, his war chariots and his cavalrymen. And the Egyptians will certainly know that I am Jehovah when I get glory for myself by means of Pharaoh, his war chariots and his cavalrymen."—Exodus 14:15-18.

[27] That night, under the light of the Passover moon, the hundreds of thousands of Israelites passed across the bed of the Red Sea with the miraculously parted waters of it on each side of them. Toward morning Jehovah permitted the Egyptian military forces to enter the dried seabed in pursuit of the Israelites. When the God of Israel began to hamper the progress of their pursuers, the Egyptian military forces sensed danger and began to feel that they were fighting against Jehovah. At last making an acknowledgment of Him by name, they said to one another: "Let us flee from any contact with Israel, because Jehovah certainly fights for them against the Egyptians." But it was too late to flee, for Jehovah sprang the trap upon them. We read:

[28] "All the while the Egyptians were fleeing from encountering it [the sea], but Jehovah shook the Egyptians off into the midst of the sea. And the waters kept coming back. Finally they covered the war chariots and the cavalrymen belonging to all of Pharaoh's military forces and who had gone into the sea after them. Not so much as one among them was let remain.

27. At what plight of theirs did the Egyptian forces finally make acknowledgment of God by name, but how timelily?
28. On that day how did Jehovah save Israel from the hand of the Egyptians?

As for the sons of Israel, they walked on dry land in the midst of the seabed, and the waters were for them a wall on their right hand and on their left. Thus on that day Jehovah saved Israel from the hand of the Egyptians, and Israel got to see the Egyptians dead on the seashore."—Exodus 14:21-30.

Chapter 2

His Own People Had to Know Who He Is

TRULY Egypt must have taken a slump as the leading military power of that ancient day. When the news of this disaster reached the Egyptians who had been left back home, they should have known at last that the God of their former slaves was Jehovah, the one living and true God. As for the liberated Israelites, at this triumphant hour they were able to appreciate what their God had said to Moses concerning them: "I shall certainly take you to me as a people, and I shall indeed prove to be God to you; and you will certainly know that I am Jehovah your God who is bringing you out from under the burdens of Egypt." (Exodus 6:7) Now they could appreciate God's name as even their forefathers had never been able to appreciate it, just as he had also said to Moses: "I am the LORD. I appeared to Abraham, Isaac, and Jacob as God Almighty. But I did not let myself be known to them by my name JEHOVAH."—Exodus 6: 2, 3, *New English Bible* of 1970.

---

1. At the disaster for the Egyptians and the triumph for their former slaves, what did each nation respectively come to know?

[2] Now the responsibility was upon those liberated Israelites to serve as witnesses to their descendants. They had come under obligation to serve as Jehovah's witnesses to their offspring, just as he had said to Moses before striking Egypt with the eighth plague, the plague of locusts: "Go in to Pharaoh, because I —I have let his heart and the hearts of his servants become unresponsive, in order that I may set these signs of mine right before him, and in order that you may declare in the ears of your son and your son's son how severely I have dealt with Egypt and my signs that I have established among them; and you will certainly know that I am Jehovah." (Exodus 10:1, 2) Good reason there now was for him to say to that nation, through his prophet Isaiah about eight hundred years later:

[3] "And now this is what Jehovah has said, your Creator, O Jacob, and your Former, O Israel: 'Do not be afraid, for I have repurchased you. I have called you by your name. You are mine. In case you should pass through the waters, I will be with you; and through the rivers, they will not flood over you. In case you should walk through the fire, you will not be scorched, neither will the flame itself singe you. For I am Jehovah your God, the Holy One of Israel your Savior. . . . You are my witnesses,' is the utterance of Jehovah, 'even my servant whom I have chosen, in order that you may know and have faith in me, and that you may understand that I am the same One. Before me there was no God formed [by the idolatrous nations], and after me there continued to be none. I—I am Jehovah, and besides me there is no savior. I myself have told forth and have saved and have caused it to be heard, when there was among you no strange god. So you are my witnesses,' is the utterance of Jehovah, 'and I am God.' "—Isaiah 43:1-12.

---

2. To whom were the liberated Israelites now under obligation to become witnesses, and concerning what?
3. Good reason there now was for Jehovah to say what to the liberated nation, in Isaiah 43:1-12?

⁴ As matters turned out, the liberated nation of Israel had yet to go through the fiery desert on their way to the Promised Land. As this wilderness was no "land of milk and honey," as the Promised Land was reported to be, the nation of his witnesses needed to learn to know Jehovah as the One who could provide for their needs all along the way. Think of providing food and water supplies for several millions of people and their livestock out in the wilderness of the Sinai Peninsula! About a month after they had left Egypt and the people were disposed to murmur about the matter of food, Jehovah declared that he would not let his name be reproached in this regard by saying to Moses: "I have heard the murmurings of the sons of Israel. Speak to them, saying, 'Between the two evenings you will eat meat and in the morning you will be satisfied with bread; and you will certainly know that I am Jehovah your God.'" Thus they learned to know him as their Provider and Sustainer when he sent an abundant supply of quail in the evening and the miraculous manna in the morning. (Exodus 16:1-18) Throughout the four decades of their journey to the Promised Land of milk and honey, Jehovah regularly provided for them the life-sustaining manna. It was no ordinary bread.

⁵ What if we of today were to have forty years of private experience with God our Creator just as the Israelites had it back there in that Middle Eastern wilderness? Would our hearts then become warmed with affection for the knowledge that God imparted? Would our eyes get to the point of seeing with understanding and appreciation what God was doing and would our ears hear what God says with an inclination to obey? Would we feel that now we knew God our Creator? We ought to do so. And yet, toward the end of the forty years of wandering in the wilderness, the proph-

---

4. During their long journey through the fiery wilderness, whom did the Israelites learn their Provider to be, and in what way?
5, 6. God's provision for Israel in the wilderness should have caused them to know what, and yet at the end of their journey what could be said about their heart, eyes and ears?

et Moses summed up the effect of God's dealings upon the Israelites, when Moses said to them:

⁶ "And yet Jehovah has not given you a heart to know and eyes to see and ears to hear down to this day. 'While I kept guiding you forty years in the wilderness, your garments did not wear out upon you, and your sandal did not wear out upon your foot. Bread you did not eat, and wine and intoxicating liquor you did not drink, in order that you might know that I am Jehovah your God.' "—Deuteronomy 29:1-6.

⁷ Early in this forty years of intimate experience with God they should have learned to know him as their Protector against violent enemies. In the second month of their journeying by stages in the wilderness they came to Rephidim. There they could have made the observation that, although they themselves might fight in self-defense, it is their God that gives them the victory over their foes. How so? What happened there? Let us read:

⁸ "The Amalekites came and attacked Israel at Rephidim. Moses said to Joshua, 'Pick your men, and march out tomorrow to fight for us against Amalek; and I will take my stand on the hill-top with the staff of God in my hand.' Joshua carried out his orders and fought against Amalek while Moses, Aaron and Hur climbed to the top of the hill. Whenever Moses raised his hands Israel had the advantage, and when he lowered his hands Amalek had the advantage. But when his arms grew heavy they took a stone and put it under him and, as he sat, Aaron and Hur held up his hands, one on each side, so that his hands remained steady till sunset. Thus Joshua defeated Amalek and put its people to the sword. The LORD said to Moses, 'Record this in writing, and tell it to Joshua in these words: "I am resolved to blot out all memory of Amalek from under heaven." ' Moses built an altar, and named it Jehovah-nissi and said, 'My oath upon it:

7, 8. At Rephidim in the wilderness, how did the Israelites learn who their Protector was, and how did the name of the newly built altar confirm this?

the LORD is at war with Amalek generation after generation.' "—Exodus 17:8-16, *New English Bible*. (The name "Jehovah-nissi" means "Jehovah Is My Signal Pole.")

⁹ It took generations, in fact, centuries, as history shows, to wipe out the last of the Amalekites, the traditional enemies of God's people. Jehovah's resolve against them was not frustrated. So history proves that it is better to gather to Jehovah as our Signal Pole rather than to rally to the aid of those who are the foes of Him and his people. We will do this if we know him.

THE SORT OF GOD THAT HE IS

¹⁰ All these historical experiences help us to appreciate what kind of God this Jehovah is. On one critical occasion he gave to Moses a description of what sort of God he is. This happened in about the fourth month after the Israelites had left their slavery in Egypt. While still at Mount Sinai thousands of the Israelites broke the first two of the Ten Commandments by committing idolatry with a golden calf. Moses as the mediator for the nation had to intercede for them to make sure that God's presence would continue with them in their journey through the wilderness. Then, while up in the mountain with God's angel, Moses made a request, and God favored Moses with a special revelation concerning the divine Name. As regards this, we read:

¹¹ "And Moses prayed, 'Show me thy glory.' The LORD answered, 'I will make all my goodness pass before you, and I will pronounce in your hearing the Name JEHOVAH. I will be gracious to whom I will be gracious, and I will have compassion on whom I will have compassion.' . . . And the LORD came down

---

9. According to later history of the Amalekites, to whom is it better to gather as to a signal pole?
10. At Mount Sinai, what showed the criticalness of the situation because of the breaking of the First and Second Commandments?
11. At Moses' request up in the mountain, what proclamation concerning God's name was made?

in the cloud and took his place beside him and pronounced the Name JEHOVAH. Then the LORD passed in front of him and called aloud, 'JEHOVAH, the LORD, a god compassionate and gracious, long-suffering, ever constant and true, maintaining constancy to thousands, forgiving iniquity, rebellion, and sin, and not sweeping the guilty clean away; but one who punishes sons and grandsons to the third and fourth generation for the iniquity of their fathers!' "—Exodus 33:18 to 34:7, *New English Bible*. (In this Bible where the expression "The LORD" occurs it also stands for the Hebrew name of God, "Jehovah.") Also, see Acts 7:37, 38, 53; Galatians 3:19.

[12] The above-given qualities distinguish Jehovah from all the so-called gods whom men and nations have worshiped. Moses was deeply moved to worship such a God as Jehovah. What reasonable person, with a proper appreciation, would not want to worship a God such as Jehovah is? He deserves to be worshiped. He has the exclusive and just right to command to be worshiped by all his creatures in heaven and on earth. He required of the Israelites whom he had liberated from oppressive Egypt to worship him. He had a sacred tent of meeting constructed at which his chosen people could worship him out in the wilderness. He provided a priesthood for them in the family of Aaron, the brother of Moses. He prescribed a list of sacrifices that they could offer to him on certain occasions and for certain reasons, these sacrifices having a special meaning and pointing forward to the Great Sacrifice that Jehovah would provide in due time to take away the sin of the whole world of mankind. Concerning this sacred tent of meeting and its priesthood, God said to Moses:

[13] "And I will present myself there to the sons of

---

12. What does such a God have the just right to command all his creatures to render to him, and what arrangements for this were made among the Israelites in the wilderness?
13. By God's sanctifying the tent of meeting, its altar and its priesthood, what would the Israelites come to know?

Israel, and it will certainly be sanctified by my glory. And I will sanctify the tent of meeting and the altar; and I shall sanctify Aaron and his sons for them to act as priests to me. And I will tabernacle in the midst of the sons of Israel, and I will prove to be their God. And they will certainly know that I am Jehovah their God, who brought them out of the land of Egypt that I may tabernacle in the midst of them. I am Jehovah their God."—Exodus 29:43-46.

[14] This transportable tent of meeting was replaced centuries later by a stationary temple built on Mount Moriah in the city of Jerusalem. King Solomon, the son of David of Bethlehem, was the builder of it, during the years 1034-1027 before our Common Era. Jehovah sanctified this temple as a place of worship just as he had done with the tent of meeting constructed by Moses. (1 Kings 6:1-38) King Solomon prayed that this might be so, and concerning the divine response to his prayer, we read, in 1 Kings 9:2, 3:

[15] "Then Jehovah appeared to Solomon the second time, the same as he had appeared to him in Gibeon. And Jehovah went on to say to him: 'I have heard your prayer and your request for favor with which you requested favor before me. I have sanctified this house that you have built by putting my name there to time indefinite; and my eyes and my heart will certainly prove to be there always.' "

[16] For that reason the name of Jehovah became associated with that temple at Jerusalem, and even far distant nations came to know this. Properly Jehovah was highly interested in what went on there at that temple, forasmuch as this would reflect upon his holy name. It was no light offense for anyone to defile his temple.

---

14. Centuries later, with what was that tent of meeting replaced, and for what did the builder thereof pray?
15. With what words did Jehovah respond to Solomon's prayer respecting the temple?
16. Properly, who was interested in what went on there at the temple, and why?

ISRAEL AND SYRIA WERE
MADE TO KNOW WHO HE IS

¹⁷ Because the temple builder, King Solomon, turned unfaithful to Jehovah in his old age, God ripped ten of the twelve tribes of Israel away from Solomon's son and successor, Rehoboam. Thus he permitted a ten-tribe Kingdom of Israel to be set up with a different royal capital city. This new kingdom quickly turned away from the worship of Jehovah at his temple in Jerusalem and established the worship of golden calves at the cities of Dan and Bethel, in the year 997 B.C.E. Fifty-seven years later Ahab the son of wicked King Omri became king of those ten tribes of Israel. He went still farther in idolatry by marrying the daughter of a foreign priest of the false god Baal and setting up Baal worship in his capital city, Samaria. (1 Kings 16:29-32) Not desiring this ten-tribe kingdom to forget him completely, Jehovah sent his prophets to them and still gave the idolatrous kingdom reason to know that he is Jehovah the God of their forefathers.

¹⁸ In the days of King Ahab there came occasions for this. Ben-hadad the king of Syria, together with thirty-two kings in league with him, came with a tremendous military force and laid siege to the capital city of Samaria. After some unsatisfactory negotiations with King Ahab, the Syrians and allies set themselves to attack Samaria with full force. Then what happened?

¹⁹ "And, look! a certain prophet approached Ahab the king of Israel and then said: 'This is what Jehovah has said, "Have you seen all this great crowd? Here I am giving it into your hand today, and you will certainly know that I am Jehovah."' "—1 Kings 20:1-13.

17. Because of Solomon's unfaithfulness, what new kingdom was established, and how did Jehovah still give it reason to know who he is?
18, 19. When Ben-hadad of Syria and his allies came to attack Samaria, what message did Jehovah's prophet give to King Ahab?

[20] Under the direct command of King Ahab, who was designated by Jehovah, the besieged Israelites moved out to the attack and were enabled to cause a great slaughter of the Syrians. King Ben-hadad of Syria managed to escape on horseback together with his horsemen. What a reason for the ten-tribe Kingdom of Israel to know that the God of victory is Jehovah! However, Jehovah knew that the Syrians had not learned their lesson but would misinterpret their humiliating defeat and that therefore King Ben-hadad would muster up new military forces and resume the attack on Samaria in the following year. By means of a prophet Jehovah mercifully forewarned King Ahab of this and told him to strengthen himself for this in advance.—1 Kings 20:22-25.

[21] Jehovah's prophecy did not fail, for in the following year King Ben-hadad did come back with apparently overwhelming military forces, to fight against the God of Israel, this time on the level land. "And," says the historic record, "the sons of Israel went into camp in front of them like two tiny flocks of goats, while the Syrians, for their part, filled the earth. Then the man of the true God approached and said to the king of Israel, yes, he went on to say: 'This is what Jehovah has said, "For the reason that the Syrians have said: 'Jehovah is a God of mountains, and he is not a God of low plains,' I shall have to give all this great crowd into your hand, and you men will certainly know that I am Jehovah." ' "—1 Kings 20:26-28.

[22] A week later the battle engagement took place, and the Syrians were proved wrong in their estimate of Jehovah. In one day the Israelites whom He was backing slaughtered a hundred thousand Syrian footmen and, by no mere accident, a wall of the city of Aphek to which the surviving Syrians had fled fell

20. Whom did the Israelites then learn the God of victory to be, but what forewarning was now given to King Ahab?
21. At King Ben-hadad's return in force, why did God say that he would intervene this time for the Israelites?
22. How did the later battle engagement turn out, and why did King Ahab return to Samaria dejected?

down upon twenty-seven thousand of them and killed them. The defeated King Ben-hadad felt obliged to hand himself over to the victors and trust to their tender mercies. Because King Ahab did not put the finishing touch to this God-given victory by acting as Jehovah's executioner and killing the God-defying King Ben-hadad, Jehovah expressed his disapproval of King Ahab. Because King Ahab now had reason to believe that what Jehovah's prophet said would come in punishment for this failure, King Ahab returned to Samaria, not flushed with victory, but dejected. —1 Kings 20:29-43.

[23] The national outcome to the ten-tribe Kingdom of Israel stands as a solemn warning to the nations of Christendom today. Because the Israelites failed to profit religiously from having learned that the God of salvation is Jehovah, they suffered national disaster in the year 740 B.C.E. In that year, because of their continuing to worship false gods and to violate the commandments of Jehovah, their ruin as an independent nation was consummated with the destruction of their capital city, not by the Syrians, but by the then Second World Power, Assyria. The surviving Israelites were carried off into exile in the distant provinces of Assyria, where the prophets of Jehovah did not visit them. Thus the Jehovah-forsaking Kingdom of Israel lasted for only 257 years. The nations of Christendom today have no reason for mistaking why this national calamity befell the ten-tribe Kingdom of Israel, for the inspired prophet and Bible writer (Jeremiah) states why, saying:

[24] "Over the fact that they had not listened to the voice of Jehovah their God, but kept overstepping his covenant, even all that Moses the servant of Jehovah had commanded. They neither listened nor performed." —2 Kings 18:11, 12.

23, 24. What national calamity did the ten-tribe Kingdom of Israel finally suffer, and what does 2 Kings 18:11, 12 state to be the reason why?

BABYLON AND OTHER NATIONS HAD TO KNOW HIM

[25] The sister kingdom composed of the two remaining tribes of Judah and Benjamin, with capital at Jerusalem, continued on for 133 years more. In this kingdom of Judah Jehovah raised up his prophet Isaiah more than thirty-five years before the destruction of Samaria by Assyria, the Second World Power. Under inspiration of the spirit of Jehovah the prophet Isaiah foretold that in course of time Jerusalem also would be destroyed by the next world power, Babylon, and that the land of Judah would be left lying desolate because the surviving inhabitants would be carried off into exile in Babylonia. But in Jehovah's due time Babylon itself would be overthrown as the Third World Power, and the conquering king, Cyrus, whom Isaiah foretold by name, would let the Jewish exiles return to their homeland and cultivate it again to become like a paradise. The returned exiles were also to rebuild the holy city of Jerusalem and its temple for the worship of Jehovah. (Isaiah 44:24 to 45:7; 35:1-10) Using this bringing back of the Jewish exiles as a prophetic picture of something still greater to occur in our own twentieth century, Isaiah went on to say:

[26] "This is what the Sovereign Lord Jehovah has said: 'Look! I shall raise up my hand even to the nations, and to the peoples I shall lift up my signal. And they will bring your sons in the bosom, and upon the shoulder they will carry your own daughters. And kings must become caretakers for you, and their princesses nursing women for you. With faces to the earth they will bow down to you, and the dust of your feet they will lick up; and you will have to know that I am Jehovah, of whom those hoping in me will not be ashamed.' "—Isaiah 49:22, 23.

[27] By the restoring of the exiles that came in the

25. What did the prophet Isaiah foretell about the exile of the people of the Kingdom of Judah and of their restoration to their homeland?
26. At whose signal were the exiles to be brought home, and how, and with what knowledge resulting?
27, 28. Knowledge of the restoration of the Jewish exiles was to become how widespread, and thereby who were to know that he is Jehovah?

year 537 B.C.E. more than merely the earthly organization of His witnesses were to know that he is Jehovah. The pagan nations were also to know this. This spread of such important knowledge internationally was foretold by the prophet Ezekiel after the desolation of Jerusalem and of Judah occurred in 607 B.C.E. and while the displaced Jews were still exiles in Babylon. To the desolated "mountains of Israel" the prophet Ezekiel was inspired to say as the spokesman for Jehovah (according to the American Standard Version Bible):

[28] "For, behold, I am for you, and I will turn unto you, and ye shall be tilled and sown; and I will multiply men upon you, all the house of Israel, even all of it; and the cities shall be inhabited, and the waste places shall be builded; and I will multiply upon you man and beast; and they shall increase and be fruitful; and I will cause you to be inhabited after your former estate, and will do better unto you than at your beginnings: and ye shall know that I am Jehovah." "Therefore say unto the house of Israel, Thus saith the Lord Jehovah: I do not this for your sake, O house of Israel, but for my holy name, which ye have profaned among the nations, whither ye went. And I will sanctify my great name, which hath been profaned among the nations, which ye have profaned in the midst of them; and the nations shall know that I am Jehovah, saith the Lord Jehovah, when I shall be sanctified in you before their eyes."—Ezekiel 36: 8-11, 22, 23.

[29] Is it important that this knowledge that he is Jehovah should be made so widespread? At least he thinks so! In the entire prophecy of Ezekiel alone the Sovereign Lord God indicates the importance of it by repeatedly declaring that nations and peoples and individuals must "know that I am Jehovah," making such a declaration sixty-two times. The last occurrence of this outstanding expression in the prophecy of Ezekiel is

---

29. How is the importance of the knowing of who God is emphasized in the prophetic book of Ezekiel alone?

in Ezekiel 39:6, 7, where the Sovereign Lord God in all earnestness says:

[30] "And I will send a fire on Magog, and on them that dwell securely in the isles; and they shall know that I am Jehovah. And my holy name will I make known in the midst of my people Israel; neither will I suffer my holy name to be profaned any more: and the nations shall know that I am Jehovah, the Holy One in Israel."—American Standard Version of the Bible. Note also Ezekiel 29:17, 21.

[31] In these critical days of our twentieth century, when the nations have militarized themselves with the deadliest of war weapons, the words of the prophet Joel seem to fit as never before, even though his words were spoken and written down in the ninth century before our Common Era and hence before Ezekiel's prophecy: "Proclaim this, you people, among the nations, 'Sanctify war! Arouse the powerful men! Let them draw near! Let them come up, all the men of war! Beat your plowshares into swords and your pruning shears into lances.'" A conflict over world domination is impending. From its outcome, what will the people on the winning side learn? This: "You people will have to know that I am Jehovah your God, residing in Zion my holy mountain. And Jerusalem must become a holy place; and as regards strangers [worldly nations], they will no more pass through her."—Joel 3:9, 10, 17.

[32] As regards the later prophet, Ezekiel, from start to finish he calls attention to the divine name. In the opening verses of his prophetic book he ascribes his prophecy to the inspiration of Jehovah. At the very end of his prophetic book, in the last two Hebrew words thereof, he gives the name of the Sovereign Lord God. According to the way that the *New English Bible* (1970) translates the very last verse, which

---

30. Who does the last expression in Ezekiel's prophecy say "shall know that I am Jehovah"?
31. How does Joel's prophecy match the militarization of the nations today, and what will those on the winning side certainly know?
32. To what extent does Ezekiel call attention to the divine name?

foretells a remarkable city on earth, he says: "The perimeter of the city shall be eighteen thousand cubits, and the city's name for ever after shall be Jehovah-shammah." This name means "Jehovah Himself Is There."—Ezekiel 48:35; *NEB; NW*.

[33] The prophet Ezekiel completed the book of his prophecy in 591 B.C.E., fifty-four years before the exiled Jews were restored to their homeland, which occurred in 537 B.C.E. (Ezekiel 29:17) This remarkable event made some impression on the pagan nations back there. After that, was it no longer important or necessary for the Sovereign Lord God to oblige the nations and peoples to know that he is Jehovah? In our day, the day of all days, does there not exist a need as never before for Him to cause all nations of the earth to know that He is Jehovah? Certainly ours is the day for the one living and true God to step forward and make himself known by his name to all nations and peoples. He needs to do this in vindication of his very existence, his Godship, his Creatorship, his truthfulness and his universal sovereignty. Yes! The very expression "Sovereign Lord Jehovah" occurs 215 times in Ezekiel's prophecy.

[34] In this the last third of the twentieth century one thing must not be overlooked with respect to that last declaration of God's purpose, in Ezekiel 39:7, that "the nations shall know that I am Jehovah." What is that? This: the prophecy must come true "in the latter years," "in the final part of the days." (Ezekiel 38:8, 16, *AS, NW*) When we take into consideration all things since World War I, which broke out in 1914 C.E., more than fifty-six years ago, the foretold latter years and days, the final part of the years and days, ought to be upon us soon! All nations of today are on the brink of coming to a knowledge of this

---

33. Since the Jewish restoration in 537 B.C.E., what about any further need for God to make himself known by name to all nations and peoples?
34. According to Ezekiel 38:8, 16, at what point of time ought we to be soon, and all nations are about to come to what knowledge as never before?

one living and true God, Jehovah, in a way that they never knew him before. Not one of us can escape it. We are all part of those nations. Do we stand to gain or to lose when there is imparted to us that highly important knowledge of Jehovah?

[35] Since He made so many declarations about what nations and peoples must come to know, then, whether we now like Jehovah and his name or not, it behooves us to peer into the prophetic book of Ezekiel. Thus we can observe how outstanding parts of it have had modern-day fulfillment. Many honest-hearted persons today are still confused about the Supreme Being, the Almighty God. They cannot do otherwise than benefit themselves by discovering his wise and timely counsel for today. Why be forced to know that he is Jehovah in the way that Pharaoh, ancient ruler of Egypt, was? Far better is it for us as lovers of life and happiness to accept his gracious invitation to come to know Him now in a peaceful, friendly way.

---

35. In view of God's oft-declared purpose, into what prophetic book does it behoove us to peer now, and in what way is it best to come to know Jehovah?

Chapter 3

God's Chariot Is on the Move!

TWO THOUSAND five hundred and seven years before the gasoline automobile began to be manufactured industrially (in 1895 C.E.), a self-moving or self-propelled chariot was seen in southwestern Asia. It was not of man's invention. It was no mere imagination. To the beholder it was awe-inspiring. Nothing like it has since been seen at the earth. It is beyond

---

1. What automotive vehicle was seen in southwestern Asia long before the gasoline automobile, and what questions arise about it?

copying by man, although over the centuries a detailed description of it has been preserved for us. It is the horseless chariot that was seen by a man whose name has gone down in history, Ezekiel the son of Buzi the priest, and he wrote down a vivid description of it for all generations to come, including our own today. What he saw was the chariot of God, and it was on the move, down from the north. Where was it headed—to somewhere in outer space or to some earthly destination? From there where did it go? Does it still exist, or something like it? Is it now on the move? Good questions these are for our locomotive twentieth century.

² Our reporter, Ezekiel, recorded where he first saw this superhuman chariot of God, and the time and the circumstances. He was by one of the canals of ancient Babylon, which was located on the Euphrates River, the canal being named Chebar. Ezekiel was a priest, not of Marduk the principal god of pagan Babylon, but of the God whose chariot he saw in vision. What was Ezekiel doing *there* instead of being active at his duties as priest far west in the temple at Jerusalem, the capital of the Kingdom of Judah? Ezekiel was there in Babylon as an exile along with the former king of Jerusalem, namely, Jehoiachin the son of the late King Jehoiakim, along with princes and mighty, valiant men and craftsmen. King Jehoiachin had surrendered to Nebuchadnezzar the king of Babylon, who was besieging Jerusalem as a rebel city. The king of Babylon spared King Jehoiachin's life and carried him and all these others, including Ezekiel, into exile in Babylon. That was in the year 617 B.C.E., as we reckon time today.

³ Accordingly, the year 613 B.C.E., the year in which Ezekiel first had the vision of the chariot of God, was the "fifth year of the exile of King Jehoiachin." Eze-

2. Where was Ezekiel when first beholding the chariot, and how did he come to be there?
3. Ezekiel's dating and locating matters indicates what concerning his prophetic book, and when first did Jehovah's hand come upon him?

kiel himself was in the thirtieth year of life. All that took place was, not imaginary or mythical, but actually historical, and so as a historian Ezekiel dated matters definitely in the opening words of his prophetic book, writing: "Now it came about in the thirtieth year, in the fourth month [the lunar month Tammuz], on the fifth day of the month, while I was in the midst of the exiled people by the river Chebar, that the heavens were opened and I began to see visions of God. On the fifth day of the month [Tammuz 5], that is, in the fifth year of the exile of King Jehoiachin, the word of Jehovah occurred specifically to Ezekiel the son of Buzi the priest in the land of the Chaldeans by the river Chebar, and upon him in that place the hand of Jehovah came to be." (Ezekiel 1:1-3) So this was near the close of spring of 613 B.C.E.

⁴ What Ezekiel now saw was no hallucination caused by the taking of some drug like LSD, but was presented to him in vision by the "hand" or applied power of Jehovah that here began to operate upon him. Evidently Ezekiel was looking northward at the time, and what he saw was something allowing for detailed description. What was seen indicated that a tempest was brewing against someone or something. What now emerged upon the scene unmistakably came from a divine source because of all the glory and fiery manifestations out of which it emerged. First of all Ezekiel draws our attention to those who are attending upon the chariot of God, as he writes this description:

⁵ "And I began to see, and, look! there was a tempestuous wind coming from the north, a great cloud mass and quivering fire, and it had a brightness all around, and out of the midst of it there was something like the look of electrum, out of the midst of the fire. And out of the midst of it there was the likeness of

---

4. What Ezekiel saw at the opening of the vision indicated what, and the thing that emerged therefrom came from what source?
5. In Ezekiel 1:4-9, how did the prophet describe the four living creatures?

four living creatures, and this was how they looked: they had the likeness of earthling man. And each one had four faces, and each one of them four wings. And their feet were straight feet, and the sole of their feet was like the sole of the foot of a calf; and they were gleaming as with the glow of burnished copper. And there were the hands of a man under their wings on their four sides, and the four of them had their faces and their wings. Their wings were joining one to the other. They would not turn when they went; they would go each one straight foward."—Ezekiel 1:4-9.

[6] Later on, when Ezekiel describes his second vision of the chariot of God at a new location, he calls these "four living creatures" by the name of "cherubs," in Ezekiel 10:1-20; 11:22.

[7] Cherubs first made their appearance to humankind at the east of the Garden of Eden to guard the entryway to that Paradise of Pleasure after the sinners, Adam and Eve, were driven out into the thorn-and-thistle-infested ground outside. (Genesis 3:17-24) As a priest Ezekiel may have here remembered that the carved cherubs of gold that were part of the lid of the sacred Ark of the Covenant in the Most Holy of the temple at Jerusalem had just two wings, stretched upward and forward to overshadow the golden cover of the Ark. (Exodus 25:18-22; 37:7-9) Since that golden lid surmounted by these cherubs pictured the throne of God, the words of Psalm 80:1, addressed to God, were appropriate: "O Shepherd of Israel, do give ear, . . . O you who are sitting upon the cherubs, do beam forth." It was therefore in nice keeping with their position and office that the four living creatures or cherubs should act as attendants upon God's chariot.

[8] Besides their upper couple of wings and their lower

6. By what name did Ezekiel later call these living creatures?
7. When did cherubs first appear to humankind, and, according to the golden carved cherubs of the Ark and Psalm 80:1, why was the position of the four living creatures by the chariot fitting?
8. The faces of the four living creatures were those of what, and what was the position of their wings?

couple of wings and their straight feet like those of a calf, gleaming like burnished copper, there were other prominent features that marked the cherubs of Ezekiel's vision. What about their heads? Ezekiel writes: "And as for the likeness of their faces, the four of them had a man's face with a lion's face to the right, and the four of them had a bull's face on the left; the four of them also had an eagle's face. That is the way their faces were. And their wings were spreading out upward. Each one had two joining to each other, and two were covering their bodies." —Ezekiel 1:10, 11.

⁹ The fact that these cherubs had the face of a man to the fore went nicely with the fact that they had the hands of a man under their wings and also that the cherubs had, in general, "the likeness of earthling man." The heavenly cherubs also have the God-given quality or attribute of love, just the same as earthling man has, the first man Adam having been created in the image and likeness of God. (Genesis 1:26-28) The face of a lion, in being on the right side of the head of each cherub, emphasized the quality of rightness, justice. This justice has power as its support, which is well pictured in that opposite the lion's face there was, to the left, a bull's face. This face well comports with the fact that the cherubs had straight feet (or limbs), the sole of each of which was "like the sole of the foot of a calf," gleaming as with the "glow of burnished copper." In his later description of the cherubs, Ezekiel calls the bull's face the "face of the cherub." (Ezekiel 10:14) Doubtless, cherubs are creatures of great power, like that of the bull.

¹⁰ Inasmuch as God, at Job 39:27-29, calls attention to the farsightedness of the eagle, the eagle's face to the rear of the cherub's head points to wisdom, the

9. What did the faces of a man, a lion and a bull represent as symbols?
10. What did the eagle's face represent as a symbol, and in what way did these four living creatures correspond with those described in Revelation 4:6-9?

heavenly wisdom, which corresponds with the heavens in which the high-flying eagle soars. This face fits in nicely with the fact that the cherubs had each four wings, enabling them to match the eagle in its flight. The eagle's face, as well as the man's face, the lion's face and the bull's face, is found among the faces of the four cherubic living creatures that were seen in vision about seven hundred years later by the Christian apostle John, these latter cherubs being located around the stationary throne of God in heaven.—Revelation 4:6-9.

¹¹ Thus, consistently, down through the centuries, the same symbols are adhered to in picturing God's wisdom (the eagle), power (the bull), justice (the lion) and love (the man). These four attributes, in perfect balance with one another, differentiate Jehovah from all the gods of mythology and false religions. He has gifted his heavenly creatures and his earthly human creatures with the suitable measure of these four attributes.

¹² Having four faces to their heads, the cherubs did not have to turn themselves if they wanted to change the direction of their movement from straight forward to the right or to the left or to reverse and go backward. Having a face looking in each direction, toward the four cardinal points, they could change directions instantly and follow the face that looked in the desired direction where the quality or attribute that was symbolized by the particular face was to be exercised and applied. They could move with the speed of lightning. Their forms were outlined or bordered with a fiery brightness surpassing that of man-made fire as then made, so bright, in fact, as to generate lightning. With the help of God's spirit of inspiration Ezekiel describes these aspects of the four cherubic living creatures, writing:

---

11. From whom do those four attributes, thus symbolized, differentiate God, and whom has he gifted with these qualities?
12. Why did those four living creatures not have to turn themselves when they desired to change direction of movement?

¹³ "And they would go each one straight forward. To wherever the spirit would incline to go, they would go. They would not turn as they went. And as for the likeness of the living creatures, their appearance was like burning coals of fire. Something like the appearance of torches was moving back and forth between the living creatures, and the fire was bright, and out of the fire there was lightning going forth. And on the part of the living creatures there was a going forth and a returning as with the appearance of the lightning."—Ezekiel 1:12-14.

THE CHARIOT WHEELS

¹⁴ Could the movements of any vehicle or chariot correspond with the movements of those four cherubic living creatures? Impossible as it is for modern automobile manufacturers to duplicate, the prophet Ezekiel saw such a maneuvering of the chariot of God, and without any steering wheel or shifting of gears. Take note as Ezekiel explains it to us:

¹⁵ "As I kept seeing the living creatures, why, look! there was one wheel on the earth beside the living creatures, by the four faces of each. As for the appearance of the wheels and their structure, it was like the glow of chrysolite; and the four of them had one likeness. And their appearance and their structure were just as when a wheel proved to be in the midst of a wheel.* When they went they would go on their four respective sides. They would not turn another way when they went. And as for their rims, they had such height that they caused fearfulness; and their rims were full of eyes all around the four of them. And when the living creatures went, the wheels would

---

* In a footnote on this the 1971 edition of the *New World Translation of the Holy Scriptures* says: "Possibly, be centered at right angles on the same axis."

---

13. With what comparisons did Ezekiel describe the brightness of the four living creatures, and their speed?
14. Who today on earth cannot duplicate God's chariot as to maneuverability?
15. How does Ezekiel describe the wheels as to their makeup and movements?

go beside them, and when the living creatures were lifted from the earth, the wheels would be lifted up. Wherever the spirit inclined to go, they would go, the spirit inclining to go there; and the wheels themselves would be lifted up close alongside them, for the spirit of the living creature was in the wheels. When they went, these would go; and when they stood still, these would stand still; and when they were lifted up from the earth, the wheels would be lifted up close alongside them, for the spirit of the living creature was in the wheels."—Ezekiel 1:15-21.

[16] A wheel being alongside each living creature would result in four wheels, not abreast of one another* nor in one long line, but in four related places,† like the four faces of the cherubs. They were thus at the four corners of a rectangle. All the wheels were alike in appearance and structure. They glowed like chrysolite when reflecting the light. Their rims were full of eyes all around, as if the wheels could see where they were going. They were not going blindly in any direction. And were the wheels high! Their height was fear-inspiring to Ezekiel. Having such a great diameter and a correspondingly big circumference, the wheels could cover a great distance with just one revolution on their axis. So, like the four cherubs, they could move like lightning.

[17] As for the structure of those wheels, there was something of an oddity about them. Each wheel had a wheel inside it, not a smaller wheel within the big wheel and in the same plane with it and turning simultaneously with it on the same hub or axle. No, but a wheel of the same diameter and fitted into the

---

* See the picture on page 119 of the book *Prophecy,* first printing, 1929. Out of print.

† See picture on page 25 of the book *Vindication,* Volume One. Now out of print and out of stock.

---

16. What was the position of the wheels with regard to one another, and how much ground could they be aware of covering with one revolution?

17. How did a wheel prove to be within a wheel, and for what maneuverableness did this allow?

base wheel crosswise, rim touching rim at a right angle. Only in this way could the wheels be said to "go on their four respective sides," one side curving frontward, another backward, another right and another left. No wonder these wheels did not have to turn around as when rounding a corner in order to go in another direction. Instantly they could change direction because there was a side of the wheel facing in each direction. Thus the wheels could conform their direction of movement to that of the four living creatures who had four faces and who therefore did not need to turn around to change directions. On four wheels of this structure the body of God's chariot could ride by invisible support just like a hovercraft that skims over water or land held up by a thin cushion of air.

[18] There were no wings on those four wheels as there were on the four living creatures, and yet they could rise from the ground and take off into space just the same as those living creatures could. Those wheels were not hitched to any team of chariot horses or other traction animals or apparatus. Where did they get this power to conform to all the movements of the living creatures? What was the force behind their locomotion? Ah, it was the spirit of the Almighty God. The same invisible active force of God was in those wheels as that within the living creatures, and they did not need any gasoline engine or electric motor to propel them. Simply stated, "the spirit of the living creature was in the wheels."

[19] Let us now, with Ezekiel, look above those fearfully high four wheels and see what is above. There is, as it were, the floor of the chariot, for Ezekiel goes on to say: "And over the heads of the living creatures there was the likeness of an expanse like the sparkle of awesome ice, stretched out over their heads up

18. What empowered these wingless wheels to conform their movements to those of the four living creatures?
19. What did Ezekiel see above the four wheels, and what sound did he hear produced by the wings of the living creatures?

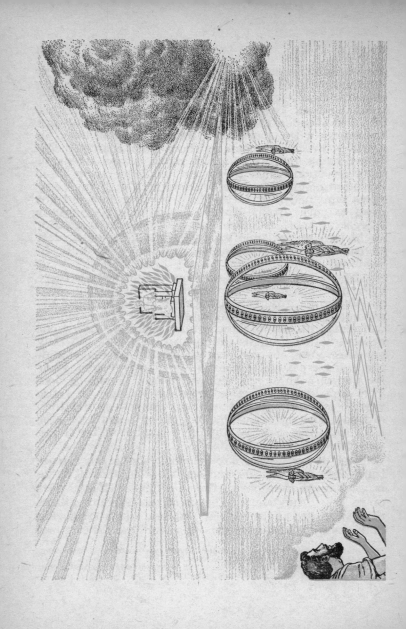

above. And under the expanse their wings were straight, one to the other. Each one had two wings covering on this side and each one had two covering on that side their bodies. And I got to hear the sound of their wings, a sound like that of vast waters, like the sound of the Almighty One, when they went, the sound of a tumult, like the sound of an encampment. When they stood still, they would let their wings down."—Ezekiel 1:22-24.

[20] The four living creatures were not as gigantic as those four wheels were. So the firmament or "expanse like the sparkle of awesome ice" that rode on invisible support above the four wheels was far above the heads of the four living creatures. Corresponding to that, the "expanse," although solid, was translucent. It was indeed awe-inspiring, a fact that fully accorded with the dignity of the One who was riding upon it.

[21] There are insects on earth that make a musical or resonant sound by rubbing their wings together. Not different from the sound-producing power of insect wings, the wings of the four cherubic living creatures in motion produced an impressive sound. We know what the sound of many waters or vast waters is when they are agitated. The sound of the wings of the living creatures was like that. Their flight was not a silent one. The sound could even be compared to the sound that the Almighty One can produce in his natural creation that can make a person start up. It was not a peaceful sound. It was like the sound of a tumult or a tumultuous crowd. The sound was far from tranquilizing, since Ezekiel says that it was like the sound of an armed camp, an encampment of soldiers. This suggested the imminence of war, of battle. So, instead of its being the four tremendous wheels that rattled noisily, it was the wings of the four living creatures that drew attention to the approach of the chariot

20. How did the wheels and the living creatures compare as to height, and the expanse above, in being like ice, had what quality?
21. By the comparing of the sound of the wings of the living creatures to different things, what is thus suggested?

of God as coming on no peaceful mission. It was coming as a war chariot! Why? We must wait to find out.

THE RIDER OF THE CELESTIAL CHARIOT

²² Our ears are now turned from the noisy sound made by the wings of the four living creatures to a voice that comes from above the floor of the celestial chariot, this calling our attention to the chariot rider. Evidently the chariot stops, as the living creatures stand still, in order that its rider may speak to this exiled priest Ezekiel. Regarding this, Ezekiel writes:

²³ "And there came to be a voice above the expanse that was over their head. (When they stood still, they would let their wings down.) And above the expanse that was over their head there was something in appearance like sapphire stone, the likeness of a throne. And upon the likeness of the throne there was a likeness of someone in appearance like an earthling man upon it, up above. And I got to see something like the glow of electrum, like the appearance of fire all around inside thereof, from the appearance of his hips and upward; and from the appearance of his hips and downward I saw something like the appearance of fire, and he had a brightness all around. There was something like the appearance of the bow that occurs in a cloud mass on the day of a pouring rain. That is how the appearance was of the brightness round about. It was the appearance of the likeness of the glory of Jehovah."—Ezekiel 1:25-28.

²⁴ For the color of it the throne of the chariot rider appeared to be of precious sapphire stone. Its color matched well the azure blue of the skies from which the chariot rider came. The throne being like an earthly throne, the One seated upon it was like earthling man in appearance. As Ezekiel was merely a human himself, the human form was the best form that he

22. The voice from above the expanse calls attention to whom?
23. How did Ezekiel describe the appearance of the glory of Jehovah above the expanse?
24. The description given of the Rider of the chariot, though given in earthly terms, indicates what about Him in reality?

could appreciate for this divine manifestation. But that human form, enveloped in glory, glowed like electrum, however, as if it were being treated by fire inside a furnace. From the waist of this manlike form there was this elegant glory extending both upward and downward, the whole form being thus encased in glory. This was a mere representation of the Almighty God, but it indicated that in actuality, in the invisible realm, he is indescribably glorious.

²⁵ Notwithstanding the mission of the divine Chariot Rider, he maintained his calm and composure. How beautifully this is pictured in his being accompanied by the lovely rainbow, "the bow that occurs in a cloud mass on the day of a pouring rain"! In that calm attitude he can keep his attributes of wisdom, justice, power and love in perfect balance. He can never be accused of being unwise, unjust, unpowerful and un-loving. His glorious appearance is never tarnished by the committing of anything wrong.

²⁶ Well, what is our impression of this description of the mere "likeness of the glory of Jehovah"? What was the effect upon Ezekiel, who actually saw these things in vision? He tells us, writing: "When I got to see it, then I fell upon my face, and I began to hear the voice of one speaking."—Ezekiel 1:28.

²⁷ The mere written description of it can never work upon us the overwhelming effect that the very sight of the vision in all its grandeur worked upon this priestly man Ezekiel. He could not do otherwise than just prostrate himself before this "likeness of the glory of Jehovah." But Ezekiel's inspired description deepens our appreciation of certain aspects of the One who desires us to know that he is Jehovah. However, the impression upon us is made even more moving and stirring when we see, in the Bible's light, the meaning of this chariot of God.

25. How is his maintaining his composure pictured, and what effect does this have on the exercise of his attributes?
26, 27. How was Ezekiel affected by the vision before being spoken to, and how does his description of it affect us?

²⁸ Certainly Jehovah does not ride on such a chariot as that seen in the vision given to Ezekiel. The ancient psalmist was inspired to say: "Bless Jehovah, O my soul. O Jehovah my God, you have proved very great. With dignity and splendor you have clothed yourself, enwrapping yourself with light as with a garment, stretching out the heavens like a tent cloth, the One building his upper chambers with beams in the very waters, making the clouds his chariot, walking upon the wings of the wind, making his angels spirits, his ministers a devouring fire." (Psalm 104:1-4) Of course, Jehovah does not make the literal clouds of earth his chariot, but he can use them as his agencies for doing certain things to or for mankind on earth. What Ezekiel saw in vision resembled a four-wheeled chariot more than clouds do. Jehovah did not inspire Ezekiel to envision that celestial chariot just to entertain him with something fantastic in appearance. He showed Ezekiel that unusual, self-propelling chariot as a picture of something still greater. There is profit for us in knowing what it signifies.

²⁹ Just as the various articles of furniture in Jehovah's temple at Jerusalem were designed by him and made according to his pattern to picture spiritual things of greater importance, so, too, the celestial chariot that wheeled up before Ezekiel in his miraculous vision pictured something vastly greater. What? The heavenly organization of Jehovah as composed of all his holy spirit creatures in that invisible realm. By the appearance of the four cherubic living creatures that had symbolic features and that accompanied the four wheels like chariot runners, we are reminded of what the psalmist David wrote, in Psalm 18:6-10:

³⁰ "In my distress I kept calling upon Jehovah, and to my God I kept crying for help. Out of his temple

---

28. How does Jehovah make clouds his chariot, as Psalm 104:1-4 says, and was the vision of a chariot (different from clouds) given to Ezekiel for his entertainment?
29, 30. The symbolic nature of the furniture in Jerusalem's temple suggests what for the visionary chariot seen by Ezekiel, and why do the living creatures beside the wheels remind us of Psalm 18:6-10?

he proceeded to hear my voice, and my own cry before him for help now came into his ears. . . . And he proceeded to bend the heavens down and descend. And thick gloom was beneath his feet. And he came riding upon a cherub and came flying, and he came darting upon the wings of a spirit."—Psalm 18:6-10; 2 Samuel 22:7-11.

[31] Jehovah does not confine himself to riding upon the one cherub mentioned by the psalmist, nor upon four cherubs as seen in his vision to Ezekiel, nor upon all the cherubs in that order of spirit creatures in heaven. He rides upon all his spirit creatures, whether cherubs, seraphs or general angels. He is the Most High God, the Supreme Being. They are all subject to him, and so he rides them in the sense of dominating them and using them according to his purpose. Instead of personally and directly going to any place himself, he can send a cherub or seraph or angel there, and by having his spirit (his invisible active force) accompany that messenger to operate through that one, Jehovah in effect rides that spirit creature. All cherubs, seraphs and angels, together, make up his united, coordinated, harmonious, obedient heavenly organization. This superhuman, spirit organization is like the celestial chariot seen in Ezekiel's vision and is pictured by it. As on a chariot he rides this organization, causing it to move to wherever his spirit impels it to move.

[32] Many years after Ezekiel had his vision of the celestial chariot, the prophet Daniel, who had been taken into exile with Ezekiel, had a marvelous vision, "in the first year of Belshazzar the king of Babylon." In the vision Daniel saw the four-wheeled throne of Jehovah in a Court scene in heaven. Daniel here makes prominent the vast body of attendants that are subject to Jehovah in heaven in the following de-

---

31. What, then, does the visionary chariot seen by Ezekiel picture, and how does Jehovah ride it?
32. How was the vastness of Jehovah's heavenly organization shown in vision to the prophet Daniel?

scription: "I kept on beholding until there were thrones placed and the Ancient of Days sat down. His clothing was white just like snow, and the hair of his head was like clean wool. His throne was flames of fire; its wheels were a burning fire. There was a stream of fire flowing and going out from before him. There were a thousand thousands that kept ministering to him, and ten thousand times ten thousand that kept standing right before him. The Court took its seat, and there were books that were opened."
—Daniel 7:1-10.

[33] In the last visions of God to be given to a Bible writer, the Christian apostle John had a vision of God's throne in the heavens around which were stationed four cherubic living creatures. In his description of what went on up there, John also calls attention to the vast throngs of spirit creatures as they all together recognize God's fairness in giving a reward to his Son who was slaughtered like a sacrificial lamb here on earth in behalf of all mankind. John writes: "And I saw, and I heard a voice of many angels around the throne and the living creatures and the elders, and the number of them was myriads of myriads [ten thousands of ten thousands] and thousands of thousands, saying with a loud voice: 'The Lamb that was slaughtered is worthy to receive the power and riches and wisdom and strength and honor and glory and blessing.'"—Revelation 5:1-12.

[34] Jehovah, who created and organized all the universe visible to our eyes, has organized all these holy heavenly spirit creatures into one vast universal organization, over which he is the Universal Sovereign. Each one of them has his own place in the organization and has his God-given duties to perform. God rides them all as his chariot. He moves over them, in control of them, as he sends them, singly or unitedly,

---

33. According to Bible record, what was the last vision given that showed the vastness of Jehovah's heavenly organization?
34. What is Jehovah to this heavenly organization, and how do its parts function, and why so?

on any mission in any part of the universe, visible or invisible. There is no friction between parts in his organization. All parts function together smoothly and efficiently in perfection, being pervaded by his holy spirit, the perfect bond of union. The marvelousness of Jehovah's heavenly organization grows on us more and more, the longer we contemplate it.

MODERN-DAY DISCERNING OF THE HEAVENLY ORGANIZATION

[35] Jehovah's Christian witnesses of this twentieth century have come to appreciate that He has such a marvelous organization. Early in the third decade of our century they were helped by His spirit to perceive this awe-inspiring fact. Before the year 1922 this was called to their attention. After that references to the heavenly organization were made in the religious publications that they used in spreading Bible instruction. For example, in the issue of *The Watch Tower* as of December 15, 1924, on page 371, under the subheading "God's Organization," we read:

The better we understand Jehovah's plan, the more fully we appreciate the fact that he has the most wonderful of all organizations. His majesty and dignity preclude him from giving direct attention to the details and the execution of his orders. From his eternal throne in the highest heaven he exercises his power as he may will. In the offices of his heavenly courts there are different creatures, as indicated by their names. Some are called cherubim, some seraphim, and some angels. It may be properly said that the angels are messengers and executive officers of the great Jehovah.—Paragraph 3 of the leading article entitled "Rapture of the Angels."

[36] In the year 1929 the Watch Tower Bible & Tract Society published the book entitled "Prophecy,"* chapter V of which bore the title "God's Organization."

---

* Now out of print and out of stock.

35. When did Jehovah's Christian witnesses begin to appreciate that He has an organization, and what did the last issue of the *Watch Tower* magazine of 1924 say about it?
36. What did the book *Prophecy*, chapter V, have to say about "God's Organization"?

Ezekiel's vision as described in the first chapter of his prophetic book was applied to God's heavenly organization of his spirit creatures. On page 121, lines 2-7, it says: "The living creatures and the inanimate objects, or instruments, appearing in the vision, together give the appearance of an enormous living chariot-like organization extending high into the heavens, and over all of which Jehovah God presides."

[37] Later, in the year 1931, the Watch Tower Bible & Tract Society published volume one of the book entitled "Vindication."* This contained a commentary on the first twenty-four chapters of Ezekiel's prophecy, and this book also applied Ezekiel's vision of the celestial chariot to Jehovah's organization. At seeing this, Jehovah's Christian witnesses were filled with such appreciation that, from the issue of October 15, 1931, to that of August 1, 1950, the front-cover design of the *Watchtower* magazine carried in its upper right-hand corner an artist's conception of Ezekiel's vision of the celestial chariot.

[38] Ezekiel had the vision of the heavenly organization of the Most High God 645 years before the organization of the Christian church or congregation in the spring of 33 C.E., on the day of Pentecost at Jerusalem. Jehovah's heavenly organization was in existence in Ezekiel's day and was on the move in that year of 613 B.C.E., when Ezekiel was favored with the marvelous symbolical vision. In the visions given to him Ezekiel was a witness of Jehovah's organization in symbol, but he actually saw how that heavenly organization operated down till Ezekiel finished his writing of prophecy in the year 591 B.C.E. Outstandingly he was one of that great "cloud of witnesses" of Jehovah that the Christian apostle Paul describes in Hebrews 11:

---

* Now out of print and out of stock.

37. How did Volume I of the book *Vindication* apply Ezekiel's vision of the celestial chariot, and how did this affect the front-cover design of the *Watchtower* magazine?
38. Measuring only from Ezekiel's vision, how long was Jehovah's heavenly organization in existence before the Christian congregation, and to what extent was Ezekiel a witness of Jehovah?

1 to 12:1. Out of the 6,961 times that the divine name Jehovah occurs in the inspired Hebrew Scriptures from Genesis through Malachi (*New World Translation*, edition of 1971), 439 of these instances occur in the prophetic book of Ezekiel, and for sixty-two times Ezekiel quotes God's statement of his steadfast purpose that nations, peoples and individuals "shall know that I am Jehovah."

[39] As regards our twentieth century, the prophet Ezekiel well pictures the anointed remnant of Jehovah's Christian witnesses since the year 1919 C.E., the critical year in which there was a revival of their public activities as foretold in Revelation 11:3-12.* It is true that in 1919 this spiritual remnant did not appreciate Jehovah's organization as they do today. It is also true that they did not then discern that Jehovah's organization was prophetically pictured by the symbolic chariot in Ezekiel's vision, not till the year 1929. Nevertheless, Jehovah's heavenly organization was, of course, in existence in the year 1919 and it got in spiritual touch with the anointed remnant in that year to revive them as Jehovah's public witnesses to all the world. That chariotlike organization was on the move then in 1919; it is on the move today, and apparently its wheels of progress are turning faster than ever. Jehovah rides again!

[40] At the visionary "likeness of the glory of Jehovah" the priestly Ezekiel was irresistibly moved to fall upon his face, prostrate. He desired to know why this celestial chariot had drawn up before him and stopped. He found out as a voice came to him from the One enthroned upon the chariot, above the "likeness of an expanse like the sparkle of awesome ice."

---

* For the explanation of these verses see the book entitled "Then Is Finished the Mystery of God," Chapter 19, on "Death and Resurrection of the 'Two Witnesses,'" page 259 and following.

39. Whom does Ezekiel picture in our day and since when, and what was then on the move the same as in Ezekiel's day?
40. At the vision of the "likeness of the glory of Jehovah," what was Ezekiel moved to do, and at discerning Jehovah's heavenly organization, what were the anointed remnant of this century moved to do?

(Ezekiel 1:22, 26-28) Likewise, at the discernment of Jehovah's heavenly organization by the anointed remnant of Jehovah's Christian witnesses of this century, they were filled with awe. More strongly they felt obliged to worship Him and to become witnesses to his gloriously historical name, Jehovah. World War I having ended on November 11, 1918, and the postwar world having set in, they keenly listened in the year 1919, after their revival, to hear what Jehovah had to say to them through his chariotlike organization.

Chapter 4

Commissioned to Speak in the Divine Name

LET us ask ourselves the question, What would I do if the emperor, king or president of my country took his official automobile and drove up to my home and, from his vehicle, made a personal delivery of a national commission to me? Well, that is somewhat of the experience that Ezekiel the son of Buzi the priest had by the bank of the river Chebar in the year 613 B.C.E., when, in vision, the celestial chariot of Jehovah, accompanied by four cherubs, wheeled down from the north and halted before him. Overwhelmed at this awe-inspiring spectacle of the "likeness of the glory of Jehovah," Ezekiel reverently prostrated himself. As he remained prostrate with his face to the ground, wondering what was the purpose of this vision, he heard the voice of the Rider of the celestial chariot speaking to

1. At the vision of the celestial chariot and its Rider at the river Chebar, why did Ezekiel prostrate himself, and about what might he have wondered?

him. (Ezekiel 1:1-28) What did it have to say? Ezekiel informs us:

² "And he proceeded to say to me: 'Son of man, stand up upon your feet that I may speak with you.'" (Ezekiel 2:1) Ezekiel is addressed, not by his personal name, but as "Son of man [*Ben adám*]." Throughout the entire book of his prophecy Ezekiel is addressed ninety-three times in this form of address. Only once again does the prophet's personal name appear in the book, and this time in chapter twenty-four, verse twenty-four, where the prophet quotes Jehovah as saying to the house of Israel: "And Ezekiel has become for you a portent. In accord with all that he has done, you will do. When it comes, you will also have to know that I am the Sovereign Lord Jehovah." In this way no prominence is given to the prophet's own name, but he is continually reminded of his lowly estate and origin. He is but an offspring of earthling man. Over six hundred and forty years later Jesus Christ is reported seventy-six times (from Matthew 8:20 to John 13:31) as speaking of himself as "the Son of man." But by this he is not comparing himself with Ezekiel, nor does this make Ezekiel a type of Christ.* Ezekiel's fellow exile Daniel is also addressed as "son of man."†

³ The command of Jehovah to Ezekiel to arise imparted active force to Ezekiel, enabling him to get up from the ground. As he tells us: "And spirit began to come into me as soon as he spoke to me, and it finally made me stand up upon my feet that I might hear the One speaking to me." (Ezekiel 2:2) Standing before the Divine Presence, Ezekiel was more alert to hear what was said.

---

* By speaking of himself as "the Son of man," Jesus Christ was not directly identifying himself as the Christ but was comparing himself with the "Son of man" seen in vision in Daniel 7:13 (*AV*). See also Acts 7:56.

† See Daniel 8:17.

---

2. By what form of address is Ezekiel spoken to, was this to make him a type of Christ, or what was its purpose?
3. The divine command to stand imparted what to Ezekiel, and why was standing before the Speaker better for Ezekiel?

⁴ "And he went on to say to me: 'Son of man, I am sending you to the sons of Israel, to rebellious nations that have rebelled against me. They themselves and their forefathers have transgressed against me down to this selfsame day. And the sons insolent of face and hard of heart—I am sending you to them, and you must say to them, "This is what the Sovereign Lord Jehovah has said." And as for them, whether they will hear or will refrain—for they are a rebellious house—they will certainly know also that a prophet himself happened to be in the midst of them.' "—Ezekiel 2:3-5.

⁵ There Ezekiel is definitely told that he is henceforth to serve as a prophet. He is commissioned to speak in the divine name, saying: "This is what the Sovereign Lord Jehovah has said." Just as Jehovah had sent Moses as his prophet nine hundred years previously, so now he was sending Ezekiel. Ezekiel was not raising himself up as a prophet and presuming to speak in the divine name. He was really a prophet sent by the Most High God. The fact that Jehovah appeared to Ezekiel in vision and spoke from his throne on his celestial chariot and directly sent Ezekiel on a definite mission with a definite message proves that Ezekiel was a true prophet, sent by God, and that what he spoke under inspiration was the real word of God. The fact, too, that he was sent on such a difficult mission adds to the proof that he did not assume to be a prophet speaking in Jehovah's name, but that the Highest Authority in all existence sent him to speak in the divine name. He was thus, in an outstanding way, made a witness of Jehovah.

⁶ Not alone were the inspired words of Ezekiel prophetic, but he himself was a prophetic figure in his action, as is later shown on occasions. (Ezekiel 24:24) Since Ezekiel himself was a "portent," or "sign" (*AV*), of someone to come, and since he was not a type or

---

4. To whom was Ezekiel told that he was sent, and after he spoke Jehovah's saying to them, what would they certainly know?
5. Therefore, what proves that Ezekiel did not presume or himself assume to be a prophet speaking in the divine name?
6. Not only were Ezekiel's words prophetic, but what was he himself at the same time?

prophetic figure of Jesus Christ, whom did the prophet Ezekiel typify in carrying out his divine commission?

[7] Although Ezekiel did not know it at the time that he was commissioned to be Jehovah's prophet, the city of Jerusalem was to be destroyed by the Babylonians just six years later, in 607 B.C.E. Ever since Ezekiel's former acquaintance, Jeremiah the son of Hilkiah the priest, was raised up back there in Jerusalem in the year 647 B.C.E., in the thirteenth year of the reign of King Josiah of Jerusalem, that city and the nation of Judah had been in their time of the end. (Jeremiah 1:1-3; 25:10, 11) In the right timing of things we today should look for the modern-day counterpart of Ezekiel as a type or prophetic figure in the "time of the end" in which we now find ourselves. Modern historians are agreed that an era ended in the year 1914 C.E., the year in which World War I began its violent, destructive course of more than four years and three months. What those historians do not take into account is that, according to the Holy Bible, the "times of the Gentiles" ended in early autumn of that very year of 1914. (Luke 21:24, AV) Since then we have been in the world's "time of the end."

[8] While the prophet Ezekiel was still an exile in Babylon, those Gentile Times began, in 607 B.C.E., when the armies of the king of Babylon brought destruction upon Jerusalem and, two months later, complete desolation came upon the whole land of Judah, including Jerusalem. (2 Kings 25:1-26; Jeremiah 39:1 to 43:7; 52:1-27) Ezekiel's fellow exile, the prophet Daniel, was used to indicate that those Gentile Times would continue for a period of seven prophetic "times," or for 2,520 years. (Daniel 4:1-28) A count of 2,520 years from the desolation of the land of Judah in the year 607 B.C.E. proves that these years of uninterrupted rule of the whole earth by the Gentile nations ended

---

7. We should look for the antitype of Ezekiel in what period of time, and since when have we been in that time period?
8. During whose exile in Babylon did those Gentile Times begin, and how, and so the time for us to look for Ezekiel's modern counterpart began when?

in 1914 C.E. Since that date the Gentile nations, including the nations of Christendom, have been in their "time of the end." Do not world events and developments since then indicate this to be true? (Matthew 24:3-44) Here, then, since 1914, and particularly since the year 1919, after World War I had ended, we should look for the modern-day counterpart of the prophet Ezekiel.

⁹ Who is Ezekiel's present-day counterpart, whose message and conduct correspond with that of that ancient prophet of Jehovah? Of whom today was he a "sign" or "portent"? Not of some individual man, but of a group of people. Being made up of a unified company of persons, the modern Ezekiel is a composite personage, made up of many members, just the same as the human body is. This reminds us of what the onetime persecutor, the Christian apostle Paul, wrote to fellow Christians in Rome, Italy, saying: "Just as we have in one body many members, but the members do not all have the same function, so we, although many, are one body in union with Christ, but members belonging individually to one another." (Romans 12:4, 5) Using the same illustration, Paul said in his letter to the congregation in Corinth, Greece: "Just as the body is one but has many members, and all the members of that body, although being many, are one body, so also is the Christ. For truly by one spirit we were all baptized into one body, whether Jews or Greeks, whether slaves or free, and we were all made to drink one spirit."—1 Corinthians 12:12, 13.

¹⁰ So it is with the modern-day counterpart of Ezekiel: it is, not one person's body, but a composite body, made up of many members. All these members were together to do the will of Jehovah, who is the Creator of this modern "Ezekiel." Who, then, are the group of persons who, toward the beginning of this "time

9. Is the modern-day Ezekiel an individual person, and how does the apostle Paul illustrate how Ezekiel's counterpart could be?
10. In order to determine which group is Ezekiel's modern counterpart, what do we have to do?

of the end," were commissioned to serve as the mouth-piece and active agent of Jehovah? In order to determine this, check the history of 1919, the first postwar year after the first world war.

[11] We do not look among the natural circumcised Jews, for they had actively taken part in World War I, the famous Zionist leader, Chaim Weizmann, lending his services as a discoverer in the chemical field to the British Government during that world conflict. In 1919 they were mainly interested in establishing a National Homeland for the Jews in Palestine, rather than in fulfilling any religious commission like that of ancient Ezekiel. But what about religious Christendom? Her appearance before Jehovah was also gruesomely blood-stained, for World War I was mainly her war, twenty-four of the twenty-eight participants in carnal warfare claiming to be Christian nations. When this first world conflict ended in 1918 (November 11), victorious Great Britain and her allies were interested in establishing a peace arrangement with the conquered nations, besides dealing with the newly arisen Communist State in Russia. Playing the modern-day role of the Bible "Ezekiel" was far from their thoughts.

[12] The churches of Christendom had taken no coura-geous Christian steps to prevent World War I. They had split into two great camps over the nationalistic war issues. The end of the war found them disunited, needing to get reconciled and to become religious friends again. According to the Treaty of London that had been signed on May 9, 1915, by Italy, Great Britain, France and Russia, "the Holy See [the pope of Rome] was not to be permitted to intervene by diplomatic action in regard to peace or questions arising from the war."* So the pro-German Vatican was not allowed to have any part in drawing up the Peace

* Quoted from *The Encyclopedia Americana,* Volume 17, edition of 1929, page 633.

11. When we look at natural Jewry and then at Christendom for the proper group, what objectionableness do we find?
12. When we look at the churches of Christendom, including the Vatican, for the proper group, what do we find?

Treaty of Versailles of 1919, which was ratified by the required national governments involved on October 13 of that year. The Covenant of the League of Nations was made a part of that peace treaty.

[13] To "save face" the bloodstained churches of Christendom who had actively backed the war in which church member fought against his fellow church member came out in favor of the proposed League of Nations, because it was put forth as an international organization for world peace and security.

[14] The Church of England supported the League of Nations inasmuch as its religious head was the King of Great Britain, the proposer and chief backer of the League of Nations. The churches of Canada, which held vows of allegiance to the Sovereign of Great Britain, also favored the League. In the allied country of the United States of America there was the Federal Council of the Churches of Christ in America, an interdenominational organization composed of representatives of various Protestant denominations.* On December 18, 1918, it sent its adopted Declaration to the American president and urged him to work for the League. The Declaration said, in part:

> Such a League is not a mere political expedient; it is rather the political expression of the Kingdom of God on earth. . . . The Church can give a spirit of good-will, without which no League of Nations can endure. . . . The League of Nations is rooted in the Gospel. Like the Gospel, its objective is "peace on earth, good-will toward men."

[15] In recommending and supporting the League of Nations as "the political expression of the Kingdom

---

* The Federal Council was superseded in the year 1950 by the organizing of the National Council of the Churches of Christ in the U.S.A., a corporate federation of 33 Protestant and Orthodox churches to advance the programs and policies of mutual interest to it.

13. To save face, what did the bloodstained churches of Christendom do respecting peace and security?
14. What was the position taken by the churches of England, Canada and the United States of America toward the League of Nations?
15. Contrary to what words of Jesus when on trial for life was the Federal Council going, and so what Kingdom of God was it that failed when World War II broke out?

of God on earth" the Federal Council of American churches went directly contrary to the words of Jesus Christ, when on trial for his life before the Roman governor, Pontius Pilate, in 33 C.E., saying: "My kingdom does not belong to this world. If it did, my followers would be fighting to save me from arrest by the Jews. My kingly authority comes from elsewhere." (John 18:36, *New English Bible*) By accepting the League of Nations as "the political expression of the Kingdom of God on earth" the members of the Federal Council of American churches were really accepting a counterfeit "Kingdom of God on earth." Hence, twenty years later when the League of Nations was knocked out of business by the outbreak of World War II and "peace on earth, good-will toward men" were taken away, it was the counterfeit "political expression" that failed, and not the real Kingdom of God as proclaimed in the Gospel of Christ.

[16] Certainly, then, back there in the postwar year of 1919 there were none among the war-guilty religious elements of Jewry and Christendom who qualified to be commissioned as the modern-day counterpart or antitype of Ezekiel. Was there no one, then, whom Jehovah could raise up to serve in a way that corresponded to that of that ancient exile in Babylon? Whom could the real "chariot" of Jehovah's organization roll up to and confront that He might bestow upon this qualified one the commission to speak as a prophet in the name of Jehovah? Ah, there was a group whose members had suffered religious persecution during World War I at the hands of Babylon the Great, the world empire of false religion, and whose members had, in fact, come out from the religious organizations of Babylon the Great. In fact, they had refused to be a party with Christendom and with all the rest of Babylon the Great in actively taking part in carnal warfare during World War I. Who were they?

---

16. What was the sort of group before which the "chariot" of Jehovah's organization could roll up in 1919 C.E. for bestowing the commission to speak in the divine name?

THE MODERN-DAY "EZEKIEL"

17 They were a small minority group of men and women who had dedicated themselves to Jehovah as God by following in the footsteps of his Son Jesus Christ. To give public evidence of this dedication to Jehovah, they had undergone water baptism just as their Leader Jesus Christ had done when he was immersed in the Jordan River by John the Baptist. (Matthew 3:13-17; 28:19, 20; 1 Peter 2:21) They were very active in preaching the good news of God's kingdom because their Leader Jesus Christ had set this preaching before them as their work in his prophecy at Matthew 24:14. They took literally the words of Jesus Christ, when before the Roman governor, that his kingdom does not belong to this world, and so they declined to have any part in the politics of this world and in its political struggles and conflicts. They took to heart Jesus' words to his followers: "You are no part of the world, but I have chosen you out of the world." (John 15:19) Hence they expected to suffer the world's hatred for their living according to that Christian rule. Hatred toward them became violent during World War I.

18 Did the ancient prophet Ezekiel mean anything to them? He did! One of the prophetic books that these students of the Bible had for years wanted to understand was that of Ezekiel. After years of waiting they felt that attention had been paid to their desire when the book entitled "The Finished Mystery" was published in July of the year 1917. This book of 608 pages, published by the Watch Tower Bible & Tract Society, contained an explanation, not only of the last book of the Bible, Revelation, but also of the twenty-sixth book of the Bible, Ezekiel. It severely criticized the religious systems of Christendom and exposed the clergy of Christendom as being false to the word of Jehovah. Can we wonder why this book had a circulation of less

17. What distinguished this group as true Christians?
18. This group was interested in what prophetic book of the Bible, and how was this interest met in 1917, with what later developments?

than nine months in the United States and Canada? It was because the book was put under ban, the wartime conditions of both countries being taken advantage of to bring this about. The Watch Tower Society's president and secretary-treasurer, together with six other members of the Society who had a connection with *The Finished Mystery,* were imprisoned in the Federal Penitentiary, Atlanta, Georgia, U.S.A.

[19] The crippling of the work of preaching God's kingdom during World War I greatly grieved these peace-loving dedicated, baptized followers of Jesus Christ. The burning question was, Would they have an opportunity to resume their peaceful activities in the service of Jehovah their God? The answer proved to be Yes! World War I did not lead on into an Armageddon for the Gentile nations but ended on November 11, 1918. They endeavored to get the imprisoned officers of the Watch Tower Society and their fellow prisoners out of the Federal Penitentiary. Their efforts were blessed from Heaven. After nine months of imprisonment these falsely charged servants of Jehovah were freed in March of 1919, never to return to prison. All the dedicated, baptized servants of Jehovah rejoiced. They recognized that their dedication to Him was for life and therefore they must do his will in the postwar period then opening up. The encouragement to be fearless and do so came through the columns of the magazine *The Watch Tower and Herald of Christ's Presence.*

[20] In the issues of August 1 and 15, 1919, of this magazine there was published a series of two articles on the subject "Blessed Are the Fearless." In the third and fifth paragraphs of this article there appeared these statements that discouraged all fear of men: "There is a fear which is very proper, and which everyone must have who is pleasing to God, and this is known as 'Godly fear'. It means a holy reverence for

19. Over what release did this group rejoice in 1919, and through what magazine did the encouragement for postwar work come?
20. How was fear of men discouraged in the series of articles in the issues of August 1 and 15, 1919, of *The Watch Tower?*

Jehovah and a fear lest we should displease him and come short of the blessings he has promised us. . . . The Scriptures abound with testimony that those whom God approves do not fear man nor any other creature, but have a holy, reverential fear of Jehovah. In times of old Jehovah justified some men to friendship with him, and the record of his dealing with them was written for the benefit of the church." Following those articles there appeared the article "Opportunities for Service," with the subheadings "Is There Work to Do?" "Work for the Little Flock," and "Benefits of Assembling Together." Also announcement was made of a General Convention to be held at Cedar Point, Lake Erie.

²¹ This general assembly at Cedar Point, Ohio, was successfully held at the appointed time, September 1-8, 1919. Thousands of dedicated, baptized servants of Jehovah were in attendance from the United States of America and Canada. The president of the Watch Tower Society there urged their fearless resumption of Jehovah's work, and this with a new magazine that would be a companion of *The Watch Tower*, namely, the thirty-two-page magazine entitled "The Golden Age." The assembled thousands of servants of Jehovah hailed this announcement of the revival of the work, and that on an enlarged scale, with tremendous joy and the spirit of dedication to Jehovah. The public address of the convention was delivered at 3 p.m., Sunday, September 7, 1919, on the subject "The Hope for Distressed Humanity." The conventioners heartily approved when the president of the Watch Tower Society, in the course of this public talk, as reported next day by the newspaper, the Sandusky (Ohio) *Star-Journal,*

declared a League of Nations formed by the political and economic forces, moved by a desire to better mankind by establishment of peace and plenty would accomplish great good, and then asserted that the Lord's dis-

21. How did this group respond to the announcement of the Cedar Point convention of 1919, and what declaration in the public lecture regarding the League of Nations did they heartily approve?

pleasure is certain to be visited upon the League, however, because the clergy—Catholic and Protestant —claiming to be God's representatives, have abandoned his plan and endorsed the League of Nations, hailing it as a political expression of Christ's kingdom on earth.*

²² The clergy of Christendom got their satisfaction when the Versailles Peace Treaty was ratified by the required nations on October 13, 1919, and thereby the League of Nations came into being. The League of Nations really began to function on January 10, 1920, when ratifications were formally exchanged by all the signatory powers at Paris, France. But the dedicated, baptized servants of Jehovah did not accept this counterfeit "political expression of the Kingdom of God on earth." They recognized that the real kingdom of God had been established in the hands of Jesus Christ in the heavens at the end of the Gentile Times in 1914, and now more vigorously than ever they undertook to preach it "in all the inhabited earth for a witness to all the nations." They did so with the additional help of *The Golden Age* (now the magazine *Awake!*).

²³ In June of 1920, when the book *The Finished Mystery* was released from under ban, these servants of Jehovah resumed the circulating of the book. With the use of it as a textbook they continued to study the Bible book of Ezekiel. Later, in the years 1931 and 1932, a more advanced, up-to-date understanding of the prophecy of Ezekiel was published in the form of three volumes of the book called "Vindication," published by the Watch Tower Bible & Tract Society. To this day their interest in the prophetic book of Ezekiel is keen, and they study it purposely in order to determine what further light it sheds on Jehovah's will for them in these closing days of the "time of the end."

* See the *Federal Council Bulletin,* Volume II, No. 1, of the year 1919, pages 12-14.

22. When the League of Nations was ratified in 1919, how did Christendom's clergy react, and how did Jehovah's servants?
23. Since the release of *The Finished Mystery* from under ban in June of 1920, Jehovah's servants have shown keen interest in what prophetic book, and how? And why?

²⁴ Why, though, are all these facts of history brought to our attention? It is to show the fulfillment of prophecy. Jehovah has found and commissioned his modern-day "Ezekiel." It is a composite Ezekiel. It is composed of those dedicated, baptized proclaimers of God's kingdom, who have been anointed with His spirit for their work. (Isaiah 61:1-3) It is manifest that in the year 1919 the invisible heavenly organization of Jehovah, like the celestial chariot seen in Ezekiel's vision, rolled up and stopped, not before Christendom's advocates of the League of Nations, but before the anointed proclaimers of the heavenly kingdom of God in the hands of Jesus Christ. From atop this celestial chariotlike organization Jehovah commissioned this dedicated, baptized, anointed class of servants to speak to all the nations in His name. Thus, like Ezekiel, they became Jehovah's witnesses. It was most fitting that, after twelve years of worldwide activity as such, they embraced the distinguishing name Jehovah's witnesses, in the summer of 1931, and that in connection with the publishing of the book *Vindication*.

WHO COMMISSIONED THE MODERN-DAY "EZEKIEL"?

²⁵ Let not the rabbis of Judaism and the clergy of Christendom say, "We did not ordain and commission these witnesses of Jehovah to be the modern antitype of the prophet Ezekiel." But what does that matter? Whoever made those rabbis and sectarian clergymen a religious body for the appointment of the official servants of the Most High God? Any ordination and commission proceeding from those religionists would be of no value and of no force in this regard. What is all-essential is for a person or group of persons to have an appointment and a commission from the Most High God, Jehovah, himself. This is what counts. As the

24. Our attention to these facts of history helps us to identify whom today, and what name was embraced at the time when the book *Vindication* was released?
25. Of what concern is it that Jewish rabbis and Christendom's clergy have not appointed Jehovah's witnesses as an antitypical Ezekiel, and what is it that counts, and why?

Supreme Being he can go over the heads of those religionists and determine for Himself who qualifies for the special work that He desires to be done in this "time of the end."

[26] Back in the year 613 B.C.E. Jehovah went over the head of the High Priest, Seraiah, and of the second priest, Zephaniah, at the temple in Jerusalem, and appointed Ezekiel the son of Buzi an underpriest to be his prophet in the land of Babylon, to speak in His name and to bear witness to Him. (2 Kings 25:18) From atop his celestial chariot Jehovah said to Ezekiel: "Son of man, I am sending you to the sons of Israel, to rebellious nations that have rebelled against me." (Ezekiel 2:3) So it was with the anointed, dedicated witnesses of Jehovah back there in the year 1919 C.E. The facts from then on down to this date prove that they received their ordination and appointment and commission for their work in this "time of the end" from Jehovah himself through his heavenly chariotlike organization. Hence they have taken their divine commission very seriously as being a real Biblical thing, and they have tried to carry it out faithfully in spite of the criticism and objections of the clergy of Christendom.

[27] Who, then, are the "sons of Israel, . . . rebellious nations that have rebelled against [Jehovah]," to whom the modern-day antitypical Ezekiel is sent in this "time of the end"? They are not the natural, circumcised "sons of Israel," who were seeking a National Jewish Homeland back in the year 1919 C.E., with Chaim Weizmann as their Zionist leader. No, but there is a modern-day counterpart of those ancient "sons of Israel, . . . rebellious nations."

[28] That counterpart is Christendom, which claims

---

26. Who were disregarded in the appointment of Ezekiel to be prophet and witness, and from whom do Jehovah's anointed witnesses of today recognize their appointment as coming?
27. What question arises as to the "sons of Israel, . . . rebellious nations," to whom the modern-day Ezekiel was sent, and what about the natural Jews back in 1919 C.E.?
28. What is the modern-day counterpart of the "sons of Israel, . . . rebellious nations," according to what religious claim?

to be a Christian Israel. To herself Christendom has applied the apostle Paul's words in Galatians 6:15, 16 (*AV*): "For in Christ Jesus neither circumcision availeth any thing, nor uncircumcision, but a new creature. And as many as walk according to this rule, peace be on them, and mercy, and upon the Israel of God." For instance, in his "A Commentary and Critical Notes" (1836 C.E. edition), the Wesleyan Methodist minister, Dr. Adam Clarke, makes this comment on the expression "The Israel of God": "The *true Christians,* called here the *Israel of God,* to distinguish them from *Israel according to the flesh.* See the notes on Rom. ii. 29, and iv. 12."

²⁹ Romans 2:29 (*AV*) reads: "But he is a Jew, which is one inwardly; and circumcision is that of the heart, in the spirit, and not in the letter; whose praise is not of men, but of God." On the expression "But he is a Jew," Dr. Adam Clarke comments: "A true member of the Church of God." On the expression "Whose praise is not of men," he comments: "It has, with great probability, been conjectured that the apostle may here refer to the signification of the name *Jew,* or *Judah,* יהודה *Yehudah,* PRAISE, from ידה *Yadah,* he PRAISED. Such a one is a true Israelite, who walks in a conformity to the spirit of his religion: his *countrymen* may *praise* him because he is a steady professor of the Jewish faith; but God *praises* him, because he has entered into the *spirit* and *design* of the covenant made with Abraham, and has got the end of his faith, the salvation of his soul. Sentiments like these, on the same subject, may be found in the ancient Jewish writers."

³⁰ Christendom, however, has not been true to her claims to be "the Israel of God." Her history since the fourth century proves that she has been like the "sons of Israel" to whom Ezekiel was sent, "rebellious na-

---

29. What does Romans 2:29 say, and how does Dr. Adam Clarke speak in comment on this?
30. How could the "sons of Israel" be then spoken of as "nations," and how did Christendom come to correspond with this in 1054 C.E.?

tions that have rebelled against me [Jehovah]." "Nations"?* Yes, because back in 997 B.C.E. there was a revolt against the rule of David's royal line and the twelve tribes of Israel were split up into two kingdoms, the Kingdom of Israel and the Kingdom of Judah, and thus there came to be two nations of Israelite stock. Many God-fearing Israelites left the rebellious Kingdom of Israel and went over to the Kingdom of Judah. Also, many exiles of the Kingdom of Israel were in the provinces that the empire of Babylon had taken over from Assyria. Correspondingly, in Christendom, in 1054 C.E., there came the final break between the Greek churches and the Latin churches, when the Roman pope's legates excommunicated Patriarch Michael Cerularius of Constantinople.

³¹ Later, in the sixteenth century there came a further split when, in the year 1529 C.E., the Protestant movement was established by the followers of the ex-priest Martin Luther. Later, in 1534 C.E., the English Parliament passed acts declaring the king of England, Henry VIII, to be the Supreme Head of the Church of England, with authority to redress errors, heresies and abuses in the Church of England. After this, non-Roman Catholic religious sects sprang up by the hundreds throughout Christendom. Religiously, Christendom can be called "nations," inasmuch as a number of so-called "Christian" lands have their own national State churches. To this twentieth-century Christendom the modern Ezekiel class was sent by Jehovah.

FEARLESSNESS NEEDED FOR THE ASSIGNMENT

³² For Ezekiel of old it was a hard mission on which Jehovah sent him, he being sent to people "insolent of

---

* Some think that "nations" here refers to the tribes of Judah and Benjamin who, together, made up the Kingdom of Judah. Each tribe could be considered a nation, according to Genesis 35:11, as addressed to Jacob or Israel.

31. What further splitting took place from the sixteenth century onward, and how can Christendom rightly be called "nations"?
32. Why was it a hard mission on which Ezekiel was sent, and what expectation according to God's prediction would comfort and strengthen Ezekiel?

face and hard of heart." In order to carry out his mission to the end he needed to have fulfilled toward him what his name Ezekiel meant, namely, "God Strengthens." At the time, they might not view or appreciate him as a prophet of Jehovah. But whether they heard him as such or refrained from hearing and paying attention to him, the occasion was to come when these rebellious people would "know also that a prophet himself happened to be in the midst of them." Jehovah would confirm him as a prophet before them by causing what Ezekiel prophesied to come true. (Ezekiel 2:3-5) The expectation of this would be a comfort and strength to Ezekiel, not to be discouraged because of the way he was being considered and treated at the moment.

33 Likewise it was a trying mission upon which the modern Ezekiel class was sent, to religious people of the same type as those in Ezekiel's day. But regardless of how Christendom views or regards this group of anointed witnesses of Jehovah, the time must come, and that shortly, when those making up Christendom will know that really a "prophet" of Jehovah was among them.

34 Would we today like to tell Jehovah's message among things that prick us and among scorpions? It would take great courage and trust in the One who sent us to do so. Into such a situation Ezekiel was sent, according to the words that Jehovah further said to him: "And you, O son of man, do not be afraid of them; and of their words do not be afraid, because there are obstinate ones and things pricking you and it is among scorpions that you are dwelling. Of their words do not you be afraid, and at their faces do not you be struck with terror, for they are a rebellious house. And you must speak my words to them, regardless of whether they hear or they refrain, for they are

33. Why is the mission of the modern-day Ezekiel class likewise a trying one, but, too, what must Christendom also come to know?
34. Ezekiel was told to speak God's word fearlessly despite what about the rebellious house of Israel, and why has the anointed remnant of Jehovah's witnesses likewise had to speak fearlessly?

a case of rebellion." (Ezekiel 2:6, 7) Since the year 1919 C.E. the anointed remnant of Jehovah's witnesses have found it to be just like that as they have spoken fearlessly the word of Jehovah in the midst of Christendom.

³⁵ The religious condition today in Christendom bears witness to the fact that, rebelliously, she has not listened to the word from Jehovah's Holy Scriptures that has been spoken to her by every means of communication, by house-to-house calls with the printed page, by recordings played on portable phonographs, by the loudspeakers of sound cars, by direct public lectures, by radio networks and by television. Regardless of Christendom's indifference or even rebelliousness, the anointed witnesses of Jehovah have done just as He told Ezekiel to do, saying: "And you, O son of man, hear what I am speaking to you. Do not become rebellious like the rebellious house. Open your mouth and eat what I am giving you."—Ezekiel 2:8.

³⁶ What was Ezekiel given to eat? His written account tells us: "And I began to see, and, look! there was a hand thrust out to me, and, look! in it there was the roll of a book. And he gradually spread it out before me, and it was written upon in front and on the back; and there were written in it dirges and moaning and wailing." (Ezekiel 2:9, 10) From what was written on the scroll Ezekiel learned the content of the message that he was to deliver to the rebellious house of Israel in the name of Jehovah.

³⁷ As no space was wasted on the scroll, but it was written upon on both sides, front and back, it was to be a full message that Ezekiel proclaimed, it was to contain a great deal of gloomy dirges, moaning and wailing. It was to be no pleasant message, and it would

35. Christendom's condition today shows that she has responded in what way to Jehovah's word presented by every means of communication, and so in what way should Christendom not be imitated?
36. What was Ezekiel given to eat, and what did it contain, for his information?
37. How was the fullness of the message to be delivered portrayed, and why was the kind of message the proper one to be delivered, both by Ezekiel and by Jehovah's witnesses of today?

not be altogether pleasant for Ezekiel to deliver it. But when rebellious people refuse to turn from their ungodly way, what other kind of message than this is there to be pronounced over them? No less so, as Jehovah's anointed witnesses of today examined the prophetic book of Ezekiel and other parts of Jehovah's Word they found just such a message for Christendom.

38 The hand that was thrust out to Ezekiel to offer him the scroll was likely a hand that was under a wing of one of the four cherubic living creatures who accompanied the celestial chariot of Jehovah. (Ezekiel 1:8) It is later reported that the hand of one of these cherubs was used to put fire into the hand of the "man clothed with the linen." (Ezekiel 10:6-8) But did Ezekiel accept from that hand the scroll despite its revealed contents and then eat it, making it a part of himself? What did he as a "sign" or "portent" for the future indicate that Jehovah's remnant of anointed witnesses would do in this twentieth century?

38. In what way was the scroll offered to Ezekiel, and what question arises as to the acceptance thereof?

Chapter 5

Appointed as a Watchman
to Christendom

A WATCHMAN should be specially appreciated in time of danger. His services by day and night, if appreciated and acted upon, result in protection and life for those over whom he acts as watchman. The people of Christendom have been in great danger ever

1. When should a watchman specially be appreciated, and into what danger had Christendom entered by the end of the Gentile Times in 1914 C.E.?

since the "time of the end" began with the expiration of the "times of the Gentiles" ("the appointed times of the nations") in early autumn of the year 1914 C.E. This being in danger has been not just because the first world war was then raging and gaining momentum, to introduce an "age of violence" that has continued on down to this day. There is a danger also for a more serious reason, as we shall see.

[2] Christendom set up first the League of Nations, and in 1945 the United Nations, as her watchman in behalf of world peace and security, but these have not worked. Rather, the spiritual interests of the people of Christendom have been endangered, the danger in this respect being particularly great because the spiritual interests have to do with one's eternal life or one's eternal death. The fact that the clergy did not stick to Christian principles so as to prevent World War I proved that, collectively, they were no reliable spiritual watchman.

[3] Consequently, at the close of that savage international conflict on November 11, 1918, the need arose or became more pressing for a spiritual watchman to be raised up by the Supreme Spirit Being in whose hands the eternal destiny of the people rests. He had to raise up such a watchman with the qualities of unrebelliousness, reliability and faithfulness, because the clergy of Christendom, Catholic, Protestant and Orthodox, could not produce such a watchman from their own ranks. That the Most High God would do so was prefigured in the case of Ezekiel the son of Buzi the priest. The year 613 B.C.E. was a late point of time in the forty-year "time of the end" for Jerusalem and its domain, the land of Judah. It was only six years more until both Jerusalem and the land of Judah should be completely desolated, without man or domestic beast. Exile in Babylon during Judah's

2. What did Christendom set up as her watchman, and what showed that her clergy could not be a reliable watchman?
3. Could Christendom's clergy raise up a spiritual watchman from their own ranks, and how did God prefigure that he would do so?

seventy years of desolation was in store for the few Jews who survived the destruction of Jerusalem. Jehovah foreknew that. He especially knew the danger to the Jewish people who were involved. Years in advance, in 613 B.C.E., He mercifully raised up a watchman among those who were already exiles in Babylon, Ezekiel the son of a priest.

[4] There was still time left for a watchman to give warning ahead of the great coming calamity. Suddenly Ezekiel found himself being favored with a vision from Jehovah the God of Israel. In the realistic vision the awe-inspiring celestial chariot of Jehovah wheeled out of the north to before Ezekiel there at the bank of the river (canal) Chebar in Babylonia. The purpose of this vision was for Jehovah, atop the chariotlike organization, to appoint Ezekiel as a prophet and a watchman in behalf of the endangered sons of Israel. As a prophet Ezekiel needed to have a message, and as a watchman he needed something to call out. Ezekiel's prophetic message and the warning that he was to cry out were contained in writing on the scroll that was now extended to Ezekiel by a hand, together with the command that he should eat this scroll. Did Ezekiel desire to proclaim the "dirges and moaning and wailing" that were written on the front side and reverse side of the scroll? Would a scroll with such a message be palatable, enjoyable to eat? Would Ezekiel be rebellious like the sons of Israel, as Jehovah told him not to be? (Ezekiel 2:8-10) What was Ezekiel's choice, as an example for the modern Ezekiel?

[5] Referring to Jehovah enthroned on his visionary chariot, Ezekiel says: "And he proceeded to say to me: 'Son of man, what you find, eat. Eat this roll, and go, speak to the house of Israel.' So I opened my mouth, and he gradually made me eat this roll.

4. What was the purpose of Jehovah's celestial chariot wheeling up before Ezekiel, and what questions come up as to Ezekiel's disposition of the scroll offered to him?
5. What was Ezekiel commanded to do, and what was the first effect when he complied?

And he went on to say to me: 'Son of man, you should cause your own belly to eat, that you may fill your very intestines with this roll that I am giving you.' And I began to eat it, and it came to be in my mouth like honey for sweetness."—Ezekiel 3:1-3.

⁶ As might be contrary to expectations, the gloom-laden roll was as sweet as honey in Ezekiel's mouth. This was because its becoming a part of Ezekiel's very system meant an acceptance of an assignment to do Jehovah's special work. This is a sweet experience for one who appreciates the honor of being appointed to serve the Most High God in a special capacity at a critical time. Seven hundred years later a like experience was to be had by the Christian apostle John, who, like Ezekiel, was an exile, on the Isle of Patmos in the Aegean Sea, far to the west of the river Chebar. In this experience John imitated Ezekiel's example. If John the beloved companion of Jesus Christ had his experience in the year 96 C.E., then it was sixty-six years after Jesus called him to be a disciple that John had his vision, whereas Ezekiel was only in his thirtieth year when he received his commission. Let us note the similarity of the two experiences as John writes:

⁷ "And the voice that I heard out of heaven is speaking again with me and saying: 'Go, take the opened scroll that is in the hand of the angel who is standing on the sea and on the earth.' And I went away to the angel and told him to give me the little scroll. And he said to me: 'Take it and eat it up, and it will make your belly bitter, but in your mouth it will be sweet as honey.' And I took the little scroll out of the hand of the angel and ate it up, and in my mouth it was sweet as honey; but when I had eaten it up, my belly was made bitter. And they say to me: 'You must prophesy again with regard to peoples and

6. Why did Ezekiel's eating the scroll bring sweetness to his mouth, and who had a like experience seven hundred years later, and where?
7. How does the apostle John describe his experience in connection with the scroll in the hand of an angel?

nations and tongues and many kings.' "—Revelation 10:8-11.

⁸ Since Ezekiel's experience was taken as a model of John's experience, it indicates that Ezekiel's experience was prophetic, prefiguring not John's experience, but the experience of the same class today as was represented by the apostle John, namely, the anointed remnant of Jehovah's Christian witnesses.

⁹ The roll that Ezekiel ate, with dirges and moaning and wailing written thereon, did not picture the prophetic book of Ezekiel. It pictured Jehovah's message that was to be delivered by Ezekiel up to when he delivered his last message against the Gentile enemies of Jerusalem and the land of Judah.—Ezekiel 35:15.

¹⁰ Similarly in the year 1919 C.E., the "roll of a book" that the anointed remnant of Jehovah's dedicated servants ate up did not picture the book of Ezekiel. It pictured all those parts of God's Holy Bible that have to do with the spiritual plagues and the "great tribulation" that are to come upon Christendom and her religious and political associates during this "time of the end." The anointed remnant of today ate up this "roll of a book" in that they accepted the commission and responsibility to deliver all these messages of God's Word as He by his spirit made them plain and understandable to His witnesses. There was unspeakable joy and rejoicing on the part of the anointed remnant back there in 1919 C.E. as they ate up Jehovah's message of the hour and resumed their public activities. It tasted sweet.

SENT, NOT TO FOREIGNERS, BUT TO HIS OWN PEOPLE

¹¹ After accepting his commission by eating the

8. Ezekiel's experience with the scroll was taken as a model for what, and whose experience did it prefigure?
9. What did the roll that contained such mournful contents and that Ezekiel ate picture?
10. In connection with the anointed remnant of Jehovah's servants, what did that "roll of a book" picture, and how did the remnant eat it and with what effect?
11, 12. After eating the roll, Ezekiel was told what about the kind of people to whom he was sent, and how was he to be adequate to face them?

"roll of a book," Ezekiel was ordered to go into action. He tells us:

[12] "And he continued saying to me: 'Son of man, go, enter in among the house of Israel, and you must speak with my words to them. For it is not to a people who are unintelligible in language or heavy of tongue that you are being sent—to the house of Israel, not to numerous peoples unintelligible in language or heavy in tongue, whose words you cannot hear understandingly. If it was to them that I had sent you, those very ones would listen to you. But as for the house of Israel, they will not want to listen to you, for they are not wanting to listen to me; because all those of the house of Israel are hardheaded and hardhearted. Look! I have made your face exactly as hard as their faces and your forehead exactly as hard as their foreheads. Like a diamond, harder than flint, I have made your forehead. You must not be afraid of them, and you must not be struck with terror at their faces, for they are a rebellious house.' "—Ezekiel 3:4-9.

[13] Ezekiel did not need to learn a new language in order to deliver his message. He was not sent to peoples whose language he did not understand and who would not understand the Hebrew that he spoke. If it were to such peoples that he was sent, they would listen to him, just as the Assyrian inhabitants of Nineveh listened to the Hebrew prophet Jonah and repented and were spared over two hundred years earlier, about the year 844 B.C.E. (Jonah 3:1 to 4:11) Ezekiel was sent to his own people, to speak to them in their holy Hebrew language. So it would not be because they did not understand what Ezekiel said that they would refrain from heeding what he said to them. Jehovah reminded Ezekiel that the house of Israel was hardheaded and hardhearted in their rebellious attitude. But Ezekiel did not need to have any trembling fear

---

13. Was Ezekiel to have a language problem with the people to whom he was sent, and why did he not need to have any trembling fear before them?

of men, that lays a snare for the frightened one. (Proverbs 29:25) Jehovah would make his forehead of a superior hardness, like that of a diamond, harder than flint, when compared with their foreheads. He could be just as determined of face as they were.

[14] After World War I ended in 1918 C.E., the revived remnant of Jehovah's anointed witnesses were sent, not to the heathen or pagans who had their own religious language, but to Christendom, that had the Christian religious idiom. They could carry on their preaching of God's kingdom well in Christendom. Why?

[15] Because they looked for the administration of their activities and for the supply of religious literature to the Watch Tower Bible & Tract Society, and already in 1919 C.E. this Society had branch offices in Great Britain, Continental Europe, Australia, South Africa and North America. The peoples in these lands of Christendom had the Holy Bible in the various languages, the same as Jehovah's witnesses did. Although the hands of these peoples were dripping with the blood of World War I, they still professed to be Christian. They claimed to believe in God the Father and in his Son Jesus Christ and in the holy spirit and in the Christian church. Consequently, the modern-day Ezekiel class could talk the religious language of these professed Christians, who, in turn, should be able to understand the Biblical language of the Ezekiel class.

[16] The anointed remnant of Jehovah's witnesses did not expect to convert Christendom from the error of her way, any more than Ezekiel had been given the hope of converting the rebellious house of Israel. Christendom really represented the foretold apostasy or rebellion against the pure religion, a rebellion that took

14. After World War I, to whom was the anointed remnant of Jehovah's witnesses sent as far as religion is concerned?
15. Due to what situation could the anointed remnant of Jehovah's witnesses carry on well the Kingdom preaching in Christendom from 1919 C.E. onward?
16, 17. As in Ezekiel's case, did Jehovah's witnesses expect to convert Christendom, and what words of Jesus did they remember about people of another speech or race?

form after the death of the twelve apostles of Jesus
Christ by the end of the first century C.E. (2 Thes-
salonians 2:3-12) So Christendom also, like ancient
Israel, was a "rebellious house." The anointed remnant
were not surprised at her indisposition to listen, for
they remembered the words of Jesus that correspond
with those of Jehovah to Ezekiel about hearing, when
Jesus said to certain Israelite cities where he had wit-
nessed:

[17] "Woe to you, Chorazin! Woe to you, Bethsaida!
because if the powerful works had taken place in Tyre
and Sidon that took place in you, they would long ago
have repented in sackcloth and ashes. Consequently
I say to you, It will be more endurable for Tyre and
Sidon on Judgment Day than for you. And you, Caper-
naum, will you perhaps be exalted to heaven? Down to
Hádes you will come; because if the powerful works
that took place in you had taken place in Sodom, it
would have remained until this very day. Consequently I say to you people, It will be more endurable for
the land of Sodom on Judgment Day than for you."
—Matthew 11:20-24.

[18] Jesus Christ also said to the "wicked and adulterous generation" of his day: "Men of Nineveh will
rise up in the judgment with this generation and will
condemn it; because they repented at what Jonah
preached, but, look! something more than Jonah is
here. The queen of the south will be raised up in the
judgment with this generation and will condemn it;
because she came from the ends of the earth to hear
the wisdom of Solomon, but, look! something more
than Solomon is here."—Matthew 12:39-42.

[19] Jehovah will not leave himself open to the accusation that he failed to give advance warning to the
people who refrained from heeding his message of
the hour. That is why he "went on to say to [Eze-

18. Also, what did Jesus say regarding the men of Nineveh and the
queen of the south as regards Judgment Day?
19. To what accusation did Jehovah not lay himself open, and, to
correspond with Ezekiel, to whom did He send the anointed remnant,
and to say what?

kiel]: 'Son of man, all my words that I shall speak to you, take into your heart and hear with your own ears. And go, enter in among the exiled people, among the sons of your people, and you must speak to them and say to them, "This is what the Sovereign Lord Jehovah has said," regardless of whether they hear or they refrain.' " (Ezekiel 3:10, 11) The anointed remnant that had survived World War I and that were familiar with the prophetic book of Ezekiel were reminded that they must take God's Word into their hearts. They must then enter in among the modern-day "exiled people," namely, the people of Christendom, which has really been taken into captivity and exile by Babylon the Great, the world empire of false Babylonish religion. To these the anointed remnant must say what Jehovah told them to say in his written Word, no matter whether they listened or refused to do so. By this course the anointed remnant would prove faithful to their God.

[20] Now was the time for action. Ezekiel was still in the presence of the visionary chariot of Jehovah with the cherubs alongside its four wheels. Now the divine spirit that was in the wheels of that celestial chariot and that made them move in the right direction began to move Ezekiel. He writes: "And a spirit proceeded to bear me along and I began to hear behind me the sound of a great rushing: 'Blessed be the glory of Jehovah from his place.' And there was the sound of the wings of the living creatures that were closely touching each other, and the sound of the wheels close beside them, and the sound of a great rushing. And the spirit bore me along and proceeded to take me, so that I went bitterly in the rage of my spirit, and the hand of Jehovah upon me was strong. So I entered in among the exiled people at Tel-abib, who were dwelling by the river Chebar, and I began to dwell where they were dwelling; and I kept dwelling there for seven days, stunned in the midst of them." (Eze-

20. To whom and where did spirit from Jehovah bear Ezekiel along, and with what temperament did he go?

kiel 3:12-15) Thus Ezekiel was irresistibly conducted to his destination.

[21] Those parting words that Ezekiel had heard, "Blessed be the glory of Jehovah from his place," were doubtless said by the four cherubic living creatures that accompanied the celestial chariot. Nominally, the temple far away in Jerusalem was "his place," Jehovah's place, but his glory was not being blessed from that now polluted, defiled religious building. Jehovah's place is with His people whom he commissions for his service, like Ezekiel himself, and blessings upon the "glory of Jehovah" should arise from them. This should be the case with Ezekiel; it should also be the case with his modern antitype, the anointed remnant of Jehovah's witnesses from 1919 C.E. onward.

GOING "BITTERLY IN THE RAGE OF MY SPIRIT"

[22] The eating of the written roll from Jehovah, that had produced sweetness like honey in the mouth of Ezekiel, worked otherwise inside him, producing a bitterness, a "rage of my spirit," because of the "dirges and moaning and wailing" that were recorded on that scroll. So his going "bitterly in the rage of my spirit" did not mean his going against his will and in objection to his difficult mission. Also Jehovah's applied power, his "hand," was strong upon Ezekiel, strengthening him to express in his ministry the spirit of what was written down on the scroll that he had eaten. He needed to enter into the feel of that divine message of God's rage in order to present it properly, zealously. The message that Ezekiel had to deliver to those Jewish exiles at the river Chebar was a stunning one, one that numbed one's senses because of shocking features that it contained. Therefore he needed time to digest it, to make it his own. Seven days, a complete period of time, he dwelt "stunned"

21. In harmony with the parting words heard by Ezekiel, from what place should the "glory of Jehovah" be blessed?
22. In what sense did Ezekiel go "bitterly in the rage of my spirit," and at what was he "stunned," remaining so for seven days?

among those Jewish exiles at Tel-abib, not making a move, like one in a daze.

23 As for modern times, the anointed remnant of Jehovah's Christian witnesses had suffered much persecution at the hands of Christendom during World War I, but it was not this that filled them with bitterness, a spirit of revenge. It was the message of Jehovah's rage against the apostate, hypocritical Christendom that made them go in bitterness to the performance of their postwar commission. But the "hand of Jehovah" that was upon them was strong, moving them to their assigned work. It was his spirit that revived them in 1919 C.E. for their postwar public activities, especially in Christendom. This was just as it had been prophetically portrayed in Revelation 11:11-14, where we read about God's "two witnesses" whose public preaching Christendom had killed during the first world war:

24 "And after the three and a half days [of lying dead in the broad way of Christendom] spirit of life from God entered into them, and they stood upon their feet, and great fear fell upon those beholding them. And they heard a loud voice out of heaven say to them: 'Come on up here.' And they went up into heaven in the cloud, and their enemies beheld them. And in that hour a great earthquake occurred, and a tenth of the city fell; and seven thousand persons were killed by the earthquake, and the rest became frightened and gave glory to the God of heaven. The second woe is past. Look! The third woe is coming quickly."

25 As in the case of Ezekiel, who remained "stunned" among the exiles at Tel-abib by the river Chebar, it took a period of time for the revived remnant of Jehovah's witnesses to adjust themselves to the awe-inspiring postwar work. It was planned by their gov-

---

23, 24. What motivated the anointed remnant of Jehovah's witnesses to go "bitterly in the rage of my spirit," and how was the entering of the reviving spirit of God into them portrayed in Revelation 11:11-14?
25. At the start of the postwar period, in what way was the anointed remnant as in a "stunned" state, and what did the magazine *The Golden Age* make a start in doing regarding Christendom?

erning body at the headquarters of the Watch Tower Bible & Tract Society at Brooklyn, New York, to publish a new magazine that would especially expose the unchristian depredations that Christendom had committed against Jehovah's people during World War I. This purpose of the new magazine, *The Golden Age,* the first issue of which appeared on October 1, 1919, was concentrated in the special issue, Number 27, under date of September 29, 1920. All thirty-two pages of this issue featured the theme article entitled " 'Distress of Nations': Cause, Warning, Remedy." Four million copies of this special issue were printed and were distributed free to the people of Christendom. This was like only a start of this magazine's exposing of the flagrant misdeeds of Christendom in violation of God's written Word, the Bible.

[26] From then on particularly *The Golden Age* was used as a companion magazine to *The Watch Tower* in exposing the ungodliness of Christendom and pointing forward to her destruction. For instance, *The Golden Age* was used with *The Watch Tower* in reporting on the international convention of the anointed remnant of Jehovah's witnesses held in Columbus, Ohio, U.S.A., on July 20-27, 1924. Thus in its issue of September 24, 1924, *The Golden Age* published that famous document that was given worldwide attention as a feature of the international convention, together with the public address that was given in support of it. This document was the resolution adopted on Friday afternoon, July 25, it being entitled "INDICTMENT." To help us to appreciate how this resolution indicated Christendom as a hypocritical apostate religious system, we quote the following paragraphs of it:

We, the International Bible Students, in convention assembled, declare our unqualified allegiance to Christ, who is now present and setting up His kingdom, and to that kingdom.

We believe that every consecrated child of God is an

---

26. Of what other magazine was *The Golden Age* a companion in exposing Christendom's ungodliness, and what did its issue of September 24, 1924, publish about Christendom, indicting her?

ambassador for Christ and is duty-bound to give a faithful and true witness on behalf of his kingdom. As ambassadors for Christ, and without assuming any self-righteousness, we believe and hold that God has commissioned us to "proclaim the day of vengeance of our God and to comfort all that mourn."—Isaiah 61:2.

. . .

We present and charge that Satan formed a conspiracy for the purpose of keeping the people in ignorance of God's provision for blessing them with life, liberty and happiness; and that others, to wit, unfaithful preachers, conscienceless profiteers, and unscrupulous politicians, have entered into said conspiracy, either willingly or unwillingly.

That unfaithful preachers have formed themselves into ecclesiastical systems, consisting of councils, synods, presbyteries, associations, etc., and have designated themselves therein as popes, cardinals, bishops, doctors of divinity, pastors, shepherds, reverends, etc., and elected themselves to such offices, which aggregation is herein designated as "the clergy"; that these have willingly made commercial giants and professional politicians the principal of their flocks.

. . .

(7) That they deny the right of the Lord to establish his kingdom on earth, well knowing that Jesus taught that He would come again at the end of the world, and that the fact of that time would be made known by the nations of Christendom engaging in a world war, quickly followed by famine, pestilence, revolutions, . . .
—Paragraphs 1, 2, 4, 5, 17, pages 820, 821 of *The Golden Age.*

²⁷ The public address that was given at that "international convention in support of the above "Indictment" on the following Sunday was entitled "Civilization Doomed." It was delivered in the Ohio State University Stadium to a visible audience estimated at 35,000 persons. In the course of this address, and after quoting from seven prominent men who sensed the impending doom, the then president of the Watch Tower Bible & Tract Society presented in much detail "the reason for Christendom's doom." And, as *The Golden Age* reported, on page 813, column two: "The

---

27. What was the title of the public lecture given in support of that "Indictment" resolution, and what publicity was given to it next day?

discourse was received with splendid attention; and while it is a pointed exposition of the fallacies of Christendom, it was received with enthusiasm and applause by the great audience. On the Monday following, the Ohio *State Journal* carried the lecture in full."*

²⁸ After the public lecture the "Indictment," as already adopted by the conventioners, was read to the public and was unanimously approved by a rising vote of this public audience. In order to inform and warn as many people of Christendom as possible, in the following October this resolution, "Indictment," began to be distributed free in tract form, finally more than 50,000,000 copies of it being printed in English and foreign languages. Certainly, then, the prophetic work that was foreshadowed by the prophet Ezekiel long ago was being carried on by his modern-day counterpart toward the antitypical rebellious "house of Israel."

HOW TO DELIVER ONE'S SOUL AS A WATCHMAN

²⁹ Ezekiel of old was no doubt waiting for further word from Jehovah in his new location at Tel-abib, Babylonia. It came, as Ezekiel reports to us: "And it came about at the end of seven days that the word of Jehovah proceeded to occur to me, saying:

³⁰ " 'Son of man, a watchman is what I have made you to the house of Israel, and you must hear from my mouth speech and you must warn them from me. When I say to someone wicked, "You will positively die," and you do not actually warn him and speak in order to warn the wicked one from his wicked way to preserve him alive, he being wicked, in his error he will die, but his blood I shall ask back from your own hand. But as for you, in case you have warned some-

* See, also, the *Watch Tower* issues of September 1, 1924, pages 262, 263, and of September 15, 1924, pages 275-281.

28. How was this "Indictment" adopted at that public meeting, what distribution of it in print was made thereafter, and in this how was the anointed remnant acting like Ezekiel?
29-31. What further words did Ezekiel receive regarding his accountability as a watchman, to warn the wicked and the righteous?

one wicked and he does not actually turn back from his wickedness and from his wicked way, he himself for his error will die; but as for you, you will have delivered your own soul.

[31] " 'And when someone righteous turns back from his righteousness and actually does injustice and I must put a stumbling block before him, he himself will die because you did not warn him. For his sin he will die, and his righteous acts that he did will not be remembered, but his blood I shall ask back from your own hand. And as for you, in case you have warned someone righteous that the righteous one should not sin, and he himself does not actually sin, he will without fail keep on living because he had been warned, and you yourself will have delivered your own soul.' "—Ezekiel 3:16-21.

[32] Ezekiel as a newly commissioned watchman to the house of Israel was not to climb up into some literal watchtower and be on the lookout for threatening dangers to them. Rather, he was to watch as to how the sons of Israel fulfilled their obligations to their God. We must remember that the house of Israel had entered into a national contract or covenant with Jehovah through his mediator Moses back in the year 1513 B.C.E. and they had agreed solemnly over sacrificial animals to keep the Ten Commandments and all the associated laws from the hand of Jehovah. (Exodus 19:3 to 24:8) In Ezekiel's day this covenant had not been replaced by a new covenant, but Jehovah still held them bound to the covenant made through Moses at Mount Sinai. The prophet Ezekiel was appointed to watch and warn the breakers of the law of this covenant about the consequences of this. Just as a soldier on sentry duty at night, if he fell asleep and failed to guard his sleeping comrades, would be sentenced to death, so Ezekiel would lose his life if he failed to give warning from Jehovah.

---

32. Was Ezekiel to be a watchman in a literal watchtower, or how, and in connection with the observance of what covenant?

[33] Especially by the curses set out in the Law covenant, Jehovah would say to the wicked violator of the covenant, "You will positively die." This did not mean one's dying a natural death such as even the non-Jews die because they are descendants of our sinful first human father, Adam; rather, it means having one's life cut short by the executional means that Jehovah will use.

[34] So the wicked one could have his life spared from such an executional death by turning completely away from his wicked life. The righteous one could have his life preserved by continuing to hold to Jehovah's righteous law as laid down in His covenant. If a righteous Israelite turned to wickedness, then all his previous righteousness would not stand in credit for him; his final state as a bad man was what determined his case, and for this reason he must die the executional death. Was there vital need, then, for Jehovah to raise up a watchman? Yes! Because now Jerusalem and the land of Judah were already far along in their "time of the end." Lives of the inhabitants were involved.

[35] Indeed, although Ezekiel was far away from the scene of coming destruction by being an exile in the land of Babylon, his own life was involved. Why so? Because he could be held responsible for the deaths of the poor victims, inasmuch as Jehovah had appointed him to be a watchman to them. Since this was so, Ezekiel had all good reason to be concerned about giving the warning that he was appointed and commanded to give to those in peril. Ezekiel's God was also involved, for he could be charged with having left his covenant people without due warning if Ezekiel, who spoke in the name of Jehovah, failed in his duty. Ezekiel must guard against letting any reproach

33. How would Jehovah say to the violators of the Law covenant, "You will positively die"? And how would they die?
34. What opportunities for life were held out to the wicked and the righteous respectively, and why was there then vital need of a watchman for Israel?
35. How were both Jehovah and Ezekiel involved with those Israelites in danger of death, and what was the wise and sensible thing for Ezekiel to do?

come upon the name of his God. The wise and sensible thing for him to do was to deliver his own soul by obediently warning those Israelite souls who were in danger of death. Jehovah had provided a way of escape, and it was Ezekiel's obligation to point people to it.

[36] Is there any less an obligation placed upon the modern-day remnant of anointed witnesses whom Jehovah has appointed as a watchman class to Christendom, which is now in its "time of the end"? No! By the Bible's time schedule they know where this world of mankind is on the stream of time. By the fulfillment of Bible prophecies since the year 1914 C.E., they know that the celestial "chariot" of Jehovah is riding to the execution of His judicial decisions against the antitypical unfaithful Jerusalem and Judah. Because they expect to have the divine protection during the coming destruction of Christendom, they are not to feel unconcerned about the souls or lives who are religiously associated with Christendom. They know that the lives of these are in danger of annihilation. These need to be warned and be directed to God's way of righteousness, that they may escape destruction with the willfully wicked. Jehovah would hold the anointed remnant responsible for the lives of those needlessly lost through the failure of his appointed watchman class. Jehovah must not be left chargeable with not having given merciful warning in advance.

THE CELESTIAL CHARIOT FOLLOWS THE PROPHET

[37] No time is to be lost! Within the sight of those "eyes" that filled the rims of the wheels of Jehovah's celestial chariot, and within the hearing of those four cherubic "living creatures" that accompanied those wheels, Ezekiel was now commanded to go and discharge his duty. From the One than whom there is no

---

36. Despite their hope of divine protection, why should the anointed remnant not be unconcerned about those associated with Christendom, and also about God's chargeableness?
37, 38. From whom and for what did Ezekiel then receive an empowering, and, as told to do, what did he do?

one higher, yes, from Jehovah, who rides supreme above all his holy heavenly organization as on a chariot, Ezekiel received an empowering to carry out his courageous service as watchman. In Ezekiel 3:22, 23, the newly appointed prophet at Tel-abib tells us:

[38] "And the hand of Jehovah came to be upon me there and he proceeded to say to me: 'Get up, go forth to the valley plain, and there I shall speak with you.' So I got up and went forth to the valley plain, and, look! the glory of Jehovah was standing there, like the glory that I had seen by the river Chebar, and I went falling upon my face."

[39] Thus the chariotlike organization of Jehovah had followed Ezekiel to this new location. This should have assured him that this divine organization would be with him in his ministry, and the further evidences show that this was so. It was no longer the time to remain merely awe-struck at the "glory of Jehovah" seen in the vision. Realizing the glorious source of his appointment to service, he must get on his feet and be on the move. But first a word of caution. He was not to expect that his service would be without opposition and outside efforts to restrain him. Concerning this God warned him, as Ezekiel himself also reports:

[40] "Then spirit entered into me and made me stand up on my feet, and he began to speak with me and say to me: 'Come, be shut up inside your house. And you, O son of man, look! they will certainly put cords upon you and bind you with them so that you cannot go forth into the midst of them. And your very tongue I will make stick to the roof of your mouth, and you will certainly become mute, and you will not become to them a man administering reproof, because they are a rebellious house. And when I speak with you I shall open your mouth, and you must say to them,

39. What assurance was Ezekiel given as far as the divine organization is concerned, and what was he not to expect as regards his ministry to the Israelites?
40. What restrictions was Ezekiel to expect to be put upon him as to movement and as to speech?

"This is what the Sovereign Lord Jehovah has said." Let the one hearing hear, and let the one refraining refrain, because they are a rebellious house.' "—Ezekiel 3:24-27.

SPEAKING DESPITE ATTEMPTED RESTRAINTS

[41] It was not the Babylonian captors of the Israelites who were to put the cords and bands upon Ezekiel. It was the Israelites themselves, Ezekiel's own people, who would try to hinder and hamper him and try to restrain him from coming out of his house and restrain him from coming into the midst of them to declare what the Sovereign Lord Jehovah had said. All this would be in expression of their rebelliousness. They did not want Ezekiel to administer reproof to them. But Ezekiel was to trust in divine inspiration. When Jehovah had no message for him to deliver, then, in that regard, Jehovah would, as it were, make Ezekiel's tongue stick to the roof of his mouth so that he would become mute. But when Jehovah had a message for him to deliver, then Jehovah would speak with him and open Ezekiel's mouth to declare it, irrespective of what those rebellious Israelites did.

[42] In this "time of the end" more than two thousand five hundred years later, Christendom has treated the anointed remnant of Jehovah's servants similarly to the way in which the rebellious Israelites treated Ezekiel. But the modern-day Ezekiel class was not left without a forewarning of this. From their previous study of the prophecy of Ezekiel they knew what to expect from Christendom. True to prophecy, Christendom tried to impose restraints upon them, as the history of those postwar years all the way down into and through World War II shows. This did not surprise the courageous Ezekiel class. Their spiritual eyes

41. Who were the ones that would try to put the restraints upon Ezekiel as a reprover, and how would his mouth be opened or his tongue be made to stick to the roof of his mouth?
42. In view of what study was the modern Ezekiel class not surprised at Christendom's treatment of them, and at their deepening discernment of what were they strengthened for their work and the right stand?

were opened to see and deeply appreciate Jehovah's chariotlike organization, his universal heavenly organization. At their discernment of this they were strengthened for their work. They realized that there were just two great organizations in existence, Jehovah's organization and that of Satan the Devil. They chose to put their services at the disposal of Jehovah's organization. They relied, not upon any divine inspiration resting upon them, but upon Jehovah's holy spirit to aid them in speaking His message.

[43] They trusted in Jesus' words to his disciples, as set out in his prophecy concerning the "conclusion of the system of things," namely: "Also, in all the nations the good news has to be preached first. But when they are leading you along to deliver you up, do not be anxious beforehand about what to speak; but whatever is given you in that hour, speak this, for you are not the ones speaking, but the holy spirit is. Furthermore, brother will deliver brother over to death, and a father a child, and children will rise up against parents and have them put to death; and you will be objects of hatred by all people on account of my name. But he that has endured to the end is the one that will be saved."—Mark 13:10-13; Matthew 24:3-14.

[44] Here we are in the decade of the 1970's, and, despite all that Christendom has attempted against them by her religious clergy and the dictators Benito Mussolini, Adolf Hitler, Joseph Stalin, and others, the anointed remnant of Jehovah's servants have endured down to this time as a watchman to Christendom. They are determined to endure to the end of their earthly ministry, and that will also be to the end of Christendom and to the end of this system of things of which Christendom has been a predominant part. They do not desire that Jehovah will have to hold them

---

43. In what words of Jesus, in Mark 13:10-13, did the Ezekiel class trust?
44. Accordingly, despite what dictatorial regimes in Christendom have the Ezekiel class endured, and what is the motive behind their determination to endure till Christendom ends?

responsible for the tremendous loss of the lives of the adherents of Christendom at the time of her destruction. Their purpose is to prove themselves a faithful, obedient watchman class. This is what they purpose, not just in order to deliver their own souls, but that Jehovah might be vindicated as having given to Christendom full and fair warning by means of them. The faithful example of ancient Ezekiel in his watchman duty is an assurance that Jehovah will likewise have a faithful watchman class now until the execution of His foretold judgment upon Christendom.

Chapter 6

The Days of Christendom Are Numbered

"WHAT time is it?" We might well ask this question with regard to that world-embracing religious organization, Christendom. The God whom she professes to worship is a Numberer of Years. He has placed within his own jurisdiction the "times and seasons" with respect to his human creatures, and especially those who religiously claim to be representatives and servants of Him. (Daniel 2:20-22; Acts 1:7) This fact should be of great comfort to all who love what is right. Why? Because it assures us that the Almighty God of righteousness will not forever put up with wickedness here on earth. He has marked off the time when he will permit false religion to prevail over all the earth, enslaving practically the entire

1. Why may the matter of time be asked with regard to Christendom, and why are her days numbered?

human family. Not even the most powerful false religious organization on earth will be able to ward off destruction at His hand, when his due time will have arrived for Him to execute his judicial decision against false religion. Christendom has been most culpable in misrepresenting Him to mankind. Therefore Christendom's days are numbered!

² This astounding fact was illustrated in the ancient type of Christendom, namely, Jerusalem and the land of Judah in the days of the prophet Ezekiel, more than six centuries before our Common Era. Ezekiel was told that he was to be a "sign" man to his people, the house of Israel. What he was told to do would be a prophetic "sign" of what would happen inside and around Jerusalem, the capital of the Kingdom of Judah. —Ezekiel 4:3; 12:6, 11.

³ It is still the year 613 B.C.E., and Ezekiel is still at Tel-abib in the land of Babylon and is still beholding the vision of the chariotlike organization of Jehovah. Ezekiel, although now fully commissioned as prophet and watchman by Jehovah, has not yet gone into action. From above the magnificent celestial "chariot," Jehovah continues to speak to Ezekiel, telling him specifically what he must now do, first. The people of Christendom today do well to listen to what he says to Ezekiel:

⁴ "And you, O son of man, take for yourself a brick, and you must put it before you and engrave upon it a city, even Jerusalem. And you must lay siege against it and build a siege wall against it and throw up a siege rampart against it and set encampments against it and put battering rams all around against it. And as for you, take to yourself an iron griddle, and you must put it as an iron wall between you and the city, and you must fix your face against it, and it must get to

2. How was Christendom's end illustrated in type, and how was Ezekiel to be a "sign" man to his people?
3. What organization does well to listen to what Jehovah tells Ezekiel from atop his chariotlike organization in 613 B.C.E.?
4. What was Ezekiel to do with the brick that he must take, as "a sign to the house of Israel"?

be in a siege, and you must besiege it. It is a sign to the house of Israel."—Ezekiel 4:1-3.

⁵ These instructions may have reminded Ezekiel that he himself had once been within Jerusalem when under siege. This was just four years earlier, back in the year 617 B.C.E. That was when, for the second time, the king of Babylon, Nebuchadnezzar by name, had come against Jerusalem and besieged it. The ruler on the throne of Jerusalem at that time was Jehoiakim, the son of good King Josiah. In the eighth year of King Jehoiakim's reign this king of Babylon had come against Jerusalem and had made Jehoiakim subject to him, to make him pay tribute to him instead of to the king of Egypt. For three years King Jehoiakim stayed subject to the king of Babylon and then rebelled against him.

⁶ So in the eleventh year of the reign of King Jehoiakim Jerusalem saw the king of Babylon come against her for the second time, in order to take King Jehoiakim captive and to carry him off to the land of Babylon and put a different king in his place on the throne of Jerusalem. So Jerusalem was under siege by the king of Babylon in the year 617 B.C.E., in the third year of the vassalage of Jehoiakim to Babylon. But before the siege was over, King Jehoiakim met his death, and his son Jehoiachin was put on the throne by the inhabitants of Jerusalem. In the besieged city of Jerusalem Jehoiachin reigned for only three months, and then he decided to surrender to the king of Babylon.

⁷ It was not then Jehovah's time for Jerusalem and its temple to be destroyed, and he did not put it into the heart of the king of Babylon to destroy the holy city at that time. Instead, we read concerning Nebuchadnezzar the king of Babylon: "He took into exile all Jerusalem and all the princes and all the valiant,

_____

5. At what time was Ezekiel in Jerusalem when under siege, and what had led up to this siege by a foreign king?
6. During the siege that followed Jehoiakim's rebellion, what happened to him, and so what did Jerusalem's inhabitants do?
7. What did the besieger Nebuchadnezzar do with Jerusalem after King Jehoiachin surrendered to him, and what happened to Ezekiel?

mighty men—ten thousand he was taking into exile —and also every craftsman and builder of bulwarks. No one had been left behind except the lowly class of the people of the land. Thus he took Jehoiachin into exile to Babylon; and the king's mother and the king's wives and his court officials and the foremost men of the land he led away as exiled people from Jerusalem to Babylon." (2 Kings 23:36 to 24:15; 2 Chronicles 36:5-10; Daniel 1:1-4; Jeremiah 22:18, 19) Ezekiel the son of Buzi the priest was taken into exile with the captured king, Jehoiachin, in 617 B.C.E.—Ezekiel 1:1-3.

[8] After that, according to the time schedule of Jehovah, the city of Jerusalem and the Kingdom of Judah were to be spared for about eleven years more. To take the place of the deported Jehoiachin, his uncle, Mattaniah, the son of good King Josiah, was put on the throne of Jerusalem by the king of Babylon, and his name was changed to Zedekiah. As he was a bad king, who favored the Egyptians as against the Babylonians, the question arose, Would King Zedekiah repeat the mistake of his brother Jehoiakim and rebel against the king of Babylon? Three years before it occurred, Jehovah revealed by a vision to Ezekiel that King Zedekiah would actually do so. (Ezekiel 17:1-6, 9-21; 2 Kings 24:18 to 25:2; Jeremiah 52:1-5) Truly, when Ezekiel was raised up as a prophet and watchman to the house of Israel, the days of Jerusalem and the Kingdom of Judah were numbered. Jehovah was keeping count.

[9] To picture in pantomime what would happen to the capital city Jerusalem after the rebellion of King Zedekiah against the king of Babylon in violation of an oath before Jehovah, Ezekiel was to lie down with his eyes fixed against the picture of the city of Jerusalem that

---

8. According to Jehovah's timetable, how much more time had Jerusalem then to go, and what did Jehovah reveal to Ezekiel that King Zedekiah would do in international matters?
9. What was Ezekiel to do to pantomime what would happen to Jerusalem and the protection to be had by the besiegers and the use of their arm for vigorous action?

he had engraved upon a brick while it was still moist. To picture the protection from behind which the attackers would lay siege to the doomed city, Ezekiel was to set an iron griddle between himself and the engraved brick. He was also to have his "arm bared," like a Babylonian soldier with his arm bared for vigorous action against the besieged city.

[10] True to the "sign" that Ezekiel was to enact before the house of Israel, the siege did take place in Jehovah's due time.

[11] The historical account of this as described by one who was actually in the besieged city at the time, namely, the prophet Jeremiah, reads as follows: "Zedekiah began to rebel against the king of Babylon. And it came about in the ninth year of his being king, in the tenth month [Tebeth] on the tenth day of the month, that Nebuchadnezzar the king of Babylon came, yes, he and all his military force, against Jerusalem and began camping against it and building against it a siege wall all around. And the city came to be under siege until the eleventh year of King Zedekiah." (2 Kings 24:20 to 25:2; Jeremiah 52:1-5) There was a short interruption of this siege when the Babylonians (Chaldeans) withdrew in order to drive back the Egyptians to whom King Zedekiah had appealed for help. But, after having taken care of this Egyptian threat, the Babylonians came back and resumed the siege, just as the prophet Jeremiah forewarned that they would do. (Jeremiah 37:5-11) Not in vain had Jehovah given a "sign" by Ezekiel.

[12] Why, though, was this siege together with its disastrous consequences to come upon the city to which the name Jehovah was attached because of his temple there? Strange to say, it was because the destruction of Jerusalem came as a punishment from the hand of

---

10, 11. How does the historic account, as written by a man who was among the besieged ones, prove that Jehovah did not give a "sign" by Ezekiel in vain?
12. Why was this disastrous siege to come upon the city to which Jehovah's name was attached, and how had Jerusalem become the capital city of but two tribes of all Israel?

Jehovah for the rebellion of his covenant people against Him. That city was for about seventy-three years the capital of the united kingdom of the twelve tribes of Israel. But after the bad end and death of King Solomon there was a revolt of ten tribes against his son and successor, King Rehoboam. The kingdom was broken into two unequal parts, ten tribes (mainly on the north) forming the Kingdom of Israel under King Jeroboam with his capital city at Shechem in the territory of the tribe of Ephraim. The two loyal tribes of Judah and Benjamin, together with the tribe of Levi whose qualified men served at the temple of Jehovah, formed the Kingdom of Judah to the south, with its capital at Jerusalem. (1 Kings 12:1-25; 2 Chronicles 10:1 to 11:16) That was in 997 B.C.E., or 384 years before Ezekiel prophesied.

THE 390 DAYS OF BEARING ISRAEL'S ERROR

13 That the destruction of Jerusalem was to be in punishment for the religious error of his chosen people, Jehovah directly stated to Ezekiel, who was depicting the siege of Jerusalem, saying: "And as for you, lie upon your left side, and you must lay the error of the house of Israel upon it. For the number of the days that you will lie upon it you will carry their error. And I myself must give to you the years of their error to the number of three hundred and ninety days, and you must carry the error of the house of Israel. And you must complete them."—Ezekiel 4:4-6.

14 By this Ezekiel was to indicate, not the length of the coming siege of Jerusalem, but the exact year in which the city was to be destroyed, at the end of its siege. The expression "the house of Israel" here stands for the Northern Kingdom of ten rebellious tribes of Israel, which did not recognize Jerusalem as its capital. Nevertheless, Jerusalem was held accountable for the

13. For how many days was Ezekiel to lie on his left side before the engraved brick, and with what purpose in view?
14. Why was Jerusalem to be held accountable for the error of "the house of Israel" for 390 days?

religious error of the Northern Kingdom of Israel, because, from the closing years of King Solomon, that city had given all twelve tribes of Israel a bad religious example, toward idolatry.

¹⁵ Also, King Solomon's son and successor, Rehoboam, had not dealt kindly with the grievances of the ten complaining tribes. So he had driven them to revolt and had alienated them from Jerusalem as the center of Jehovah's worship. Hence Jerusalem was not guiltless as respects the religious error of the Northern Kingdom of Israel. This rebellious kingdom did not last three hundred and ninety (390) years from its start in 997 B.C.E., for it was destroyed by the Assyrian World Power about the year 740 B.C.E. Although this served as a direct punishment for its departure from the worship of Jehovah as God, the destruction of the Northern Kingdom of Israel, with its final capital at Samaria, did not settle the matter as far as Jehovah was concerned. There was still a measure of accounting to be settled with the mother capital, Jerusalem. When was it to be settled?

¹⁶ At the end of three hundred and ninety years from the start of the Northern Kingdom of Israel. That "error" could not start any earlier than the start of that kingdom itself, in 997 B.C.E. It did start then. In that year of revolt, what did King Jeroboam do?

¹⁷ "And Jeroboam began to say in his heart: 'Now the kingdom will return to the house of David. If this people continues going up to render sacrifices in the house of Jehovah in Jerusalem, the heart of this people will also be bound to return to their Lord, Rehoboam the king of Judah; and they will certainly kill me and return to Rehoboam the king of Judah.' Consequently the king took counsel and made two golden calves and said to the people: 'It is too much for you to go up to

---

15. How was King Rehoboam implicated in the "error" of the Northern Kingdom of Israel, and so was the matter of accountability settled with Jehovah by destruction of Samaria in 740 B.C.E.?
16. When was the matter of accounting for the "error" of the Northern Kingdom of Israel to be settled?
17, 18. According to the record in 1 Kings 12:26-33, what did King Jeroboam of the revolted tribes do?

Jerusalem. Here is your God, O Israel, that brought you up out of the land of Egypt.'

[18] "Then he placed the one in Bethel, and the other he put in Dan. And this thing came to be a cause for sin, and the people began to go before the one as far as Dan. And he began to make a house of high places and to make priests from the people in general, who did not happen to be of the sons of Levi. . . . And he began to make offerings upon the altar that he had made in Bethel on the fifteenth day in the eighth month, in the month that he had invented by himself; and he proceeded to make a festival for the sons of Israel and to make offerings upon the altar to make sacrificial smoke."—1 Kings 12:26-33; 2 Chronicles 11:14, 15.

[19] The year of the start of the "error" of the house of Israel having been found, namely, 997 B.C.E., then if we measure three hundred and ninety years from then we arrive at the date for the destruction of Jerusalem. It is the year 607 B.C.E.* Whether the prophet Ezekiel figured out that date on his receiving the prophecy six years before Jerusalem suffered destruction, we do not know. But the exactness of the matter proves that Jehovah indeed is a Numberer of Years and that he had fixed in advance the year in which he was to execute his judicial decision to the full upon unfaithful Jerusalem. This is something for the modern-day counterpart of unfaithful Jerusalem, namely, Christendom, to take seriously to heart at this late date. Does she realize from examining the Bible that her days are numbered?

THE FORTY DAYS OF BEARING JUDAH'S ERROR

[20] However, was there no "error" on the part of the Southern Kingdom of Judah, the punishment for which

---

* Compare *Aid to Bible Understanding,* page 338, paragraphs 7-9.

19. When would those 390 years end, and what does this timing of matters show Jehovah to be?
20. In the second case, how many days was Ezekiel to lie on his right side, and with what purpose in view?

was to be executed upon Jerusalem to the point of destroying her? Yes. Jehovah did not overlook this, for he went on to say to Ezekiel, who was pantomiming the siege of Jerusalem: "And you must lie upon your right side in the second case, and you must carry the error of the house of Judah forty days. A day for a year, a day for a year, is what I have given you. And to the siege of Jerusalem you will fix your face, with your arm bared, and you must prophesy against it. And, look! I will put cords upon you that you may not turn yourself from your one side to your other side, until you will have completed the days of your siege." —Ezekiel 4:6-8.

[21] If Ezekiel was lying with the head to the east in his mimic siege of Jerusalem, then his left side would be to the north, the direction of the former Northern Kingdom of Israel, and his right side would be to the south. So it was fitting for him to lie upon his right side when carrying the "error" of the Southern Kingdom of Judah. Of course, Ezekiel's lying on his right side for forty days came after his lying on the left side for three hundred and ninety days, which would mean four hundred and thirty days of lying down as in a siege.

[22] However, in the actual fulfillment upon ancient Jerusalem, the forty days for the "error" of the "house of Judah" would run concurrently with the last forty days of the three hundred and ninety days for the "error" of the "house of Israel." The unit of time measurement that Jehovah gave to Ezekiel was, "a day for a year," made emphatic by being repeated. This was the same unit of time measurement that Jehovah gave when he required the rebellious Israelites to wander forty years in the wilderness after coming up out of Egypt. (Numbers 14:34) So that time unit

---

21. If Ezekiel faced east, his left and right sides would be turned to what kingdoms respectively, and what was the sum of the days of his lying down in this mimic siege of Jerusalem?
22. How did the forty days respecting the "error" of the kingdom of Judah apply with reference to the 390 days for Israel's "error," and so how did the forty years respecting Judah apply with respect to the 390 years for Israel?

as stated back there in 1512 B.C.E. was at least 899 years old when Jehovah restated it to Ezekiel. Accordingly the forty years for the "error" of the "house of Judah" were to run concurrently with the last forty years of the 390-year period for the "error" of the "house of Israel." The last forty years of that time period began in the year 647 B.C.E. (350 years after 997 B.C.E.) Those forty years ended in 607 B.C.E. Both time periods, the longer one and the shorter one, had to converge on the same date, for ancient Jerusalem was destroyed only once, namely, in 607 B.C.E.

²³ A question now arises, Was the beginning of those forty years for the "error of the house of Judah" marked by anything to indicate a start of counting religious "error"? Yes, the opening year of that period was the thirteenth year of the reign of good King Josiah of Jerusalem, and that was the year when Jehovah appointed Jeremiah the son of Hilkiah the priest to serve as His prophet in the land of Judah. (Jeremiah 1:1-3; 25:3) But at that time was not good King Josiah restoring the pure worship of Jehovah throughout the land of Judah? Why, then, should Jehovah start to reckon "error" against the "house of Judah" in that year? It was because of the sins of King Manasseh, the grandfather of King Josiah, sins that had been so plentiful and shocking that Jehovah could not clear them from the account that he held against Jerusalem as a bloodstained, idolatrous city. We read:

²⁴ "It was only by the order of Jehovah that it took place against Judah, to remove it from his sight for the sins of Manasseh, according to all that he had done; and also for the innocent blood that he had shed, so that he filled Jerusalem with innocent blood, and Jehovah did not consent to grant forgiveness."—2 Kings 24:3, 4; 21:16.

²⁵ Even after the noble efforts of King Josiah to

<hr>

23, 24. How was the forty-year period of bearing the "error" of Judah marked, and how does 2 Kings 24:3, 4; 21:16 indicate why it began then despite Josiah's restoring of pure worship at that time?
25. How does 2 Kings 23:25-27 indicate that, despite the noble efforts of King Josiah, an account remained for Jehovah to settle with Jerusalem?

enforce the law of Jehovah in Judah and Jerusalem, we read: "And like him there did not prove to be a king prior to him who returned to Jehovah with all his heart and with all his soul and with all his vital force, according to all the law of Moses; neither after him has there risen up one like him. Nevertheless, Jehovah did not turn back from the great burning of his anger, with which his anger burned against Judah over all the offensive things with which Manasseh had made them offend. But Jehovah said: 'Judah, too, I shall remove from my sight, just as I have removed Israel; and I shall certainly reject this city that I have chosen, even Jerusalem, and the house [temple] of which I have said, "My name will continue there."' " —2 Kings 23:25-27.

²⁶ Josiah's father, King Amon, had not improved matters in Judah and Jerusalem, for with regard to King Amon it is written: "And he proceeded to do what was bad in Jehovah's eyes, just as Manasseh his father had done; and to all the graven images that Manasseh his father had made Amon sacrificed, and he continued serving them. And he did not humble himself because of Jehovah the same as Manasseh his father humbled himself, for Amon was one that made guiltiness increase. Finally his servants conspired against him and put him to death in his own house." (2 Chronicles 33:22-25) Thus King Amon left Judah and Jerusalem with an ugly record and a heavy amount of unpardonable accountability before Jehovah when his son and successor, Josiah, became king in 659 B.C.E.

²⁷ In the thirteenth year of Josiah's reign Jehovah raised up Jeremiah the son of Hilkiah the priest as his prophet, in 647 B.C.E. By Jeremiah's prophesying Jehovah definitely made known his purpose to bring utter desolation upon Judah and Jerusalem without

26. How had King Amon not improved matters in Judah, so leaving a heavy amount of unpardonable accountability for Jerusalem when his son became king?
27. Had the forty years begun counting when King Manasseh was taken captive to Babylon, why might those forty years have ended during Josiah's reign, and why would this have been inappropriate?

fail. (Jeremiah 19:1-5; 25:1-11) In accord with this, Jehovah made the thirteenth year of King Josiah's reign the beginning of the count of the forty years of bearing the "error of the house of Judah." This forty-year period ended in 607 B.C.E., or twenty-one years after the death of King Josiah. If the forty-year period had begun during the reign of his grandfather, King Manasseh, especially from the time that King Manasseh was taken captive to Babylon by the king of Assyria, then the forty years might have ended during the reign of King Josiah. How so? Because the reign of King Manasseh lasted for fifty-five years, and his son Amon's reign lasted for two years, and that of King Josiah for thirty-one years. (2 Chronicles 33:10 to 34:2, 19-28) Josiah's reign was good all the way through, and so the calamity due at the end of forty years was not allowed to come in his day.—2 Kings 22:11-20; 2 Chronicles 34:14-33.

²⁸ However, what especially concerns us today is the fulfillment of the calamity upon the modern-day counterpart of idolatrous, bloodstained Jerusalem and Judah, namely, Christendom. No less so than in the ancient type, Christendom is filled with idolized things, with religious images and with nationalistic statues and emblems to which idolatrous devotions are paid. No less so than in the case of Jerusalem, Christendom has been filled with "innocent blood" in great quantity "from end to end." (2 Kings 21:16) From its very beginning Christendom has been befouled with bloodshed. After the Roman emperor, Constantine the Great, had accepted the Christianity of his day, making it the religion of the State, yes, after he had presided over the religious Council of Nicaea, he had his oldest son put to death and thereafter his own wife, Fausta. In this way the very foundations of Christendom were befouled with blood.—*The Encyclopædia Britannica,* 11th Edition, Volume 6, page 989, paragraph 4.

---

28. However, with the calamity coming upon whom are we concerned today, and how does the modern antitype correspond with ancient Jerusalem as to idolatry and bloodshed?

²⁹ Throughout the centuries that followed, Christendom's skirts have dripped with blood. If that blood could cry out, it would testify against the ten religious crusades that she carried on vainly against the "infidel" Mohammedans of the Middle East, the crimes of the religious inquisition, the religious wars between Roman Catholics and Protestants, her Hundred Years' War, her Thirty Years' War, and now, finally, her two world wars of this twentieth century by means of which more blood was shed than has been shed since the founding of ancient Babylon by Nimrod, "a mighty hunter in opposition to Jehovah" four thousand two hundred years ago! Has not the "error" of Christendom come to be far greater than that of ancient Jerusalem and Judah? From all the facts the answer is plainly Yes! And if Jehovah held ancient Jerusalem responsible, ought He not to do the same with Christendom?

CHRISTENDOM WORSE THAN "HEATHENDOM"

³⁰ Christendom cannot deny that she has acted far worse than that religious realm which she called "heathendom" or "pagandom." Jehovah's estimate of her must be the same as that which he expressed to the prophet Ezekiel concerning the city where the temple of His worship was located: "This is what the Sovereign Lord Jehovah has said, 'This is Jerusalem. In the midst of the nations I have set her, with lands all around her. And she proceeded to behave rebelliously against my judicial decisions in wickedness more than the nations, and against my statutes more than the lands that are all around her, for my judicial decisions they rejected and, as for my statutes, they did not walk in them.'

³¹ "Therefore this is what the Sovereign Lord Jehovah has said, 'For the reason that you people were more turbulent than the nations that are all around

---

29. If Jehovah held ancient Jerusalem responsible for bloodguiltiness, what cases of large-scale bloodshed on the part of Christendom since Emperor Constantine's day may Jehovah consider?
30, 31. A comparison of Christendom with heathendom corresponds with what estimate that Jehovah expressed to Ezekiel about Jerusalem when compared with surrounding lands, and so what was Jehovah determined to do to Jerusalem?

you, in my statutes you did not walk and my judicial decisions you did not perform; but according to the judicial decisions of the nations that are all around you, you performed, did you not? therefore this is what the Sovereign Lord Jehovah has said: "Here I am against you, O city, even I, and I will execute in the midst of you judicial decisions in the eyes of the nations. And I will do in you that which I have not done and the like of which I shall not do anymore by reason of all your detestable things." ' "—Ezekiel 5:5-9.

³² When we recall that it was late in the forty-year period of bearing "error" for the house of Judah that Jehovah appointed Ezekiel as his prophet and watchman, we see reason to believe that it is likewise late in Jehovah's appointed period of time for bearing the error of Christendom. Here we are more than half a century from the end of the Gentile Times in the year 1914, and Christendom's two world wars are now shameful history and nothing seems to deter her from preparing for a third one. From her own internal state of affairs the days of Christendom must be numbered. But from Jehovah's count of time her days are for a certainty numbered. And when the number thereof ends, then what?

³³ To the prophet Ezekiel Jehovah indicated what the ending of the 390 "days" (years) and of the 40 "days" (years) simultaneously would mean for Jerusalem and Judah. After telling Ezekiel how to pantomime the approaching siege of Jerusalem, Jehovah went on to say to him: "And as for you, take for yourself wheat and barley and broad beans and lentils and millet and spelt, and you must put them in one utensil and make them into bread for you, for the number of the days that you are lying upon your side; three hundred and ninety days you will eat it. And your food

---

32. As in the raising up of Ezekiel as a prophet, how far along is it now in the bearing of the "error" of Christendom, and from all standpoints what must be true about her remaining days?
33. What and how was Ezekiel to eat and drink during the days of the mimic siege of Jerusalem?

that you will eat will be by weight—twenty shekels a day. From time to time you will eat it. And water you will drink merely by measure, the sixth part of a hin. From time to time you will drink."—Ezekiel 4:9-11.

BAD FOOD AND HEALTH CONDITIONS

34 Think of it—eating just twenty shekels' weight (slightly over eight ounces) of food a day, and drinking just one-sixth of a hin measure (about a pint) of water a day, for three hundred and ninety days! A starvation diet like that indicated a critical food shortage, a famine, yes, just like that to which the besieged city of Jerusalem was to be reduced. This was enough, also, to bring on pestilence among the starving inhabitants! And yet these are the very things that Ezekiel was instructed to pantomime and that Jehovah clearly said, by way of interpretation, would befall Jerusalem under siege. Even cannibalism would result, he said:

35 " 'Therefore fathers themselves will eat sons in the midst of you, and sons themselves will eat their fathers, and I will execute in you acts of judgment and scatter all the remainder of you to every wind. Therefore as I am alive,' is the utterance of the Sovereign Lord Jehovah, 'surely for the reason that it was my sanctuary that you defiled with all your disgusting things and with all your detestable things, I myself also am the One that will diminish you and my eye will not feel sorry and I myself also will not show compassion. A third of you—by the pestilence they will die, and by famine they will come to their end in the midst of you.' "—Ezekiel 5:10-12.

36 Those who would die as a result of the famine and the pestilence inside besieged Jerusalem were to be like the third of the hair that Ezekiel would shave off his head and beard, not with a razor, but with a sword of

34. What did such a starvation diet for Ezekiel indicate for Jerusalem during her siege, with what health effects therefrom?
35. According to what Jehovah said to Ezekiel, how extreme was the famine to become?
36. How did Ezekiel illustrate that the famine and pestilence would consume their victims like fire?

war, and that Ezekiel was to "burn in the very fire in the midst of the city as soon as the days of the [mimic] siege have come to the full." (Ezekiel 5:1, 2) The famine and pestilence were to consume their victims like fire!

[37] What a miserable diet the cooped-up inhabitants of besieged Jerusalem were to have! It was bad enough to have to eat bread made up of a variety of ingredients, of wheat, barley, broad beans, lentils, millet and spelt. For a Jew like Ezekiel the son of a temple priest such a bread would be unclean, for its makeup violated the principle that Jehovah had set down in the law given through Moses, in Leviticus 19:19: "You must not sow your field with seeds of two sorts, and you must not put upon yourself a garment of two sorts of thread, mixed together." (Also, Deuteronomy 22:9) But look at the combustible material that the inhabitants of besieged Jerusalem might have to use in baking this ritually unclean bread! Jehovah hinted at it when he said to Ezekiel about how to bake the bread mixture: "And as a round cake of barley you will eat it; and as for it, upon dung cakes of the excrement of mankind you will bake it before their eyes." Ezekiel was hereby to enact a prophetic picture, for he tells us: "And Jehovah went on to say: 'Just like this the sons of Israel will eat their bread unclean among the nations to which I shall disperse them.'"—Ezekiel 4:12, 13.

[38] Baked in such a way, bread would be doubly unclean. Does such a baking process seem revolting to us of modern civilization? Twenty-five centuries ago it was even revolting to Ezekiel. He just could not help but express his horror, as he tells us: "And I proceeded to say: 'Alas, O Sovereign Lord Jehovah! Look! My soul is not a defiled one; neither a body already dead nor a torn animal have I eaten from my youth up,

---

37. How was illustrated the ceremonially unclean bread that the inhabitants of Jerusalem would be obliged to eat?
38. How did Ezekiel express horror at eating bread of that kind prepared in such a way, and what did it mean for Jerusalem to have to eat such objectionable bread?

even until now, and into my mouth there has come no foul flesh.' " (Ezekiel 4:14) Over six hundred years later the Jewish Christian, the apostle Peter, had a similar revulsion of feelings at the instructions given to him in a vision from God. (Acts 10:9-17; 11:5-10) Ezekiel, of a priestly family, would not desire, even under the dire famine conditions of a siege, to defile himself ceremonially, although it might mean death by starvation. It gives one just an inkling of the dire straits to which the besieged Jerusalem might be brought down.

[39] However, a bread mixture, whether baked over dung cakes made of human excrement or not, would still be unclean as well as be in short supply. This was the main point to be stressed. Hence Jehovah could show consideration for Ezekiel's feelings and make the baking process more normal for Middle Easterners. "Accordingly," says Ezekiel, "he said to me: 'See, I have given you cattle manure instead of the dung cakes of mankind, and you must make your bread upon it.' " Then Jehovah gives his own explanation, for Ezekiel writes: "And he continued saying to me: 'Son of man, here I am breaking the rods around which ring-shaped loaves are suspended, in Jerusalem, and they will have to eat bread by weight and in anxious care, and it will be by measure and in horror that they will drink water itself, to the intent that they may be lacking bread and water and they may look astonished at one another and rot away in their error.' "—Ezekiel 4:15-17.

[40] This was no overdrawn statement. During the actual siege, the prophet Jeremiah, imprisoned inside Jerusalem, was finally given a round loaf of bread "daily from the street of the bakers, until all the bread was exhausted from the city." (Jeremiah 37:21) Finally, Jeremiah could write concerning the last year of the reign of wicked King Zedekiah in besieged Jeru-

---

39. Why could Jehovah show consideration for Ezekiel's feelings in this regard, and yet how was Jerusalem to fare as to food and drink?
40. How did the later developments in Jerusalem prove that Jehovah had not made an overdrawn statement about food and drink?

salem: "On the ninth day of the fourth month the famine was severe in the city, and there proved to be no bread for the people of the land. And the city got to be breached, and all the men of war fled by night by the way of the gate between the double wall that is by the king's garden, while the Chaldeans were all around against the city; and the king began to go in the direction of the Arabah. And a military force of Chaldeans went chasing after the king, and they got to overtake him in the desert plains of Jericho; and all his own military force was scattered from his side." (2 Kings 25:3-5; Jeremiah 39:3-5; 52:6-8) The warning "sign" that Jehovah gave by Ezekiel proved to be all too true!

⁴¹ What, though, about those survivors of the eighteen-month-long siege of Jerusalem? They were, as Jehovah told Ezekiel, to "eat their bread unclean among the nations to which I shall disperse them." (Ezekiel 4:13) They were to be dispersed, scattered to non-Israelite lands as exiles, leaving the land of Judah and Jerusalem a complete desolation. They left behind at Jerusalem, not only the victims of the famine and pestilence, but also those who had been killed off by the weapons and military equipment of the Chaldeans or Babylonians. These latter war casualties and the survivors themselves were like the other two parts of the hair that Ezekiel had shaved off his head and beard by a sword. The war dead were like the third of his hair that Ezekiel was to strike with the sword all around, on all sides. As for the survivors, who were to be dispersed among the Gentile nations, they were like the remaining third of Ezekiel's hair that he was to scatter to the wind, not for a peaceful life in exile, but, as Jehovah said to Ezekiel, "I shall draw out a sword itself after them." (Ezekiel 5:2) Explaining Ezekiel's symbolic actions toward these latter two portions of hair, Jehovah said to his prophet:

---

41. How were the survivors of the siege of Jerusalem to get along in the lands to which they were scattered?

[42] "And another third [the second third of the hair] —by the sword [of war] they will fall all around you. And the last third I shall scatter even to every wind, and a sword is what I shall draw out after them. And my anger will certainly come to its finish and I will appease my rage on them and comfort myself; and they will have to know that I myself, Jehovah, have spoken in my insistence on exclusive devotion, when I bring my rage to its finish upon them."—Ezekiel 5:12, 13.

[43] Some exiles were to be like the few hairs that Ezekiel would take from the third portion of shaved hair and would wrap up in the skirts of his garment. Such exiles would go through their hard experience and come back from the dispersion to take up a purified worship of Jehovah after the land of Judah had lain desolate for seventy years. But as for the exiles in general, it was to be no easy experience. The consuming fire of Jehovah's anger would be against them. Like human hair, they would be very combustible. So, concerning the remaining hairs that were not bound up in Ezekiel's skirts, Jehovah said to him: "And others of them you will take and you must pitch them into the midst of the fire and incinerate them in the fire. From one [fire] a fire will go forth to all the house of Israel." —Ezekiel 5:3, 4.

[44] So those who try to worship the true God hypocritically will not escape for long. Jehovah hates being treated by religious hypocrites like a God who can be fooled. Therefore to such partway survivors this God who requires exclusive devotion said:

[45] "And I shall make you a devastated place and a reproach among the nations that are all around you before the eyes of every passerby. And you must become a reproach and an object of reviling words, a

---

42. How did Jehovah explain it according to the way in which Ezekiel treated the last third of his shaved-off hair, and what were the survivors to know?
43. What was to be the experience of those pictured by the hairs bound in Ezekiel's skirts and of those pictured by the hair thrown into the fire?
44, 45. What kind of example was Jehovah to make of the people of Jerusalem, and what acts of judgment was he to do toward the partway survivors of Jerusalem?

warning example and a horror to the nations that are all around you, when I do in you acts of judgment in anger and in rage and in raging reproofs. I myself, Jehovah, have spoken. When I send the injurious arrows of the famine upon them, which must prove to be for ruination, which arrows I shall send to bring you people to ruin, even famine I shall increase upon you people and I will break your rods around which ring-shaped loaves are suspended. And I will send upon you people famine and injurious wild beasts, and they must bereave you of children, and pestilence and blood themselves will pass along through you, and a sword I shall bring in upon you. I myself, Jehovah, have spoken."—Ezekiel 5:14-17.

46 Cruel words! So that declaration of Jehovah's purpose may appear to be to sentimentalists and to those who do not heartily detest religious hypocrisy and who do not appreciate the dignity of the true God that has been outraged. But those words were not more cruel than the actual experiences that befell the dispersed survivors of Jerusalem's destruction in 607 B.C.E. Jehovah did not speak in vain, nor had he overstated matters. His words are not to be taken lightly. When religious pretenders bring reproach upon Him and his sacred name, it is sure to result in reproach coming upon them from the worldly nations. Jehovah exposes their religious hypocrisy before the nations of the world.

ARROWS OF FAMINE AND PESTILENCE TO HIT CHRISTENDOM

47 Let not this historic lesson be lost upon us. Why should we suffer with Christendom, who has not taken to heart this "warning example" that is so plainly recorded in Jehovah's Word? Of course, famine and pestilence are predicted to come, not just on Christen-

46. Were the later facts more cruel than those prophetic words, and so what results to religious pretenders who bring reproach upon Jehovah and his name?
47. For not heeding this "warning example" of Bible history, what food and health conditions are due to come upon Christendom?

dom alone, but upon all the world of mankind, according to the warnings of today's ecologists and economists and statisticians who are worried at the way the population increase is outstripping the production of food and also the spreading of diseases due to the increasing pollution of man's environment. But when Jehovah lets loose the "great tribulation" as predicted by his Son Jesus Christ, in Matthew 24:21, 22, and when it strikes the modern-day counterpart of ancient Judah and Jerusalem, then Christendom will experience famine and pestilence in an *added* sense.

[48] Christendom's salaried clergymen, even those of the highest ecclesiastical dignity, will no longer receive the financial and material support of the people. Her religious churches and related seminaries and other institutions will suffer and perish from lack of contributions and patronage; in fact, they will be violently despoiled. Not being fed and nourished on the sound doctrine of Jehovah's written Word, both the clergy and their religious organizations will prove to be mortally sick spiritually, smitten with an epidemic of venereal diseases that result from committing religious fornication with the political and secular elements of this unclean system of things.

[49] Because she has misrepresented him to the nations, Jehovah will not shield her from violence at the hands of disgusted worldly elements. The number of her days will have come to their full. She will be destroyed as surely as was Jerusalem back in 607 B.C.E. Any associates of Christendom who survive her destruction in the "great tribulation" will not come through to any improved, long-lived future, any more than did those hypocritical survivors of ancient Jerusalem's destruction. They face only further hardship and eventual destruction in the further and concluding part of the "great tribulation." Jehovah's symbolic "sword" of

48. How will Christendom experience famine and pestilence in an added sense?
49. Because of being misrepresented, from what will Jehovah not shield Christendom, and how will He bring his rage to a finish upon any hypocritical survivors of Christendom's destruction?

judicial execution will be brandished against them in the "war of the great day of God the Almighty" at the world situation called Har–Magedon. (Revelation 16: 14-16; 19:11-21) In this way he will bring his righteous rage against religious hypocrisy and ungodliness to a finish upon them.

⁵⁰ Does this seem a gloomy picture, one setting out in sharp detail the "dirges and moaning and wailing" that were written in the "roll" that Ezekiel ate? There is, nevertheless, a bright side to the picture! What did the utter desolating of the land of Judah and Jerusalem back there accomplish? It cleared off all false religion from that God-given land. The land lay clean for the reestablishment of the pure religion there in Jehovah's due time. (Ezekiel 2:9 to 3:2) Similarly down here in this twentieth century. If Christendom must go in the approaching "great tribulation," so must all the rest of false religion. The entire earth must be cleansed of all false religion and its defiling, corruptive influence and power.

⁵¹ But this will not leave a religious vacuum, a godless emptiness. The true religion of the one living and true God will survive under his protection. Without the opposition and persecution by the promoters of false religion, it will flourish under divine blessing and spread to all parts of the earth. After the destruction of Jerusalem in 607 B.C.E., Ezekiel was appointed to prophesy about this blessed future for all mankind.—See Ezekiel's prophecy in chapters thirty-six through forty-eight.

---

50. The desolating of the land of Judah and Jerusalem back there accomplished what religiously, and likewise to what will Christendom's removal lead religiously?
51. Why will the destruction of Christendom and all other false religion not leave a godless vacuum on the earth?

Chapter 7

Christendom Will Know
—at Her End

THE Creator does not enjoy seeing this earth defiled, polluted. It is *his* creation and was meant to be a credit to him. It was his original purpose that this earth, as a home for mankind, should be everywhere a paradise such as would make this terrestrial globe a decoration in the gorgeous celestial Milky Way of which it is a tiny part.

2 The first human couple were started off in a paradise that went beautifully with their human perfection. Before them and their offspring to be, there lay the opportunity to extend their original paradise home to the complete circumference of the earth. (Genesis 1:26 to 2:25) Today, after six thousand years of man's existence on earth, look at it! Its condition is far from being the happy paradise of life, health and beauty that its Creator purposed it to be. This could hardly be any cause of pleasure to Him any more than it is to us humans. In fact, does He have any right to be angry about this? If *He* does not have a right to be angered over this, who else does?

3 However, what does a Creator do when his creation has been defiled and its surface has been spoiled, ruined, by the creatures who were meant to take care of it? Does he destroy this whole creation, together with the living creatures upon it?

---

1. What is the Creator's purpose concerning the earth, making the defiling of it something not enjoyable to Him?
2. How does the earth's condition today compare with the possible condition that was set before man in his original paradise home, and so what questions come up as to the Creator's pleasure or anger?
3. What question arises as to the procedure of a Creator when creatures living on it defile it?

⁴ Any doing of such a thing would be a waste of his creative activity, a sign of defeat. What he should do, and what he purposes to do, he illustrated by what he did to the land of Judah and Jerusalem back there in the seventh century before our Common Era. Jehovah had brought his people into the Promised Land in the year 1473 B.C.E. It was then, as Jehovah said, "a land that I had spied out for them, one flowing with milk and honey. It was the decoration of all the lands." (Ezekiel 20:6, 15) The generation of those Israelites that Jehovah brought into this beautiful land remained faithful to Him. But their descendants began to defile the land by adopting idolatry and unrighteously shedding innocent blood. Repeated religious purgings followed, but the Israelites would always fall back into idolatry. Finally, in 607 B.C.E., Jehovah cleared off all the Jewish idolaters and thus left the land of Judah utterly desolate.

⁵ The land of Judah and Jerusalem did not then go out of existence. For seventy years it lay desolate, Jehovah not permitting even pagan, non-Israelite idolaters to move in and continue the defilement of it. Jehovah purposed for his pure worship to be reestablished in that land which was undergoing a purging. At the end of the seventy years of desolation Jehovah brought back to the land a repentant purified remnant of Israelites to reoccupy the land of Judah and Jerusalem and to restore the clean worship of their God there. Jehovah repeopled the land with his worshipers who would use it in harmony with the sacred purpose for which he had given them the land. By his prophet Ezekiel he foretold this.

⁶ Ezekiel first had the difficult task of prophesying against the inhabitants of the land of Judah and Jerusalem who were defiling their God-given possession.

4. As to what was to be done, why does the land of Judah here come under consideration, and what happened to that land in 607 B.C.E.?
5. How did Jehovah let the land of Judah undergo a purging, and how was it put to use again for the purpose for which it was given?
6. First, what difficult task did Ezekiel have, and why did Jehovah have Ezekiel address the land itself?

Jehovah used Ezekiel to make an address to the land itself to indicate what would befall it because of its idolatrous God-defying occupants. Ezekiel, still referring to the year 613 B.C.E., tells us of this in these words:

7 "And the word of Jehovah continued to occur to me, saying: 'Son of man, set your face toward the mountains of Israel and prophesy to them. And you must say, "O mountains of Israel, hear the word of the Sovereign Lord Jehovah: This is what the Sovereign Lord Jehovah has said to the mountains and to the hills, to the stream beds and to the valleys:

8 " ' " 'Here I am! I am bringing upon you a sword, and I shall certainly destroy your high places. And your altars must be made desolate and your incense stands must be broken, and I will cause your slain ones to fall before your dungy idols. And I will put the carcasses of the sons of Israel before their dungy idols, and I will scatter your bones all around your altars. In all your dwelling places the very cities will become devastated and the high places themselves will become desolated, in order that they may lie devastated and your altars may lie desolated and be actually broken and your dungy idols may be actually made to cease and your incense stands cut down and your works wiped out. And the slain one will certainly fall in the midst of you, and you will have to know that I am Jehovah.' " ' "—Ezekiel 6:1-7.*

IDOL WORSHIPERS WILL HAVE TO KNOW WHO HE IS

9 Idolatrous high places, idolatrous altars, idolatrous

---

* Here begins the series of sixty-two occurrences in the book of Ezekiel where Jehovah declares that others will "have to know that I am Jehovah," as follows: Ezekiel 6:7, 10, 13, 14; 7:4, 9, 27; 11:10, 12; 12:15, 16, 20; 13:9, 14, 21, 23; 14:8; 15:7; 16:62; 20:12, 20, 26, 38, 42, 44; 22:16; 23:49; 24:24, 27; 25:5, 7, 11, 17; 26:6; 28:22, 23, 24, 26; 29:6, 9, 16, 21; 30:8, 19, 25, 26; 32:15; 33:29; 34:27; 35:4, 9, 15; 36:11, 23, 38; 37:6, 13; 38:23; 39:6, 7, 22, 28.

7, 8. What was Ezekiel told to say to Israel's mountains, hills, stream beds and valleys regarding a purging, and so what would the land have to know?
9. What had Jehovah meant for that beautiful land to be religiously, and what was now infringing upon exclusive worship at his temple?

incense stands, dungy idols—those are the vile things by means of which the unfaithful inhabitants of the mountains and hills and valleys and banks of the stream beds of the land of Judah are polluting their God-given possession. He had meant for that beautiful land to be sanctified as a place of his clean worship, but now, after 860 years of occupancy, look at it! Desecrated by those corrupt high places, altars, incense stands, dungy idols, whereas Jehovah's temple was ignored as the only right place of worship with the help of his priesthood there!

¹⁰ Little wonder, therefore, that Jehovah determined to bring the "sword" of aggressive warfare upon those mountains, hills, stream beds and valleys of the land of Judah, to cause the slain bodies of the idolaters to fall around their idols that were filthy like the dung of animals. Their high places, incense stands and altars with which they carried on their idolatrous worship were to be wrecked by the highly militarized invaders whom Jehovah would bring against this land to purge it of its idolatrous inhabitants.

¹¹ It had to take such drastic action as that to rid those mountains, hills, stream beds and valleys of the land of Judah of those rebels against the pure worship of the one living and true God. They had chosen to leave Jehovah out of their minds, and they had caused the mountains, hills, stream beds and valleys of the God-given land to be identified with false worship and the names of false deities. Now, by his purging work, he would cause those mountains, hills, stream beds and valleys to know once again who is the true God: "You will have to know that I am Jehovah."—Ezekiel 6:7.

¹² Bodily immorality is unclean. Spiritual immorality, or spiritual fornication, is still worse. Spiritual

10. Why was Jehovah bringing the sword of aggressive warfare upon that land?
11. Why was such drastic action with the sword of war necessary, but thereby what would the land come to know?
12. How had the Israelites become guilty of spiritual immorality, and according to what rule was this punishable?

fornication—that is what those ancient Israelites were guilty of to a shocking degree. By means of the covenant that Jehovah had established by means of the prophet Moses in 1513 B.C.E., Jehovah had brought the nation of Israel into a marriage relationship with him. He was as a heavenly Husband to the nation. (Jeremiah 31:31, 32) But the nation did not appreciate its blessed relationship to him, but united itself to false gods in idolatrous worship. By this the nation committed spiritual immorality. Was physical fornication punishable according to the law of Jehovah? Yes. Likewise, spiritual fornication or immorality was punishable, for it meant unfaithfulness to the nation's covenant with him. How the disloyal Israelites would be punished and would suffer for their spiritual immorality, Jehovah went on to say by Ezekiel:

¹³ "And when it occurs I will let you have as a remnant the ones escaping from the sword among the nations, when you get scattered among the lands. And your escaped ones will certainly remember me among the nations to which they will have been taken captive, because I have been broken up at their fornicating heart that has turned aside from me and at their eyes that are going in fornication after their dungy idols; and they will certainly feel a loathing in their faces at the bad things that they have done in all their detestable things. And they will have to know that I am Jehovah; not in vain did I speak about doing to them this calamitous thing."—Ezekiel 6:8-10.

¹⁴ The escapees of the sword of execution right there in the land of Judah will be but a remnant of these idolatrous spiritual fornicators. But into slavish captivity they will be led away from the mountains, hills, stream beds and valleys in which they committed the things detestable to Jehovah, the One to whom

---

13. By Ezekiel, what did Jehovah say regarding the scattered ones that escaped from the sword, and what would they have to know?
14. Comparatively, what would the escapees of the idolatrous Israelites constitute, and for what feeling will they take up residence in exile, and what will they have to know?

they had been married by their national covenant. But it will be only for shame of face that they will take up residence in the lands of their captors. Their false gods will prove to be no saviors to them. Since they abandoned Jehovah in order to pursue spiritual immorality, he abandons them to their enemies. Then this captive remnant of escaped ones will know that he is Jehovah, who cannot be tampered with in a disregard of their matrimonial covenant. By hard experiences in the distant lands of their captors they will know that, in the terms of his covenant with them, he did not speak in vain to warn them that he would bring upon them the terrible consequences of their forsaking his pure worship.

[15] Like the mountains, hills, stream beds and valleys of the land of Judah, the realm of Christendom has been polluted by the religious things that she adopted from the idolatrous pagans in order to carry on her spiritual immorality. She should have kept her realm clean of all false worship, because she paraded herself before all the nations as being Christian and so as being in the "new covenant" with God through the Mediator, Jesus Christ. But her standing as Christian before the eyes of the world she profaned by imitating the "heathen" in religious idolatry both in teaching and in practice. She is wrongly occupying any standing as *Christian*. She has no right to the name Christian. She must be removed from such a standing and name. At her destruction Jehovah will deprive her of such a standing and name. Any adherents who escape execution at her destruction have no prospect of a future free life. They will be taken over and brought under the control of the secular elements of this world. They will have to know that their executioner is really Jehovah and that he did not speak amiss in his holy written Word, the Sacred Bible.

15. Similarly how has Christendom committed spiritual immorality, what will happen to her as to a place in the realm called Christian, and what will she have to know concerning her executioner?

DRASTIC MEANS BY WHICH TO MAKE THEM KNOW

[16] The knowledge that He is Jehovah will have to be forced upon the spiritual fornicators of Christendom, just as it had to be in the case of the polluters of the mountains, hills, stream beds and valleys of the land of Judah. To emphasize this fact still more, the Lord God went on to say to his prophet Ezekiel:

[17] "This is what the Sovereign Lord Jehovah has said, 'Clap your hands and stamp with your foot, and say: "Alas!" on account of all the bad detestable things of the house of Israel, because by the sword, by the famine and by the pestilence they will fall. As for the one far away, by the pestilence he will die; and as for the one that is nearby, by the sword he will fall; and as for the one that has been left remaining and that has been safeguarded, by the famine he will die, and I will bring to its finish my rage against them. And you people will have to know that I am Jehovah, when their slain ones come to be in the midst of their dungy idols, all around their altars, upon every high hill, on all the tops of the mountains and under every luxuriant tree and under every branchy big tree, the place where they have offered a restful odor to all their dungy idols. And I will stretch out my hand against them and make the land a desolate waste, even a desolation worse than the wilderness toward Diblah, in all their dwelling places. And they will have to know that I am Jehovah.' "—Ezekiel 6:11-14.

[18] To think of all the destruction that was to come upon the inhabitants of the land of Judah by the famine, the pestilence and the sword of war was enough to make a person cry out, "Alas!" Yes, enough to move a person to make this exclamation emphatic by clapping the hands and stamping with the foot! There would be no escaping by the guilty ones from the

16, 17. As in Israel's case, Christendom must come to know that He is Jehovah in what way, and Ezekiel was told to describe this way with what details?
18. Why was Ezekiel told to cry out, clap his hands and stamp with his foot, and for the spiritual fornicators why would no place at all be safe from execution of God's judgment?

execution of the judicial decisions of the Sovereign Lord Jehovah. If a spiritual fornicator escaped one form of execution, another form was certain to strike him. Near or far, wherever a person happened to be physically located would not safeguard him. He is marked for annihilation. And famine and pestilence that would take their toll of victims would not be plagues that spread to the land of Judah from outside lands, but such disasters would arise within as the result of activity from the outside by the sword of the aggressive invader. Only by the execution of the divine judicial decision to the full will Jehovah's rage against them come to a finish and subside.

¹⁹ What a sight there is to behold! Dead bodies of the spiritual fornicators all around their idolatrous altars, by their incense stands upon which they offered incense emitting restful odors to their false gods, at their religious "high places" on the hilltops and mountaintops, and in the shade under the trees of luxuriant foliage and branchy big trees! A ghastly silent testimony to the mournful end to which the God who requires exclusive devotion to Him brings the spiritual fornicators! They have been *made* to know that the one living and true God is Jehovah. A covenant with Him is not a mere scrap of manuscript to be torn to pieces and canceled unilaterally by the unfaithful party to the covenant at any time that he likes! A covenanter should not think that Jehovah does not care about his covenants, that he forgets about them, or that he does not hold the covenanter as well as himself to the covenant as being a binding one. He is true to His covenant. Not only does he bless the covenanter who is true to the covenant, but he punishes the covenanter who is untrue to the covenant according to the punishments specified in the covenant.

19. The sight of the dead bodies lying at the locations for idolatrous worship silently testifies to what fact, and it emphasizes what things about a covenant with God?

[20] Left behind are the putrefying corpses of all these slain ones when the remnant of survivors are led away by their captors into alien lands. The mountains, hills, stream beds and valleys of the land of Judah are cleansed of all the polluting idolatry and idolatrous spiritual fornicators by being left a desolation. Why, the desolate waste is worse than the wilderness that stretches "toward Diblah." (Ezekiel 6:14, *NW; LXX; Vg; Aramaic; Syriac; Arabic*) By lying desolate for seventy years, without man or domestic animal, the land would be considered cleansed and rested up from its pollution, according to the decree of Jehovah. He was obliged to vindicate his unbreakable word. He had to uphold the reality of his own Godship. Said he, in connection with those covenant breakers, those spiritual fornicators: "And they will have to know that I am Jehovah."

[21] That ancient type will not fail of fulfillment upon its modern, antitypical counterpart. Christendom will be uprooted from where she has been deeply entrenched for sixteen centuries. Her realm will be desolated, without her hypocritically Christian clergymen and church institutions. Men will look at the place where she used to exist and to flourish, and she will be no more. (Psalm 37:9, 10) Like her ancient type, she will have to feel the full force of the words of the God whom she has misrepresented: "And they will have to know that I am Jehovah." (Ezekiel 6:14) His pure worship will survive Christendom's destruction everlastingly from the earth.

THE END OF HER IS NEAR!

[22] Should the destruction of an idolatrous system of false, hypocritical religion call for pity from the

---

20. Thus how were the mountains, hills, stream beds and valleys of Judah to be cleansed and rested up from all the misuse, and what were the covenant breakers to know?
21. How will that ancient type have a modern fulfillment, all this resulting in what vital knowledge to whom?
22. Should sorrow or pity be felt at the destruction of Christendom, and at what result thereof will lovers of truth and righteousness rejoice?

eyes of persons who love truth and righteousness, or even pity from the eyes of the God of true worship? The great oppression and the blinding and misguidance of the people that have resulted from such false religion keep the lovers of truth and righteousness from feeling sorry. To the contrary, they rejoice at the clearing of the way for the prevalence of pure and true worship throughout the whole earth. The approaching end of Christendom does not fill these with sorrow or dismay. The Sovereign Lord God himself will feel no more sorrow at this than he felt when he brought destruction upon her ancient type, the inhabitants of the land of Judah and Jerusalem. In evidence of this the prophet Ezekiel writes:

[23] "And the word of Jehovah continued to occur to me, saying: 'And as for you, O son of man, this is what the Sovereign Lord Jehovah has said to the soil of Israel, "An end, the end, has come upon the four extremities of the land. Now the end is upon you, and I must send my anger against you, and I will judge you according to your ways and bring upon you all your detestable things. And my eye will not feel sorry for you, neither will I feel compassion, for upon you I shall bring your own ways, and in the midst of you your own detestable things will come to be; and you people will have to know that I am Jehovah." ' " —Ezekiel 7:1-4.

[24] It is still the year 613 B.C.E. as Jehovah makes that statement. The destruction of the city of Jerusalem and its defiled temple was therefore just six years off, the closing six years of a period of forty years of bearing the "error" of the house of Judah. (Ezekiel 4:6) Quite precisely, then, Jehovah could say that "an end, the end" has come upon the four extremities of the land, "the soil of Israel." He himself feels the urgency of the progress of events as he says:

---

23. Though not feeling sorry or pitiful, Jehovah can bring what upon doers of detestable things and thus make them know what?
24. Why was Jehovah precise in saying that "an end, the end," had come upon the land, and what is it really that He brings to an end?

"Now the end is upon you." It means that the time has come for him to take judicial action as respects the "soil of Israel" to its four corners. So he adds: "And I must send my anger against you, and I will judge you according to your ways and bring upon you all your detestable things." It is not the "soil of Israel," "the four extremities of the land," that He brings to an end. The lifeless soil is not responsible to Him. Rightly, it is the unfaithful religious system that has for more than three centuries been operating upon this soil that Jehovah brings to an end in his righteous anger.

[25] He will not be held back by sorrow and compassion from putting an end to that religious system with its detestable things. He will not change his law that, as a person or nation sows, it must also reap. The consequences of its own unfaithful ways must be brought upon it, to make the religious system eat the fruitage of its own doings. In this way the religious adherents of that system must be made to know that he is Jehovah, that he is the same Jehovah who said to his covenant people by the mouth of the prophet Moses: "If you will not do this way, you will also certainly sin against Jehovah. In that case know that your sin will catch up with you [will find you out]." —Numbers 32:23, NW; AS.

[26] Even those whom Jehovah uses as his executioners on earth might appreciate that the detestable religious system is getting nothing but its just deserts and deserves no pity. Listen in on the prophet Jeremiah as he tells us what a Babylonian army officer said to him after the destruction of Jerusalem in the year 607 B.C.E.: "The word that occurred to Jeremiah from Jehovah after Nebuzaradan the chief of the

25. What divine law concerning consequences will Jehovah not change toward the detestable religious system, and what will its religious adherents be brought to know as regards their covenant?
26. As to discerning that one gets one's deserts, what is indicated by the observation that Nebuzaradan made to Jeremiah concerning Jerusalem's destruction?

bodyguard sent him from Ramah, when he took him while he was bound with handcuffs in the midst of all the exiles of Jerusalem and of Judah, who were being taken into exile in Babylon. Then the chief of the bodyguard took Jeremiah and said to him: 'Jehovah your God himself spoke this calamity against this place, that Jehovah might bring it true and do just as he has spoken, because you people have sinned against Jehovah and have not obeyed his voice. And this thing has happened to you.' "—Jeremiah 40:1-3.

²⁷ Today Christendom has been longer in existence than the 860 years that the house of Israel was in the Promised Land by the time that Ezekiel was appointed as a prophet and a watchman over Israel. She has a longer record of committing detestable things in her religious realm. She has been a longer time in coming to her day of reckoning. But now at last her sin has found her out, has caught up with her. The end that Jehovah has decreed for her is about to come upon her, and she may expect no mercy from Him. She is past all possibility of repenting and converting to Him.

²⁸ Just as it was foretold concerning these last days, Christendom has had a "form of godliness," a "form of godly devotion," but she has all along been "denying the power thereof," or "proving false to its power." (2 Timothy 3:1-5, *AV; NW*) By not holding true to the Holy Bible, she ignored the God who is set forth in the Bible, Jehovah. He does her no injustice by bringing upon her the consequences of her ways and by showing her how detestable to Him her religious things are. At her end it is proper for her to know that there is indeed a God named Jehovah, who gives due rewards.

---

27. How does Christendom's existence compare with that of Israel upon the Promised Land down to Ezekiel's appointment, and now what is about to come upon her?
28. As foretold, what has been the religious course of Christendom, and does Jehovah do her any injustice by bringing her ways upon her?

²⁹ Never can Christendom rightly scream out to Jehovah, "Calamity howler!" because he told Ezekiel to say, with her as well as the unfaithful house of Israel in mind:

³⁰ "This is what the Sovereign Lord Jehovah has said, 'A calamity, a unique calamity, look! it is coming. An end itself must come. The end must come; it must awaken for you. Look! It is coming. The garland must come to you, O inhabiter of the land, the time must come, the day is near. There is confusion, and not the shouting of the mountains. Now shortly I shall pour out my rage upon you, and I will bring my anger against you to its finish, and I will judge you according to your ways and bring upon you all your detestable things. Neither will my eye feel sorry nor shall I feel compassion. According to your ways shall I do the bringing upon you yourself, and your own detestable things will come to be right in the midst of you; and you people will have to know that I am Jehovah doing the smiting.' "—Ezekiel 7:5-9.

³¹ No, there was no mistake about what we heard when Jehovah spoke the first time. He meant what he said in the first place. So for the sake of emphasis he repeats himself in many respects, with some new details added, about the end. A "garland" will indeed come to the idolatrous inhabiter of the land, but it will encircle the inhabiter's head with calamitous things, not with the nice-looking decoration of an idolater who is enjoying a festival. It will be a time, not of well-arranged ceremonies, but of confusion, false religion not being able to unite the people in any self-helpful measures, even against a common enemy. What shouting will then be heard will be that of wild confusion, not that of revelers at the religious "high places" on the mountains or the shouting of men treading the grapes gathered from the vineyards

---

29, 30. A calamity must come because Jehovah brings what upon the inhabiter of the land, and the one doing the striking shall be known to be who?
31. What kind of garland will it be that will come upon the inhabiter of the land, and the shouting then will not be for what causes?

on the mountainsides. There will be the noise foretold for this time by the prophet Isaiah:

³² "There is a sound of uproar out of the city [of Jerusalem], a sound out of the temple! It is the sound of Jehovah repaying what is deserved to his enemies." —Isaiah 66:6.

³³ If, in their dire distress, people finally call to Jehovah as a last source of relief, he will not hear them. His eye will not feel sorry, nor will he feel compassion for these idolatrous worshipers who have continually refrained from listening to him. When he fails to answer their prayers, they will come to sense that he is against them. By his prophets and by his Bible instructors he has foretold this calamitous end upon the unfaithful religious system. Hence when it comes upon them, they will be able to attribute it to no one else but Him. Just as he said to the stubborn, heedless religionists: "You people will have to know that I am Jehovah doing the smiting."

THE "ROD" FOR DIVINE USE ON THAT DAY

³⁴ Back in Ezekiel's day Jehovah had his executional forces ready, and He foretold who they would be, namely, the military forces of the Third World Power of Bible history, namely, Babylon, of whom the mighty Nebuchadnezzar was then king. Correspondingly, Jehovah has his visible executional forces ready now, poised to strike Christendom, the present-day counterpart of the land of Judah and Jerusalem. Jehovah refers to these in his next words:

³⁵ "Look! The day! Look! It is coming. The garland has gone forth. The rod has blossomed. Presumptuousness has sprouted. Violence itself has risen up into a rod of wickedness. It is not from them, nor is it from

---

32. The noise then will be due to what, according to Isaiah 66:6?
33. Why will no pity then be deserved, and to whom will they then knowingly be able to attribute the calamitous end?
34. What executional forces did Jehovah have ready for his use back in Ezekiel's day?
35. To what time period does Jehovah now repeatedly call attention, and in view of it what should the buyer and the seller respectively not do for certain reasons?

their wealth; and it is not from their own selves, nor is there any eminency in them. The time must come, the day must arrive. As regards the buyer, let him not rejoice; and as regards the seller, let him not go into mourning, for there is hot feeling against all its crowd. For to what was sold the seller himself will not return, while their life is yet among the living ones; for the vision is for all its crowd. No one will return, and they will not possess themselves each one of his own life by his own error."—Ezekiel 7:10-13.

[36] Let the hypocritical religionists who claim to be in a relationship with the Sovereign Lord God by a covenant through his mediator not forget that this extraordinary day is coming. It must be a terrible day; otherwise, Jehovah would not so repeatedly call attention to it. From the description that he gives of it by Ezekiel, it does prove to be a most tragic day! On that day the "garland" is to be put as a circlet upon the head of the doomed people, to crown them with calamity. The symbolic "rod" for the applying of punishment is at hand, for Jehovah's use, for it has blossomed. In Ezekiel's day it was King Nebuchadnezzar together with his then invincible Babylonian military forces. Babylon, as represented by her king and his armies, was going to do the presumptuous thing against Jehovah's chosen people and his temple.

[37] On this account Jehovah addresses Babylon as Presumptuousness personified, saying: " 'Look! I am against you, O Presumptuousness,' is the utterance of the Sovereign Lord, Jehovah of armies, 'for your day must come, the time that I must give you attention. And Presumptuousness will certainly stumble and fall, and it will have no one to cause it to rise up.' " (Jeremiah 50:31, 32) Since Babylonish PRESUMPTUOUSNESS had "sprouted," it was in position to exert itself and was ready to do so.

36. On whose head was the "garland" to be placed, what was the "rod" that had blossomed and so was ready to be applied, and against whom was presumptuous action to be taken?
37. By what term does Jehovah address Babylon, and what does its having "sprouted" mean for it?

[38] The violence that marked the Jerusalem and Judah of Ezekiel's day reminds us that, since the year 1914 C.E., we too have entered into an "age of violence," especially so in Christendom. Has such violence "risen up into a rod of wickedness"? Most assuredly, Yes! A violent "wind" is what the violent religionists keep sowing, and "a stormwind is what they will reap." (Hosea 8:7) Violence brings on its own punishment as by a "rod" for its own wickedness. In the case of these violent religionists the truth of Proverbs 13:21 must be demonstrated: "Sinners are the ones whom calamity pursues, but the righteous are the ones whom good rewards." From the "rod" of punishment the violent religionists do not deserve to be shielded. There is no "eminency" to be found in them, no worthiness of being spared from the execution of Jehovah's judicial decisions. There is no excusableness that proceeds from them, nor from their wealth, nor from their very own selves. They deserve to feel the "rod" for their wickedness.

[39] Learn, now, the long-range effects of the coming of that day of deserved punishment. There is no reason for a buyer to rejoice because he has bought the hereditary land-property of a fellow Israelite and thus expects to reap the produce from that land down till the Jubilee year. Let not the indebted Israelite who is economically forced to sell his hereditary property mourn because of his loss till the next Jubilee year in the land of Judah. Why not? Because the feeling of Jehovah is hot against "all its crowd," buyers and sellers alike. When the calamitous day arrives, either they will be killed off or else they will be taken off the land into distant exile. Even if the sellers were to survive until the next Jubilee year, even though "their life is yet among the living ones"

---

38. What does the mention of violence remind us of that has set in since 1914 C.E., and how has "violence" resulted in being a "rod" for punishing wickedness?
39, 40. Why was the seller not to mourn, and the buyer not to rejoice, and was that "crowd" to expect that by committing error each one could possess himself of his own life?

when that year of liberation falls due, no seller will return to the hereditary possession that he sold to pay off his debt. Why is that to be so?

. ⁴⁰ Because the exile of the violent religionist would extend beyond the time of the next Jubilee year. The exile would be longer than the Jubilee cycle of fifty years. (Leviticus 25:8-54) Jehovah would enforce his decree that the land of Judah should lie desolate, without man or domestic animal, for seventy years. (Jeremiah 25:11, 12; 29:10) Furthermore, after the long-desolated land would begin to be occupied again, the Jubilee system would not be put in operation again in the land of Judah. Each hereditary possession that was sold before that calamitous day would be gone for good. So why should the seller of it mourn? He would have to part with it anyhow when that day of recompense came. And so, too, would the buyer of it, for which reason he had no cause to rejoice at his purchase. The "vision" of coming catastrophe is meant "for all its crowd," without distinction. They are not to expect that by the committing of some planned "error" they can or "will possess themselves each one of his own life."

⁴¹ From such an outcome of things we can draw one conclusion for today: Any adherent of Christendom who suffers material loss by her destruction in the coming calamitous day will never recover his loss. According to the ancient prophetic model in Ezekiel's day, Christendom is to be besieged by her desolators. It will be a time of great fear on the part of her members. They will be afraid to come to her defense or to do battle with those bent on her destruction. Let the military trumpet be blown to summon her defenders to their defensive posts. The response thereto will be like that foretold by Jehovah in further describing the events of that "day" to Ezekiel, saying:

41. What does the seller's permanent loss suggest as to adherents of Christendom, and to what extent will fear affect the defense of Christendom?

⁴² "They have blown the trumpet and there has been a preparing of everybody, but there is no one going to the battle, because my hot feeling is against all its crowd. The sword is outside, and the pestilence and the famine are inside. Whoever is in the field, by the sword he will die, and whoever are in the city, famine and pestilence themselves will devour them. And their escapees will certainly make their escape and become on the mountains like the doves of the valleys, all of which are moaning, each one in his own error. As for all the hands, they keep dropping down; and as for all knees, they keep dripping with water. And they have girded on sackcloth, and shuddering has covered them; and on all faces there is shame and on all their heads there is baldness."—Ezekiel 7:14-18.

⁴³ The refusal of Jehovah to fight for them against their besiegers will dishearten the religionists who are under attack. Those who manage to keep alive will have their hands drop from sheer faintness, as if paralyzed. Out of fear their limbs will perspire so heavily that their knees will drip from perspiration. It will be no day of glory for false religionists, but one of shame for them. At the overthrow of their cherished religious system they will, as it were, shave their heads bald in mourning.

MATERIAL RICHES THEN OF NO AVAIL!

⁴⁴ Wait, though! What about the tremendous wealth that the system of false hypocritical religion has amassed? Will not the religious controllers of all this material wealth be able to use these vast riches in buying their way out to safety or to buy food and drink to stave off starvation? Jehovah will not let silver or gold bribe him or his executional forces so

42. How did Jehovah describe what responsiveness there would be to the call to defense, and also the effects of fear and grief?
43. Such disheartenment will be due to the refusal of whom to fight for them?
44. What questions arise as to the use of the material wealth that the system of false religion has amassed, in that day of calamity, and what must the answers be?

as to spare religious systems that have trusted in material riches to save them in the day of reckoning. By His prophet Ezekiel he says:

[45] "Into the streets they will throw their very silver, and an abhorrent thing their own gold will become. Neither their silver nor their gold will be able to deliver them in the day of Jehovah's fury. Their souls they will not satisfy, and their intestines they will not fill, for it has become a stumbling block causing their error. And the decoration of one's ornament —one has set it as reason for pride; and their detestable images, their disgusting things, they have made with it. That is why I will make it to them an abhorrent thing. And I will give it into the hand of the strangers for plunder and to the wicked ones of the earth for spoil, and they will certainly profane it. And I shall have to turn away my face from them, and they will actually profane my concealed place, and into it robbers will really come and profane it."—Ezekiel 7:19-22.

[46] Imagine silver money being thrown into the streets of the city of Jerusalem! Imagine gold money becoming like a thing abhorred! And yet once these material riches were the things highly prized and hungrily sought after. But putting money ahead of spiritual interests and the craving of money became a stumbling block over which the hypocritical religionists stumbled and fell into committing "error" just to make unjust gain. How shameful it was for the prophet Micah to have to report: "Her own head ones judge merely for a bribe, and her own priests instruct just for a price, and her own prophets practice divination simply for money; yet upon Jehovah they keep supporting themselves, saying: 'Is not Jehovah in the midst of us? There will come upon us no calamity.' Therefore on account of you men Zion will be plowed

45. What did Jehovah say as to the gaining of deliverance by means of silver and gold on the day of His fury, and what are the things that he will then let be profaned?
46. To the hypocritical religionists, what has become a "stumbling block causing their error," and what shameful report did the prophet Micah make about such religionists of his day?

up as a mere field, and Jerusalem herself will become mere heaps of ruins, and the mountain of the house [of Jehovah] will be as the high places of a forest"! —Micah 3:11, 12.

⁴⁷ As regards the religious leaders of Christendom, they also have charged money for their ecclesiastical services to the church members. They have charged for performing baptisms and marriages, for blessing homes and properties of church members, for saying masses in church and for praying in behalf of the "souls of the dead in Purgatory," for granting indulgences, for admission into church or for seats therein, for education at religious schools, for serving as chaplains in the armies, for carrying of images of "saints" in processions, at the same time accepting money from the political State where there happens to be a union of Church and State or a State Church. Countless other ways have been devised to take in money from the people. And much of such money has been invested in the financial center of Wall Street, New York city, and in other commercial enterprises for the sake of money profits. Scandalously this greed for money and material riches has caused the religious leaders of Christendom to stumble into erroneous conduct before God.—1 Timothy 6:10.

⁴⁸ But a human creature cannot eat gold or silver or paper stocks and bonds! In Jehovah's day of accounting for them the hypocritical religionists will not be able to consume gold and silver to fill their intestines with needed food amid famine conditions. They will not be able to ransom their lives with gold and silver by bribing Jehovah and his executional agents in the earth. Did not the Christian apostle Peter tell Simon, the professional magician in the city of Samaria: "May your silver perish with you, because

---

47. How have the religious leaders of Christendom charged for ecclesiastical services, and such materialism has proved to be a stumbling block to fall into what error?
48. How valueless will gold and silver, though coined, be in the day of Jehovah's fury, and how will it become an "abhorrent thing" to the possessors?

you thought through money to get possession of the free gift of God"? (Acts 8:9-20) Yes! And as respects those who think they will be able to buy their way out and satisfy the animalistic cravings of their souls, the Sovereign Lord God says: "Neither their silver nor their gold will be able to deliver them in the day of Jehovah's fury." (Ezekiel 7:19) Such coined metal will be valueless. To its owners even gold will become an "abhorrent thing," when they now at last reflect that their greed for it has brought on their destruction.

49 X

⁴⁹ The religious leaders of Christendom have adorned themselves with gold and silver crucifixes, rings, miters, crosiers, regalia, thrones, and other paraphernalia. They have made such costly things the "decoration of one's ornament," and they have set such as a reason for priding themselves, considering themselves as somebodies higher than the common, ordinary laity.

⁵⁰ They have also used such gold and silver and jewels for decorating the images and emblems used in their churches. "Detestable images," "disgusting things," Jehovah calls them, despite their artistic construction. As in the case of ancient Jerusalem in the day of Jehovah's fury against her, those gold and silver and bejeweled articles of false worship will be plundered by the antireligious "strangers" and will be seized as "spoil" by the irreligious "wicked ones." They will not consider as untouchable the things, even religious images, held sacred by Christendom. They will profane such reputedly holy things. What enormous accumulations of wealth in Christendom will fall to the greedy irreligious despoilers in the "day of Jehovah's fury"!

⁵¹ Shocking profanation of things once regarded as most holy took place back there in the year 607 B.C.E.,

49. What "decoration of one's ornament" have the religious leaders set as a "reason for pride" in comparison with whom?
50. What else besides themselves have the religious leaders used gold, silver and jewels in decorating, and how will such things be profaned in the day of Jehovah's fury?
51. How did shocking profanation of things considered most holy come in 607 B.C.E., and for that reason where did Jehovah have to turn his face?

just six years after the giving of this prophecy. Those things had to do with Jehovah himself, a house, a temple, dedicated to Him, and a city where he had placed his holy name! No wonder he had to say regarding the religionists who formalistically worshiped there: "I shall have to turn away my face from them"! (Ezekiel 7:22) This reminds us of what Jesus Christ himself said to the Jews about their temple at Jerusalem, which was to be destroyed in the year 70 C.E.: "Look! Your house is abandoned to you." (Matthew 23:38) Abandoned by Jehovah as a place of his pure worship!

⁵² For what did that abandoned state of Jerusalem's temple open the way back there in Ezekiel's day? Having in mind the Babylonian military forces, Jehovah said: "And they will actually profane my concealed place, and into it robbers will really come and profane it."—Ezekiel 7:22.

⁵³ Jehovah's "concealed place" was the innermost chamber of the temple and was called "the Most Holy." In the "day of Jehovah's fury" the Babylonian invaders would be permitted to profane even this most sacred compartment. For then invading it in search of loot no pagan Babylonian would be struck down dead immediately by Jehovah or be smitten with leprosy. Those Babylonian or Chaldean "robbers" would be allowed, actually without divine punishment then, to profane the temple even to its most sacred compartment. It was because Jehovah's presence was no longer there! The Chaldean "robbers" were permitted to make away with the sacred utensils and paraphernalia of Jerusalem's temple and cart them off and display them in the temples of their pagan gods and goddesses in idolatrous Babylon. Behind them they left the smoldering ruins of the looted temple that they had burned down.—2 Kings 25:8-17; 2 Chronicles 36:17-19; Daniel 5:2, 3, 22, 23.

52, 53. What was then Jehovah's "concealed place," and why did he allow even the profanation of it by the pagan "robbers" without punishment then?

[54] Those shocking events of ancient history were prophetic and reflect the now not distant future. When Jehovah turns away his face from the hypocritical worshipers of Christendom, what can we expect, in the light of the past? The profanation, misuse and destruction of the things now rated as sacred by Christendom, even her most sacred things, be they the very heart and center of Christendom, such as Vatican City, or the palatial residences of the patriarchs of the various sister church systems, Greek Orthodox, Constantinopolitan, Armenian, Coptic, or palace of the Anglican archbishop. Nothing will be sacred to the looters!

THE DIVINE PURPOSE IN ALL THIS

[55] In all this the Sovereign Lord God who thus executes his judicial decisions against false religion has a valid purpose. He leads up to the plain declaration of this purpose in what he next says to his prophet Ezekiel:

[56] "Make the chain, for the land itself has become full of bloodstained judgment and the city itself has become full of violence. And I will bring in the worst ones of the nations, and they will certainly take possession of their houses, and I will cause the pride of the strong ones to cease, and their sanctuaries must be profaned. There will come anguish, and they will certainly seek peace but there will be none. There will come adversity upon adversity, and there will occur report upon report, and people will actually seek a vision from a prophet, and the law itself will perish from a priest and counsel from elderly men. The king himself will go into mourning; even a chieftain will clothe himself with desolation, and the very hands of the people of the land will get disturbed. According to their way I shall act toward them, and with their

54. Of what was such ancient profanation of sacred things prophetic for the now not distant future?
55, 56. The consequences of what will Jehovah bring upon the false religionists, and what is Jehovah's valid purpose in all of this?

judgments I shall judge them; and they will have to know that I am Jehovah."—Ezekiel 7:23-27.

[57] In the chains of captivity the survivors of the destruction of Jerusalem in 607 B.C.E. could well meditate on what had happened to their land and nation. They could painfully realize that there is indeed a God that intervenes in the affairs of men and that his name is Jehovah. "Make the chain," Ezekiel was commanded by Jehovah, in order to indicate what Jehovah had in store for the survivors of the national catastrophe. Six years more, and those survivors did find themselves in chains, being dragged off into distant exile in a pagan land. Speaking for the survivors after the destruction of Jerusalem, the prophet Jeremiah said in lamentation: "He has blocked me up as with a stone wall, that I may not go forth. He has made my copper fetters heavy." (Lamentations 3:7) Jeremiah also tells what the king of Babylon did to King Zedekiah, who had fled from the breached city and was nonetheless captured: "And the eyes of Zedekiah he blinded, after which the king of Babylon bound him with copper fetters and brought him to Babylon and put him in the house of custody until the day of his death."—Jeremiah 52:11; 39:7.

[58] Why was the "chain" of captives and exiles to be forged for the house of Judah? Jehovah explained to Ezekiel the reason for making this symbolic chain, saying: "For the land itself has become full of bloodstained judgment and the city itself has become full of violence." Inhabitants who were guilty of such wicked things deserved to be chained and dragged off the land that they were defiling.

[59] Whom, though, was Jehovah about to use to fasten the chain upon them? The answer makes one shudder, as Jehovah continues on to say: "And I will bring in

57. Jehovah's command to Ezekiel, "Make the chain," was fulfilled how in actuality?
58. For what reasons was the "chain" to be forged for the house of Judah?
59. Why were those whom Jehovah used to forge the chain for Judah called "the worst ones of the nations"?

the worst ones of the nations, and they will certainly take possession of their houses." Aha! "the worst ones of the nations." The Babylonian armies matched that description, for Babylon then held the position of the Third World Power of Bible history. Not even Egypt could hold them in check. Later, in prophesying against the king of Egypt, Ezekiel speaks of the aggressive Babylonians as "the tyrants of the nations." (Ezekiel 30:11) In prophesying against the "leader" of ancient Tyre, Ezekiel says: "Here I am bringing upon you strangers, the tyrants of the nations, and they will certainly draw their swords against the beauty of your wisdom and profane your beaming splendor." —Ezekiel 28:1, 2, 7.

⁶⁰ For about eighteen lunar months the city of Jerusalem held out against the siege by the "worst ones of the nations," and then the city was breached. (2 Kings 25:1-4) Then, in fact, Jehovah did "cause the pride of the strong ones to cease." Their anointed King Zedekiah, of the royal house of David, was captured while in flight. (2 Kings 25:4-7) The chief ones of their priesthood of the family of Moses' brother Aaron were slaughtered. (2 Kings 25:18-21) In addition to that, as Jehovah said, "their sanctuaries must be profaned" by the "worst ones of the nations," and that did not exclude the gorgeous temple that had been built by wise King Solomon at Jerusalem.—Ezekiel 7:24; 2 Kings 25:8-17.

⁶¹ What, though, about the situation inside Jerusalem during the siege by the "worst ones of the nations"? With the sword of punitive warfare outside and with famine and pestilence taking their toll inside, there must have been anguish inside the besieged city, just as Jehovah had foretold. Why was it that He said: "They will certainly seek peace and there will be none"? It was because they did not seek peace in the way

60. How did Jehovah "cause the pride of the strong ones to cease" and fulfill his determination that "their sanctuaries must be profaned"? 61. Why was it that, among the besieged inhabitants, they would not find peace although they sought it?

that Jehovah had instructed through the prophet Jeremiah, namely, go out in unconditional surrender to the Babylonians. (Jeremiah 21:7-9; 38:1-3, 9-23) Consequently, what followed?

[62] There was to "come adversity upon adversity," and there was to "occur report upon report," but no good news from any quarter. It was of no use to "seek a vision from a prophet," aside from Jehovah's true prophet Jeremiah, who was held in custody. The law as given by the priest, who was against priest Jeremiah, was of no avail; it was to perish. The counsel as given by the elderly men of experience was impractical; it also was to perish. Stubborn King Zedekiah, who was in fear of his own princes, had no other course to take but "go into mourning." Each chieftain could not do anything but rip his garments apart in expression of inward despair and grief and thus "clothe himself with desolation." With their leaders in such a mental, spiritual and nervous state, what could the common "people of the land" do but get disturbed as to using their hands, not knowing how and with what to employ them? (Ezekiel 7:25-27) They had only themselves to blame!

[63] Continually those beleaguered inhabitants of the land of Judah and Jerusalem had ignored the counsel of the God of Israel. They had persecuted his prophets, including Jeremiah the priest. The judgments that their courts handed down and executed caused the shedding of innocent blood, or because of the wickedness of the people those courts had to handle capital crimes involving blood. "Bloodstained judgment," indeed, resulted! The capital city itself, Jerusalem, was "full of violence," despite its being the center of religious worship at the temple of Jehovah. Under such circumstances was Jehovah obliged to deal lightly with those religious rebels by condoning and overlooking

62. What would be the case as to getting information or an effective law or practical advice and knowing how to use one's hands?
63. Why did the besieged inhabitants have only themselves to blame in the light of their judgments and conduct, and what questions arise as to Jehovah's obligations in this regard?

their terrible "error"? Was he to act as if he did not exist? Was he to deal with them as if he were some god different from the Sovereign Lord Jehovah with whom their forefathers had made a solemn covenant through the mediator Moses? What must we say in all fairness?

[64] Jehovah was obliged to fulfill His part of the solemn covenant and act toward them "according to their way." Also, "with their judgments." That is to say, with the judgments that apply to them according to the law of His covenant, Jehovah was obliged to "judge them," to give to them according to their deserts. It was fair and equitable for Him to do so. He must be true to Himself. He must leave no misimpressions in their minds about Him. He is the same Jehovah as the One with whom their forefathers entered into their solemn obligations under the law given through Moses. They needed to be forced to know that He is Jehovah. The righteous way that He chose was the way to bring this about.

WHAT ABOUT CHRISTENDOM?

[65] Is Christendom of today to be treated in any different way? Is not her realm likewise "full of blood-stained judgment"? Is she not, even in her religious centers and strongholds, "full of violence"? Why, then, should any different treatment be expected for her?

[66] When in the coming "great tribulation" the siege takes place that results in her destruction at the hands of the "worst ones of the nations," she will continue to do just as she is already doing. She will persist in seeking peace and making terms according to her ways, but "there will be none" in that way. There will be more extreme anguish than what she feels

---

64. What was Jehovah, as party to a covenant with Israel, obliged to do, in order to leave no misimpression about himself in their minds?
65. What questions therefore arise with regard to Christendom as to the treatment that she merits?
66. As in ancient Jerusalem's case, when Christendom's siege sets in at the "great tribulation" she will be carrying on in what way, and what will be the outcome with her?

already. Further visions of her false prophets will perish in failure. The law of her priesthood and clergy will perish, disregarded; likewise, the counsel of her worldly-wise elders. Ecclesiastical rulers will mourn. Religious chieftains will lose confidence in their own leadership and take on an appearance of desolation as regards their hopes. Their hosts of laymen will have nervous hands, uncertain as to how to apply their powers to save their religious institutions. The outcome will be the same with Christendom as it was with typical Jerusalem.

[67] The ways of Christendom are written down on the pages of history from her beginning in the fourth century down till now. Since she has given all the world to understand that she represents the Sovereign Lord God, Jehovah must take her at her word and act toward her according to her ways. His judgments that apply to her are written in his sacred Word, the Bible; and in full accord with these He must judge her. Those judgments are unchangeable. By His executing them upon her and thus bringing about her end, Christendom will learn that He has not changed. He is still the same God in this twentieth century. She will have to know that He is Jehovah.

---

67. Since Christendom has all along claimed to represent God, in what, then, will his taking her at her word result?

Chapter 8

Detestable Religious Things
over Which to Sigh

TIME moved on one year and two months closer to the day of Jehovah's fury against ancient Jerusalem when Ezekiel as an exile in Babylon received his next revelation from the Sovereign Lord Jehovah. If that year had an intercalary or thirteenth lunar month in it, that lunar year and the two lunar months offered more time than the prophet Ezekiel had been commanded to lie on the ground, 390 days on his left side and 40 days on his right side, in a mimic siege of Jerusalem. (Ezekiel 4:4-7) Thus Ezekiel received the revelation on the fifth day of the lunar month Elul of the year 612 before our Common Era, or in the sixth year of Ezekiel's exile in Babylon. He dates the time in these words:

2 "And it came about in the sixth year, in the sixth month, on the fifth day of the month, that I was sitting in my house and the older men of Judah were sitting before me, when the hand of the Sovereign Lord Jehovah fell upon me there."—Ezekiel 8:1.

3 Evidently Jehovah had something special to bring to the attention of those fellow exiles of Ezekiel who were sitting before him in his house at Tel-abib in Babylon. These older men had likely come to "inquire

1. After his visions in 613 B.C.E., how long was it before Ezekiel received his next vision?
2. At the time of the vision, who were sitting before Ezekiel, and where?
3. Why were those elders there, and how long did they have to wait until they learned what Ezekiel now saw?

142

of Jehovah," by means of Ezekiel, just as turned out to be the case over a year later. (Ezekiel 20:1-3) When the "hand" of applied power of Jehovah fell upon Ezekiel, to make him experience an exciting vision, they had to wait until the divine power was lifted from him at the close of the vision in order to learn what Ezekiel had seen. Here is what he could tell them:

⁴ "And I began to see, and, look! a likeness similar to the appearance of fire; from the appearance of his hips even downward there was fire, and from his hips even upward there was something like the appearance of a shining, like the glow of electrum. Then he thrust out the representation of a hand and took me by a tuft of hair of my head, and a spirit carried me between the earth and the heavens and brought me to Jerusalem in the visions of God, to the entrance of the inner gate that is facing northward, where the dwelling place is of the symbol of jealousy that is inciting to jealousy. And, look! the glory of the God of Israel was there, like the appearance that I had seen in the valley plain."—Ezekiel 8:2-4.

⁵ The appearance that Jehovah assumed in this vision is not described in great detail by Ezekiel. He had a fiery appearance, and from his hips downward there was an appearance of fire. From his hips upward there was a shining, "like the glow of electrum." The appearance is hard for Ezekiel to describe because it bears no resemblance to the form of a man. But it is awe-inspiring, glorious, just as was the case of Ezekiel's first vision of the celestial chariot at the river Chebar. (Ezekiel 1:26-28) When this appearance of Jehovah thrust out what corresponds with a human hand ("the representation of a hand") and took Ezekiel by a "tuft of hair" of his head, did he feel like those Israelites whose hair Governor Nehemiah pulled

4. What did Ezekiel first see, and to where was he transported, and how?
5. How does Ezekiel try to describe the glorious appearance assumed by Jehovah, and what kind of spirit was it that transported him to Jerusalem?

out because he was displeased at their disobeying God's law? (Nehemiah 13:25) Of course, God was not displeased with his prophet Ezekiel, but he was displeased at the things that He was going to show Ezekiel in vision. Being lifted up by this means, Ezekiel was transported in spirit from Babylon to Jerusalem hundreds of miles to the west. Evidently the "spirit" that carried him there was the spirit of inspiration.

⁶ Thus, "in the visions of God," Ezekiel was set down in the temple that had been built by King Solomon in Jerusalem. That temple was now 415 years old. It had an inner court and an outer court, the altar of sacrifice being located in the inner court. The façade of the temple was toward the east, but Ezekiel was deposited in the outer court at the "entrance of the inner gate that is facing northward." Behind Ezekiel was the outer gate through which a person entered into the outer court. What did he see there at the entrance of the gate that leads into the inner court? A lifeless, motionless "symbol of jealousy that is inciting to jealousy." How this must have shocked Ezekiel!

⁷ In stark contrast with that idolatrous "symbol of jealousy" near the inner gate, "look!" as Ezekiel tells us, "the glory of the God of Israel was there, like the appearance that I had seen in the valley plain." (Ezekiel 8:4) The celestial chariot of Jehovah had moved—from the river Chebar in Babylonia where Ezekiel had first seen it in vision, westward to the doomed city of Jerusalem in the land of Judah. (Ezekiel 1:4-28) This movement of the celestial chariot was ominous for Jerusalem!

⁸ From his celestial chariot Jehovah began to speak to Ezekiel there at the northern inner gate that led

---

6. By whom had the real temple, as seen by Ezekiel in vision, been built, and what did Ezekiel see at the entrance of the northern inner gate?
7. What was nearby in stark contrast with that "symbol of jealousy," and for whom was its movement there ominous?
8. Ezekiel was asked whether he saw what, and what effect would its being there have upon Jehovah?

to the altar of sacrifice. "And," says Ezekiel, "he proceeded to say to me: 'Son of man, please, raise your eyes in the direction of the north.' So I raised my eyes in the direction of the north, and, look! to the north of the gate of the altar there was this symbol of jealousy in the entranceway. And he went on to say to me: 'Son of man, are you seeing what great detestable things they are doing, the things that the house of Israel are doing here for me to become far off from my sanctuary? And yet you will see again great detestable things.' "—Ezekiel 8:5, 6.

⁹ Just what kind of idolatrous thing this "symbol of jealousy" was we are not told. It is thought that it was an "asherah," or sacred pole, that represented the false goddess who was the wife of the Canaanite god Baal. Whatever it was, it incited the living God Jehovah to jealousy, for it divided the exclusive devotion of the Israelites to Jehovah and it was in violation of the first two of the Ten Commandments, namely: "I am Jehovah your God, who have brought you out of the land of Egypt, out of the house of slaves. You must not have any other gods against my face. You must not make for yourself a carved image or a form like anything that is in the heavens above or that is on the earth underneath or that is in the waters under the earth. You must not bow down to them nor be induced to serve them, because I Jehovah your God am a God exacting exclusive devotion, bringing punishment for the error." (Exodus 20:2-5) Hence worship of that "symbol of jealousy" in Jehovah's own temple in Jerusalem was one of the "great detestable things" that the apostate Israelites were doing.

¹⁰ Was such a material temple, defiled by the worship of this "symbol of jealousy," a proper "sanctuary" for Jehovah to continue occupying by his spirit and favor?

9. What effect did that "symbol of jealousy" in his temple have upon Jehovah, and of what divine commandments was its presence there a violation?

10. The presence of that "symbol of jealousy" there obliged the Lord God to do what as regards the temple, and what similar action by him took place in 33 C.E.?

No, indeed! That idolatrous symbol, together with other "great detestable things," made it necessary for him to withdraw his spiritual presence. It obliged him, as he said, "to become far off from my sanctuary." This meant for him to abandon it to destruction. The same thing occurred in the year 33 of our Common Era, when Jesus Christ said to the Jews concerning their temple in Jerusalem: "Look! Your house is abandoned to you." (Matthew 23:38) That desecrated temple was destroyed in 70 C.E.

¹¹ Today Christendom has defiled its religious houses with many symbols that divide its exclusive devotion to the God whom it professes to serve, professedly the God of the Bible. By such idolatrous things Christendom, which takes the name of the Son of God, incites Jehovah the heavenly Father to jealousy. It would be well, therefore, for churchgoing people of Christendom to take note of what Jehovah showed his prophet Ezekiel, to see whether they and their church systems are guilty of these very same things, in modern style. They might thus learn what to do now without delay in order to save themselves from destruction in the "great tribulation" that is shortly to come upon the modern-day antitypical Jerusalem, namely, Christendom. (Matthew 24:21, 22) Not yet have we noted all the "great detestable things" that turned away Jehovah from those who long ago pretended to worship him, for, as he said to Ezekiel at the temple of Jerusalem, "yet you will see again great detestable things." Let us see them also.

OUTRAGEOUS WORSHIP OF CREATURES INFERIOR TO MAN

¹² Ezekiel followed Jehovah on this tour of inspection of the temple conditions. He says: "Accordingly he brought me to the entrance of the courtyard, and

11. What other religious system has defiled its houses in a way like that of Jerusalem's temple, and what should adherents thereof do therefore in order to take proper action?
12, 13. Where did Jehovah now bring Ezekiel, and what did he do on being told?

I began to see, and, look! a certain hole in the wall. He now said to me: 'Son of man, bore, please, through the wall.' And I gradually bored through the wall, and, look! there was a certain entrance. And he further said to me: 'Go in and see the bad detestable things that they are doing here.' "—Ezekiel 8:7-9.

¹³ According to this, Jehovah brought Ezekiel through the northern inner gate right on into the inner courtyard where the altar was located. Inside this courtyard Ezekiel was shown a chamber at or near the inner gate through which he had come. Do we now see that hole in its wall? Ezekiel is told to bore through it, enlarging the opening in order to get through to the inside. Either through this bored entrance or through another "certain entrance" near the bored hole, Ezekiel is told to go in and see what those inside are doing. What Ezekiel saw after doing so he tells us:

¹⁴ "So I went in and began to see, and, look! there was every representation of creeping things and loathsome beasts, and all the dungy idols of the house of Israel, the carving being upon the wall all round about. And seventy men of the elderly ones of the house of Israel, with Jaazaniah the son of Shaphan standing in among them, were standing before them, each one with his censer in his hand, and the perfume of the cloud of the incense was ascending. And he proceeded to say to me: 'Have you seen, O son of man, what the elderly ones of the house of Israel are doing in the darkness, each one in the inner rooms of his showpiece? For they are saying, "Jehovah is not seeing us. Jehovah has left the land." ' "—Ezekiel 8:10-12.

¹⁵ This was taking place in the inner courtyard near the temple altar! There may have been individual chambers inside this structure into which Ezekiel had bored his way, and the walls of all these had carvings of creeping things, ceremonially unclean loathsome

---

14. Inside, what did Ezekiel see seventy men carrying on, and what were they saying?
15. The things that those elderly men worshiped were the things worshiped by what kind of nations?

beasts and "dungy idols" such as the pagan Egyptians in particular worshiped along the Nile River.

¹⁶ Outrageously in the very temple of Jehovah, those seventy elders of the house of Israel were offering up incense to the false gods represented by those carvings on the wall! To them it did not matter that they were doing such degraded false worship in the temple of Jehovah. They quieted any fears of receiving punishment therefor by saying to themselves that Jehovah was not seeing what they were doing in the darkness, behind closed doors. In fact, Jaazaniah the son of Shaphan and the sixty-nine other elders of the house of Israel may have felt that Jerusalem and the Kingdom of Judah had had so much trouble recently at the hands of Babylon that Jehovah had apparently "left the land" of Judah. And, as far as having further interest in the land, Jehovah was dead!

¹⁷ Today, in this so-called Brain Age, does Christendom show herself so smart as to keep from offering up the incense of worship to "every representation of creeping things and loathsome beasts, and all the dungy idols," such as those seventy elders of Israel were perfuming? Well, look at the wild animals and birds by which the nations of Christendom represent or symbolize their respective countries, to which symbols they give their heart's devotion. Look at the animalistic and birdlike names that the sports teams of Christendom call themselves, the heroes of such sports becoming popular idols for even churchgoing people. And what about the Evolution Theory, which even most of the clergy of Christendom have adopted instead of holding to the Bible explanation of God's direct creation of man as distinct from the lower animals and fishes! Thus Jehovah is shoved out of the picture as man's divine Creator, and the evolutionist

---

16. How did those seventy elders quiet any fears of being punished for carrying on such worship there?
17. In this "Brain Age," how does Christendom show the inclination of those seventy elders in worshiping beasts, birds and fish?

clergy of Christendom lead their church people in worshiping a theoretical evolutionary force as man's creator, at the same time speaking of Mother Nature instead of the Heavenly Father as Creator and God.

[18] If these hypocritical religionists of Christendom think that Jehovah is paying no attention to what is going on in the earth and is no longer interested, not even in Christendom, and that thus "God is dead," they are greatly mistaken. He is as alive as ever, being immortal, and he is highly offended at what is going on among those who claim to represent him and to be in a Christian relationship with him. These facts he will shortly make them painfully feel.

[19] Consequently church people who are under the influence and guidance of these clergy elders of Christendom have all good reason to consider the things that Jehovah showed to his prophet Ezekiel. He sees what the clergy are doing "in the darkness," behind closed doors. He hears and knows what they are saying to themselves in self-assurance. Why should he not be able to do this? Think of how, by means of visions, he was able to uncover to Ezekiel what was going on in the temple of Jerusalem, although Ezekiel was bodily in Tel-abib in Babylonia five hundred miles east of Jerusalem. Distance is no barrier to Jehovah's vision and hearing. Let us, then, read about what is next shown to Ezekiel:

[20] "And he [Jehovah] continued on to say to me: 'You will yet see again great detestable things that they are doing.' So he brought me to the entrance of the gate of the house of Jehovah, which is toward the north, and, look! there the women were sitting, weeping over the god Tammuz."—Ezekiel 8:13, 14.

---

18. Are those hypocritical religionists correct in their way of thinking, and Jehovah will shortly make them feel that he feels how toward them?
19. Who today have good reason to consider what Jehovah showed here to Ezekiel, and how do his visions to Ezekiel prove that he sees and hears what is done and said in the dark?
20, 21. The false god over whom Ezekiel saw the women weeping furnished the name for what lunar month, and what did he represent to his worshipers in southwest Asia?

WORSHIP OF THE FALSE GOD TAMMUZ

²¹ Tammuz—ah! we recall that the fourth month of the lunar year is named after this false god. According to the Babylonians and the Syrians he was the god of vegetation that grows during the rainy season with its kindly floods and dies during the dry season of southwest Asia. Death of the vegetation pictured the death of Tammuz, and it was his death that was bewailed annually at the time of the greatest heat, by the idolatrous worshipers of Tammuz. At return of the rainy season Tammuz was supposed to return from the Underworld, as symbolized by the growth again of the vegetation. Worship of Tammuz is understood to be one of the oldest forms of false religious worship in human history, and has not altogether disappeared from certain parts of the earth even now.

²² However, in his book entitled "The Two Babylons" Dr. Alexander Hislop identifies Tammuz with Nimrod, the founder of the city of Babylon, about 180 years after the flood of Noah's day.

²³ Nimrod was the great-grandson of Noah. According to Genesis 10:1, 6, 8-12, Nimrod became known as "a mighty hunter in opposition to Jehovah." According to religious tradition, Nimrod was executed for his rebelliousness against Jehovah, the God of Noah. Nimrod's followers considered his violent death a tragedy or calamity, and deified him. Annually they memorialized his death on the first or second day of the lunar month Tammuz, when the idolatrous women wept over his idol. So among the ancient classical writers he was given the name Bacchus, which means "Bewept One," "Lamented One." This weeping over him corresponds with that carried on over the legendary Adonis, a beautiful youth who was loved by Venus or Ishtar and who was killed by a wild boar in the

22. With whom does the book *The Two Babylons* identify Tammuz?
23. Who, Biblically, was Nimrod, what did his followers do about him after his death, and how do the mythical characters Bacchus and Adonis correspond with him?

mountains of Lebanon. In fact, the Latin Vulgate Bible and the English Douay Version Bible use the name Adonis instead of Tammuz in Ezekiel 8:14: "Behold women sat there mourning for Adonis," or, "Lord."

²⁴ *The Two Babylons* (page 245, footnote) derives the name Tammuz from the words *tam* ("to make perfect") and *muz* ("fire") so as to mean "Perfecting Fire" or "Fire the Perfecter." Another derivation gives it the meaning "Hidden" or "Obscure," and this corresponds with the fact that the worship of the image of Tammuz was carried on in a secret place, as pictured at Ezekiel 8:14.* He was represented by the first letter of his name, which is an ancient *tau*, that was a cross. The "sign of the cross" was the religious symbol of Tammuz. So there was an attempt to introduce the worship of the idolatrous pagan cross into the temple of Jehovah at Jerusalem. How scandalous it was for those Israelite women, on the pavement of the inner court of Jehovah's temple, to be religiously weeping over the executional death of Tammuz, in reality over "Nimrod a mighty hunter in opposition to Jehovah"!

²⁵ What today in Christendom, since its founding in the fourth century by Roman Emperor Constantine the Great, derives itself from all religious things having to do with Nimrod alias Tammuz? Let us bear in mind that "the beginning of his kingdom came to be Babel [or Babylon] and Erech and Accad and Calneh, in the land of Shinar. Out of that land he went forth into Assyria and set himself to building Nineveh and Rehoboth-Ir and Calah and Resen between Nineveh and Calah: this is the great city." (Genesis 10:10-12) Thus

---

* Others derive the name Tammuz from the Akkadian word *Duzu*, which is associated with the Sumerian word *Dumuzi*, meaning "Faithful son," or, "Sprouting of life."

24. What derivations have been given for the name Tammuz, what letter became a symbol of him, and why was it scandalous for women to bewail Tammuz in Jehovah's temple?
25. According to Genesis 10:10-12, Nimrod was a founder of what, and what type of religion stems from the "beginning of his kingdom"?

Nimrod was the founder of cities and of political systems of rule, contrary to the will of Jehovah God. All false religion stemmed from Babylon after the flood of the days of Noah. Genesis 10:8, 9 says that "he [Nimrod] displayed himself a mighty hunter in opposition to Jehovah."

²⁶ The term "hunting," according to the ancient Babylonian and Assyrian custom, was applied not only to hunting for wild animals but also to military campaigns against human creatures as the prey. So Nimrod made himself a shedder of human blood in warfare.

²⁷ How well these details about Nimrod fit also to Christendom! Like Nimrod, she also has established her own religious systems. These are generally thought of as being in harmony with the Holy Bible of Jehovah but in actuality being in harmony with religious teachings of ancient Babylon, including the adoration of the cross, the symbol of Tammuz. Like Nimrod, Christendom has not confined herself to religion purely; she has mixed herself in worldly politics, setting up, wherever possible, a union of Church and State, with the Church trying to tell the State what to do. She has claimed that her political emperors and kings have ruled "By the grace of God." Even her bishops, archbishops and popes have been honored with material thrones and are still said to "reign" over their bishoprics and papal sees.

²⁸ The politicians of this world are given prominent positions and considerations in the church systems. What a contrast this to the example of Jesus Christ, who refused to be made a king on earth by men! To the Roman governor, Pontius Pilate, he said: "My kingdom is no part of this world. If my kingdom were part of this world, my attendants would have fought

26. According to the Babylonian and Assyrian custom of applying the word "hunter," in what way was Nimrod a shedder of blood?
27. What has Christendom done as regards setting up religious systems, and how has she not confined herself to religion purely as her realm?
28. How have the politicians been favored by Christendom, and how has she gone contrary politically to the words and example of Jesus Christ?

that I should not be delivered up to the Jews. But, as it is, my kingdom is not from this source." (John 18:36) To the contrary of this, Christendom insists that it is the duty of her church members to engage in politics. At times and in some places, she endeavors to dictate to them as to the political candidates for whom they shall cast their election ballots. Members of her clergy have even acted as political rulers, as president, or prime minister, and so on.

²⁹ And what about wanton bloodshed as committed by "Nimrod a mighty hunter in opposition to Jehovah"? Nimrod was merely a small prototype for Christendom! She too has engaged as a "hunter" in military campaigns with carnal weapons. The most sanguinary wars of all human history have been waged by the members of Christendom, between themselves and with the so-called infidels and pagans. All this is not Christlike. It is Babylonish and smacks of Nimrod.

³⁰ The loss of human lives in these wars has caused untold weeping by the womenfolk of Christendom. Memorial days are held annually when the ones bereaved by war go to the graveyards to decorate the burial plots of their slain warriors. The deaths of the mighty war generals and other high-ranking warlords are mourned by the patriotic, nationalistic members of Christendom, these being eulogized in the churches in which the funeral services are held. All this in full agreement with the notorious fact that churches have been used as recruiting stations and propaganda centers in times of war. Such connecting up of all these political and military doings with the "house of God" (the Church) in Christendom well reminds us of those Israelite women sitting and weeping over Tammuz inside the inner court of the temple of the Sovereign Lord God in Ezekiel's day.

---

29. How does Christendom find in Nimrod the "mighty hunter" a small prototype of herself as regards bloodshed?
30. How have the wars of Christendom caused further weeping on the part of the womenfolk and the paying of special respects by the churches to high-ranking war figures?

WORSHIPING A SYMBOLIC SUN

[31] However, is that all? Ezekiel says not, for he goes on to tell us what further Jehovah showed to him, saying: "And he further said to me: 'Have you seen this, O son of man? You will yet see again great detestable things worse than these.' So he brought me to the inner courtyard of the house of Jehovah, and, look! at the entrance of the temple of Jehovah, between the porch and the altar, there were about twenty-five men with their backs to the temple of Jehovah and their faces to the east, and they were bowing down to the east, to the sun. And he went on to say to me: 'Have you seen this, O son of man? Is it such a light thing to the house of Judah to do the detestable things that they have done here, that they have to fill the land with violence and that they should offend me again, and here they are thrusting out the shoot [twig] to my nose? And I myself also shall act in rage. My eye will not feel sorry, neither shall I feel compassion. And they will certainly call out in my ears with a loud voice, but I shall not hear them.'"
—Ezekiel 8:15-18; footnote reading.

[32] The conduct of those twenty-five Israelite men was specially outrageous toward Jehovah. There they were, in the inner court of the temple dedicated to him and in the space between the porch of the temple and the altar of sacrifice at the center of the inner court. But they were not worshiping Jehovah at that place, nor were they bowing to his altar of sacrifice that was to the east of them. Instead of facing west, toward the temple where the presence of Jehovah was symbolized by the Shekinah light that hovered over the sacred Ark of the Covenant in the innermost compartment, the Most Holy, those twenty-five men turned their backs toward the Divine Presence and faced east. Horrors! They were bowing down in worship to the

31. What worship did Jehovah show to Ezekiel as being carried on by about twenty-five men between temple porch and altar, and what was also being done so that Jehovah should not hear their prayers?
32, 33. On whose worship were those men turning their backs, and what warning through Moses were they violating?

sun in the sky! They were expressly violating the warning that Jehovah gave through the prophet Moses:

[33] "You must take good care of your souls, . . . that you may not raise your eyes to the heavens and indeed see the sun and the moon and the stars, all the army of the heavens, and actually get seduced and bow down to them and serve them."—Deuteronomy 4:15-19.

[34] In the year 642 B.C.E., or thirty years before this, good King Josiah had publicly read those words to the people who were assembled at the temple, and after that he promptly abolished and destroyed all worship of the sun-god out of the Kingdom of Judah. (2 Kings 22:3 to 23:11) But now, after Josiah's death, the men of Judah acted like washed swine that returned to their wallowing in the mire and they reintroduced sun worship and practiced it right inside the temple of Jehovah, without interference on the part of the priests of the tribe of Levi. They renounced the words of the "sons of Korah [the Levite]," as recorded in Psalm 84:11: "Jehovah God is a sun and a shield; favor and glory are what he gives. Jehovah himself will not hold back anything good from those walking in faultlessness." Those twenty-five renegade Israelites looked to a mere creation of Jehovah, the sun, as their source of "favor and glory," as their source for "anything good." That was enough to insult Jehovah.

[35] Yet those men added further insult to this. "Here," said Jehovah, "they are thrusting out the shoot [or, twig] to my nose." (Ezekiel 8:17) This shoot or twig was used in idolatrous worship and may have been carved to a certain shape to represent the human male organ. At least it must have been something very offensive or obscene to be held out to Jehovah's nose, as if he would find pleasure in smelling it. Such idolatrous sun worship on the part of those twenty-five men was

_____

34. Earlier, what had good King Josiah done regarding sun worship, but now how were those twenty-five men renouncing Psalm 84:11?
35. Why was their holding out the shoot or twig to Jehovah's nose offensive to him, and with what were they filling the land, thus obliging Jehovah to act in what way toward them?

accompanied by their filling "the land with violence." It was enough for Jehovah to find good reason to "act in rage." This it was his purpose to do at the approaching destruction of Jerusalem and its temple. Then, when the sun-god failed those twenty-five apostate Israelites, they would fall back on Jehovah and call out to him with a loud voice to try to make him hear, but he would have no cause for paying attention to their selfish cries. As he looked upon their destruction by his executional forces his eye would feel no sorrow, for he himself would feel no compassion. He hates hypocrites!

[36] No, the religionists of Christendom today do not actually worship the sun, for they know from their scientists something of what the sun is, so as to know that it is no god. Even after World War II ended in 1945 the emperor of non-Christian Japan was intelligent enough to renounce the claim made for emperors of Nippon that they were descendants of the sun-goddess, Amaterasu. Be that as it may, yet there is a prominent group in Christendom, including the Modernist clergyman of her churches, that has turned from worshiping the God of the Holy Bible, Jehovah, to a substitute of their own choice. They even deny his existence. In place of looking to Him as the source of enlightenment and energy and of the warmth of material comforts, they look to modern science and human philosophy. They pay more respect to these modern scientists and intellectuals, they attribute more to these, than they do to Jehovah. These have become the symbolic "sun" that Christendom worships and to which she looks for salvation. Christendom's general acceptance of the unprovable Theory of Evolution is one of the evidences betraying her as a worshiper of such a "sun."

[37] Modern science has come to be treated like a "sa-

---

36. In what way are members of Christendom today engaging in a symbolic worship of the sun?
37. How has modern science been treated by awed human creatures, and how has Christendom displayed the tendency noted in Romans 1:23?

cred cow," that must be treated with reverence and that must be considered ahead of the Bible and its God. Modern intellectuality with all its theories has been treated as the up-to-date form of enlightenment that has made the Bible out-of-date, obsolete. This high-speed, nuclear, space age has come to be rated as having advanced beyond the so-called "camel train" philosophy of the Bible. To modern technology is given the credit for all the material comforts and labor-saving devices and communication systems that are at our disposal today. All this has focused the attention upon the human creature. For all these marvelous accomplishments of modern times Christendom's worship has been directed to the creature. She has turned her back on the Creator, who endowed the human creature with the mental and physical powers to accomplish these things. This constant human tendency to do so was mentioned nineteen centuries ago in Romans, chapter 1, verse 23.

[38] Christendom's infection with the worship of false gods, the gods of demonism, betrays itself very slyly. For instance, on July 20, 1969, when for the first time a human astronaut set foot upon the moon, who was glorified thereby, according to the way that the scientific group responsible for it named things that were involved? Certainly not Jehovah, the Creator of the moon, but the mythological sun-god. How so? Because the man-made spacecraft with which the successful moon-shot for putting Americans on our lunar satellite was made was named Apollo, Number Eleven. Phoebus Apollo was the sun-god of the ancient Greeks and was also the twin brother of Artemis (or Diana), the moon-goddess. This Apollo of the Greeks has been traced back as being the first king of Babylon, namely, Nimrod, the "mighty hunter in opposition to Jehovah." (Genesis 10:8-10)* Since that first landing on the

---

* See page 32, with footnotes, of *The Two Babylons*, by Dr. Alexander Hislop, the edition of 1926.

38. How has Christendom's infection with worship of the demon gods been betrayed, even in connection with putting men on the moon?

moon, further moon-shots have been made in space-crafts of the "Apollo" series. All a part of sun worship!

[39] Has this sun worship proved to be beneficial to mankind? Back in the days of the prophet Ezekiel it did not prove to be so. Neither has it proved to be so in this modern twentieth century. The violence that has resulted has vastly exceeded that of Ezekiel's day. (Ezekiel 8:17) The clergymen of Christendom have not halted the application of modern-day science to the invention and use of the most fiendish weapons of war, culminating in the developing of biological and radiological and atomic-nuclear weapons. The fighting of World Wars I and II was heavily dependent upon activity of scientists. Violence that has filled the earth has not been limited to those two world wars that were fought mainly by Christendom. The much-worshiped modern philosophy has robbed churchgoing people of a real fear of God, and violence is being employed widely, even in peacetime. The time period since 1914 C.E. has been officially termed an "Age of Violence."

[40] The technology of modern science has been applied to modern industry and commercialism, and this has resulted in a growing pollution that is ruining man's natural environment. Fears are expressed that this earth will become shortly a place unfit for humans in which to exist. And what about man's moral environment?

[41] A new morality has been adopted that views even fornication, adultery, and homosexuality with indulgence and makes legal allowances for them. Christendom's clergymen refrain from declaring what the Bible has to say against these things. In fact, many prominent clergymen have come out publicly in favor of legislation that relieves immoral persons of punishment for committing such unclean things. Venereal disease continues to increase as a result, in fact, has

39. What must be said as to whether this symbolic worship of the sun has been beneficial to mankind?
40, 41. How have the techniques of modern science in industry and communication affected man's natural environment, and what must be said about the offensiveness of man's moral environment today?

become an epidemic! If this is offensive to many God-fearing people today, what must it be to God himself? It is just as offensive as when those twenty-five sun worshipers in Jehovah's temple in Jerusalem were obscenely "thrusting out the shoot" to His nose. (Ezekiel 8:17) Should he hear such hypocritical Christians when they soon cry to Him? No!

CHRISTENDOM INFECTED WITH DEADLY DEMONISM

⁴² There is every justification for Jehovah to "act in rage," without feeling compassion, when he shortly brings upon Christendom and her worldly associates the "great tribulation" with which this system of things will come to its end. Our tour of inspection regarding the religious conditions of Christendom has been just as revealing as that which Ezekiel made in the polluted temple of Jehovah in Jerusalem. It has disclosed that Christendom's house of worship is so infected with demonism and so loaded with the appendages of demonism as to be inseparable from it. This was admitted almost a hundred years ago by one of Christendom's famous clergymen. In the year 1878 the Roman Catholic prelate, John Cardinal Newman, published his book entitled "Essay on the Development of Christian Doctrine." In this he expressed his belief that the early professed Christians had not been infected with spiritual disease by any adopting into their religious organization the things that had to do with the worship of devilish demons. Accordingly he wrote:

> Confiding then in the power of Christianity to resist the infection of evil, and to transmute the very instruments and appendages of demon-worship to an evangelical use, and feeling also that these usages had originally come from primitive revelations and from the instinct of nature, though they had been corrupted; and that they must invent what they needed, if they did not use what they found; and that they were moreover possessed of the very archetypes, of which paganism attempted the shadows; the rulers of the Church from early times

---

42. How has our tour of inspection of the house of worship of Christendom shown that Jehovah is justified in acting shortly in rage against her, and as to her what did Cardinal Newman write?

were prepared, should the occasion arise, to adopt, or imitate, or sanction the existing rites and customs of the populace, as well as the philosophy of the educated class.

Proceeding now to show the origin of Christendom's things, he says:

> The use of temples, and these dedicated to particular saints, and ornamented on occasions with branches of trees; incense, lamps, and candles; votive offerings on recovery from illness; holy water; asylums; holydays and seasons, use of calendars, processions, blessings on the fields; sacerdotal vestments, the tonsure, the ring in marriage, turning to the East, images at a later date, perhaps the ecclesiastical chant, and the [song] Kyrie Eleison [Lord, have mercy], are all of pagan origin, and sanctified by their adoption into the Church.—Pages 355, 371, 373, of the edition of 1881.

[43] Expressing the same spirit of compromise as continuing into this twentieth century is the statement made to newspapermen in Rome, Italy, by the late Pope Pius XI (died 1939):

> The head of the Catholic Church would consider it his duty to deal with the Devil himself, to say nothing about any mortals who, hypothetically, or in reality, were merely agents of the Dictator of Diabolism, if reasonable grounds existed to support the hope that such dealings would protect, or advance, the interests of religion among mankind.—Quoted by Michael Williams, in the February 21, 1943, issue of the Brooklyn *Eagle*, New York.

[44] Even the Eastern Orthodox churches and the Protestant churches of Christendom have not discarded the practices and the "misleading inspired utterances and teachings of demons" that were to mark "later periods of time." (1 Timothy 4:1) As regards the Israelites in the days of the prophet Ezekiel, there was no Biblical excuse for them to adopt the rites and teachings of demon worship, as this course was for-

---

43. How did the late Pope Pius XI express the same spirit of compromise religiously to newspapermen regarding dealing with others for church interests?

44, 45. Have the Eastern Orthodox and Protestant churches discarded the inspired expressions and teachings of demons, and in the light of 2 Corinthians 6:14 to 7:1 what excuse do professed Christians have for contaminating themselves with the things of demonism?

bidden even back in the Law of Moses. (Deuteronomy 18:9-14) Likewise, as respects those who profess to be Christians, there is no excuse for them to contaminate themselves with the teachings, practices, instruments and appendages of demonism, especially in view of the apostolic command:

⁴⁵ "Do not become unevenly yoked with unbelievers. For what fellowship do righteousness and lawlessness have? Or what sharing does light have with darkness? Further, what harmony is there between Christ and Belial? Or what portion does a faithful person have with an unbeliever? And what agreement does God's temple have with idols? For we are a temple of a living God; just as God said: 'I shall reside among them and walk among them, and I shall be their God, and they will be my people.' ' "Therefore get out from among them, and separate yourselves," says Jehovah, "and quit touching the unclean thing" '; ' "and I will take you in." ' ' "And I shall be a father to you, and you will be sons and daughters to me," says Jehovah the Almighty.' Therefore, since we have these promises, beloved ones, let us cleanse ourselves of every defilement of flesh and spirit, perfecting holiness in God's fear."—2 Corinthians 6:14 to 7:1; Isaiah 52:11; Jeremiah 31:9.

⁴⁶ Disobedience to such inspired commands has resulted in the confused, contaminated religious condition of Christendom today. She is beyond recovery. Like her ancient prototype, ancient Jerusalem, she is bound to suffer execution at the hands of the God against whom she has so greatly offended. A "great tribulation" exceeding even that which came upon Jerusalem in the days of the apostles of Jesus Christ is prophesied to come upon her. (Matthew 24:15-22; Mark 13:14-20) In view of this, searching questions present themselves to each one of us: Am I an active

46, 47. Disobedience to those divine commands has resulted in what religious condition in Christendom, and what is prophesied to come upon her, so that we should ask ourselves what searching questions and seek for answers where?

member of Christendom's religious organization? Or, Am I in sympathy with her and cooperating with her? If so, how will the "great tribulation" that is coming upon her affect me? Is there any way to escape sharing with her in that destructive "great tribulation"? Will even anyone who is in the midst of Christendom but who is not a sympathetic part of her be spared alive?

⁴⁷ What Jehovah showed to Ezekiel in vision after he inspected the temple in Jerusalem furnishes answers to these questions.

Chapter 9

Marking Foreheads of Those to Be Spared

JEHOVAH and his prophet Ezekiel were still, in vision, at the defiled temple of Jerusalem when what Ezekiel next describes took place: "And he proceeded to call out in my ears with a loud voice, saying: 'Have those giving their attention to the city come near, each one with his weapon in his hand for bringing ruin!'"—Ezekiel 9:1.

² Here "those giving their attention to the city" were not members of the city government of Jerusalem. So those whom Jehovah called did not include King Zedekiah, who was then governing Jerusalem and all the Kingdom of Judah in that year 612 B.C.E. Certainly King Zedekiah and his princes did not try to destroy Jerusalem. In fact, they appealed to Pharaoh of Egypt to come and help to save the city. Those

1. What does Jehovah, while still at the temple, call out in Ezekiel's hearing as a summons?
2. To whom did the expression "those giving their attention to the city" not apply, and what was their mission?

whom Jehovah called were those "giving their attention to the city," not to preserve and govern it, but to destroy inhabitants of it with those weapons "for bringing ruin." They were not Jews. Who, then, were they?

³ Let us take a look at them with Ezekiel, as he goes on to say: "And, look! there were six men coming from the direction of the upper gate that faces to the north, each one with his weapon for smashing in his hand; and there was one man in among them clothed with linen, with a secretary's inkhorn at his hips, and they proceeded to come in and stand beside the copper altar."—Ezekiel 9:2.

⁴ Forebodingly, they came in from the north, for that was the direction from which the mighty armies of Babylon came against Jerusalem three years later, in 609 B.C.E. By the northern inner gate of Jehovah's temple they passed into its inner courtyard and stood beside the copper altar at its center, but not to offer sacrifice to Jehovah. There, at the north side of the altar, they might be seen by the twenty-five men who were between the altar and the temple porch and who were bowing down in worship to the sun to the east. (Ezekiel 8:16) Being seven in number, they were a complete team for united action. But the man "clothed with linen" was singled out from among the other six by his garment. He also got to be separated from them by being sent ahead of them.

⁵ The "six men" in the vision were evidently supernatural persons, like materialized angels. It is not said that they were Babylonians, even though the Babylonians were used to destroy the literal Jerusalem. Since the "six men" had each one a "weapon for smashing" in the hand, they represent the heavenly executional forces of Jehovah who are subject to his command. They represent a heavenly army, soldiers, as it were.

3. Whom did Ezekiel now see come in and stand beside the altar, and how were they distinguished?
4. Why was it foreboding that the seven men came from the north into the temple, and how was the one man singled out from the other six?
5. Who evidently were those "six men," and whom did they represent?

These could, in actuality, use Babylonian soldiers as earthly agents.

THE MARKER OF FOREHEADS

⁶ The seventh individual, the man "clothed with linen," was of a higher rank (not meaning hereby of a higher nature) in comparison with the "six men" armed with weapons. He is observed to have a "secretary's inkhorn" at his waist, evidently held there by his girdle. But it is not said that he is the "secretary of the chief of the army" so as to be associated with military matters. (Jeremiah 52:25) He could be a peaceful governmental secretary. (2 Samuel 8:17; 20:25; 1 Kings 4:3) In the vision, on what kind of mission is this man in linen sent? This is made manifest by the commission that he receives from Jehovah, who rides on his celestial chariot. On this Ezekiel says:

⁷ "And as regards the glory of the God of Israel, it was taken up from over the cherubs over which it happened to be to the threshold of the house, and he began calling out to the man that was clothed with the linen, at whose hips there was the secretary's inkhorn. And Jehovah went on to say to him: 'Pass through the midst of the city, through the midst of Jerusalem, and you must put a mark on the foreheads of the men that are sighing and groaning over all the detestable things that are being done in the midst of it.' "—Ezekiel 9:3, 4.

⁸ Ah, the man in linen is sent on a peaceful, life-saving mission. At this point the Divine Presence moved from above the awesome icelike platform that was above the four wheels and the heads of the four cherubs at the north entrance of the temple. To where? "To the threshold of the house." (Ezekiel 8:3, 4; 9:3)

---

6. What kind of individual is the man "clothed with linen," and what question arises as to his part?
7. From where does Jehovah call out to the man "clothed with linen," and what does He tell the man to do?
8. What was the "threshold of the house" to above which Jehovah's glory moved, and on what kind of mission was the man "clothed with linen" sent?

This was not the porch of the temple, in front of which the twenty-five sun worshipers were standing. Appropriately it would be the threshold of the innermost compartment of the temple, the threshold of the Holy of Holies in which the Ark of the Covenant was located. On the golden lid of that gold-covered Ark there were the two golden cherubs, facing each other with upraised wings. Between or above the cherubs there appeared the miraculous Shekinah light as a symbol of God's presence in the Most Holy. (Numbers 7:89) From this position above the inner threshold of the temple Jehovah issued his orders to the "man that was clothed with the linen." He was to go through Jerusalem ahead of the "six men." He was to use his pen and ink to do a marking work.

WHOSE FOREHEADS ARE MARKED, AND HOW

⁹ All the people in Jerusalem were in danger of their lives, because Jehovah was about to 'act in his rage' in executing his judicial decision against the city. Despite his justified "rage," he would have compassion upon some of its inhabitants. Upon whom? Upon those who were not in sympathy with the detestable things that were being committed at Jehovah's temple nor with the violence with which the unfaithful religionists were filling the land. (Ezekiel 8:17, 18) There were "men that are sighing and groaning over all the detestable things that are being done" in Jerusalem.

¹⁰ All these the man with the inkhorn at his waist was to mark in their foreheads, where the mark could be openly seen. For the man in linen to do this, it would require him to go from house to house, from home to home, in order to locate men who were grieved at the way that their God Jehovah was being offended. In order that these sighing and groaning men might be distinguished from the offenders against

9. Who were in danger, and upon whom did Jehovah purpose to have compassion?
10. As to those upon whom Jehovah was to have compassion, what was required of the man "clothed with linen" to carry out his mission toward them?

God, they needed to be marked in their foreheads. This would mark them as true worshipers of Jehovah.

[11] Of what value would that mark with ink on the foreheads of such pure worshipers of the one living and true God be? This becomes apparent from the official orders that Jehovah next gave to the "six men" armed with weapons for smashing. The prophet Ezekiel tells us what he heard: "And to these others he said in my ears: 'Pass through the city after him and strike. Let not your eye feel sorry, and do not feel any compassion. Old man, young man and virgin and little child and women you should kill off—to a ruination. But to any man upon whom there is the mark do not go near, and from my sanctuary you should start.' "—Ezekiel 9:5, 6.

[12] According to those divine instructions any Israelites having their foreheads marked would not be killed off by the "six men." Since the instrument used for killing the unmarked Israelites was a "weapon for smashing," it was likely used in smashing the skulls of those deserving to be executed. How fitting it was, then, that the foreheads of Jehovah's worshipers were marked, for the "six men" would strike at the head! Seeing a mark on the forehead would hold them back from smashing that head. Age or sex was no reason for an offender against Jehovah to be spared, neither singleness nor marriage. Unmarked parents would not have their minor children marked in the forehead. Hence they would be the ones responsible for the killing of their little children, the Ten Commandments plainly stating that "punishment for the error of fathers" would be brought upon the "sons, upon the third generation and upon the fourth generation." The failure of parents to bring up their children in the pure worship of Jehovah would make such delinquent

---

11. Of what value to the bearer was the mark with ink in the forehead, according to Jehovah's orders to the "six men"?
12. In view of the executional instruments of the "six men," why was the mark in the forehead appropriate, and who became responsible for the killing of the unmarked minor children?

parents responsible for the outworking of God's righteous law against their minor children.—Exodus 20:5.

WHERE THE SMASHING OF HEADS BEGINS

[13] Since Jehovah said, "From my sanctuary you should start," the armed "six men" did not have to shrink from the thought of smashing persons to death inside His temple. All the idolatrous Israelites may have felt safe inside the temple, because they thought that slain dead bodies defiled Jehovah's sanctuary but their false worship with idols did not defile his sanctuary. However, Jehovah had moved far off from his nominal sanctuary, and in evidence of that he wanted it to be defiled by the slain bodies of those who were defiling the sanctuary with their idolatries. Accordingly Ezekiel tells us concerning the "six men" with their smashing weapons: "So they started with the old men that were before the house. And he said further to them: 'Defile the house and fill the courtyards with the slain ones. Go forth!' And they went forth and struck in the city."—Ezekiel 9:6, 7.

[14] Consequently, one's being inside the premises of the temple sanctuary of Jehovah was not like having a "Saint Christopher's medal" or amulet around one's neck to protect one from being killed by Jehovah's executioners. That polluted temple was no longer any sanctuary of refuge for hypocritical religionists. So, what about those seventy "elderly ones of the house of Israel, with Jaazaniah the son of Shaphan," who were burning incense to idolatrous carvings that were on the inside walls of the house that was before the sanctuary? (Ezekiel 8:7-11) They were the ones with whom the "six men" started their executional work. Then there were the women "sitting, weeping over the god Tammuz." These also were brained to death with

13. Why did the idolatrous Israelites feel safe inside Jehovah's nominal sanctuary, but what were Jehovah's orders to the "six men" as to defiling the house?
14. Why was being in the temple premises no longer like a charm of protection against being killed, and upon whom did the "six men" start their executional work, going on to whom afterward?

the smashing weapons. The "twenty-five men" who were between the porch and the altar and who were worshiping the sun are not called "old men" or "elderly ones," but they also were killed by the "six men." (Ezekiel 8:14-16) Thus the house and the courtyards of the temple were defiled with the slain ones. This left Ezekiel remaining alive alone there!

¹⁵ The gory sight inside the temple may have raised this question in Ezekiel's mind: If no one in such a sacred place as the temple is spared alive, how will anybody outside in the secular city of Jerusalem have an opportunity to be spared alive? Ezekiel tells us how he reacted at the impression made upon him, saying: "And it came about that, while they were striking and I was left remaining, I proceeded to fall upon my face and cry out and say: 'Alas, O Sovereign Lord Jehovah! Are you bringing to ruin all the remaining ones of Israel while you are pouring out your rage upon Jerusalem?' "—Ezekiel 9:8.

¹⁶ Was the whole nation of Israel to be wiped out at that time? At the most there was just a remnant or "remaining ones of Israel," seeing that the Assyrians had conquered the ten-tribe Kingdom of Israel to the north and had deported all survivors off to distant parts of the Assyrian Empire. Later, the Babylonians had come and besieged Jerusalem and had taken King Jehoiachin and his household and thousands of other Jews, including Ezekiel, into exile in Babylon. Remembering how the promises of Jehovah for the benefit of all mankind were tied in with the nation of Israel, Ezekiel became so frightened that he fell prostrate and cried out.

¹⁷ Ezekiel informs us what Jehovah said in response: "So he said to me: 'The error of the house of Israel and Judah is very, very great, and the land is filled with bloodshed and the city is full of crookedness;

15. The sight of the slaughter in the temple premises may have raised what question in Ezekiel's mind, and what did he cry out and say?
16. Why was it the "remaining ones of Israel" about whom Ezekiel asked while Jehovah was pouring out his rage upon Jerusalem?
17. What did Jehovah say in response to Ezekiel?

for they have said, "Jehovah has left the land, and Jehovah is not seeing." And as for me also, my eye will not feel sorry, neither shall I show compassion. Their way I shall certainly bring upon their own head.' "—Ezekiel 9:9, 10.

[18] When we consider without sentimentalism the bad things that Jehovah here sets out, was he not justified in bringing his executional forces upon the offending "house of Israel and Judah"? He had long shown that he was looking with a sorrowful eye upon them and was feeling compassion for them by repeatedly sending his faithful prophets to warn them, but they had refrained from listening and had persecuted and killed his obedient spokesmen. So why should his eye feel sorry now and he show compassion now? It was at last the time for Him to let the punishment of "their way" fall where it belonged, upon their own responsible heads.

[19] History actually worked out in harmony with this vision to Ezekiel. The city of Jerusalem and its temple were destroyed and the land of the Kingdom of Judah was laid desolate five years later, or in 607 B.C.E. Among those killed off during and after the siege of Jerusalem there were "old man, young man and virgin and little child and women." Who it was that was slain did not matter with the Babylonian soldiers. They showed no pity. How the death-dealing conditions in the "city that was abundant with people" affected all without respect of age we can read for ourselves in the Book of Lamentations written by the prophet-priest Jeremiah, who survived the destruction of Jerusalem only under divine protection. His lamentations, despite their beautiful poetry, portray to us the heart-rending conditions and events that beset the doomed city, mothers even boiling their own children and

18. What shall we say as to whether Jehovah was justified in now bringing his executional forces upon the house of Israel and Judah, and that without sorrow and compassion?
19. How did history work out in harmony with the vision to Ezekiel, and how also do the Lamentations written by Jeremiah bear out the indiscriminateness of the slaughter?

eating them to satisfy the gnawing pangs of starvation.
—Lamentations 1:1, 4, 6, 15, 18; 2:10, 20, 21; 4:10, 4, 16; 5:11-14.

20 Neither was high rank or sacred position respected. Jehovah's command to the executioners was: "From my sanctuary you should start." (Ezekiel 9:6) Even so, the topmost officials of Jehovah's temple were destined for violent death because of failing to keep His sanctuary free from idolatrous worship. That they and other responsible men of eminence did not escape execution, the doleful record in 2 Kings 25:18-21 testifies, in these words:

21 "Furthermore, the chief of the bodyguard took Seraiah the chief priest and Zephaniah the second priest and three [temple] doorkeepers; and from the city he took one court official that had a command over the men of war, and five men from those having access to the king that were found in the city; and the secretary of the chief of the army, the one mustering the people of the land, and sixty men of the people of the land that were to be found in the city; and Nebuzaradan the chief of the bodyguard then took them and conducted them to the king of Babylon at Riblah. And the king of Babylon proceeded to strike them down and put them to death at Riblah in the land of Hamath. Thus Judah went into exile from off its soil."

22 Away back there no inhabitant of Jerusalem bore a literal mark on his forehead to notify the executioners whom Jehovah used that he was to be spared from violent death. There is no record in the Bible to show that some commissioned servant of Jehovah went through the midst of Jerusalem and used pen and ink to mark the "foreheads of the men that are sighing and groaning over all the detestable things that are being done in the midst of it." (Ezekiel 9:4) The prophet-priest Jeremiah did not do it; the prophet

20, 21. From the historic record, how did the command to the executioners work out, "From my sanctuary you should start"?
22. Among the survivors of Jerusalem's destruction, who were the ones that really had divine promise and protection, and the facts about these show the marking of foreheads to be what kind of work?

Ezekiel himself did not do it, for he himself was an exile in Babylon during all the reign of Zedekiah, the last king of Jerusalem. According to divine promise and protection certain ones did escape execution, like Baruch the secretary of Jeremiah, and Ebed-melech the Ethiopian and the Rechabites. (Jeremiah 45:1-5; 39:15-18; 35:1-19) But these survivors bore no ink mark on their literal foreheads. Evidently, then, marking of foreheads as forevisioned by Ezekiel is a symbolic work.

[23] Also, the man "clothed with linen, with a secretary's inkhorn at his hips," is a prophetic figure, and he finds his fulfillment down here in this twentieth century in connection with the antitypical unfaithful Jerusalem, namely, Christendom. And amazingly enough, a work that closely corresponds with that of the linen-clad man with the secretary's inkhorn at his waist began and is still in progress throughout Christendom during this "time of the end." Who, then, fulfills the picture of this man who engages in this lifesaving work throughout antitypical Jerusalem? Let, now, the historic facts speak for themselves to identify him.

THE MODERN-DAY MARKER OF FOREHEADS

[24] Not too long ago, in the year 1931, a Biblical book was published entitled "Vindication."* This book, which had a wide distribution throughout Christendom, was published by the Watch Tower Bible & Tract Society. It was a commentary on the first twenty-four chapters of the prophecy of Ezekiel. It made clear that the prophecy of the man "clothed with linen" had not been fulfilled in any one man in contact with Christendom, say, for instance, in Charles Taze Russell,

---

* Now out of print and out of stock.

23. What sort of figure is this linen-clad man with the secretary's inkhorn, and where does the fulfillment of his lifesaving work take place in reality?
24. What book was published by the Watch Tower Society in 1931, and according to it whom did this man with the inkhorn picture?

the first president of the Watch Tower Bible & Tract Society, who died October 31, 1916, thereby finishing his earthly work as a Christian, in the midst of World War I. Concerning this, *Vindication* (Volume I) said, on pages 99, 100, under the subheading "Man with Inkhorn," the following:

> Aside from the Lord Jesus Christ, God has never since committed to any one individual on earth an exclusive work to be done by that individual. From the very beginning of his ministry Christ Jesus had a visible organization, and his apostles, acting collectively under his direction, formed the visible part thereof. There was unity of action by the faithful apostles; . . . 'The man with the writer's inkhorn by his side,' therefore, clearly represented the anointed "servant" class of the Lord on earth, which class is a part of God's organization.

[25] It was on the afternoon of July 30, 1931, that the above book was released, after the delivery of a talk on "Man with the Writer's Inkhorn" to the many thousands attending the international convention of International Bible Students that was in session at Columbus, Ohio, U.S.A. Just the preceding Sunday afternoon, July 26, this international gathering had adopted unanimously the Resolution by which they embraced the Scriptural name for themselves of "Jehovah's Witnesses."—Isaiah 43:1, 10-12, *AS*.

[26] Thus these dedicated, anointed followers of Jesus recognized themselves as the Christian witnesses of Jehovah, whereas the prophet Ezekiel was a pre-Christian witness of Jehovah. They were very grateful that their God, Jehovah, had definitely revealed to them the work for them to do as indicated in the vision to Ezekiel concerning the man "clothed with linen, with a secretary's inkhorn at his hips." They were highly elated at the prospect of engaging in the work of marking the foreheads of those who were to be spared on the day when Jehovah executes his judicial

25. Where, to whom and when was this book released, and four days after the adoption of what identifying Resolution?
26. Those adopting that Resolution thus identified themselves as being what, and at what prospect were they now elated, and from whom were they receiving a commission of work?

decision against antitypical unfaithful Jerusalem, namely, Christendom. By doing so they, as an anointed class, were fulfilling the role of the envisioned man with the inkhorn. In fact, this visionary man with the inkhorn found his modern counterpart in this united class of Jehovah's anointed, dedicated, baptized servants. It was as if Jehovah, from atop his chariotlike heavenly organization were saying thenceforth to this modern-day 'man with the inkhorn' the words of command: "Pass through the midst of the city, through the midst of Jerusalem [as typical of Christendom], and you must put a mark on the foreheads of the men that are sighing and groaning over all the detestable things that are being done in the midst of it."—Ezekiel 9:4.

THE ONES BEING MARKED IN THEIR FOREHEADS

27 Who are those men who were sighing and groaning over all the detestable religious things that were being done in and by Christendom? They were not members of the modern-time Ezekiel class, a class of dedicated Christians anointed with God's spirit. (Isaiah 61:1-3) They were not part of the 'man with the inkhorn' class, which is the same dedicated, baptized, anointed class of Jehovah's united servants. So they were not expecting to die and have a spiritual resurrection into the heavenly realm as spiritual sons of God and as joint heirs with Jesus Christ in his heavenly kingdom. They were persons who were associated with Christendom but who had a sincere reverence for the things of God and who were sick at heart because of all the unchristian teachings and actions of Christendom, all of which brought reproach upon God's holy name. As for their hope of eternal life, they were satisfied to live in a cleansed earth, restored to a Paradise state and under the heavenly kingdom of God. They desired to have the Son of God, Jesus Christ,

---

27. Who, then, are the ones pictured by the men that sigh and groan over all the detestable things being done in Jerusalem, and what is their hope?

over them as their "Fine Shepherd" and to follow in his footsteps as his disciples.

[28] In Jesus' parable on the Fine Shepherd he indicated that he would have such a flock of sheeplike persons on the earth. He spoke of them as his "other sheep," for, after speaking about the "fold" containing those who will be joint heirs with him in the heavenly kingdom, he went on to say: "And I have other sheep, which are not of this fold; those also I must bring, and they will listen to my voice, and they will become one flock, one shepherd." (John 10:16) The 'man with the inkhorn' class also speak of these as the "other sheep." These "other sheep" who are living in this "time of the end" for Christendom are the ones that need to have their foreheads marked in order to be spared at the time when Jehovah's executional "six men" go throughout Christendom to destroy all the unmarked ones.—Ezekiel 9:5, 6.

THE "MARK"

[29] What, then, is the symbolic "mark" that is penned upon their foreheads? In ancient time, the times of Ezekiel, it was the custom for worshipers of a certain god or goddess to identify themselves as such by putting the mark or name of such deity upon the brow of their face. Likewise, slaves had branded upon their foreheads, if not also in their hand, the name of their owner so as openly to indicate to whom they belonged. It would be just as fitting today for these symbolic "other sheep" to be marked in such a way as to show publicly whom they worshiped as God and to whom they belonged as spiritual slaves. Is the "mark," then, the having of Bible knowledge in one's head, and is the marking work that of putting Bible knowledge in the minds of people?

---

28. In his parable of the Fine Shepherd, how did Jesus refer to persons of that kind, and why do they now have to get their foreheads symbolically marked?
29. In accord with the ancient purpose of marking persons, why would such a mark be fitting for these symbolic "other sheep" of today?

[30] Not exactly, although that may be an important part of the matter. It is not what a religionist has in his head that counts, but what he proves himself to be. What about "Seraiah the chief priest and Zephaniah the second priest and the three doorkeepers," all of whom the king of Babylon killed off at Riblah after the destruction of Jerusalem and its temple? (Jeremiah 52:24-27) All of these temple officials had in their heads the required knowledge of Jehovah's written Word, but what were they personally? Despite all this head knowledge, they permitted all those detestable idolatrous things to be carried on by apostate Jews in the temple dedicated to the one living and true God, Jehovah. They had not been "sighing and groaning over all the detestable things" being done in Jerusalem. In the same way, all the knowledge that the religious clergy of Christendom have in their heads from their schooling in religious seminaries will not save them when Jehovah's "six men" go through Christendom with their smashing weapons. It becomes manifest, therefore, that mere Biblical knowledge could not be the "mark."

[31] In actuality, the symbolic mark is the evidence, as if it were displayed on a person's uncovered forehead, that he is a dedicated, baptized disciple of Jesus Christ and has a Christlike personality that differentiates him from all hypocritical Christians. It is not a mere outwardly "having of a form of godly devotion," but is an inwardly and outwardly proving true to "its power," a having of true faith accompanied by works in proof thereof. (2 Timothy 3:5; James 2:18-26) This visible or discernible "mark" makes it plain to Jehovah's executional forces that the marked ones are not in sympathy with all the detestable religious things that are being said and done in the midst of Christendom, things that are untrue to the name of Christ

---

30. Why could merely having Biblical knowledge not be the symbolic "mark," as illustrated in the case of the temple officials whom Neb-uchadnezzar killed off at Riblah after Jerusalem was destroyed? 31. What in actuality is the symbolic "mark," and what divine command about dissociating themselves have they obeyed?

that she bears. In fact, they have been "sighing and groaning" over all such God-dishonoring things, and in protest thereat they have come out of Christendom and have renounced all membership in her. They come to appreciate that she is an integral part of Babylon the Great, the world empire of false religion, for which reason they must obey the divine command, "Get out of her my people."—Revelation 18:4; Isaiah 52:11.

[32] Necessarily, then, the work of marking foreheads, as done by the anointed remnant of heirs to Jehovah's heavenly kingdom, must do more than simply impart Bible knowledge to people by putting the Bible and Bible literature in their hands to read for themselves and get what they are mentally able to get out of reading it. It includes helping these persons to understand what they read and then to conform their lives to what they read in God's Word. It means teaching such persons and building up in them a truly Christian personality, a personality built up on Jesus Christ as the Foundation and sticking to all the Bible rules and principles for Christlike conduct. Jesus' instructions to his apostles and disciples after his resurrection from the dead were:

[33] "Go therefore and make disciples of people of all the nations, baptizing them in the name of the Father and of the Son and of the holy spirit, teaching them to observe all the things I have commanded you. And, look! I am with you all the days until the conclusion of the system of things."—Matthew 28:16-20.

[34] All the proof necessary is available to establish that we have been living in the "conclusion of the system of things" since the end of the "appointed times of the [Gentile] nations" in early autumn of 1914 C.E. (Luke 21:24) Today many persons feel that the only reasonable thing open for them to do is to become

---

32, 33. So what really is this work of marking foreheads, and how was this work indicated by Jesus' command after his resurrection from the dead?

34. Since when have we been living in the "conclusion of the system of things," and so what is it yet proper for those to do even though only an earthly prospect seems available to them?

one of the "other sheep" of the Fine Shepherd Jesus Christ. To that end what must they do? This: obey him as the Fine Shepherd and become one of his disciples. Sheep, whether of the royal "little flock" or of the "other" fold, must follow the one Shepherd, who died in surrender of his human soul for all of them. This means that in the present "conclusion of the system of things" those whom God assigns to be of the "other sheep" must become his disciples and get baptized in water and be taught all the things that he commanded his disciples to observe. (Luke 12:32; John 10:14-16) Inasmuch as he is their Model and got baptized in water, so they also must get baptized in symbol of their coming to God to do His will. —Hebrews 10:5-10; 1 Peter 2:21.

[35] Consistently, then, in 1934, or three years after the release of the book *Vindication* (Volume I), the magazine *The Watchtower* published in its issue of August 15, 1934, the article entitled "His Kindness." In this it clearly set forth, on pages 249, 250, that even the "other sheep" of the present time must be made up of those who have dedicated themselves to God through Christ and who have symbolized that unconditional dedication by being immersed in water, like Jesus. This, at the earliest, marks the point where the work of the anointed remnant began in marking the foreheads of those whom God would choose to spare alive during the "great tribulation" upon antitypical unfaithful Jerusalem, Christendom. Why? Because prior to that the work toward these consisted merely of imparting Biblical knowledge to them. (Matthew 24:15-22; Mark 13:14-20) But even at that time the "other sheep" of the present time were not identified as being the same ones as those who make up the "great multitude" or "great crowd" as foretold in Revelation 7:9-17. Hence up till that time no organized effort was made to gather the "other sheep."

35. By reason of what disclosure in *The Watchtower* in 1934 could the work of marking foreheads begin in effect, and why up till that time was no organized effort made to gather "other sheep"?

[36] In the following spring, however, there came an event that definitely marked out that the work of the modern-day man "clothed with linen, with a secretary's inkhorn at his hips," had at last begun. Where was this? At a general convention of Jehovah's witnesses at Washington, D.C. There hundreds of persons who did not feel entitled to a heavenly inheritance with Christ presented themselves for water baptism to symbolize that they had decided to enter into a dedicated relationship with Jehovah through Christ. What was it that powerfully moved them to do this in a mass baptism? This: On Friday afternoon, May 31, 1935, the then president of the Watch Tower Bible & Tract Society gave to the conventioners an address on "The Great Multitude," and in this he explained Revelation 7:9-17 (*AV*). He showed that the ones making up that "great multitude" would not be a spiritual class with a heavenly hope under the 144,000 joint heirs of Jesus Christ. (Revelation 7:1-8) Instead, they would be an earthly class, with an earthly Paradise hope, namely, the "other sheep" of the Fine Shepherd Jesus Christ. Next day came the baptism.

[37] Now, indeed, there needed to be no hesitation on the part of anyone to make a full dedication of himself to Jehovah through the Fine Shepherd Jesus Christ and undergo water baptism as a symbol of that unconditional dedication. It was not surprising, then, that the next day, Saturday, June 1, 1935, there were 840 that were immersed at this Washington (D.C.) convention. (See *The Golden Age,* as of July 17, 1935, page 655, column 2.)

[38] They were baptized by total submersion of the body in water as dedicated disciples of the Lamb of

---

36. In the year 1935, what was it that definitely marked out that the work of the man with the inkhorn had at last begun, and so who presented themselves to enter -a dedicated relationship with God through Christ?
37. What occurred next day at the Washington convention to show that there need be no further hesitation about making and symbolizing a full dedication to God through Christ?
38. As being what were all those 840 candidates baptized, and there has since been a large participation in what event at the various assemblies of Jehovah's witnesses?

God, Jesus Christ, in obedience to Matthew 28:19, 20. This was regardless of whether Jehovah would later reveal to them that he had assigned them to be of the "little flock" of Christ's joint heirs or had assigned them to be "other sheep" who make up the present-day "great multitude" or "great crowd." The Lamb's shepherding of this "great crowd" of the "other sheep" is beautifully described in Revelation 7:16, 17. Baptismal services with a notably large participation by newly dedicated persons have since taken place at the circuit, district, national and international assemblies of Jehovah's witnesses down till now.

[39] Since the end of World War II in 1945 more than a million newly dedicated persons have thus been baptized world wide as disciples of Jesus Christ the Fine Shepherd. During the 1970 service year alone of Jehovah's witnesses, 164,193 were thus baptized in symbol of their dedication to Jehovah regardless of where he chooses to place them within his theocratic organization. This increasing "great crowd" of baptized disciples of Christ are now aiding the modern-day 'man with the inkhorn,' the small remnant yet on earth of the 144,000 joint heirs of Jesus Christ. Under the supervision of this anointed remnant they are sharing in the work of marking the foreheads of those who are "sighing and groaning over all the detestable things" that take place in the midst of Christendom. Even in lands outside Christendom the marking goes on.

[40] Indeed, in 206 lands and island groups around the globe Jehovah's witnesses are active. Many adherents of non-Christian religions are hearing and taking heed to the good news of God's kingdom and are forsaking such non-Christian religions in response to Jehovah's call for those who desire to be his people to get out of Babylon the Great, the world empire of false re-

39. Since World War II, how many have thus been baptized, and in what work are these now taking part and under whose supervision?
40. How extensively active are Jehovah's witnesses at present, and who besides those of Christendom are now getting marked in their foreheads symbolically?

ligion. By accepting Christ's teachings and by dedication and water baptism these also are qualifying to be marked in their foreheads as being true disciples of Jesus Christ.

[41] They will need this symbolic mark then when Babylon the Great, of which Christendom has been the dominant part, is destroyed in the approaching "great tribulation" so that their lives may be spared by Jehovah's executional forces. (Revelation 17:1 to 19:2) Reasonably, if false hypocritical religionists inside Christendom who are not marked in the forehead as true Christians are not to be spared, all unmarked persons outside Christendom will not be spared alive, for they are no more true disciples of Christ than are the religious hypocrites of Christendom.

ACCOMPLISHMENT OF THE WORK REPORTED ON

[42] In the vision given to the prophet Ezekiel the lifesaving work of marking foreheads in doomed Jerusalem was brought to an end. Just as surely, then, although the marking work has been going on now for more than thirty-five years, it will come to its end throughout the earth, inside and outside of Christendom. The certainty of this is forevisioned by what the prophet Ezekiel says as to whether the man charged with the marking work carried out his commission or not: "And, look! the man clothed with the linen, at whose hips there was the inkhorn, was bringing back word, saying: 'I have done just as you have commanded me.' " (Ezekiel 9:11) If the man had failed to carry out his commission he would have been held responsible for the slaughter of those "sighing and groaning" men whose foreheads he had not marked. He would have been like Ezekiel, who would have been held accountable for the blood of the exe-

41. When, and why, will such ones from outside Christendom need that symbolic mark in their foreheads?
42. What indicates whether the marking work inside and outside Christendom will be fully accomplished, and for what would the man with the inkhorn have been held accountable had he failed to carry out his commission?

cuted Israelites if he had failed to give them warning
from Jehovah as a watchman.—Ezekiel 3:17-21.

⁴³ The anointed remnant of Jehovah's servants today
are determined to be just as faithful as was the linen-
clad man in the vision. With that end in view they continue, despite opposition and persecution, to go from
house to house, presenting the good news of God's
kingdom, to get in touch with all persons who are
"sighing and groaning over all the detestable things"
that are being done within and without Christendom
and that are detestable to Jehovah the one living and
true God. Jesus Christ prophesied: "This good news
of the kingdom will be preached in all the inhabited
earth for a witness to all the nations; and then the
end will come." (Matthew 24:14) When that "end"
does come and the marking work is completed, the
anointed remnant desire to be able to bring back word
to their Commissioner, Jehovah, and to say: "I have
done just as you have commanded me."

⁴⁴ The "other sheep" who are cooperating with them
in the work of marking foreheads are no less desirous
of proving faithful at the side of the anointed remnant,
the present-day man "clothed with linen, with a secretary's inkhorn at his hips." For these "other sheep"
to be spared by Jehovah's executional "six men" in
the approaching "great tribulation" they must keep
this symbolic "mark" in their foreheads, that the "six
men" may never come near them to use their smashing
weapons upon their heads. They can retain this lifesaving "mark" on their foreheads by loyally and obediently sharing in the marking work with the anointed
remnant who are clothed with the symbolic linen of
God's righteousness. This will ensure that the "great
crowd" of these marked "other sheep" will "come out
of the great tribulation" and enter into Jehovah's
further service in His new system of things under
the Lamb Jesus Christ.—Revelation 7:17.

---

43. What are the anointed remant of Jehovah's servants determined
to carry on doing, and to that end what do they continue doing?
44. What are the "other sheep" now desirous of doing, and why must
they keep the "mark" upon their foreheads, and how?

Chapter 10

Christendom's Fiery Destruction from the Celestial Chariot

THE celestial chariot of Jehovah is still standing outside the northern gate that leads up into the inner court of Jerusalem's temple as new things are revealed in the vision to the Levite prophet Ezekiel. From a rider's position above the celestial chariot the "glory of the God of Israel" had moved to above the threshold of the Most Holy of the temple. (Ezekiel 8:3, 4; 9:3) His presence there was rightly the occasion for him to inspect this house dedicated to him and to see what was going on there and then to express his judicial decision. It set the pattern for what was to take place later with regard to a greater temple, as foretold by a later prophet in these words:

2 " 'Look! I am sending my messenger, and he must clear up a way before me. And suddenly there will come to His temple the true Lord, whom you people are seeking, and the messenger of the covenant in whom you are delighting. Look! He will certainly come,' Jehovah of armies has said. 'But who will be putting up with the day of his coming, and who will be the one standing when he appears? For he will be like the fire of a refiner and like the lye of laundrymen. And he must sit as a refiner and cleanser of silver and must cleanse the sons of Levi; and he must clarify them like gold and like silver, and they will certainly become to Jehovah people presenting a gift offering

---

1-3. Jehovah's position at the temple was rightly the occasion for him to do what, and for what did this set the pattern as foretold in Malachi 3:1-5?

in righteousness. And the gift offering of Judah and of Jerusalem will actually be gratifying to Jehovah, as in the days of long ago and as in the years of antiquity.

³ " 'And I will come near to you people for the judgment, and I will become a speedy witness against the sorcerers, and against the adulterers, and against those swearing falsely, and against those acting fraudulently with the wages of a wage worker, with the widow and with the fatherless boy, and those turning away the alien resident, while they have not feared me,' Jehovah of armies has said."—Malachi 3:1-5; written 443 B.C.E., after Jerusalem's temple was rebuilt.

⁴ In the vision to Ezekiel at the temple Jehovah had indeed been a "speedy witness" against the seventy older men who had been burning incense to idolatrous carvings and against the women who sat weeping over the false god Tammuz and against the twenty-five men who had their backs to Jehovah's temple as they bowed in worship to the eastern sun. The man "clothed with linen, with a secretary's inkhorn at his hips," had not put a saving mark on their foreheads, and so Jehovah's "six men" with smashing weapons had killed off those defilers of Jehovah's temple. From their work at the temple those six executioners had gone out through the city of Jerusalem and had smashed to death all the unmarked persons, regardless of age, sex or civil status. Now what was to happen to the city itself, filled as it was with the corpses of the slain? Ezekiel was under command to tell us:

⁵ "And I continued to see, and, look! upon the expanse that was over the head of the cherubs there was something like sapphire stone, like the appearance of the likeness of a throne, appearing above them. And he proceeded to say to the man clothed with the linen, even to say: 'Enter in between the wheel-

4. According to the vision to Ezekiel, against whom had Jehovah been a speedy witness at the temple, and from there to where else had the "six men" carried on their smashing work to the finish?
5. What was the man "clothed with linen" now told to do, and did he do so?

work, in under the cherubs, and fill the hollows of both your hands with coals of fire from between the cherubs and toss them over the city.' So he entered in before my eyes."—Ezekiel 10:1, 2.

⁶ Thus we have indicated to us the judicial decision of Jehovah from the temple: the city of Jerusalem must be destroyed, burned with fire, not even its temple being spared! From where would the incendiary material proceed? From between the chariot wheels, beside which the four cherubs were standing. There the coals of fire were to be found. However, the cherubic living creatures were not the ones directly commanded to toss the fiery coals over corpse-filled Jerusalem. They were not to leave their place beside the wheels of the celestial chariot, but were to use an agent. Whom? The man "clothed with linen, with a secretary's inkhorn at his hips." In this way the fiery destruction of Jerusalem and its temple is traced back to Jehovah's celestial chariot, and the tossing of the fiery coals therefrom is done at Jehovah's command. The prophet Ezekiel saw the linen-clad man go in to where the fire was to get both hands filled with the fiery coals. Miraculously his hands were not to be hurt thereby.

⁷ As Ezekiel watches, he proceeds to give us the background of the exciting scene by saying: "And the cherubs were standing to the right of the house when the man entered, and the cloud was filling the inner courtyard."—Ezekiel 10:3.

⁸ By the expression "right of the house" did Ezekiel mean his right side as he faced the temple? Traditionally, the right side represents the south to the Hebrews. But here he speaks of the "right of the house when the man entered," which would seem to have reference to the right side of the man as he entered, his right side being to the north. Taking this

6. What was Jehovah's judicial decision from the temple, and from where were the means for this to be done to be procured, and then used by whom?
7, 8. Where were the four cherubs alongside the chariot wheels standing, and how do we figure that out?

viewpoint of the matter, *The New English Bible* (1970) translates this part of verse three: "The cherubim stood on the right side of the temple as a man enters." This would place the cherubs on the north side, where the description in Ezekiel 8:3, 4 stations them. Otherwise, we must understand (although Ezekiel does not say so) that the celestial chariot with its wheels and cherubs had moved from north of the temple to the south side (the right side when one faces east) of the sanctuary.

⁹ Now apparently Ezekiel repeats what he had described previously (in Ezekiel 9:3) as he goes on to say: "And the glory of Jehovah proceeded to rise up from the cherubs to the threshold of the house, and the house gradually became filled with the cloud, and the courtyard itself was full of the brightness of the glory of Jehovah. And the very sound of the wings of the cherubs made itself heard to the outer courtyard, like the sound of God Almighty when he speaks." —Ezekiel 10:4, 5.

¹⁰ As indicating that there had not been a movement of Jehovah away from the threshold of the temple to above the celestial chariot and then back again to the threshold of the temple, Young's Literal Translation of the Holy Bible reads: "And become high doth the honour of Jehovah above the cherub, over the threshold of the house, and the house is filled with the cloud, and the court hath been filled with the brightness of the honour of Jehovah." Also, *An American Translation* renders Ezekiel 10:3, 4: " . . . and the cloud filled the inner court; for when the glory of the LORD had gone up from the cherubim to the threshold of the house, the house was filled with the cloud, while the court was filled with the radiance of the glory of the LORD." Also, *A New Translation of the Bible* (by Dr. James Moffatt) here reads: " . . . a cloud filled the inner

9. How does Ezekiel apparently repeat Ezekiel 9:3 regarding the movement of Jehovah's glory and the sound of the cherubs' wings?
10. How do three modern translators indicate there had been no interim movement of Jehovah's glory?

court. When the Splendour of the Eternal ascended from the kherubs and went to the threshold of the temple, the temple was filled with the cloud, and the inner court was filled with radiance from the Splendour of the Eternal."

[11] Thus the glory of Jehovah had left the sapphire throne above that icelike expanse that was above the wheels and the cherubs alongside them and was still over the threshold of the Most Holy of the temple when the linen-clad man was told to get coals of fire. (Ezekiel 1:25-27; 10:1, 2) As for the temple down under the glory of Jehovah, it became filled with a miraculous cloud, this showing that Jehovah dominated the temple and no one else could enter it. (Compare 1 Kings 8:10-13; Revelation 15:8.) So bright was the glory of Jehovah above the temple that its radiance filled the courtyard in front of the temple sanctuary. Jehovah's presence at the temple for the executing of his judicial decision was highly important. So deserving of attention was it that the four cherubs alongside the chariot wheels put their wings in motion, not to fly away with the chariot, but to make a mighty sound. If anyone had been in the outer courtyard, he could have heard the sound. It might have been like ear-shattering thunder, as when God Almighty speaks. —Compare Exodus 20:18, 19; John 12:28-30.

[12] The man "clothed with linen, with a secretary's inkhorn at his hips," now turned his attention to those cherubs. Regarding his previous work of marking foreheads he had reported to Jehovah at the temple, saying: "I have done just as you have commanded me." (Ezekiel 9:11) Now he turns to the "right [side] of the house," to go to the celestial chariot, as Ezekiel next tells us:

[13] "And it came about, when he commanded the

---

11. When the linen-clad man went in to get the fiery coals, where was Jehovah's glory, and what was the effect of this on the temple, so that the cherubs called attention to it in what way?
12. Where had the man with the inkhorn made his report, and to what did he now give his attention?
13. What did the man "clothed with linen" receive from one of the cherubs, and how?

man clothed with the linen, saying: 'Take fire from between the wheelwork, from between the cherubs,' that he proceeded to enter and stand beside the wheel. Then the cherub thrust his hand out from between the cherubs to the fire that was between the cherubs and carried and put it into the hollows of the hands of the one clothed with the linen, who now took it and went out. And there was seen belonging to the cherubs the representation of a hand of earthling man under their wings."—Ezekiel 10:6-8.

SYMBOLIC "COALS OF FIRE" TOSSED OVER JERUSALEM

[14] This is the last that the prophet Ezekiel sees of the man "clothed with linen" in the vision. Ezekiel's eyes turn from following this man in the execution of his mission to a further contemplation of the celestial chariot. Ezekiel thus spares us the sight of the burning of the city of Jerusalem, as this linen-clad man turns his hands from the lifesaving work of marking foreheads to the destructive work of tossing "coals of fire" over the city. It is not man-made fire with which he sets the city afire; it is miraculous fire from God's heavenly organization. Not a man, but a cherub that belonged to that organization, put this fire into the hands of the linen-clad man. What does this signify? This: that the utter destruction of Jerusalem as IF with fire could be an expression of Jehovah's wrath and fury against that capital city of the Kingdom of Judah. The prophet Ezekiel saw this miraculous fire "between the wheelwork," not when he first saw the celestial chariot the previous year in Babylon, but *now* when he sees that chariot on location at Jerusalem. When that chariot reached Jerusalem, it was the time for her destruction!

[15] The prophet Jeremiah, when lamenting bitterly

---

14. What kind of fiery coals does the linen-clad man toss over the city, and this fact signifies what concerning the destruction of Jerusalem?
15. Correspondingly, to what does Jeremiah in the Lamentations liken the anger and rage poured out by Jehovah on Jerusalem?

over the destruction of Jerusalem, likens Jehovah's anger and rage to fire. Mournfully he says: "Jehovah has swallowed up, he has shown no compassion upon any abiding places of Jacob [Israel]. In his fury he has torn down the fortified places of the daughter of Judah. He has brought into contact with the earth, he has profaned the kingdom and her princes. In the heat of anger he has cut down every horn of Israel. He has turned his right hand back from before the enemy; and in Jacob he keeps burning like a flaming fire that has devoured all around. He has trodden his bow like an enemy. His right hand has taken its position like an adversary, and he kept killing all those desirable to the eyes. Into the tent of the daughter of Zion he has poured out his rage, just like fire." (Lamentations 2:2-4) With fitting figures of speech Jeremiah continues on to say: "Jehovah has accomplished his rage. He has poured out his burning anger. And he sets a fire ablaze in Zion, which eats up her foundations."—Lamentations 4:11.

[16] Even the inspired Chronicler, evidently the priestly scribe Ezra, words his account to remind us that the destruction of Jerusalem and its temple in 607 B.C.E. was the unmistakable expression of God's justified rage against the unfaithful city. So, in 2 Chronicles 36:16-20, we read about the unresponsive Jews:

[17] "They were continually making jest at the messengers of the true God and despising his words and mocking at his prophets, until the rage of Jehovah came up against his people, until there was no healing. So he brought up against them the king of the Chaldeans, who proceeded to kill their young men with the sword in the house of their sanctuary, neither did he feel compassion for young man or virgin, old or decrepit. Everything He gave into his hand. And all the utensils, great and small, of the house of the true God and the treasures of the house of Jehovah and the

16, 17. The account in 2 Chronicles 36:16-20 is so worded as to indicate that destruction of Jerusalem and her temple was the expression of whose rage?

treasures of the king and of his princes, everything he brought to Babylon. And he proceeded to burn the house of the true God and pull down the wall of Jerusalem; and all its dwelling towers they burned with fire and also all its desirable articles, so as to cause ruin. Furthermore, he carried off those remaining from the sword captive to Babylon, and they came to be servants to him and his sons until the royalty of Persia began to reign."

[18] That account, and the fuller account in 2 Kings 25:8-21, show that it was the armies of the king of Babylon that actually burned down the city of Jerusalem. This does not mean, however, that such Babylonians were prefigured by the man "clothed with linen" who, in Ezekiel's vision, tossed fiery coals over Jerusalem. No, but this visionary man continued to picture the faithful remnant of Jehovah's baptized, anointed witnesses who do the symbolic marking of foreheads down at this "time of the end" for Christendom. Hence the man's tossing coals of fire over Jerusalem pictured first that Jehovah would pour out his fiery rage upon Jerusalem. By the linen-clad man he was serving advance notice of this upon the inhabitants of Jerusalem. This pouring out of divine wrath was carried out by means of the Babylonian armies that really did burn the city. In like manner the modern-day counterpart of the linen-clad man scatter the fiery message from God's Word all over Christendom, and this serves as advance notification to her that Jehovah's fiery anger will be vented upon her in the coming "great tribulation."

[19] Hence, in the actual working out of things in the near future, the anointed remnant pictured by the man "clothed in linen" will not actually set fire to

18. Were those who actually burned Jerusalem down prefigured by the man "clothed with linen," and so what was really implied by this man's tossing the fiery coals over Jerusalem?
19. So, then, what relation does the anointed remnant pictured by the linen-clad man have with Christendom's destruction, and, aside from his invisible, heavenly organization, what agencies will Jehovah use to wreak destruction upon Christendom?

Christendom, nor will they have any active hand in destroying her. They merely now proclaim the "day of vengeance on the part of our God" against Christendom. (Isaiah 61:1, 2) They got this fiery message from Jehovah through his heavenly organization, his celestial chariot. As it were, one of the heavenly cherubs belonging to that celestial chariot put these symbolic "coals of fire from between the cherubs" into the hollows of their hands to go and toss them out over the city of Christendom as warning notice. Aside from what Jehovah's invisible heavenly organization under the glorified Jesus Christ will do toward the literal wiping out of Christendom, he will use earthly agencies to wreak violent destruction upon Christendom like what the Babylonians did to hypocritical Jerusalem back in 607 B.C.E.

[20] When we call to mind that Christendom is the outstanding part of modern-day Babylon the Great, the world empire of false Babylonish religion, we can see that Christendom is in line for destruction as if by being burned with all-consuming fire.

[21] Unavoidably, then, Christendom comes within the range of the prophetic words from heaven, as heard by the Christian apostle John: "That is why in one day her plagues will come, death and mourning and famine, and she will be completely burned with fire, because Jehovah God, who judged her, is strong." Then, in a description of those who suffer personal selfish loss at the destruction of the world empire of false religion (including Christendom), the apostle John goes on to say: "And the kings of the earth who committed fornication with her and lived in shameless luxury will weep and beat themselves in grief over her, when they look at the smoke from the burning of her, while they stand at a distance because of their fear of her torment and say, 'Too bad, too bad, you great city, Bab-

---

20. Since Christendom is the outstanding part of Babylon the Great, she is in line for what kind of destruction?
21. Unavoidably, then, Christendom comes within the range of what words expressed in Revelation, chapter eighteen, concerning Babylon the Great?

ylon you strong city, because in one hour your judgment has arrived!' ''—Revelation 18:8-10.

[22] Even the last writer of the Bible recognizes this destruction of the hypocritical religious organization as a fiery destruction from the One who rides upon the celestial chariot. Accordingly the apostle John, after describing the sorrow of many at this destruction, says: "Be glad over her, O heaven, also you holy ones and you apostles and you prophets, because God has judicially exacted punishment for you from her!" (Revelation 18:20) All those marked in the forehead by the modern-day man "clothed with linen," will rejoice with these at the fiery destruction that proceeded from Jehovah's celestial chariot against hypocritical Christendom and all the rest of Babylon the Great. Surely all of us want to be on the side of those who rejoice when that occurs.

THE WHEELWORK AND CHERUBS THAT ARE INVOLVED

[23] Along with the prophet Ezekiel let us take another look at Jehovah's celestial chariot from which this fiery destruction flames forth against Christendom. How Ezekiel now describes it corresponds closely with what he said about it in Ezekiel 1:5-28. To identify it as being the same chariot, Ezekiel writes:

[24] "And I continued to see, and, look! there were four wheels beside the cherubs, one wheel beside the one cherub and one wheel beside the other cherub, and the appearance of the wheels was like the glow of a chrysolite stone. And as for their appearance, the four of them had one likeness, just as when a wheel proves to be in the midst of a wheel. When they would go, to their four sides they would go. They would not change direction when they went, because the place

22. According to the words of Revelation, chapter eighteen, the destruction is recognized as coming from whom, and how will those symbolically marked in the forehead react to it?
23, 24. What description does Ezekiel now give of the wheels and cherubs, and what does its correspondency with the previous description indicate as to the source of destruction?

to which the head would face, after it they would go. They would not change direction when they went. And all their flesh and their backs and their hands and their wings and the wheels were full of eyes all around. The four of them had their wheels. As regards the wheels, to them it was called out in my ears, 'O wheelwork [*hag-Galgal,* Hebrew]!' "—Ezekiel 10:9-13.

[25] It may have startled Ezekiel to hear a name called out to the wheels, "Wheelwork!" (Ezekiel 10:2) This name was evidently occasioned by what the wheel does, namely, it rolls along or whirls. So it could be called a roller or whirler. This feature is emphasized in *The Emphasised Bible,* by J. B. Rotherham, which translates Ezekiel 10:13 in this way: "To the wheels, to them was made the cry, O whirling wheel!" Or, according to the marginal reading: "O thou that whirlest!" Correspondingly, the name of the Israelite city Gilgal means "A Rolling Away."—Joshua 5:9.

[26] The naming of this part of the celestial chariot by such a name calls attention to the speed with which the celestial chariot, Jehovah's heavenly organization, moves. It moves as with "wheels [*galgal* (used here in the plural)] as a stormwind." "His wheels are like a storm-wind." (Isaiah 5:28, *Ro*) The war chariots of the Assyrian capital, Nineveh, never moved faster than this celestial chariot, even if it is said of those Assyrian war chariots: "Like the lightnings they keep running." (Nahum 2:4) Although the celestial chariot wheels whirled with so many revolutions per minute, they had eyes to see their way.

[27] From the wheels the prophet Ezekiel now turned his consideration to the accompanying cherubs. Evidently looking first at the left side of the cherubic living creature, Ezekiel remarks as follows about them: "And each one had four faces. The first face was the

25. What was the name given to the wheels, and to what feature about a wheel does it call attention?
26. The naming of this feature about the celestial chariot with such a name called attention to what about Jehovah's heavenly organization?
27. What observation did Ezekiel now make about the cherubs, and what does the movement of the wheels alongside them indicate?

face of the cherub [a bull's face, in Ezekiel 1:10], and the second face was the face of earthling man, and the third was the face of a lion, and the fourth was the face of an eagle. And the cherubs would rise—it was the same living creature that I had seen at the river Chebar—and when the cherubs went, the wheels would go alongside them; and when the cherubs lifted up their wings to be high above the earth, the wheels would not change direction, even they themselves, from alongside them. When these stood still, they would stand still; and when these rose, they would rise with them, for the spirit of the living creature was in them." (Ezekiel 10:14-17) There was thus perfect cooperation between the wheels and the cherubs. There was no disharmony or disorganization about this celestial chariot of Jehovah.

[28] The "fire" taken from between the cherubs of this chariot and tossed by the linen-clad man over the city of Jerusalem had not yet reached the temple. So, in the vision, the "glory of Jehovah" still continues to maneuver in that area, just as Ezekiel now tells us: "And the glory of Jehovah proceeded to go forth from over the threshold of the house and to stand still over the cherubs. And the cherubs now lifted up their wings and rose from the earth before my eyes. When they went forth, the wheels also were close alongside them; and they began standing at the eastern entrance of the gate of the house of Jehovah, and the glory of the God of Israel was over them, from above. This is the living creature that I had seen under the God of Israel at the river Chebar [in Babylonia], so that I came to know that they were cherubs. As for the four, each one had four faces and each one had four wings, and the likeness of the hands of earthling man was under their wings. And as for the likeness of their faces, they were the faces the appearance of which I had seen by the river Chebar, the very ones. They would go each one straight forward."—Ezekiel 10:18-22.

---

28. To what new position did the "glory of Jehovah" and the celestial chariot now move?

[29] As the celestial chariot, with Jehovah seated upon the sapphire throne above it, stands at the outer eastern entrance of the temple, what instructions are to be given to the prophet Ezekiel? But first he must be brought from his position in the inner court of the temple in order to view what may be seen from the outer eastern gate that looked toward the Mount of Olives. We are interested to learn what he sees and hears there.

29. To where must the prophet Ezekiel now be brought, and what are we interested to learn respecting him now?

Chapter 11

Disappointment in Store for Overconfident Ones

IN HIS next vision, what does Ezekiel see happen? Listen: "And a spirit proceeded to lift me up and bring me to the eastern gate of the house of Jehovah that is facing eastward, and, look! in the entrance of the gate there were twenty-five men, and I got to see in the midst of them Jaazaniah the son of Azzur and Pelatiah the son of Benaiah, princes of the people. Then he [Jehovah] said to me: 'Son of man, these are the men that are scheming hurtfulness and advising bad counsel against this city; that are saying, "Is not the building of houses close at hand? She is the wide-mouthed cooking pot, and we are the flesh."'"—Ezekiel 11:1-3.

[2] Apparently these are not the twenty-five men

1. Whom, in vision, did Ezekiel now get to see in the eastern gate of the temple, and what were they saying?
2. What do we note about the identity of these twenty-five men, and what political movement were they scheming?

whom Ezekiel saw earlier in the inner court of the temple, worshiping the sun to the east, before the slaughter work was ordered to begin upon the unmarked inhabitants of Jerusalem. (Ezekiel 8:16) Nor is this Jaazaniah the son of Azzur the same as the Jaazaniah the son of Shaphan whom Ezekiel saw engaged in idolatrous worship inside a temple building. (Ezekiel 8:11) These latter twenty-five men are said to be "princes of the people," hence governmental princes and not religious princes of the temple. Evidently, in this year 612 B.C.E., more than three years before the Babylonian siege of Jerusalem began, King Zedekiah of Jerusalem had not yet rebelled against the king of Babylonia to whom he had pledged submission. (2 Chronicles 36:11-13; 2 Kings 24:18 to 25:1) But these twenty-five "princes of the people" were likely scheming in favor of such a rebellion, for they were "advising bad counsel against this city." But they were confident that no harm would come.

[3] Those schemers and bad counselors of the king of Jerusalem likened the city to a widemouthed cooking pot or caldron, one made of iron. The city walls were like the sides of that metallic pot, unbreachable. Inside those walls, like flesh that is to be cooked, those twenty-five princes would be safe. Safe inside, they would never be dispossessed, and so was it not the time to build houses for permanent occupancy? They could make sure of their permanent residence by appealing to Egypt against the king of Babylon. They did not believe the predictions of the prophet-priest Jeremiah concerning the coming destruction of Jerusalem. They needed to have a double warning of this from Jehovah. "Therefore," said Jehovah to Ezekiel, "prophesy against them. Prophesy, O son of man." —Ezekiel 11:4.

[4] What now happened to Ezekiel proves how true

---

3. To what did those twenty-five men liken Jerusalem's walls and therefore themselves, how were they reasoning, and what did they now need?
4. What now happened to Ezekiel proved the truth of what action of the spirit as mentioned in 2 Peter 1:21?

were the later words of the Christian apostle Peter: "Prophecy was at no time brought by man's will, but men spoke from God as they were borne along by holy spirit." (2 Peter 1:21) Note what Ezekiel tells us:

5 "Then the spirit of Jehovah fell upon me, and he went on to say to me: 'Say, "This is what Jehovah has said: 'You people said the right thing, O house of Israel; and as regards the things that come up in your spirit, I myself have known it. You have caused your slain ones in this city to be many, and you have filled her streets with the slain ones.' " "Therefore this is what the Sovereign Lord Jehovah has said, 'As regards your slain ones whom you people have put in the midst of her, they are the flesh, and she is the widemouthed cooking pot; and there will be a bringing forth of you yourselves out of the midst of her.' " ' "—Ezekiel 1:5-7.

6 In order to try to make sure of their permanent position inside Jerusalem, those pro-Egyptian princes had killed off those who were in favor of continuing submissive to Babylon. If Jerusalem were to be likened to a cooking pot, then those slain ones were the ones to stay inside, on the site of the city, and not be dragged out of her by the Babylonians. They were to be like the flesh in the caldron. But the walls of Jerusalem would be no metallic cooking pot for the pro-Egyptian murderous princes. They were the ones who were to be brought out of her by the Babylonians. They would have to leave vacant the houses that they had built.

7 The fiery destruction that was symbolized by the "coals of fire" that the linen-clad man tossed over the city was certain to reach their newly built houses and all the city of Jerusalem. (Ezekiel 10:2-7) If they

---

5. In what Jehovah now told Ezekiel to say, how did he use the likeness drawn by the twenty-five men but show a reverse outcome for them themselves?
6. Why were so many slain by those princes, and who were to remain inside the symbolic cooking pot, the slain ones or the princes?
7. What was to happen to the newly built houses of those princes, and what did they have reason to fear as to Egypt's ability against Babylon?

put through their scheme to induce King Zedekiah to break his oath and rebel against Babylon, they had good reason to fear that the king of Babylon would come back against Jerusalem with the sword of punishment. Even militarized Egypt would not prove strong enough to hold back the king of Babylon. Hence Ezekiel must continue on to say to those scheming princes:

8 " 'A sword you have feared, and a sword I shall bring upon you,' is the utterance of the Sovereign Lord Jehovah. 'And I shall certainly bring you forth out of the midst of her and give you into the hand of strangers and execute upon you acts of judgment. By the sword you will fall. On the border of Israel I shall judge you people; and you will have to know that I am Jehovah. She [Jerusalem] herself will not prove to be for you a widemouthed cooking pot, and you yourselves will not prove to be flesh in the midst of her. On the border of Israel I shall judge you, and you will have to know that I am Jehovah, because in my regulations you did not walk and my judgments you did not do, but according to the judgments of the nations that are round about you, you have done.' "—Ezekiel 11:8-12.

9 The high hopes of those overconfident schemers were to be disappointed. The judicial decision to be executed upon them was to be from Jehovah, but he would use the "sword" in the hands of those foreign "strangers" to do the executing. By this "sword" of punitive warfare many of them would fall in death. Those who survived would not remain safe inside Jerusalem's walls. Her walls would not prove to be like the impenetrable side of an iron cooking pot, safely protecting the "flesh" inside her. Those rebellious scheming survivors would be brought out as captives from behind the breached walls of Jerusalem to suffer acts of judgment. These miserable survivors were to

8. What instrument did Jehovah say he would bring against them, and in what region would he judge them?
9. In the execution of his judicial decisions, what would Jehovah use, and the use of it in execution would take place in what part of the land?

be dragged off the territory of the Kingdom of Judah, for Jehovah had said that "on the border of Israel" he would judge them. At the northern tip of the territory that had been conquered by King David, namely, at Riblah toward Hamath, Jehovah would have them executed by the Babylonian king wielding the "sword." On this Jeremiah 52:24-27 informs us:

[10] "Furthermore, the chief of the bodyguard took Seraiah the chief priest and Zephaniah the second priest and the three doorkeepers, and from the city he took one court official that happened to be commissioner over the men of war, and seven men of those having access to the king, who were found in the city, and the secretary of the chief of the army, the one mustering the people of the land, and sixty men of the people of the land, who were found in the midst of the city. So these Nebuzaradan the chief of the bodyguard took and conducted them to the king of Babylon at Riblah. And these the king of Babylon proceeded to strike down and to put them to death in Riblah in the land of Hamath. Thus Judah went into exile from off its soil."

[11] What was Jehovah's purpose in letting the Babylonian "strangers" treat his chosen people in such a harsh, merciless way? "And you will have to know that I am Jehovah," is His answer. Twice, in close succession, he here makes that declaration of his purpose. His chosen people were trying to ignore him, and he had to show them forcefully that he had not released them from their sacred covenant with him long ago through the prophet Moses. As a matter of fact, that Mosaic covenant was to continue in force for almost 639 years after the destruction of Jerusalem in 607 B.C.E., or down till the spring of 33 C.E. He had to force them to know that he still held them to account for breaking their side of this two-way covenant. Invisible though he was because of being spirit,

10. Concerning that execution, what does Jeremiah 52:24-27 say?
11. What was Jehovah's purpose in letting the Babylonians treat his people so harshly, and what connection did this purpose have with the Mosaic law covenant?

he was not to be treated as someone that did not exist. He was Jehovah, the very same God to whom their forefathers had repeatedly said at Mount Sinai in Arabia: "All that Jehovah has spoken we are willing to do." (Exodus 19:1-8; 24:1-7) Jehovah would in this way demonstrate before all creation in heaven and in earth that he faithfully lives up to his side of any solemn contract or covenant.

[12] Because Jehovah by his prophets had forewarned them that he would bring upon the Israelites such consequences of their breaking of their covenant with him, they would know that it was the action of Jehovah himself when these foretold things actually came upon them. He was plain spoken when he pointed out to them just why he had to execute these acts of judgment upon them, saying: "On the border of Israel I shall judge you, and you will have to know that I am Jehovah." Why? "Because in my regulations you did not walk and my judgments you did not do, but according to the judgments of the nations that are round about you, you have done."—Ezekiel 11:11, 12.

WHY CHRISTENDOM ALSO
WILL NOT ESCAPE FROM KNOWING

[13] Modern-day Christendom has let this warning example of history be lost on her. Regardless of how she feels about it today, she has claimed to be like ancient Israel, in a solemn compact or covenant with the God of the Holy Bible. The copies of the Bible that she has printed and circulated by the hundreds of millions in over a thousand languages establish his divine name as being Jehovah or Yahweh. Only she claims her mediator between this God and men to be Jesus Christ the Son of God, and her covenant with God to be the new covenant. (Jeremiah 31:31-34; Luke 22:20; 1 Timothy 2:5, 6) In all this, Christendom

---

12. What did Jehovah do toward helping them to know that it was he who was taking the action and why he had to do so?
13. In what respects does Christendom claim to be like ancient Israel, and therefore, despite her hypocrisy, how should she expect to be treated?

is hypocritical. Nevertheless, Jehovah God takes her according to her claims and pretensions, and he must deal with her accordingly. He is not going to let her misrepresent him shamefully before all the world and not be exposed finally as a hypocrite and be duly punished for it.

[14] Christendom's claimed Mediator, Jesus Christ, will not plead before God for mercy upon her. She will have to know painfully that he is Jehovah. In fact, all mankind will have to know that He is not the God that Christendom has represented Him to be.

[15] Similar to ancient Israel, Christendom has preferred to make her own chosen alliances with this world. She has not put her trust in the God of the new covenant. In lack of faith, she has paid no attention to the divine warning, in Isaiah 31:1: "Woe to those going down to Egypt for assistance, those who rely on mere horses, and who put their trust in war chariots, because they are numerous, and in steeds, because they are very mighty, but who have not looked to the Holy One of Israel and have not searched for Jehovah himself." Christendom's religious leaders may have felt that they are the "flesh" in the midst of the widemouthed cooking pot, safe behind her walls of protection and defense. But will the secular elements of modern-day Egypt, this worldly system of things, be able to save her from the execution of Jehovah's judicial decisions against her? No! Her symbolic walls of defense will fail under the assaults of Jehovah's executional forces. Her overconfident leaders, who trust in man-made security within their ironlike "cooking pot," will surely be taken out of her and destroyed by Jehovah's executional "sword."

[16] Is it not therefore dangerous before God for re-

14. What will Christendom's claimed Mediator not do for her in the judgment, and what will all mankind have to know on her account?
15. How has Christendom ignored Isaiah 31:1 as regards alliances, and what will be her experience as regards the symbolic ironlike cooking pot?
16. Because of the dangerousness of connections with Christendom, what is it urgent for each church member or moral supporter of her to ask himself now?

ligiously inclined persons to continue their membership in Christendom or their close association with her on a sort of "interfaith" basis? Each church member or moral supporter of Christendom is now under a growing urgency to ask himself, 'When shortly God carries out his stated purpose, "You will have to know that I am Jehovah," will the execution of his judicial decision bring about my own destruction along with Christendom?' This is no academic, theoretical question; it is practical, realistic and now most timely!

[17] Let every honest person compare what the Bible says about true Christianity and what Christendom has adopted as her religious regulations. Then he will see that Jehovah can appeal to the same reason for destroying Christendom as he did for destroying Jerusalem in the year 607 B.C.E. What reason? "Because," as Jehovah said, "in my regulations you did not walk and my judgments you did not do, but according to the judgments of the nations that are round about you, you have done." (Ezekiel 11:12) If we share with Christendom in that course, can we evade her destruction?

[18] The fact that the destruction comes from Jehovah enthroned on his celestial chariotlike organization was illustrated in the experience that the prophet Ezekiel had respecting the twenty-five men who schemed what proved to be disastrous for Jerusalem: "And it came about that as soon as I prophesied Pelatiah the son of Benaiah himself died, and I proceeded to fall upon my face and cry with a loud voice and say: 'Alas, O Sovereign Lord Jehovah! Is it an extermination that you are executing with the remaining ones of Israel?' " (Ezekiel 11:13) In this vision, what caused Pelatiah the prince to drop dead after Ezekiel had prophesied and served notice upon the twenty-five

---

17. What is the reason to which Jehovah can appeal for destroying Christendom just as in the case of destroying ancient Jerusalem?
18. The fact that the destruction comes from Jehovah was illustrated in the sudden death of which prince, and of what did Ezekiel, according to his outcry, take this to be a sign?

"princes of the people"? The prophet Ezekiel according to what he cried out in fear took it to be a direct execution of judgment from Jehovah. He took it as a sign, not only of impending death for the other twenty-four princes, but also of a coming extermination of all the "remaining ones of Israel." He did not, however, challenge God's right to exterminate them all.

[19] Just as Ezekiel feared the destruction of all of Jehovah's covenant people during the threatening destruction of Jerusalem, so a fear might be excited in the hearts of religiously minded persons who do not appreciate the distinction between Christendom and true Christianity. Their frightened question might be, 'If in the coming "great tribulation" upon the whole system of things Jehovah exterminates all of Christendom and her worldly allies, will this mean the destruction of true Christianity?' Communist and other radical elements of this system of things who hate the Christianity of the Holy Bible would like to have it so and would like to have a part in making it so. They would like to have wiped out, not only the hypocritical Christianity of Christendom, but also the "pure religion," the true Christian worship of the Sovereign Lord Jehovah. (James 1:27, *AV; NW*) Will these irreligious radicals have the satisfaction of seeing such a thing realized, in substantiation of the fears of some religious people?

CHRISTENDOM'S DESTRUCTION
NOT THAT OF CHRISTIANITY

[20] The fear-inspired question of Ezekiel could be answered only by Jehovah, whose covenant had been broken by the house of Israel. His answer to Ezekiel exemplified what would be the case with regard to true Christianity in this modern "time of the end."

---

19. What fear of religiously inclined people today compares with Ezekiel's outcry, and in view of the Communists' attitude, what question arises as to the future of religion?
20, 21. Who only could answer Ezekiel's fearful question, and what did he promise to become to the exiled brothers of Ezekiel who had the right to a repurchase?

Ezekiel gives us the divine answer as he now writes:

21 "And the word of Jehovah continued to occur to me, saying: 'Son of man, as regards your brothers, your brothers, the men concerned with your right to repurchase, and all the house of Israel, all of it, are the ones to whom the inhabitants of Jerusalem have said, "Get far away from Jehovah. To us it belongs; the land has been given us as a thing to possess"; therefore say, "This is what the Sovereign Lord Jehovah has said: 'Although I have put them far away among the nations, and although I have scattered them among the lands, yet I shall become to them a sanctuary for a little while [or, in a little way] among the lands to which they have come.' " ' "—Ezekiel 11:14-16, and marginal reading.

22 This divine promise had reference to Ezekiel himself and to his fellow exiles in Babylon hundreds of miles away from Jerusalem. They were Ezekiel's Israelite brothers. They were the ones who in the year 617 B.C.E. had been put far away among the nations and scattered among the lands because of Jehovah's judicial decision. They had thus been obliged to leave their hereditary possessions in the land of Israel. Besides these ones, Jehovah's expression "all the house of Israel, all of it" might include the Israelites who had been carried into exile by the Assyrians back in 740 B.C.E. (2 Kings 17:6-18; 18:9-12) According to God's law as set out in Leviticus 25:13-38, hereditary land in Israel that was sold to an alien resident could be repurchased for the landless Israelite by a close Israelite relative before the Year of Jubilee arrived, and thereby the original landowner could be reinstated on his God-given property. But did the inhabitants of Jerusalem in Ezekiel's day have that loving spirit of a redeemer or repurchaser toward their exiled brothers scattered throughout the Babylonian Empire?

_____

22. As regards the exiles, whom might the expression "all the house of Israel, all of it" include, and how did the matter of a repurchase enter into the case of these exiles?

²³ Not according to the way in which Jehovah described those Jews still occupying Jerusalem and the land of Judah. They did not desire their unfortunate brothers to be restored from exile in Babylon and to reoccupy estates in the land of Israel. They were pleased to have their brothers unwillingly get as far away from Jehovah as possible, in order that they might have all the land for themselves in the land of Israel where Jehovah was understood to be. They felt that by His act of providence all the land had now been given to them to possess. Like Pelatiah the son of Benaiah, they felt that they were secure in the land and that it was the time to build houses therein for permanent occupancy. They felt snug and safe like flesh in a widemouthed cooking pot. (Ezekiel 11:1-3, 13) In a lack of brotherly affection they were unwilling to share the God-given land once again with any restored exiles.

²⁴ However, Jehovah had other thoughts than theirs in mind. He was not disposed to favor those land-greedy inhabitants of Jerusalem and Judah by letting them have continued occupancy of the land at the expense of their brothers in exile. The repentant ones among those exiles he was mercifully disposed to favor. During their exile he became for them a "sanctuary for a little while [or, in a little way] among the lands to which they have come." (Ezekiel 11:16) For the "little while," for the limited time of their being exiled, he would be a holy place in which they could take refuge and be safe and be preserved for his future good purposes.

²⁵ Jehovah would be such a "sanctuary" to some extent, "in a little way," inasmuch as he could not shield them from all the deserved consequences of their past

---

23. Did Jerusalem's inhabitants have the loving spirit of a redeemer toward their exiled brothers, and what is the evidence according to the way her inhabitants talked and planned?
24. How were Jehovah's thoughts different from those of Jerusalem's inhabitants, and what did he promise to be to those exiles?
25. Besides being a "sanctuary" to those exiles "for a little while," how could he be such to them only "in a little way"?

bad conduct toward him. He had brought their exile upon them as a due recompense, and he was not going to shorten the time of exile in Babylon that he had decreed and foretold for them. His being a sanctuary to them was therefore limited. But greater mercy was to be shown them as he now told Ezekiel to explain to them, in these words:

²⁶ "Therefore say, 'This is what the Sovereign Lord Jehovah has said: "I will also collect you from the peoples and gather you from the lands among which you have been scattered, and I will give you the soil of Israel. And they will certainly come there and re-move all its disgusting things and all its detestable things out of it. And I will give them one heart, and a new spirit I shall put inside them; and I shall cer-tainly remove the heart of stone from their flesh and give them a heart of flesh, in order that they may walk in my own statutes and keep my own judicial decisions and actually carry them out; and they may really become my people and I myself may become their God."'"—Ezekiel 11:17-20.

²⁷ What, though, about those inhabitants of Jeru-salem and Judah who were not desirous of having the exiles get back on the land of Israel? Concerning these selfish princes and people Jehovah went on to say by Ezekiel: "'But as for those whose heart is walking in their disgusting things and their detestable things, upon their head I shall certainly bring their own way,' is the utterance of the Sovereign Lord Jehovah." —Ezekiel 11:21.

²⁸ By the year 607 B.C.E. and through the destruc-tion of Jerusalem and her temple and the desolating of the land of Judah, Jehovah brought upon those covenant-breaking idolatrous Jews the fruitage of their disgusting, detestable way. With his sword of judicial

---

26. What greater mercy was to be shown to those exiles as Jehovah now told Ezekiel to say to them?
27. What, though, did Jehovah say about those inhabitants of Jerusalem who did not want the exiles to get back on the land of Israel?
28. How did Jehovah bring upon the loveless greedy ones the fruitage of their detestable ways, and how did he show mercy upon the repentant exiles?

execution he cut them down by means of the Babylonian "strangers." Thus they lost the "soil of Israel" that they hugged so greedily to themselves. But what about those far-off exiles in Babylon? In 537 B.C.E., after the full appointed time of seventy years of desolation of the land of Judah, the repentant remnant of those exiled Israelites were collected together and restored to the "soil of Israel." There Jehovah did for them just as he had promised through his prophet Ezekiel. In this way he proved that they were his people and that he was their God. Jerusalem was rebuilt and another temple was built on the old site.

IS CHRISTENDOM TO BE RESTORED?

[29] What did this prefigure for our modern day? Could it really mean that Christendom, which is to be destroyed in the oncoming "great tribulation," will be restored to earth sometime after the "war of the great day of God the Almighty" at Har–Magedon? (Matthew 24:21, 22; Revelation 16:14-16) No, this could not be meant! We need here to correct any wrong understanding of what Christendom is. Her church members may understand Christendom to mean Christ's kingdom and to be the same as Christ's kingdom. But this is not so, and hence there can be no true Christendom and counterfeit Christendom.

[30] There is only the one Christendom, and it is a false, hypocritical religious organization. Let us never forget that Christendom is and always has been a part of what the Bible calls Babylon the Great, which is the world empire of false Babylonish religion. She is the most populous and powerful part of Babylon the Great. Christendom will no more be restored to earth than will the rest of Babylon the Great. Concerning Babylon the Great, all of her, including Christen-

---

29. Does this prefigure that Christendom will be restored after Har–Magedon, and what misunderstanding as to what Christendom is here needs to be corrected?

30, 31. Of what greater religious organization has Christendom always been a part, and what does Revelation 18:21 to 19:3 say about that greater organization?

dom, we read, in Revelation 18:21 to 19:3, these words:

[31] "And a strong angel lifted up a stone like a great millstone and hurled it into the sea, saying: 'Thus with a swift pitch will Babylon the great city be hurled down, and she will never be found again.' . . . 'Praise Jah, you people! And the smoke from her goes on ascending forever and ever.' "—Compare Jeremiah 51:58-64.

[32] The total destruction of Christendom along with the rest of Babylon the Great does not take away one iota from God's true Christian religion in the earth; it does not leave Him without his pure, undefiled religion in the earth. The fact is, the annihilation of Christendom will leave a live, flourishing true Christianity, standing forth in glorious purity under God's protection. This Christianity has been flourishing in the earth more and more since the year 1919 C.E. Among whom, if not in Christendom? Among the dedicated, baptized, anointed remnant of Jehovah's worshipers. It is these who were prefigured by the exiled prophet Ezekiel himself.

[33] Indeed, it is these in whom Jehovah has fulfilled his prophecy by Ezekiel about the collecting and gathering of his people from their scattered condition and giving them the "soil of Israel," in this "time of the end." (Ezekiel 11:17-20) These dedicated worshipers, anointed with Jehovah's spirit, were brought into a Babylonish captivity and exile during the world war of 1914-1918 and underwent a severe disciplining then. Their spiritual condition and their prospects of being reactivated in God's service were pictured and foretold in the vision that was given to Ezekiel about 606 B.C.E., after the destruction of Jerusalem, and in which vision he saw a valley plain full of dry bones

---

32. Will Christendom's destruction leave Jehovah without his pure religion in the earth, and how is this matter affected by what has been flourishing on earth in a religious way since 1919?
33. In whom during this twentieth century has Jehovah fulfilled his prophecy by Ezekiel concerning the gathering of his people and restoring them to the "soil of Israel" and how, by what train of events?

and what happened to make them live again. (Ezekiel 37:1-28; 33:21, 22; 32:1) In the spring of the year 1919 C.E. the faithful anointed remnant of Jehovah's Christian worshipers were delivered from this Babylonish bondage and shook off the shackles of Babylon, thus being restored to the symbolic "soil" of spiritual Israel. This repeopling of the desolated "soil" of spiritual Israel was also foretold after Jerusalem's destruction, in chapter thirty-six of Ezekiel's prophecy.

³⁴ These anointed spiritual Israelites Jehovah has purified still more since their deliverance from Babylonish bondage in 1919 C.E. Under the guidance of his holy spirit these restored ones have done just as he foretold: "They will certainly come there and remove all its disgusting things and all its detestable things out of it."

³⁵ To that end Jehovah has given them a better heart condition spiritually just as he had foretold: "And I will give them one heart, and a new spirit I shall put inside them; and I shall certainly remove the heart of stone from their flesh and give them a heart of flesh, in order that they may walk in my own statutes and keep my own judicial decisions and actually carry them out; and they may really become my people and I myself may become their God." (Ezekiel 11:18-20) These purified anointed worshipers of Jehovah as God are the ones who, as a class, fulfill the prophetic picture of the man "clothed with the linen, at whose hips there was the secretary's inkhorn." In so serving they mark the foreheads of persons who will be spared alive when there comes upon Christendom fiery destruction from Jehovah enthroned on his celestial chariot.

³⁶ Those marked in the forehead for preservation through the coming "great tribulation" upon Christen-

34. How has Jehovah purified still more the anointed spiritual Israelites since 1919 C.E.?
35. According to what promise has Jehovah given the restored ones a better heart condition spiritually, and they have been fulfilling the work of whom as seen in Ezekiel's vision?
36. Who are now enjoying Jehovah's favor along with the restored remnant?

dom are now enjoying Jehovah's favor along with the restored anointed remnant of spiritual Israelites on the symbolic "soil" of spiritual Israel.

[37] Especially since the year 1935 C.E. has the constantly increasing "great crowd" of sheeplike persons been gathered there into association with the anointed remnant of Jehovah's Christian witnesses.* They also have had to leave behind the detestable and disgusting things of Christendom and the rest of Babylon the Great in order to take up the pure, undefiled worship of the one living and true God. This has required a change of heart on their part. More and more it has become clearly marked in their lives that they too are dedicated worshipers of Jehovah as their God. Until now they are greatly aiding the anointed spiritual remnant in the work of symbolically marking the foreheads of all who seek pure religion.

THE CHARIOT MOVES TO AN OBSERVATION POST

[38] Not against these marked ones, but against all those remaining in active and sympathetic association with Christendom and all the remainder of Babylon the Great, will Jehovah's angelic executional forces start using their weapons of destruction at His appointed time. He observes and directs the lifesaving work from a fine observation post. (2 Peter 3:9-14) It is as if his celestial chariotlike organization has moved to the top of the Mount of Olives that lies to the east of Jerusalem and overlooks it.

[39] This is the significant location where the prophet Ezekiel finally saw the high-wheeled chariot of Jeho-

---

* See *The Watchtower* under the dates of August 1 and 15, 1935, containing Parts One and Two of the article entitled "The Great Multitude."

37. Why and how has this required a change of heart on the part of the "great crowd" gathered since 1935 C.E., and in what lifesaving work have they been aiding the spiritual remnant?
38. Against whom, at his time, does Jehovah's executional force use their weapons, and as if from where can he observe the lifesaving work, as it goes on?
39. To what final location did Ezekiel see Jehovah's celestial chariot move, and from that same location, when and by whom was destruction of a later Jerusalem foretold?

vah, according to what he tells us at the close of this series of visions, saying: "And the cherubs now lifted up their wings, and the wheels were close by them, and the glory of the God of Israel was over them, from above. And the glory of Jehovah went ascending from over the midst of the city and began to stand over the mountain that is to the east of the city." (Ezekiel 11:22, 23) It was from this same Mount of Olives that, 644 years later, Jesus Christ the Son of God foretold the fiery destruction that was to come upon the Jerusalem of that day in the year 70 C.E., a destruction that in itself was prophetic of the destruction that is coming upon Christendom as the antitypical unfaithful Jerusalem of modern times.—Matthew 24:1-22; Mark 13:1-20; Luke 21:5-24.

⁴⁰ After Jehovah's celestial chariot took its position over the Mount of Olives Ezekiel himself was put in position to declare the prophetic visions concerning the Jerusalem of his day. Not till eighteen and a half years later, which was thirteen and a half years after Jerusalem's destruction, did Ezekiel see Jehovah's symbolic "chariot" again. (Ezekiel 40:1-6; 43:1-17) At this latter time he received a prophetic message of another kind from the Divine Rider of the celestial chariot. Ezekiel continued to be Jehovah's prophet up till the beginning of the twenty-seventh year of his exile in Babylon. (Ezekiel 29:17-21) So for twenty-one years and nine months he served as a prophetic witness of Jehovah.—Ezekiel 1:1-3.

TELLING TO OTHERS THE SERIES OF VISIONS

⁴¹ It is one thing to see inspired visions; it is another thing to be obedient to Jehovah's command to tell forth to others what one saw and heard in such visions. By being privileged to see the visions Ezekiel was not just being entertained; he was being equipped for the

40. After that movement of Jehovah's celestial chariot to the mountain-top, what was Ezekiel put in position to do, when did he see the chariot again, and how long did he prophesy?
41. By being given this series of visions, for what was Ezekiel being equipped, and when, now, did he begin doing this and toward whom?

work of preaching and teaching that he was commissioned to do. With that purpose in view he is at length released from the power of inspiration and brought back to the realm of reality where he must do his work. Hence, after describing his then final view of Jehovah's celestial chariot, he tells us: "And a spirit itself lifted me up and finally brought me to Chaldea to the exiled people, in the vision by the spirit of God; and the vision that I had seen went ascending from upon me. And I began to speak to the exiled people all the things of Jehovah that he had caused me to see."—Ezekiel 11:24, 25.

[42] All through this series of visions Ezekiel had been "sitting in [his] house and the older men of Judah were sitting before [him]." He did not leave the company of those older men of Judah in his house, but the hand of Jehovah, with inspirational power, came upon Ezekiel and caused him to see such remarkable visions. How long those older men were obliged to wait until Ezekiel came out from under this visualizing spirit of God is not stated. In vision he became transported hundreds of miles away from the Chebar River in Chaldea (Babylonia), but now by the same inspirational spirit he was brought back to his real location in his house of exile. So when the final part of the vision "went ascending" from him, he became conscious again of where he actually was.

[43] It was no fanciful dream that Ezekiel had seen. It was nothing that Ezekiel had conjured up in his own mind. It was not by means of any modern-day hallucinogenic drug that he went mentally traveling and seeing what he did. The visions given to him were from Jehovah, the God of true prophecy. That the visions were no idle imaginations is proved by the fact that what the visions presented symbolically came true in actual human history. Consequently Ezekiel took

42. During this series of visions where had Ezekiel been, but where had he remained physically, and who were sitting before him?
43. By what means was Ezekiel caused to see those visions, how did he take his commission to tell out those visions, and to whom did he tell them?

the visions seriously; he took his commission to reveal and tell them seriously. Immediately upon coming out from under the visualizing power of inspiration he began telling those older men of Judah sitting in his house what he had seen and been commanded to say. He did not confine his revealing of the divine prophecies to those older men in his house, but went out telling it to still others. All the exiled people there in Chaldea were concerned. This was potent reason for him to do as he reports of himself: "I began to speak to the exiled people all the things of Jehovah that he had caused me to see."—Ezekiel 11:25.

[44] By the enlightening power of Jehovah's spirit we today have been given an understanding of what those prophetic visions of Ezekiel mean. The giving of such understanding of those prophetic revelations is not for our personal self-enjoyment. Rather, it lays upon us the obligation to imitate Ezekiel and tell out to everybody who is involved what Jehovah through his chariotlike heavenly organization has made known to our understanding. For our own sakes, for others' sakes, it is now more urgent than ever before that we do this. The time for Christendom's fiery destruction from Jehovah enthroned on his celestial chariot was never nearer!

44. What obligation is laid upon us by the giving to us of the understanding of Ezekiel's visions, and why is it urgent for us now to carry out that obligation?

Chapter 12

"Until He Comes Who Has the Legal Right"

ALTHOUGH man has made a failure of human government, man's Creator holds onto his marvelous purpose to have a successful government of righteousness ruling over all mankind on a paradisaic earth. Man's Creator is not the kind of Person that a recent book author imagined him to be, when he wrote: "If I were God, I'd quit."* The true God will not quit until he has realized the glorious purpose with which he started out when he put man on the earth. What was that purpose? The whole earth comfortably filled, with the human family enjoying peace and happiness in human perfection under God's heavenly government.

[2] Sad it is, indeed, to see the failure of a government that starts out with bright prospects and good promise. In the face of such failure it is comforting for us to get the assurance that, in God's due time, he will produce the longed-for ruler and put him in power so as to satisfy the righteous desire of every human heart. This is the hope that was given to the prophet Ezekiel at the time that God told him to declare the approaching ruin of the royal government of Jerusalem. Ezekiel's message sounded a death knell for

---

* See the book entitled "Rock 2000," by Hiley H. Ward, 1970 edition.

1. Regardless of man's failure at government, what is God's attitude toward his original purpose for the earth, and what is that purpose?
2. It was sad to see the failure of what promising government of long ago, but it is comforting to have what assurance, as indicated in Ezekiel 21:27?

Jerusalem, but this was followed by the sounding forth of a life-giving hope, in these words: "A ruin, a ruin, a ruin I shall make it. As for this also, it will certainly become no one's until he comes who has the legal right, and I must give it to him."—Ezekiel 21:27.

³ At that time it was the seventh year of the exile of Ezekiel in the land of Babylon, or the year 611 B.C.E., likely in the fifth lunar month (named Ab) and on the tenth day of that month. (Ezekiel 20:1) Ever since Ezekiel had last seen the celestial chariot of Jehovah in vision the preceding year, he continued prophesying. In the course of the divine prophecies given to him during that time he had repeatedly declared God's announced purpose, that the hearers of His prophecies "will have to know that I am Jehovah." (Ezekiel 12:15, 16, 20; 13:9, 14, 21, 23; 14:8; 15:7; 16:62; 20:12, 20, 26, 38, 42, 44) The time had now moved one year closer to when Jehovah would make those words come true, so that the Israelites would have to know that Jehovah had spoken and that he had taken action in fulfillment of what he had spoken. —Ezekiel 5:13; 12:15; 21:5; 22:22; 37:14, 28.

⁴ As surely as Jehovah's prophecies by means of Ezekiel were to come true, just so surely the news about the fulfillment of those prophecies would reach Ezekiel's fellow Jewish exiles in Babylon. The news was bound to shake those exiles out of their unbelieving attitude toward Ezekiel and would vindicate the word of his God, Jehovah. That time was then not far off. Less than two and a half years from then the "battle in the day of Jehovah" would start against Jerusalem and the land of Judah. (Ezekiel 13:5) Quite properly, therefore, Jehovah the Warrior now used war phraseology in the prophecy that he gave to Ezekiel. Hence Ezekiel writes:

---

3. When was Ezekiel given this prophetic message, and what had he been doing till then, with emphasis on what divine purpose?
4. If Ezekiel's prophecies came true, then what about the news thereof, and what effect would this have upon the hearers of the prophecies, and why so before not very long?

⁵ "And the word of Jehovah continued to occur to me, saying: 'Son of man, set your face toward Jerusalem and drip words toward the holy places, and prophesy against the soil of Israel. And you must say to the soil of Israel, "This is what Jehovah has said: 'Here I am against you, and I will bring forth my sword out of its sheath and cut off from you righteous one and wicked one. In order that I may actually cut off from you righteous one and wicked one, therefore my sword will go forth from its sheath against all flesh from south to north. And all those of flesh will have to know that I myself, Jehovah, have brought forth my sword from its sheath. No more will it go back.' " ' " —Ezekiel 21:1-5.

⁶ Jehovah speaks of it as His war. He is the One that draws from its sheath His sword, which is his instrument for the execution of his judicial decision against those upon whom he makes war. His "sword" signifies the earthly agency that he uses, but it could also include his unseen heavenly chariotlike organization.

⁷ When this symbolic "sword" of Jehovah strikes, woe to all the occupiers of the "soil of Israel"! That sword will cut off "righteous" occupant as well as "wicked" occupant, just as when a forest fire devours the "still-moist" tree as well as the "dry tree." (Ezekiel 20:47, 48) When Jehovah begins to wield that sword, it will not stop with cutting off those in the Kingdom of Judah, which lay southward from Babylon as a "southern quarter," Judah being also a southern kingdom in contrast with the northern kingdom of the revolted ten tribes of Israel. (Ezekiel 20:45, 46) Jehovah's "sword" would also continue its activity northward, going forth "from its sheath against all flesh

5. With what war phraseology does Jehovah give the prophecy of Ezekiel 21:1-5 against the "soil of Israel"?
6. How is it determined from that prophecy whose war it is, and what is the instrument of warfare?
7. Why did the unsheathing of that "sword" mean woe to all occupants of the "soil of Israel," and what was the purpose of having the "sword" do its work from the south on to the north?

from south to north." What is the purpose of such extensive use of this "sword"? The heavenly Wielder of the "sword" explains, saying: "And all those of flesh will have to know that I myself, Jehovah, have brought forth my sword from its sheath. No more will it go back."—Ezekiel 21:5.

[8] Those on the "soil of Israel" and in Jerusalem were not the only sinners against Jehovah. "All flesh," all humanity, were then sinners against him, even though they were not directly in a covenant with him as was the nation of Israel. They deserved to be punished also. They were not to be left in the position where they could exult over Israel and boast that Israel's God, Jehovah, had taken drastic action against his own people but that they themselves, not being of Israelite flesh, had escaped Jehovah's attention. They were not to be left with the idea that they were more righteous than Israel. Hence all those nations who had ill-will against Jehovah's chosen people were also to fall by the edge of Jehovah's sword as sinners against Him as well as against his people. His unsheathed "sword" was not to go back to its resting-place until it had executed his judicial decision upon non-Israelite flesh also. In this way "all those of flesh" would be made to know that it is the God of Israel, Jehovah, that battles against them with his "sword."

JEHOVAH'S "SWORD" AGAINST "ALL THOSE OF FLESH"

[9] Shortly, within our twentieth century, the "battle in the day of Jehovah" will begin against the modern antitype of Jerusalem, Christendom. The ancient "soil of Israel" pictures the realm in which Christendom has operated. It pictures the standing and relationship that Christendom has claimed to occupy with God by means of his "new covenant" of which Jesus Christ is the

---

8. Thus, how were "all those of flesh" to know that Jehovah had brought forth His sword from its sheath, and what was the reason for this?
9. What today is pictured by the "soil of Israel," and whom will Jehovah's "sword" cut off from it?

mediator. Now is no time for anyone in Christendom to rely on any righteousness on the basis of his own merits and to boast of his own self-righteousness. Jehovah's "sword" of warfare will cut off from this position that Christendom's clergy claim for her all religionists who depend upon her having an acceptable standing with God.

[10] However, Jehovah's "sword" will not be applied merely to those adhering to Christendom. It will also be brandished against "all flesh from south [Christendom] to north." Religionists belonging to all the rest of the world empire of false religion will feel the cutting edge of Jehovah's "sword." Their being non-Christians will not cause them to be spared. They will not be left to gloat over the destruction of Christendom as a rival religious system.

[11] Righteousness before the one living and true God, Jehovah, is not to be gained through Christendom or through any other religious system of the world that offers the hope of self-merit by means of one's own works of self-righteousness. As the "battle in the day of Jehovah" against all false religion gets closer, the urgency increases for us to accept His way of gaining true righteousness.

[12] That way is through faith in the ransom sacrifice for sins as provided in His Son, Jesus Christ. Since Christendom claims to be the "house of God," it is appropriate for the execution of His judicial decision to start with her. This is the thing to expect in line with these words of 1 Peter 4:17, 18: "It is the appointed time for the judgment to start with the house of God. Now if it starts first with us, what will the end be of those who are not obedient to the good news of God? 'And if the righteous man is being saved with difficulty, where will the ungodly man and the sinner

---

10. What religionists besides those of Christendom are foretold to be cut off by Jehovah's "sword," and why?
11. True righteousness cannot be gained through what religious agencies, and whose way of gaining it is it now urgent for us to accept?
12. Why is it appropriate for Jehovah's execution of his judicial decision to begin at Christendom, but why not stop there?

make a showing?' " They will make no showing in the "battle in the day of Jehovah." His "sword" will not go back to its sheath until he makes "all those of flesh" know that He has taken action.

¹³ Is it any wonder that the anointed remnant of Jehovah's Christian witnesses of today are moved to such intense activity in warning people everywhere about such a prospect? No, for in this way it is shown that they feel just the same as the prophet Ezekiel was told to express himself, in these words of Jehovah: "And as for you, O son of man, sigh with shaking hips. Even with bitterness you should sigh before their eyes. And it must occur that, in case they say to you, 'On account of what are you sighing?' you must say, 'At a report.' For it will certainly come, and every heart must melt and all hands must drop down and every spirit must become dejected and all knees themselves will drip with water. 'Look! It will certainly come and be brought to occur,' is the utterance of the Sovereign Lord Jehovah."—Ezekiel 21:6, 7.

¹⁴ After Jehovah's "sword" did bring about the destruction of Jerusalem and the utter desolation of the "soil of Israel" in the year 607 B.C.E., the bitter "report" did come, even as far as to the Jewish exiles in Babylon. (Ezekiel 33:21, 22) Doubtless the "report" as delivered by an escapee from the destroyed Jerusalem did affect the hitherto unbelieving Jewish exiles in the very way that Jehovah foretold to Ezekiel. Doubtless their knees dripped with more than the mere sweat of horrified excitement. They were likely so weakened in spirit that their kidneys could not control themselves and their knees dripped with their own urine! They had to acknowledge that Jehovah's word as spoken through Ezekiel had been vindicated. He was proved to be the truth-telling God. When, not before very long, the authentic report is published that

13. The anointed remnant's being intensely active in trying to warn everybody portrays what in Ezekiel's case, according to Ezekiel 21:6, 7?
14. When the "report" finally came to the Jewish exiles, what effects of it upon them were to be expected, and what effects upon religionists may be expected from the report of Christendom's ruin?

Jehovah's executional "sword" has actually brought about the utter ruin of Christendom, it will produce similar effects upon many religionists.

[15] Skeptical as people may be about it today like those Jewish fellow exiles of Ezekiel, yet Jehovah really has a "sword" that He will use as his agency in executing her just deserts upon Christendom. The modern-day remnant of Jehovah's anointed witnesses are calling attention to this notable "sword" that Jehovah will unsheath against the organization of hypocritical Christianity, as the prophet Ezekiel was told to do, when Jehovah said to him: "And the word of Jehovah continued to occur to me, saying: 'Son of man, prophesy, and you must say, "This is what Jehovah has said: 'Say, "A sword, a sword! It has been sharpened, and it is also polished. For the purpose of organizing a slaughter it has been sharpened; for the purpose of its getting a glitter it has been polished." ' " ' "—Ezekiel 21:8-10.

NO BASIS FOR EXULTING OVER FALSE PREMISES

[16] No religious basis exists for self-assuring persons to exult, using the argument: "We are God's people. We have in our midst the house of God at which we worship. Jehovah's executional sword will not come 'organizing a slaughter' among us!" Such an argument was suggested by the question that was interjected in the description of Jehovah's sword to Ezekiel: "Or shall we exult?"—Ezekiel 21:10.

[17] Those Israelites who were inclined to exult would remember that their capital was the city of Jerusalem with its holy status because of its having the temple built by King Solomon. Also, its king was a descendant of King David, with whom Jehovah had made a cov-

---

15. Does Jehovah really have such a symbolic "sword" today for his use, and, according to Ezekiel 21:8-10, what should Jehovah's anointed remnant today do in that regard?
16. The interjection "Or shall we exult?" suggested what question on the part of religionists who assure themselves respecting God's "sword"?
17. By those inclined to exult, why was the question raised as to whether the "sword" would reject the scepter of Jerusalem's king?

enant for an everlasting kingdom. Also, this Davidic king was anointed with oil into office and accordingly was called "the anointed one of Jehovah," or "the Messiah" (Hebrew) or "the Christ" (Greek). And as a descendant of King David this anointed king was said to sit upon the throne of God, "to sit upon Jehovah's throne as king in place of David his father." (2 Samuel 7:4-16; Lamentations 4:20; 1 Chronicles 29:23) Would it be likely, then, that Jehovah's "sword" would reject the scepter of such a king?

18 Ah, but Jehovah's sword was going to do just that, according to his own words concerning the sword: "Is it rejecting the scepter of my own son, as it does every tree?" (Ezekiel 21:10) For reasons that are stated soon afterward, Jehovah's sword does not fail to reject that royal scepter of the Kingdom of Judah any more than it rejects every other scepter, every other "tree." The fact that Jehovah said that the successors of David on the royal throne of Jerusalem would be like sons to him was not going to save them from the sword in case they were stubbornly disobedient. So, too, Christendom's kings are not to be spared in the 'battle in the day of Jehovah' just because the religious clergy have anointed these kings to reign "By the Grace of God." The claims of such rulers to exemption from execution by Jehovah's "sword" will be rejected by the agency that Jehovah uses as his executional "sword."—2 Samuel 7:14.

19 Back in Ezekiel's day Jehovah is the One who gave his executional "sword" into the hand of the agency whom he used in bringing ruin upon Jerusalem and the Kingdom of Judah. Jehovah makes this fact very plain in telling Ezekiel to say: "And one gives it to be polished, in order to wield it with the hand. It—a sword has been sharpened, and it—it has been

18. Was the "sword" of Jehovah going to reject "the scepter of my own son, as it does every tree," and in view of the answer will Christendom's political rulers receive exemption from execution by Jehovah's "sword"?
19. According to Ezekiel 21:11, who is it that gives the "sword" into the hand of the killer?

polished, in order to give it into the hand of a killer."
—Ezekiel 21:11.

[20] In this case the "killer" or slayer is the agency
that directly acts as the executioner for Jehovah, but
Jehovah's giving the "sword" into the hand of the
killer is Jehovah's appointment and authorization of
that agency to do the killing. The fact, too, that those
who were to be "hurled to the sword" were found
among those whom Jehovah calls "my people" proves
further that this use of the sword "against my people"
was by Jehovah's permission, indeed, by His direction.
Not even the "chieftains of Israel" were to be spared
by the executional sword, not even the highest earthly
chieftain of Israel, namely, King Zedekiah. His scepter
would be rejected from being spared. The bare thought
of such a thing was enough to make a man of Israel
cry out and howl and to slap his right thigh instead of
beating his bosom like a woman. This is why Jehovah
said to Ezekiel as an illustration:

[21] " 'Cry out and howl, O son of man, for it itself
[the sword] has come to be against my people; it is
against all the chieftains of Israel. The very ones
hurled to the sword have come to be with my people.
Therefore make a slap on the thigh. For an extermination has been made, and what of it if it is rejecting
also the scepter? This will not continue existing,' is the
utterance of the Sovereign Lord Jehovah."—Ezekiel
21:12, 13.

THE THING THAT WAS NOT TO "CONTINUE EXISTING"

[22] What was it that was not to "continue existing"?
It was the scepter of the kings of Israel, the rod or
wand that is the emblem of royal power and authority
in an active sense. That meant that the Kingdom of

20. What does Jehovah's giving the "sword" into the hand of the
"killer" constitute, against whom was it to be used under Jehovah's
supervision, and not even who were to be spared?
21. Consequently, Jehovah told Ezekiel to act in what way, giving
what reasons for his doing so?
22. The failure of the thing mentioned to "continue existing" meant
what as to rulerships world wide, but what did it not mean as to
the royal line of King David?

Judah was to go down, to disappear. Jehovah's throne in Jerusalem was to be overturned, to be left unoccupied by a royal descendant of King David. The typical or miniature kingdom of Jehovah God among the Israelites was to be suspended, to cease functioning. This would leave only kingdoms of this world, Gentile kingdoms, functioning on the earth. Nevertheless, this did not mean that every rightful descendant in the royal line of David would be cut off, so that David's royal line would cease to exist. Although no surviving descendant of the royal house of David would ever again wield a material scepter on a material throne in earthly Jerusalem, someone of David's royal line would yet come who would have the natural right to the kingdom of David over the twelve tribes of Israel. Ezekiel waited for God to assure him of this.

²³ Jehovah's "sword" was to be so active in its destructive movements that it would appear to encircle the doomed Israelites. This was enough to make an Israelite slap his hands together in astonishment, if not in fear. The highly polished and sharpened sword was to be a noteworthy one, one of international importance. For this reason Jehovah commanded Ezekiel to call further attention to it, saying: "And you, O son of man—prophesy, and strike palm against palm, and 'A sword!' should be repeated for three times. The sword [1] of the slain ones it is. It is the sword [2] of someone slain who is great, which is making an encirclement of them. In order for the heart to melt and in order to multiply those who are overthrown at all their gates, I will make a slaughter by the sword [3]. Alas, it is made for a glittering, polished for a slaughter!"—Ezekiel 21:14, 15.

²⁴ Note that Jehovah himself takes the responsibility for the slaughter despite his using an executional agency. He says: "I will make a slaughter by the

---

23. How could the "sword" be said to make an encirclement of the Israelites, and how was Ezekiel told to emphasize the notableness of this "sword"?
24. Responsibility for the slaughter is taken by whom, and at what strategic points will the slaughter therefore be multiplied?

sword." So when the besieged Jews in Jerusalem rush to her gates to defend their holy city, it will be in vain; they will be overthrown. The slain there at such strategic points Jehovah will multiply. As the polished sword against them continues to be brandished, it will produce a repeated glittering. Sharpened to a keen cutting edge, it will cause fearsome slaughter.

25 As if the sword were alive and able to take orders as to where to direct itself, Ezekiel is told to speak to it in an apostrophe: "Show yourself sharp; go to the right! Set your position; go to the left! To wherever your face is directed!" Thus, according to Jehovah's will, it is a directed slaughter. He knows upon whom to use his executional sword. There will be no rest for his sword until he has carried out to the full his judicial sentence. Just as he says: "And I myself also shall strike my one palm against my other palm, and I will bring my rage to its rest. I myself, Jehovah, have spoken."—Ezekiel 21:16, 17.

INTERFERENCE BY DEMONS TO BE THWARTED

26 Are the spirit demons, under the control of their ruler, Satan the Devil, going to be permitted to turn Jehovah's "sword" aside, to turn it in a different direction from where he wants it to go first and directly? Try to do so, the demons might, according to the appeals of spiritualists, astrologers, fortune-tellers and false prophets under demon influence. But this will never succeed, according to what Ezekiel now tells us: "And the word of Jehovah continued to occur to me, saying: 'And as for you, O son of man, set for yourself two ways for the sword of the king of Babylon to enter. From the one land both of them should go forth, and an index hand should be cut out; at the head of the way to the city it should be cut out. A way you should

25. To what is Ezekiel told to turn and direct his speech in order to indicate what kind of a slaughter, and when will Jehovah bring his rage to its rest?
26. What road indexes was Ezekiel told to set up, and what question respecting the directive power of the demons here comes up?

set for the sword to enter against Rabbah of the sons of Ammon, and one against Judah, against Jerusalem fortified. For the king of Babylon stood still at the crossways, at the head of the two ways, in order to resort to divination.' "—Ezekiel 21:18-21.

²⁷ Aha! Here we have identified for us the "killer" into whose hand Jehovah would give the executional sword to carry forward visibly the "battle in the day of Jehovah" against Jerusalem. It is the king of Babylon. Since Babylon was then a world power, the Third World Power in Bible history, no wonder that the "sword" of warfare that it wielded was such an internationally notable sword, well deserving of Ezekiel's calling such attention to it! At the time of Ezekiel's prophecy the king of Babylon was named Nebuchadnezzar. According to secular history, he was a very religious man, and much devoted to the demon god named Marduk. This meant that Nebuchadnezzar was very superstitious, relying for his official guidance upon demonistic practices, such as divination.

²⁸ This reminds us of how political rulers of even Christendom rely upon demonism for guidance in their political activities and decisions, the fortune-tellers and clairvoyants of Washington, D.C., for example, being heavily patronized by the national politicians who have their offices there. The Nazi dictator of the Third German Reich, Adolf Hitler, in his day was notorious for his dependence upon astrology, having a special official astrologer. They no more look to Jehovah for guidance than did Nebuchadnezzar.

²⁹ Coming into the land of Palestine from the north, Nebuchadnezzar at the head of his mighty army came to a fork in the line of march. This was a place for decision. Just as Ezekiel had been told to illustrate it

---

27. Who is the "killer" here identified as being, and what kind of person was this "killer"?
28. Of what does this remind us of the politicians of Christendom and resorting to forms of demonism?
29. As he marched down from the north, at what crossways was a decision forced upon Nebuchadnezzar, and how was he to decide?

before the Jewish exiles back in Babylon, one branch of this crossways led to Rabbah of the sons of Ammon, which lay to the east of the Jordan River. The other branch led to Jerusalem in the mountains west of the Jordan River and the Dead Sea. The Ammonite capital city, Rabbah, was the less fortified city, easier to capture, and should Nebuchadnezzar direct his military campaign first against that city? On the other hand, the Judean capital was called "Jerusalem fortified." It should be much harder to capture, requiring a longer siege that might discourage the Babylonian soldiers. Should Nebuchadnezzar postpone attacking it till after his troops were elated with a capture of Ammonite Rabbah? A tough choice! How was he to decide? By divination!

[30] One method of divination was not enough for King Nebuchadnezzar. He must make sure by using three. By this means would the demons, of which Babylon was a superstitious worshiper, make the threefold divination result in such a way as to steer him contrary to Jehovah's will—against Ammonite Rabbah first? Not when the Almighty God Jehovah had declared his purpose for His own executional "sword" to go first against Jerusalem. He outmaneuvered the demons, and hence Ezekiel was told to say of Nebuchadnezzar's divination:

[31] "He [1] has shaken the arrows [one marked for Rabbah and the other for Jerusalem, to be drawn out of a vessel after being shaken]. He [2] has asked by means of the teraphim; he [3] has looked into the liver [of a slain animal victim]. In his right hand the divination proved to be for Jerusalem, to set battering-rams, to open one's mouth for a slaying, to raise the sound in an alarm signal, to set battering-rams against gates, to throw up a siege rampart, to build a siege wall."—Ezekiel 21:21, 22.

---

30. To how many forms of demonism did Nebuchadnezzar resort and why, and who now was to show superiority—the demons or Jehovah? 31. How does Jehovah describe to Ezekiel Nebuchadnezzar's resort to divination, and what course would a drawing by his right hand favor?

[32] What King Nebuchadnezzar drew forth with his right hand was the favored choice, to indicate the most auspicious course. In agreement with Jehovah's will it directed the king of Babylon against Jerusalem first. That meant bringing up against Jerusalem all the Babylonian heavy siege equipment and using all the devices for besieging a strongly fortified city.

[33] How, though, did the foretelling of such an outcome to King Nebuchadnezzar's divination sound to the inhabitants of Judah and Jerusalem? Jehovah foresaw how it would seem to them, and so he said further to Ezekiel: "And it has become to them like an untrue divination in their eyes—those who are sworn with oaths to them; and he is calling error to remembrance, in order for them to be caught." —Ezekiel 21:23.

[34] The foretold divination of King Nebuchadnezzar seemed to these Jews in the land of Judah to be "untrue," because they felt that the king of Babylon would not desire to come against such a strongly walled city as Jerusalem. They felt that he could never take it if he tried. Furthermore, they could call upon the powerful international rival of Babylon, namely, Pharaoh of Egypt, to come to their assistance and turn back the military hordes of Babylon. What did they care about the oaths that they had sworn to the king of Babylon to be subject to him as vassals? They disregarded the fact that they had taken these oaths of submission to King Nebuchadnezzar as their suzerain lord in the name of Jehovah their God. So, in their self-assurance, they favored breaking their oaths to the king of Babylon by rebelling against him and relying, not upon Jehovah, but upon the Pharaoh

---

32. The drawing by the right hand directed Nebuchadnezzar against which city, and so what did this mean for him?
33. According to Ezekiel 21:23, how would the foretelling of such an outcome to Nebuchadnezzar's divination seem to the inhabitants of Judah and Jerusalem in an oath-bound relationship to him?
34. Why did Nebuchadnezzar's divination, as foretold, seem untrue to the inhabitants of the land of Judah, and what was their attitude toward the oaths that they had sworn to him?

of Egypt. They would influence their king, Zedekiah, to take this perjured, rebellious course.

[35] Through Ezekiel, Jehovah foretold that this would occur. Speaking of how King Nebuchadnezzar had put Zedekiah on the throne of Jerusalem instead of his nephew Jehoiachin in 617 B.C.E., and foretelling how King Zedekiah would treat his oath, Jehovah said to Ezekiel: "Furthermore, he [Nebuchadnezzar] took one [Zedekiah] of the royal seed and concluded a covenant with him and brought him into an oath; and the foremost men of the land he [Nebuchadnezzar] took away, in order that the kingdom might become low, unable to lift itself up, that by keeping his covenant it might stand. But he [Zedekiah] finally rebelled against him in sending his messengers to Egypt, for it to give him horses and a multitudinous people. Will he [Zedekiah] have success? Will he escape, he who is doing these things, and who has broken a covenant? And will he actually escape?" These questions Jehovah at once answers by saying:

[36] " ' "As I am alive," is the utterance of the Sovereign Lord Jehovah, "in the place of the king [Nebuchadnezzar] who put in as king the one [Zedekiah] that despised his oath and that broke his covenant, with him in the midst of Babylon he will die. And by a great military force and by a multitudinous congregation Pharaoh will not make him effective in the war, by throwing up a siege rampart and by building a siege wall, in order to cut off many souls. And he [Zedekiah] has despised an oath in breaking a covenant, and, look! he had given his hand [in a pledge of covenant keeping] and has done even all these things. He will not make his escape." ' ' "Therefore this is what the Sovereign Lord Jehovah has said: 'As I am alive, surely my oath that he has despised and my covenant that he has broken—I will even bring

---

35. How did Jehovah foretell King Zedekiah's oath-breaking rebellion, and what questions did Jehovah therefore ask?
36. What answers to those questions did Jehovah give to Ezekiel as regards oath-breaking Zedekiah and the Pharaoh of Egypt?

it upon his head.' " ' "—Ezekiel 17:13-19; 2 Chronicles 36:11-13.

[37] This rebellion against his Babylonian overlord would be an erroneous course on the part of King Zedekiah of Jerusalem. But the king of Babylon would not overlook this or forget about it. "He is calling error to remembrance, in order for them to be caught." (Ezekiel 21:23) In this way the oath-breaking Zedekiah and his counselors were to be caught in the bitter results of their own erroneous action. Hence Jehovah goes on to say to those self-deceiving oath breakers: "Therefore this is what the Sovereign Lord Jehovah has said, 'By reason of your causing your error to be remembered by your transgressions being uncovered, in order that your sins may be seen according to all your dealings, by reason of your being called to remembrance you people will be seized even by the hand.'" (Ezekiel 21:24) Their transgressions against proper covenant-keeping came out into the open or were uncovered, and this caused the offended king of Babylon to remember their error.

[38] In due time the Jews deserved to be called to remembrance for the attention that covenant breakers deserve. So their rebellion would fail, the stout walls of Jerusalem would fail them, and they would be "seized even by the hand" and led captive to Babylon.

[39] In view of this, what would King Zedekiah, as "chieftain of Israel," be obliged to do? Through the prophet Ezekiel, Jehovah tells him straight to his face, saying: "And as for you, O deadly wounded, wicked chieftain of Israel, whose day has come in the time of the error of the end, this is what the Sovereign Lord Jehovah has said, 'Remove the turban, and lift off the crown. This will not be the same. Put on high even what is low, and bring low even the high one.

---

37. What was the "error" that was to be remembered, and what caused the king of Babylon to remember it?
38. The prophecy that the covenant breakers should be "seized even by the hand" meant what?
39. What would Zedekiah, "chieftain of Israel," be obliged to do, according to the words Jehovah directed to him?

A ruin, a ruin, a ruin I shall make it. As for this also, it will certainly become no one's until he comes who has the legal right, and I must give it to him.' " —Ezekiel 21:25-27.

DOWN WITH THE "HIGH ONE"!

[40] By his rebellious course King Zedekiah deadly wounded himself, thereby making certain his death, not in peace as king in Jerusalem under the suzerainty of the king of Babylon, but as a dethroned, childless, sightless, imprisoned exile in Babylon. By breaking his oath given in the name of Jehovah and by violating his covenant with the king of Babylon, he showed his wickedness. His day for eating the bitter fruitage of his badness as "chieftain of Israel" had come. It was now the "time of the error of the end," not alone the "error" of King Zedekiah, but also the "error" of all the kingdom of Judah and Jerusalem. The time of this "end" began in the thirteenth year of Josiah as king of Jerusalem, which was also the year when the priest, "Jeremiah the son of Hilkiah," began to prophesy. (Jeremiah 1:1, 2; 25:3-11) In order to illustrate those final forty years, the prophet Ezekiel had been instructed to lie publicly on his right side before a model of Jerusalem, that thus he might "carry the error of the house of Judah." (Ezekiel 4:6, 7) Zedekiah shared in that "error of the end."

[41] King Zedekiah wore a royal turban, distinctive of his royal office, wearing also a crown. He did not voluntarily "remove the turban, and lift off the crown" from his head in obedience to the command of Jehovah through Ezekiel. This was done for him by the king of Babylon when he captured the fleeing Zedekiah and deposed him as king, destroying his royal throne and his royal city. (2 Kings 25:1-7; Ezekiel 17:19, 20)

---

40. Through what course was Zedekiah a "deadly wounded" chieftain, how did he show himself to be "wicked," and how had his "day" come in regard to the "time of the error of the end"?
41. In fulfillment of Jehovah's command, how were the turban removed and the crown lifted off, and thereby what was brought to an end, this introducing what world situation?

With that event the typical kingdom of God on earth, with a descendant of King David sitting on "Jehovah's throne" in Jerusalem, came to an end. It had stood for 463 years, from 1070 to 607 B.C.E. This left the world stage in complete control of the non-Jewish or Gentile kingdoms, with no interference or restriction by a typical, miniature kingdom of Jehovah God on earth. What a world situation that introduced!

⁴² It was Jehovah's due time for a change. This he indicated when he added: "This will not be the same. Put on high even what is low, and bring low even the high one."—Ezekiel 21:26.

⁴³ By this turning of things upside down things would not be the same for a long while. What was the "low" thing that was put on high by this destruction of the Kingdom of Judah, and what was the "high one" that was brought low? Not the family of King Zedekiah who was once high on the throne of Jerusalem in contrast with his nephew Jehoiachin's family who were then exiles in Babylon, with Jehoiachin himself lying in prison. (2 Kings 24:8-16; 25:27-30) Nor was it the high family line of King Solomon the son of David in contrast with the low obscure family line of Nathan the son of King David. (Matthew 1:6-16; Luke 3:23-31) Both of these latter family lines became involved, genealogically, with the birth of Jesus Christ at Bethlehem-Judah, for the names of Shealtiel and Zerubbabel appear in the genealogies from both Solomon and Nathan. (Matthew 1:12; Luke 3:27) So there was no special abasement of one family in favor of the other as regards producing the Messiah.

⁴⁴ Instead of the foregoing, it was the Kingdom of Judah that was the "high one" in being the miniature kingdom of Jehovah God on earth, so that it was the Kingdom of Judah that was made low by being de-

---

42. With what words did Jehovah indicate it was time for a change?
43. As to putting on high what is low and bringing low the high one, what must be said as regards Zedekiah's family in contrast with Jehoiachin's, and Solomon's family in contrast with Nathan's?
44. Hence what was the high thing that was brought low, and what was the low thing that was put on high? And how?

stroyed in 607 B.C.E. It was the non-Jewish or Gentile kingdoms of this world that were the "low" thing that was "put on high" by the destruction of the Kingdom of Judah and leaving Gentile rule in complete control of all the earth, Jehovah's chosen people of Israel being thenceforth subject to such Gentile rule.

45 So, to begin with at this point, the Babylonian World Power, the Third World Power in Bible history, dominated the entire earthly scene of international politics. Long previously, in the year 1473 B.C.E., the prophet Moses had foretold this, saying under divine inspiration to the nation of Israel: "Jehovah will indeed put you at the head and not at the tail; and you must come to be only on top, and you will not come to be on the bottom, because you keep obeying the commandments of Jehovah your God, which I am commanding you today to observe and to do.

46 "And it must occur that if you will not listen to the voice of Jehovah your God by taking care to do all his commandments and his statutes that I am commanding you today, all these maledictions must also come upon you and overtake you: Jehovah will march you and your king whom you will set up over you to a nation whom you have not known, neither you nor your forefathers; and there you will have to serve other gods, of wood and of stone. The alien resident who is in your midst will keep ascending higher and higher above you, while you—you will keep descending lower and lower. He will be the one to lend to you, while you—you will not lend to him. He will become the head, while you—you will become the tail." —Deuteronomy 28:13, 15, 36, 43, 44.

47 Being put on high in the year 607 B.C.E. when the Babylonians destroyed Jerusalem and unseated the royal line of David, the Gentile nations began to tread down or trample upon Jerusalem as signifying

45, 46. So what world power then dominated the earthly scene politically, and how had Jehovah foretold this reversal through Moses in Deuteronomy, chapter twenty-eight?
47. Thus in 607 B.C.E., what treading down or trampling began?

a kingdom of Jehovah God with a royal descendant of David seated upon "Jehovah's throne."

[48] The Gentile Times for thus trampling upon the right of the royal line of David to the throne in a kingdom set up by Jehovah God were to last for only a measured period of time. Jehovah, who caused those Gentile Times to begin, had also appointed the time for them to end. In the year 33 of our Common Era Jesus Christ spoke prophetically about those Gentile Times that were still running in his day. Foretelling a destruction of the Jerusalem of his day, he said: "There will be great necessity upon the land and wrath on this people; and they will fall by the edge of the sword and be led captive into all the nations; and Jerusalem will be trampled on by the nations, until the appointed times of the nations are fulfilled." (Luke 21:20-24) Hence the year would come when those Gentile Times would end.

[49] When? In the year when a remarkable event should take place. Not for all time would the kingship of a rightful descendant of King David seated on "Jehovah's throne" continue as a "ruin." Jehovah said: "A ruin, a ruin, a ruin I shall make it. As for this also, it will certainly become no one's until he comes who has the legal right, and I must give it to him."—Ezekiel 21:27.

"HE COMES WHO HAS THE LEGAL RIGHT"

[50] The year when the descendant of King David with the legal right should come and when Jehovah should give the kingship to that one would be at the close of the Gentile Times, or at the end of the "appointed times of the nations." Those Gentile Times did not end in the days of Jesus Christ when on earth in the first century of our Common Era. No; for Jesus said that

---

48. Who caused those Gentile Times to begin, what had he also appointed for those Times, and how did Jesus speak of them in prophecy?
49. With what words, in Ezekiel 21:27, did Jehovah foretell the event at which those Gentile Times would end?
50. Why did Jesus Christ not seek any kingship during his days on earth?

Jerusalem must be destroyed a second time and thereafter the Gentile Times must continue on still farther until they are fulfilled. That is why Jesus Christ did not seek any kingship in his days on earth. (John 6:14, 15) This is why Jehovah did not give to Jesus Christ the Davidic kingship at his sacrificial death, resurrection and ascension to Jehovah's right hand in heaven.—Acts 1:6, 7; 2:29-37.

[51] Jerusalem's second destruction occurred in the year 70 C.E. at the hands of the Roman legions, and Jesus Christ foretold that the Gentile Times were to keep on running for a time after that. (Luke 21:24) So, after his ascension to heaven in 33 C.E., Jesus Christ must wait in heaven until those Gentile Times ended. Then was God's appointed time for the Gentile nations to be brought low and for God's Messianic kingdom of a descendant of King David to be put on high. Then was the due time for Jesus Christ to come with his legal right to the kingship and ask Jehovah and for Jehovah to give him the kingship. This is what the Hebrew Christians were told, in Hebrews 10:12, 13, concerning Jesus Christ: "This man offered one sacrifice for sins perpetually and sat down at the right hand of God, from then on awaiting until his enemies should be placed as a stool for his feet." (Psalm 110:1, 2; 2:7-9; Acts 2:34-36) Knowing from Daniel's prophecy (4:16-27) the length of those "appointed times of the [Gentile] nations" enabled Jesus Christ to calculate when they would end, namely, in 1914 C.E.

[52] The prophet Daniel was a fellow exile of Ezekiel, and very appropriately, then, Jehovah as the "Ancient of Days" gave Daniel a vision of the coming of the Messiah to him at the end of the Gentile Times to receive the kingship as the Permanent Heir of King David. Daniel writes: "But as for the rest of the

51. After his ascension, how long was Jesus Christ due to wait on Jehovah's right hand, and then what action was due to take place?
52. What vision was Daniel given of the coming of David's descendant to receive the kingship, and in whom did Jesus Christ look for that vision to be fulfilled, and when?

[Gentile] beasts, their rulerships were taken away, . . . I kept on beholding in the visions of the night, and, see there! with the clouds of the heavens someone like a son of man happened to be coming; and to the Ancient of Days he gained access, and they brought him up close even before that One. And to him there were given rulership and dignity and kingdom, that the peoples, national groups and languages should all serve even him. His rulership is an indefinitely lasting rulership that will not pass away, and his kingdom one that will not be brought to ruin." (Daniel 7:12-14) Jesus Christ looked forward to the fulfillment of that prophetic vision in himself in heaven when the Gentile Times ended in 1914.

[53] With the end of the Gentile Times in 1914, in the lunar month of Tishri (September-October), the appointed time arrived for Jehovah to put a stop to the Gentile nations (including Christendom) in their trampling upon what ancient Jerusalem symbolized, namely, the kingdom in the hands of the anointed descendant of King David reigning on "Jehovah's throne." Jehovah did this by then giving the active Davidic kingship to the one "who has the legal right," that is to say, to His anointed Son, Jesus Christ. Thereafter the Gentile nations could tread down and trample upon the Middle Eastern site of ancient Jerusalem all they wanted to in a literal sense, but they would no longer be trampling upon the real kingdom of the anointed descendant of King David, who has the legal right to it. He sits on "Jehovah's throne" in the heavens, and the heavily armed nations of today can never overturn and destroy that heavenly throne or the "city of the living God, heavenly Jerusalem."—Hebrews 12:22.

[54] How refreshing it is to the spirits of true lovers

---

53. At the end of the Gentile Times, how did Jehovah put an end to the trampling carried on by the Gentile nations, despite their occupying the site of earthly Jerusalem?
54. What will happen shortly to the modern-day antitypical unfaithful Jerusalem, and how will this affect the Messianic kingdom of God as set up at the end of the Gentile Times?

of God's Messianic kingdom to know these wonderful facts! Shortly the modern antitype of ancient unfaithful Jerusalem will be brought to her perpetual ruin as pictured by the ruin of Jerusalem in the year 607 B.C.E. But that will not signify the ruin and destruction of the Messianic kingdom of God, inasmuch as Christendom's claim to be Christ's kingdom is false and has greatly misrepresented the Biblical facts. The hypocritical Christ's kingdom on earth must go! The true heavenly kingdom of Christ must remain in heavenly power for the blessing of all mankind for whom Jesus Christ died as a ransom sacrifice. The Gentile nations, as well as Christendom, will not be able to interfere with this blessing. Their "appointed times" having run out in 1914 C.E., they will be brought to eternal ruin in the "war of the great day of God the Almighty" at the now-shaping-up world situation called Har–Magedon.—Revelation 16:14-16.

AFTER THE DESTRUCTION OF CHRISTENDOM, WHAT?

[55] Destruction of the political Gentile nations follows that of Christendom. In an ancient parallel to this, destruction of the Ammonite capital of Rabbah followed that of ancient Jerusalem in 607 B.C.E. It was Jehovah's will that Jerusalem should fall first. That is why he took care that King Nebuchadnezzar's divination should send him first against Jerusalem, down the right-hand branch of the crossroads. (Ezekiel 21: 19-22; Jeremiah 25:17-29) In a warning for Rabbah of the sons of Ammon not to gloat over the ruin of Jerusalem, Jehovah told Ezekiel what to say:

[56] "And you, O son of man, prophesy, and you must say, 'This is what the Sovereign Lord Jehovah has said concerning the sons of Ammon and concerning the reproach from them.' And you must say, 'A sword, a sword drawn for a slaughter, polished to cause it to

---

55. Destruction on whom follows that of Christendom, and how was a parallel of this given in Ezekiel's day?
56. In order that Rabbah of Ammon might not gloat over ruined Jerusalem, what did Jehovah tell Ezekiel to say to Ammon in warning?

devour, in order to glitter, because of their beholding for you an unreality, because of their divining for you a lie, in order to put you on the necks of the slain ones, the wicked men whose day has come in the time of the error of the end. Return it to its sheath. In the place that you were created, in the land of your origin, I shall judge you. And I will pour out upon you my denunciation. With the fire of my fury I shall blow upon you, and I will give you into the hand of men who are unreasoning, the craftsmen of ruination. For the fire you will become fuel. Your own blood will prove to be in the midst of the land. You will not be remembered, for I myself, Jehovah, have spoken.'" —Ezekiel 21:28-32.

[57] In due time the king of Babylon was used to bring ruin upon the land of the sons of Ammon. This occurred because the prophets of Ammon were "beholding" an escape for Rabbah from the "sword" of King Nebuchadnezzar, and this had to be proved "an unreality." The diviners of Ammon were predicting that Rabbah would be spared, and this needed to be proved "a lie." The purpose of this was to "put" the slain ones of Ammon, as it were, "on the necks" of the slain wicked Israelites, as if in one pile of dead ones. From this historic example, let all reproachers of the Sovereign Lord Jehovah take warning. The "sword" of the "war of the great day of God the Almighty" will reach them in their own land. In the land of their origin their blood will be poured out. The death that they divined and desired for Jehovah's true people will come upon their own selves as a denunciation from Jehovah. Let them imagine no unreality about this; let them make no mistake about this. It is Jehovah who has spoken it. It will therefore not fail to come true, to His vindication.

---

57. From that prophecy as historically fulfilled, what warning should all reproachers of Jehovah take, and why will the prophecy not fail of fulfillment upon them?

Chapter 13

Christendom's Associates
Turn upon Her!

IT IS often said that history has the habit of repeating itself. Or, the future is only the past entered into a new case. As far as the general features are concerned, it is true that world events that form the subject matter of a history do repeat themselves. Similar causes would produce such repeating of events.

² If we study the calamitous events of human history, we can take them as warning examples and can learn their inducing causes. Thus we can know what to avoid in order not to have those calamitous events repeat themselves upon us. This is one of the benefits that we can get from studying Bible history, just as the Christian apostle Paul suggests. When writing about the calamitous happenings of the nation of Israel in their journey of forty years from Egypt to the Promised Land, he expressed it this way:

³ "Now these things became our examples, for us not to be persons desiring injurious things, even as they [the Israelites] desired them. . . . Now these things went on befalling them as examples, and they were written for a warning to us upon whom the ends of the systems of things have arrived. Consequently let him that thinks he is standing beware that he does not fall."—1 Corinthians 10:6-12.

---

1. To what extent is it that history repeats itself?
2, 3. From history how can we learn to avoid calamitous events such as occurred to others previously, and, in 1 Corinthians 10:6-12, how does Paul point to the benefits of studying Bible history?

⁴ The ancient city of Jerusalem was one that did not beware and so did not profit by the warning example of history, even in her own family relationship. What wonder, then, that her God, when telling of the calamity that would come upon her for her unfaithfulness to Him, went on to say: "And you will certainly be profaned within yourself before the eyes of the nations, and you will have to know that I am Jehovah." (Ezekiel 22:16) Centuries-old Christendom has been just as heedless of the warning examples of Bible history. There is only one outcome to be expected. Just as surely as ancient Jerusalem was made to know, in a disastrous way, the God with whom she was dealing, so Christendom will have Jerusalem's terrible experience repeat itself upon her, and that very soon.

⁵ Keeping Christendom in mind as the modern-day antitype, let us now consider the deserved punishment that God foretold, years in advance, and that was to come upon ancient Jerusalem. Making a written record of this divine prophecy, the prophet Ezekiel in exile in Babylon says: "And the word of Jehovah proceeded to come to me, saying: 'Son of man, two women, the daughters of one mother, there happened to be. And they began to prostitute themselves in Egypt. In their youth they committed prostitution. There their breasts were squeezed, and there they pressed the bosoms of their virginity. And their names were Oholah the older one and Oholibah her sister, and they came to be mine and began to give birth to sons and daughters. And as for their names, Oholah is Samaria, and Oholibah is Jerusalem.' "—Ezekiel 23:1-4.

⁶ Up to the time of its destruction by the Assyrians in the year 740 B.C.E., Samaria was the capital city

4. What did Jehovah say would happen to Jerusalem for not heeding the warning example of history in her own family relationship, and so what will Christendom experience for likewise being heedless?
5. Where did the symbolic Oholah and Oholibah begin to commit prostitution, but to whom did they come to belong, and what did they produce for that owner?
6. As cities, what were Samaria and Jerusalem respectively, who was their "mother," and how was it that in Egypt they practiced prostitution spiritually?

of the Northern Kingdom of Israel, composed out of ten of the twelve secular tribes of Israel. On the other hand, Jerusalem was the capital of the Southern Kingdom of Judah, composed of the remaining tribes of the Jewish people. So their two capital cities are used to represent or picture their respective kingdoms. They both came from one parent organization or "mother," namely, the national organization that descended from Abraham, Isaac and Jacob and the twelve sons of Jacob. Symbolically they were spoken of as the "daughters" of that mother organization. Jacob and his sons and their families moved down from Palestine into Egypt in the year 1728 B.C.E., in the days when his son Joseph was the prime minister and food administrator of Egypt under Pharaoh. There the tribes that descended from Jacob's twelve sons and that make up the two daughter organizations were influenced to practice spiritual prostitution. In what way?

⁷ By defiling themselves with the idol worship that was then prevalent in Egypt. By doing this they were having unclean, immoral connection with the false gods and idols of pagan Egypt. In the prophecy of Ezekiel 20:4-8 Jehovah reminded certain exiled elders of Israel about such spiritual prostitution on the part of their forefathers in Egypt. Of course, away back there the Northern Kingdom of Israel with its capital at Samaria did not exist. (1 Kings 16:23-28) But the ten tribes that eventually rebelled to form that kingdom did exist, and thus the symbolic woman Oholah was in formation. She was composed of the most of the tribes of Israel, and these included the tribes that descended from the two oldest sons of Jacob, namely, Reuben and Simeon, and also the tribes of Manasseh and Ephraim that descended from Joseph, Jacob's first-born son by his beloved wife Rachel. Rightly, then, the symbolic Oholah could be spoken of as the "older

7. How did the symbolic Oholah and Oholibah practice spiritual prostitution down in Egypt, and how could the symbolic Oholah be rightly spoken of as the older of the two sisters?

one" of the two symbolic daughters of the one mother.
—Genesis 29:32-35; 30:22-24.

⁸ The name given to her, Oholah, means "Her Tent,"
that is, a tent for carrying on religious worship. When
the Northern Kingdom of Israel was established in 997
B.C.E., it went over to the worship of the golden calf and
later added to this idolatrous worship the worship of the
false god Baal. In this way the symbolic Oholah forgot
Jehovah and cast him behind her back and set up her
own tent for idolatrous worship. Jehovah's tent was not
in her.

⁹ The name of her symbolic sister was Oholibah.
This name is understood to mean "My Tent Is in Her."
It being a God-given name, it signified that Jehovah's
tent of worship was in the symbolic Oholibah, the
Southern Kingdom of Judah. This kingdom ruled over
the two tribes of Judah and Benjamin and also had
the support of the religious tribe of Levi. Levi was
the third son of the patriarch Jacob, Judah was the
fourth son, and Benjamin the twelfth and last son, so
that the symbolic Oholibah was well pictured as the
younger of the two daughters of the "one mother."
The tent containing Jehovah's ark of the covenant was
served by the qualified men of the tribe of Levi and
came to be located at Jerusalem after King David captured that city in 1070 B.C.E. and made it his capital.
In that city, also, David's son Solomon built the gorgeous temple for Jehovah's worship, and it was still
standing in the day of Ezekiel's prophecy about the
symbolic Oholah and Oholibah. So the name Oholibah
fitted the Southern Kingdom of Judah, for Jehovah's
tent or temple of worship was in her.—2 Samuel 5:
1-9; 6:11 to 7:13.

¹⁰ "And they came to be mine," said Jehovah concerning those two symbolic women. (Ezekiel 23:4)

8. What does Oholah's name mean, and how did it fit her?
9. Why did the name Oholibah fit the younger "sister" even in Ezekiel's day of prophesying about her?
10. When did the two symbolic women become Jehovah's, how did
they give to him sons and daughters, and why would unfaithfulness to
him be adulterous?

When was that? It was in the year 1513 B.C.E., when Jehovah delivered the "mother" organization, the twelve tribes of Israel, from bondage to Egypt on the night of the first celebration of the Passover, and more specifically so when Jehovah brought the twelve tribes formally into a covenant with him through the mediator Moses at Mount Sinai in Arabia. (Exodus 12:50 to 13:21; 19:3 to 24:8) Thereafter sons and daughters were brought forth in covenant relationship with Jehovah as their God. How? This was by reason of the action of their fathers in making this national covenant with Jehovah, the Deliverer of His people. They were all subject to Him because of being the children of the nation that was married to Him like a wife to a husband or husbandly owner. (Jeremiah 3:14; 31:32) Unfaithfulness to Him was adulterous.

[11] The symbolic "two women, the daughters of one mother," definitely took form in the year 997 B.C.E., or 516 years after the rescue of the nation of Israel from the slave-driving Egypt. In that year ten of the tribes of Israel refused further allegiance to the royal house of David and set up their own kingdom, the final capital of which proved to be Samaria, some thirty-five miles to the north of Jerusalem. This Northern Kingdom, with capital at Samaria, was symbolized by Oholah. The Southern Kingdom, with capital at Jerusalem, was symbolized by Oholibah. —Ezekiel 23:4.

"OHOLAH" SETS A BAD HISTORICAL EXAMPLE

[12] This crackup of the twelve-tribe nation of Israel did not dissolve its covenant with Jehovah as entered into through the mediator Moses at Mount Sinai. Both of the new kingdoms were still in this covenant of the Mosaic Law and were therefore still subject to Jehovah as to a spiritual Husband. (1 Kings 11:29-39)

---

11. In what year did those two symbolic "women" definitely take form, and in what way?
12. Did the cracking up of Israel dissolve Jehovah's covenant toward the two resulting nations, and how did the symbolic Oholah refuse wifely subjection to her husbandly Owner?

But the Northern Kingdom, the symbolic Oholah, refused wifelike subjection to Jehovah and became idolatrous. She lost her trust in Him as her Protector and began to play politics with the pagan nations round about, especially imperial Assyria to the northeast. (2 Kings 15:17-22; Hosea 5:13; 12:1) Did this getting on friendly terms with the militarized political world power of Assyria work out well for the ten-tribe Kingdom of Israel? Did Assyria prove to be a staunch, true friend to this symbolic Oholah? Note what Jehovah goes on to say, in Ezekiel 23:5-10:

¹³ "And Oholah began to prostitute herself, while subject to me, and kept lusting after those passionately loving her, after the Assyrians, who were near, governors clothed with blue material, and their deputy rulers—desirable young men all of them, cavalrymen riding horses. And she continued giving forth her prostitutions upon them, the choicest sons of Assyria all of them; and with all those after whom she lusted —with their dungy idols—she defiled herself. And her prostitutions carried from Egypt she did not leave, for with her they had lain down in her youth, and they were the ones that pressed the bosoms of her virginity and they kept pouring out their immoral intercourse upon her. Therefore I gave her into the hand of those passionately loving her, into the hand of the sons of Assyria, toward whom she had lusted. They were the ones that uncovered her nakedness. Her sons and her daughters they took, and her they killed even with sword. And she came to be infamy to women, and acts of judgment were what they executed upon her."

¹⁴ Losing her faith in the invisible Jehovah and putting her trust in the impressive-looking military might of idolatrous Assyria did not save and preserve the spiritually adulterous Oholah, the ten-tribe Kingdom of Israel. Abandoning the One who had delivered her

---

13. What do Jehovah's words in Ezekiel 23:5-10 show as to whether Assyria proved to be a staunch, true friend to symbolic Oholah?
14. So the trusting of "Oholah" in Assyria caused Jehovah to do what to her?

out of Egypt, she was abandoned by Him to the brutal Assyrians who had passionately loved to force a worldly alliance upon her.

[15] Jehovah let "Oholah" fall into the violent hands of those with whom she had preferred to be in a covenant, the Assyrians. These acted as executioners of divine judgment upon her, giving her the treatment that an adulterous wife deserved. With the sword of war they punitively killed her as a political nation, destroying her national capital, Samaria. But first they took captive her sons and daughters, herding them away into slavery in another land. They made no allowance for her to be revived and restored as a people and kingdom. They "uncovered her nakedness" by stripping the land of her Israelite children, deporting them afar off; and then, to take their place on the land, Assyria imported pagan peoples from various parts of the Assyrian Empire.—2 Kings 18:8-12; 17:1-24.

[16] Good reason this was for the criminally executed "Oholah" to become "infamy to women," that is, to pagan kingdoms of that time. They looked down upon her as a nation that had gained shameful infamy for herself and they shuddered at her fate. Her kingdom ceased to exist permanently in 740 B.C.E. at the destruction of Samaria and the deportation of her surviving sons and daughters.

HISTORIC FORECAST FOR OUR DAY

[17] Did symbolic Oholah come to be "infamy" to her sister Oholibah, the Southern Kingdom of Judah? Did Oholibah appreciate this warning example of history and profit by it? Did she therefore avoid the spiritually adulterous course of her sister in order that history might not repeat itself upon her and she might not have to drink the cup of judgment that her sister had been obliged to drink? What did Oholibah indicate that

---

15. As executioners of what did the Assyrians act toward symbolic Oholah, and how did they expose her nakedness?
16. How did "Oholah" come to be "infamy to women"?
17. In view of "Oholah" as a warning example, what questions arise as to the symbolic Oholibah?

her modern-day counterpart Christendom would do in our times? Jehovah pointed to the course that Oholah's sister kingdom was pursuing, saying, in Ezekiel 23:11-17:

[18] "When her sister Oholibah got to see it, then she exercised her sensual desire more ruinously than she, and her prostitution more than the fornication of her sister. For the sons of Assyria she lusted, governors and deputy rulers who were near, clothed with perfect taste, cavalrymen riding horses—desirable young men all of them. And I got to see that, because she had defiled herself, both of them had one way. And she kept adding to her acts of prostitution when she got to see the men in carvings upon the wall, images of Chaldeans carved in vermilion, girded with belts on their hips, with pendant turbans on their heads, having the appearance of warriors, all of them, the likeness of the sons of Babylon, Chaldeans as respects the land of their birth. And she began to lust after them at the sight of her eyes and proceeded to send messengers to them in Chaldea. And the sons of Babylon kept coming in to her, to the bed of expressions of love, and defiling her with their immoral intercourse; and she continued getting defiled by them, and her soul began to turn away disgusted from them."

[19] Oholibah defied the warning example in the history of her sister kingdom, Oholah. Jehovah got to see that both Oholibah and Oholah "had one way," only that Oholibah pursued the way in a more extreme fashion. Forgetting Jehovah and her marriage-like covenant with Him, she went playing politics with that mighty military world power, Assyria. This was notoriously so in the days of King Ahaz of Jerusalem. Despite the counsel of Jehovah by the prophet Isaiah, King Ahaz called the Assyrian conqueror Tiglath-pileser to his aid against the allied kingdoms of Syria

18. In what words, in Ezekiel 23:11-17, did Jehovah point to the course that the symbolic Oholibah was then pursuing?
19. How did the symbolic Oholibah defy the warning example of her sister Oholah, and what outcome for Assyria posed a problem for Oholibah?

and Israel. (Isaiah 7:1-20; 2 Kings 16:5-10, 17, 18) King Hezekiah, successor to Ahaz, saw how disastrously Oholah's courting the political favor of Assyria ended in the year 740 B.C.E., with the destruction of Samaria and its kingdom. Although King Hezekiah was delivered from the Assyrian king Sennacherib, he entertained the friendly advances made by the Babylonians. For this he was rebuked by Jehovah. (Isaiah 37:36 to 39:7; 2 Kings 19:35 to 20:18) After the Babylonians overthrew the Assyrian World Power by destroying its capital Nineveh about 632 B.C.E., this posed a serious problem for Jerusalem.

²⁰ Four years later, in 628 B.C.E., the conquering king of Egypt put King Jehoiakim upon the throne of Jerusalem in place of his brother Jehoahaz. But in the year 620 B.C.E. the king of Babylon subjected Jehoiakim as a king tributary to Babylon. In the year 617 B.C.E. the king of Babylon installed Jehoiakim's brother Zedekiah as king on the throne of Jerusalem. (2 Kings 23:31 to 24:18) During the reigns of these two kings the symbolic Oholibah "exercised her sensual desire more ruinously" than did her sister Oholah by courting the political favor of the Babylonian World Power. This international intercourse kept up in both cases until at last Jerusalem tired of the domination of Babylon. So "her soul began to turn away disgusted" from the Babylonians by rebellion against the king of Babylon.—2 Kings 24:1, 18-20.

²¹ How, though, did Jehovah feel about this spiritually adulterous course on the part of the symbolic Oholibah? This is something that her modern-day counterpart Christendom should have considered long ago. In Ezekiel 23:18-21 Jehovah tells how he felt by saying: "And she went on uncovering her acts of prostitution and uncovering her nakedness, so that my soul turned away disgusted from company with her, just as my

20. How did the king of Babylon undo the political action of the king of Egypt toward Jerusalem, how did the symbolic Oholibah court Babylon's political favor, and how did she show her tiring of this?
21. In Ezekiel 23:18-21, how did Jehovah say how he felt about the adulterous course of the symbolic Oholibah?

soul had turned away disgusted from company with her sister [Oholah]. And she kept multiplying her acts of prostitution to the point of calling to mind the days of her youth, when she prostituted herself in the land of Egypt. And she kept lusting in the style of concubines belonging to those whose fleshly member is as the fleshly member of male asses and whose genital organ is as the genital organ of male horses. And you continued calling attention to the loose conduct of your youth by the pressing of your bosoms from Egypt onward, for the sake of the breasts of your youth."

²² Since Jehovah's very being had turned away in disgust from company with her adulterous sister Oholah, why should not his soul turn away in disgust from company with Oholibah because of like loose conduct with the idolatrous Babylonians? Jehovah is consistent with himself and so harmonized his actions toward both sisters, Oholah and Oholibah.

²³ How did Oholibah go "calling to mind the days of her youth, when she prostituted herself in the land of Egypt"? She did so by looking southward to Egypt for military aid when "her soul began to turn away disgusted" from the Babylonians by rebelling against the king of Babylon. (Ezekiel 17:7-10, 15-17) In the language Jehovah here uses, what contempt he expresses for her animalistically passionate course that was unbecoming to a wife but quite usual with a readily available concubine. He says: "And she kept lusting in the style of concubines belonging to those whose fleshly member is as the fleshly member of male asses and whose genital organ is as the genital organ of male horses." Or, as the *New English Bible* of 1970 words it: "She was infatuated with their male prostitutes, whose members were like those of asses and whose seed came in floods like that of horses."—Ezekiel 23: 20, *NW; NEB*.

---

22. How did Jehovah harmonize his course toward Oholibah with that toward Oholah?
23. How did Oholibah call to mind the days of her youth when she prostituted herself in Egypt, and her passion became like that of concubines belonging to whom?

THE SLIGHTED POLITICAL LOVERS REACT

[24] In the light of what happened to the symbolic Oholah for her spiritually immoral course, what was her sister Oholibah consistently to receive at the hand of Jehovah in his disgust? It was yet some time, possibly two years, to the beginning of the final Babylonian siege of Jerusalem, when Jehovah answered the question by saying to that unfaithful city in which His "tent" was still standing:

[25] "Therefore, O Oholibah, this is what the Sovereign Lord Jehovah has said, 'Here I am rousing up your passionate lovers against you, those from whom your soul has turned away in disgust, and I will bring them in against you on all sides, the sons of Babylon and all the Chaldeans, Pekod and Shoa and Koa, all the sons of Assyria with them, desirable young men, governors and deputy rulers all of them, warriors and summoned ones, riding on horses, all of them. And they must come in against you with rattling of war chariots and wheels, and a congregation of peoples, with large shield and buckler and helmet. They will set themselves against you all around, and I will give judgment over to them, and they must judge you with their judgments. And I will express my ardor against you, and they must take action against you in rage.

[26] " 'Your nose and your ears they will remove, and the remainder of you will fall even by the sword. Your sons and your daughters they themselves will take, and the remainder of you will be devoured by the fire. And they will certainly strip off you your garments and take away your beautiful articles. And I shall actually cause your loose conduct to cease from you, and your prostitution carried from the land of Egypt; and you will not raise your eyes to them, and Egypt you will remember no more.' "—Ezekiel 23:22-27.

24, 25. Consistent with what happened to the symbolic Oholah for her spiritual adultery, what did Jehovah say, in Ezekiel 23:22-25a, he would do to her sister Oholibah?

26. According to Jehovah's words in Ezekiel 23:25b-27, what would the Babylonians and their allies do to symbolic Oholibah?

²⁷ What a horrible shock to have one's passionate lovers turn suddenly upon one! How could such a change of sentiment occur so quickly? It is Jehovah who brings this about against the wifelike organization that has proved false to him. It is he who raises up and brings down upon her those whom we would hardly think he would use as his instrument in executing judgment upon her, her associates or allies who once passionately loved her as a vassal kingdom. They are not just the common rabble, but are governors, deputy rulers, professional warriors, summoned ones called in for counsel, men of equestrian rank. There will be no escaping for her, inasmuch as they will come in against her on all sides. The war chariots, the rattling of the wheels of which she hears, can dart like the lightning and overtake her. The congregation of well-protected military peoples can hem her in. Are they to execute the judgments judicially handed down by men? No, for they are mere instruments of execution!

²⁸ The judicial decisions are those of Jehovah, and he turns over the execution of these to his chosen human agencies. But they are allowed to apply these judicial decisions according to their own cruel way of execution judgment. Jehovah has jealous ardor against the symbolic Oholibah, and his executional forces on earth have rage; and when divine ardor and Assyro-Babylonian rage combine in one united action, it really means woe for Oholibah.

²⁹ Is it ghastly cruel to cut off a woman's nose and her ears, horribly disfiguring her? Yes, but that was the way those ancient world imperialists punished adulteresses. Oholibah had turned adulterously away from her husbandly owner, Jehovah. Like an outraged

27. Who is it that raises up against "Oholibah" those least expected, and how is escape barred for her, and are mere judicial decisions as handed down by men executed upon her?
28. Whose judicial decisions are executed, how are they applied, and with what emotions are they executed?
29. The cutting off of nose and ears was the penalty for what moral crime, and how was this punishment inflicted upon the symbolic Oholibah?

jealous husband, he set his mark upon the face of his unfaithful mate. Her beautiful national appearance was ruined. Her anointed king and other prominent officials, who were like the "very breath of our nostrils," were taken away. (Lamentations 4:20) Her priests and judges and literary men, who were like ears to listen and give balance to the headship of the nation, were also violently removed. With so mutilated a national appearance, how could she "save face" before other nations? She could not!

³⁰ After she had thus been mutilated, what was remaining of adulterous Oholibah was to fall by the executional sword of the victorious Babylonians, her former passionate lovers. Alas, then, for her sons and daughters! Those of them surviving were to be taken captive and enslaved. The remainder of her, in the way of nonportable material properties, was to be "devoured by the fire." She was to be exposed naked, stripped of her garments and beautiful articles with which she had practiced her allurements as a nation. Such spiritual adultery as hers must cease from the earth forever!

³¹ Oholibah's tiring of certain ones like the Babylonians with whom she had committed spiritual prostitution did not mean that she had turned in heartfelt repentance to Jehovah to become reconciled with him. She was still given over to committing spiritual immorality with idolatrous gods. She was still inclined to violate her covenant with Jehovah and adulterously enter alliances with a pagan nation if she felt that this would save her as a nation. Fully aware of this, Jehovah went on to say to symbolic Oholibah:

³² "For this is what the Sovereign Lord Jehovah has said, 'Here I am giving you into the hand of those whom you have hated, into the hand of those from

---

30. What was to be done with what remained of her, human and inanimate, irremovable, leaving her in what appearance?
31. What indicates whether Oholibah's tiring of the Babylonians meant her repenting for reconciliation with Jehovah or not?
32. Into whose hand did Jehovah tell Oholibah, in Ezekiel 23:28-31, that he would give her, and what would then happen to her, and why?

whom your soul has turned away disgusted. And they must take action against you in hatred and take away all your product of toil and leave you naked and nude; and the nudeness of your acts of fornication and your loose conduct and your acts of prostitution must be uncovered. There will be a doing of these things to you because of your going like a prostitute after the nations, on account of the fact that you defiled yourself with their dungy idols. In the way of your sister [Oholah] you have walked; and I shall have to give her cup into your hand.' "—Ezekiel 23:28-31.

[33] Oholibah, representing unfaithful Jerusalem, was not to think that by her coming to hate the Babylonians and turning away from them in soulful disgust she could escape the consequences of her past spiritually immoral connections with them. It was not as easy as all that. The hated Babylonians were not willing to forget her engagements with them. And what about her superior engagements to Jehovah, her husbandly owner? Repentance over her loose conduct with the Babylonians was not repentance toward Jehovah. So He was disposed to let Oholibah settle for the violation of both her obligations to the Babylonians and her obligations to Him by surrendering her into the hands of her estranged lovers, the Babylonians.

[34] Her nakedness ought to be exposed to all nations by the laying bare of her record as a shameless "streetwalker," a prostitute out hunting for suckers on a national scale. Her God, whose religious "tent" was in her, must be punishing her for something! If her infidelity and her crimes against him had not been so enormous, her punishment would not have been so great! That was the case with her sister Oholah. So now why not also with her herself?

[35] Oholibah was not to think that she was an excep-

33. Could Oholibah escape consequences by taking one-sided action, and for what engagements till now was Jehovah disposed to let her make a settlement?
34. Oholibah's being made naked caused the nations to reason how as to the cause therefor?
35. What false reasoning was Oholibah not to indulge in as to there being an exception to the rule concerning consequences?

tion to the rule. Irreversibly her sister Oholah had suffered for certain causes. What historical basis was there, then, for her to think that history would not repeat itself upon her for just the same causes, yes, aggravated causes? Like crimes, like punishment! Jehovah showed in advance that he would make no exception of Oholibah, even though she represented Jerusalem, by saying to her:

[36] "This is what the Sovereign Lord Jehovah has said, 'The cup of your sister you will drink, the deep and wide one. You will become an object of laughter and derision, the cup containing much. With drunkenness and grief you will be filled, with the cup of astonishment and of desolation, the cup of your sister Samaria. And you will have to drink it and drain it out, and its earthenware fragments you will gnaw, and your breasts you will tear out. "For I myself have spoken," is the utterance of the Sovereign Lord Jehovah.' "—Ezekiel 23:32-34.

[37] Apparently for ninety-three years, from the time of Samaria's destruction in 740 B.C.E. to the beginning of Jerusalem's "time of the error of the end" in 647 B.C.E., the adulterous Oholibah had time to profit from the historical warning example of her sister Oholah. Unhappily, she did not do so. (Ezekiel 4:6, 7; 21:25) At the hand of her forsaken husbandly owner, Jehovah, she must drink the same kind of potion that her sister Oholah (Samaria) did in 740 B.C.E. Only the cupful thereof will be larger in quantity, "the cup containing much" because it is "the deep and wide one." She will drink the potion of becoming an "object of laughter and derision" to all the maliciously minded nations round about. She will be astonished at the shame and desolation that will come upon her. Just to think that Jehovah would let this come upon her!

---

36. Because he would make no exception, what cup did Jehovah say Oholibah would drink, and to what extent?
37. Jehovah's description of the "cup" indicated what about the amount of the potion that Oholibah was to drink, and at what she had to drink why would she be astonished, made drunk, grieved?

The cupful of national destruction, deportation from her God-given homeland and the international disgrace will be enough to make her feel drunk. She will be filled with grief at her own undone condition, not at the reproach that she brought upon the name of her husbandly owner, Jehovah. However great the potion, it will not be more than her due.

[38] Not a drop of the potion must she fail to drink. Even the moisture that has soaked into the porous absorbent material of the cup she must imbibe by gnawing and crunching the "earthenware fragments" of the cup. To the full she must pay the divine penalty for her unfaithful, adulterous course toward the God of her covenant. What Jehovah spoke concerning her she must undergo. The warning example in the case of her sister was nothing to be flouted!

HOW THE RULE WORKS UPON CHRISTENDOM

[39] Since this rule worked so unerringly with the symbolic Oholah and Oholibah, what now is to be expected with regard to Christendom, the present-day counterpart of these two symbolic sisters, Samaria and Jerusalem? Will Bible history fail to repeat itself upon Christendom? Whereas Oholibah (Jerusalem) drank the same cup as her sister Oholah (Samaria) did for imitating Oholah's conduct toward Jehovah, will Christendom escape drinking the same cup even though she has imitated the conduct of both Oholah and Oholibah? If the religious clergy and church people of Christendom think so, they are terribly mistaken, forasmuch as the true God, Jehovah, is consistent in all his ways. What makes it more certain that Christendom will experience the repeating of history and drink the same cup as her ancient prototypes is that Jehovah has spoken it in his written Word, in the recorded prophecies of the last book of the Bible.

---

38. How did Jehovah figuratively describe how the symbolic Oholibah would pay the full penalty for unfaithfulness to Him?
39. In view of the experience of symbolic Oholibah and Oholah, what questions arise as to the future of Christendom, and what gives us certainty as to the answers to these questions?

⁴⁰ What was it that Oholibah, like her sister Oholah, was to experience by 607 B.C.E.? For one thing, the turning of her passionate lovers upon her. Their action would result in her being stripped naked; she will be rendered childless, her children being led away captive or falling by the sword of punitive warfare; she will be burned with fire; her queenly dignity will be disgraced, as her royal position among the nations disintegrates. Is anything like that to be repeated in modern history? Listen now to what Jehovah has spoken through Jesus Christ as it booms forth more loudly than ever from the sound track of his written Word:

⁴¹ "The waters that you saw, where the harlot is sitting, mean peoples and crowds and nations and tongues. And the ten horns that you saw, and the wild beast [that bears the ten horns upon its seven heads], these will hate the harlot and will make her devastated and naked, and will eat up her fleshy parts and will completely burn her with fire. For God put it into their hearts to carry out his thought, even to carry out their one thought by giving their kingdom to the wild beast, until the words of God will have been accomplished. And the woman whom you saw means the great city that has a kingdom over the kings of the earth."

⁴² "Get out of her, my people, if you do not want to share with her in her sins, and if you do not want to receive part of her plagues. For her sins have massed together clear up to heaven, and God has called her acts of injustice to mind. Render to her even as she herself rendered, and do to her twice as much, yes, twice the number of the things she did; in the cup in which she put a mixture put twice as much of the mixture for her. To the extent that she glorified herself and lived in shameless luxury, to that extent give her torment and mourning. For in her heart she keeps

40. What was it that the symbolic Oholibah would experience by 607 B.C.E. at the hands of her alienated lovers, and to learn about any repeating of history to what must we turn?
41, 42. What does Revelation 17:15-18 and 18:4-8 say about similar calamities befalling an immoral person?

saying, 'I sit a queen, and I am no widow, and I shall never see mourning.' That is why in one day her plagues will come, death and mourning and famine, and she will be completely burned with fire, because Jehovah God, who judged her, is strong."

⁴³ To whom do those words of Revelation 17:15-18 and 18:4-8 apply? Who is the "harlot" in this case? From that last book of the Bible Jehovah by his angel speaks in answer: "Come, I will show you the judgment upon the great harlot who sits on many waters, with whom the kings of the earth committed fornication, whereas those who inhabit the earth were made drunk with the wine of her fornication." "And he carried me away in the power of the spirit into a wilderness. And I caught sight of a woman sitting upon a scarlet-colored wild beast that was full of blasphemous names and that had seven heads and ten horns. And the woman was arrayed in purple and scarlet, and was adorned with gold and precious stone and pearls and had in her hand a golden cup that was full of disgusting things and the unclean things of her fornication. And upon her forehead was written a name, a mystery: 'Babylon the Great, the mother of the harlots and of the disgusting things of the earth.' And I saw that the woman was drunk with the blood of the holy ones and with the blood of the witnesses of Jesus."—Revelation 17:1-6.

⁴⁴ Here indeed is foretold a repeating of history that reproduces the historical features of what befell the ancient prostitute, Oholibah. The Biblically described treatment of adulteresses and harlots is seen not to change from what it was in 607 B.C.E., when Oholibah (Jerusalem) was destroyed by the Babylonians, to what is prescribed for adulteresses and harlots in the year 96 C.E., about which time the Christian apostle John wrote the last book of the Bible, Revelation. More

43. With what portrayal of her, whom does Jehovah by his angel identify the harlot as being, in Revelation 17:1-6?
44. According to that, had the style of punishing women for adultery and fornication changed with the passing of years, and so punishment like that of whom is Babylon the Great to suffer?

than seven hundred years of the passing of time and yet no change! And there is no change foreseen and foretold after the passing of more than eighteen centuries of time since then till now in our twentieth century; for Revelation, chapters seventeen and eighteen, forecasts the events of our present century. Regardless of whatever the symbolic harlot, Babylon the Great, may say in her heart, she must suffer the punishment of women of loose conduct, like ancient Oholah, like Oholibah, at the hands of Jehovah God, who judges her. His style of punishment has not changed!

[45] Wishful thinking is it for Christendom to say in her heart that she will not suffer the fate of Babylon the Great of today. For years now she has been notified that Babylon the Great stands for the world empire of false Babylonish religion, and of this worldwide religious organization Christendom is the most populous and powerful part. As such she is one of those religious "harlots" of which Babylon the Great is the mother organization.—Revelation 17:5.

[46] Consequently, as fares Babylon the Great at the hands of Jehovah God, so must Christendom fare. And inasmuch as Christendom was specifically typed or foreshadowed by the adulterous Oholibah (Jerusalem), this makes it certain that she will share in the disastrous finale of Babylon the Great, which finale closely parallels that of the prostitute Oholibah. Has Christendom shared in the sins of Babylon the Great which have massed together clear up to heaven? Since she has done so, then she must receive part of the plagues of Babylon the Great that are divinely decreed to come "in one day," namely, death, mourning, famine, "and she will be completely burned with fire," and this at the hand of her former associates.—Revelation 18:4-8; 17:16.

45. Why is it wishful thinking for Christendom to say within herself that she will not suffer the fate of Babylon the Great of today?
46. Consequently, how must Christendom fare at the hands of Jehovah, and since she has share in the sins of Babylon the Great she must also receive part of what?

⁴⁷ We might well think of Christendom as Jehovah goes on to relate to his prophet Ezekiel the ungodly conduct of Oholibah (Jerusalem) toward Him, saying: "Therefore this is what the Sovereign Lord Jehovah has said, 'For the reason that you have forgotten me and you proceeded to cast me behind your back, then you yourself also bear your loose conduct and your acts of prostitution.'"

⁴⁸ Ancient Oholibah did what she was told to do in these words of Ezekiel 23:35, that is to say, she had to bear the bitter consequences of her spiritually loose conduct and acts of prostitution. Christendom will have to do the same, without fail.

⁴⁹ We do not have to peer too deeply into the historic record that Christendom has made for herself in order to discern that she has forgotten Jehovah and has cast him behind her back. It is not with Him that she has allied herself and aligned herself in hope of protection and preservation. She has carried on spiritual immorality with the politicians of all the nations. Along with them she has promoted and endorsed that idolatrous "image" of the symbolic wild beast, namely, the United Nations, as the necessary organization for world peace and security. This political "image" is the scarlet-colored wild beast with seven heads and ten horns that Babylon the Great has been riding since it came into existence, originally as the League of Nations in 1919. Since she looks away from Jehovah, she will get no protection and deliverance from Him when her political and secular associates turn upon her in rage to destroy her.—Revelation 13:14, 15; 14:9-11; 17:3-7.

⁵⁰ This drastic punishment will strike Christendom, shortly now, in the approaching "great tribulation such

47, 48. In the words of Ezekiel 23:35, what did Jehovah tell the symbolic Oholibah to do, and so what will Christendom have to do?
49. According to the historic record, how has Christendom since 1919 shown that she has forgotten Jehovah and cast him behind her back as regards world peace and security, and so what will she not get when her associates turn upon her?
50-52. When will this drastic punishment come upon Christendom, and, before then, what must the anointed Ezekiel class do, as indicated in Ezekiel 23:36-42?

as has not occurred since the world's beginning." (Matthew 24:15, 21, 22) But before then, the anointed Ezekiel class whom Jehovah is using today must declare abroad His judicial decisions against Christendom as if pronouncing divine judgment upon her. Indicative of this is what the ancient prophet Ezekiel next tells us, in his account in Ezekiel 23:36-42:

[51] "And Jehovah went on to say to me: 'Son of man, will you judge Oholah and Oholibah and tell them their detestable things? For they have committed adultery and there is blood on their hands, and with their dungy idols they have committed adultery. And, besides that, their sons whom they had borne to me they made pass through the fire to them as food. What is more, this is what they have done to me: They have defiled my sanctuary in that day, and my sabbaths they have profaned. And when they had slaughtered their sons to their dungy idols they even proceeded to come into my sanctuary on that day to profane it, and, look! that is what they have done in the midst of my house. And in addition to that, when they began to send to the men coming from far away, to whom there was sent a messenger, then, look! they came, for whom you had washed yourself, painted your eyes and decked yourself with ornaments. And you sat down upon a glorious couch, with a table set in order before it, and my incense and my oil you put upon it.

[52] "'And the sound of a crowd at ease was in her, and to the men out of the mass of mankind there were drunkards being brought in from the wilderness, and they proceeded to put bracelets on the hands of the women and beautiful crowns upon their heads.'"

FORMAL ACCUSATION
AS PRESENTED AGAINST CHRISTENDOM

[53] What an indictment this is of Christendom, as reflected from the ancient prototype of her! This indict-

---

53, 54. Those words of judgment against Oholah and Oholibah are an indictment also against whom today, and how has the latter been guilty of what is denounced in James 4:4?

ment has been presented by the Ezekiel class of today, the anointed Christian witnesses of Ezekiel's God, Jehovah. Like ancient Oholah and Oholibah, Christendom has committed spiritual adultery against the God whom she professes to worship, the God of the Bible. Deserving of her consideration, therefore, is the Bible question raised in James 4:4, which reads: "Adulteresses, do you not know that the friendship with the world is enmity with God? Whoever, therefore, wants to be a friend of the world is constituting himself an enemy of God."

[54] Christendom's perpetual friendliness with the politicians, and military forces and the big business profiteers of this world is a public scandal. As the dominant member of the "great harlot," Babylon the Great, Christendom has been a religious organization "with whom the kings of the earth committed fornication, whereas those who inhabit the earth were made drunk with the wine of her fornication." Christendom dominates in the symbolic "city that has a kingdom over the kings of the earth."—Revelation 17:1, 2, 18.

[55] The religious sects of Christendom have committed spiritual adultery also "with their dungy idols." One of the latest and biggest things to be idolized by her is the "image" of the symbolic wild beast of world politics, namely, the United Nations, to which most of the professedly Christian nations belong.—Ezekiel 23:37; Revelation 13:14, 15; 14:9-11; 16:2.

[56] And of the religious sects of Christendom can it be said that "there is blood on their hands"? As the ancient Oholah and Oholibah made their sons pass through the sacrificial fire to the dungy idol image of the false god Molech, so the sects of Christendom have caused their sons to shed their blood in sacrifice to the bloodthirsty god Mars, the Roman god of war. All this in the name of what they call Christianity! Chris-

55. What outstanding modern instance is there of the committing of spiritual adultery with idols by the sects of Christendom?
56. How is it true of the sects of Christendom in a sacrificial way that "there is blood on their hands"?

tendom's bloodstained hands testify to the sacrifice of her religious sons by the fanatical savage crusades against the Mohammedans of the Middle East, yes, by wars within her own ranks between Catholics and Protestants, by religious inquisitions with fiendish tortures of those viewed as heretics, by wars between the nations of Christendom that pitted Catholic against Catholic and Protestant against Protestant, by two world wars both of which began right inside Christendom!

[57] Worse still, with utter disrespect for the Bible God, they have, on the day of committing such atrocities, come with blood-drenched hands into what they call God's sanctuary, even on what they called their sabbath day. In this way they have, in effect, defiled and profaned God's sanctuary, thus grossly misrepresenting what the true house of God stands for. In disapproval of all this, what a blood account there is for Him to settle with Christendom!

[58] As portrayed by Oholibah (Jerusalem), we can picture Christendom acting like a professional harlot. She has sought customers, sending out for them to come into alliance with her for unchristian intercourse. See her washing herself to remove any offensive smells! See her making her eyes appear larger and more lustrous by painting them! See her decking herself with ornaments to make herself look irresistibly enticing! See her putting herself in a reclining position upon a glorious couch with a table put in front of it! The incense burning upon it and the perfumed oil put upon it for rubbing purposes she took away from what really belongs to God. In response to the messenger she sent out, her enticed customers were to come from all the secular parts of this world that is at enmity with Jehovah God. Her brothel becomes the location from which, despite closed doors and windows, issues the

---

57. How have they misrepresented what God's sanctuary stands for by how they have proceeded to do despite being defiled with blood?
58. How does Oholibah portray Christendom as trying to entice immoral customers, and who are not excluded from the mass of mankind that flocks to her?

sound of a crowd at ease and yielding themselves to sensual pleasures. A mass of mankind have flocked to her as for sexual satisfaction. Have drunkards been added to that indiscriminate mass as welcome? Yes, even though they come from such a low class as is to be found in the wilderness.

[59] Because Christendom's sects made religion easy for such worldlings, and because they could join her as church members and at the same time continue to be a part of this selfish, idolatrous, bloodstained world, all these elements of human society let themselves be herded into harlot-like Christendom. As payment for whatever religious favors that brought them sensual pleasure, they glorified her. As it were, to beautify her blood-reddened hands they put bracelets on her wrists, and they set beautiful crowns upon the heads of her sects, thereby giving the clergy some religious headship over their lives. This has become an old custom.

[60] Yet, is this to go on forever, or will it go beyond this generation of ours? Not according to what Jehovah now tells Ezekiel in these words: "Then I said respecting her who was worn out with adultery, 'Now she will keep on committing her prostitution, even she herself.' And they kept on coming in to her, just as one comes in to a woman that is a prostitute; in that manner they came in to Oholah and to Oholibah as women of loose conduct. But as regards righteous men, they are the ones that will judge her with the judgment for adulteresses and with the judgment for female shedders of blood; for adulteresses are what they are, and there is blood on their hands." (Ezekiel 23:43-45) Accordingly, since Christendom will not stop "committing her prostitution, even she herself," then a stop must be put to her committing spiritual prostitu-

---

59. Because Christendom has made religion an easy thing, what elements of human society have been herded to her, and in what sense have they put bracelets on her wrists and crowns on her head? 60. What are the indications as to whether Christendom will stop her spiritual immorality, and to what end must "righteous men" be used, these executing the judgments applied to what sort of women?

tion by having others execute upon her the judgment for adulteresses and the judgment for women guilty of shedding blood willfully.

THE "RIGHTEOUS MEN" FOR JUDGING CHRISTENDOM

⁶¹ Who, though, are those "righteous men" that will execute judgment upon her? Not Ezekiel and his fellow exiles Daniel, Hananiah, Mishael and Azariah, nor the prophet Jeremiah at Jerusalem and his secretary Baruch and his friends Ebed-melech the Ethiopian and the household of the Rechabites. (Ezekiel 14:14, 20; Daniel 1:1-7; Jeremiah 35:1-19; 36:4-32; 45:1-5) These approved men had no part whatsoever in executing the judgment of Jehovah upon Oholibah (Jerusalem) in the years 609-607 B.C.E. Rather, it was the Assyrians who destroyed Oholah (Samaria) in 740 B.C.E., and Babylonians who destroyed Oholibah (Jerusalem) in 607 B.C.E.

⁶² Consequently, the "righteous men" here meant are the former passionate lovers of Oholibah (Jerusalem) from whom her soul finally turns away in disgust and who therefore turn upon her and bring her to ruin. But how could such ones, the Babylonian executioners of judgment, be called "righteous men" inasmuch as they were pagans? It was in a comparative sense. So great was the wickedness of Oholibah (Jerusalem) in Jehovah's sight, that the Babylonians whom He used as his executioners were comparatively "righteous" in His sight. Because of so flagrantly violating her sacred covenant with Jehovah as her God, Oholibah (Jerusalem) was far more reprehensible than the pagan Babylonians. Furthermore, they were executing the "righteous" judgment of Jehovah upon Oholibah (Jerusalem), the judgment that is deserving for adulteresses and female shedders of blood. (Ezekiel 23: 22-27) Similarly, in our day the "righteous men" are

61. Who, then, are the "righteous men" that execute judgment upon the symbolic Oholibah?
62. Since Jehovah's executioners back there were pagans, in what way could they be called "righteous men," and, similarly who are the "righteous men" used as executioners in our day?

not Jehovah's Christian witnesses, but are Christendom's onetime worldly associates who get to hating her and who turn upon her to execute God's sentence upon her.

[63] That this is the correct understanding of who those "righteous men" are is confirmed by Jehovah's final words concerning Oholibah: "For this is what the Sovereign Lord Jehovah has said, 'There will be the bringing up of a congregation against them and a making of them a frightful object and something to plunder. And the congregation must pelt them with stones, and there will be a cutting of them down with their swords. Their sons and their daughters they will kill, and with fire their houses they will burn. And I shall certainly cause loose conduct to cease out of the land, and all the women will have to let themselves be corrected, so that they will not do according to your loose conduct. And they must bring your loose conduct upon you, and the sins of your dungy idols you will bear; and you people will have to know that I am the Sovereign Lord Jehovah.' "—Ezekiel 23:46-49.

[64] The congregation of Babylonian soldiers that Jehovah brought up against Oholibah (Jerusalem) did make her a frightful object in 607 B.C.E., breaching her sturdy walls, invading her, looting her, carrying away the plunder, and burning her with fire. (2 Kings 25:1-17; 2 Chronicles 36:17-19; Jeremiah 52:6-23) Doubtless the stones that the Babylonians hurled into the city during the long siege were of considerable size, doing much damage and causing many deaths. Besides that, many of Jerusalem's sons and daughters were dispatched by Babylonian swords upon the breakthrough into the city and thereafter. The firing of all the combustible houses that remained completed the desolation. Thus spiritually loose conduct and idolatry were made

---

63. How is the identity of those "righteous men" confirmed in Jehovah's final words concerning Oholibah?
64. How did Jehovah bring up against Oholibah a "congregation" of plunderers, wielders of swords, stoners, desolaters and burners, and cleansers of immoral conduct, and to whom did she become a frightful, corrective warning example?

to cease out of the land of Judah by the destruction of Oholibah (Jerusalem). Terrible were the consequences that came upon her for committing such detestable things in Jehovah's sight. What befell her should have been a warning to other "women," that is, nations, not to follow her example.

65 Has Christendom let herself be corrected by the warning example of Oholibah (Jerusalem) so as not to imitate her spiritually loose conduct and worship of dungy idols? In answer it must be said that Oholibah did not take heed to the warning example of her sister Oholah (Samaria), and neither will Christendom take heed to the warning example of the heedless Oholibah (Jerusalem). She is doomed to be plundered and made a frightful object mass of ruins. Not for long will her present friendship and sharing of her bed of immoral love with the worldly elements of this system of things continue. Her political, military, and other secular lovers will see reason to hate this worn-out old harlot and will turn upon her in rage. Jehovah will bring them up against her as an army of executioners of his righteous judgment, and false hypocritical Christianity will be burned out of the earth. Frightful will be the ruin of this symbolic woman, Christendom, that did not let herself be corrected by the warning examples recorded in Jehovah's Word. No one can ignore those warning examples and get by with it!

66 There is a purpose behind having all this take place. What is it? It is the divine purpose: "And you people will have to know that I am the Sovereign Lord Jehovah." (Ezekiel 23:49) Those words should be taken to heart by us. It was the name of the Sovereign Lord Jehovah that was involved with the terrible events of divine judgment in the year 607 B.C.E. In his own

65. In view of the warning example of Oholibah, what question arises as to Christendom, and whom will Jehovah bring up against her because of her course?
66. What is the purpose behind having all this take place, what will Christendom experience according to Jehovah's warning examples, and who today should take note respecting this?

name Jehovah had foretold those events by his prophets. In vindication of his own name He as Sovereign Lord irresistibly caused them to occur as the execution of His judicial decisions. Let all ignorers of Jehovah today take note. Relish it or not, the approaching destruction of Christendom will be according to His warning examples, his prophecies and his irreversible decrees. Thereby people will have to know that He, the Fulfiller of his unchangeable Word, is Jehovah.

[67] All those of us who have already come peacefully to a knowledge of this Sovereign Lord will thereby have that divine purpose mightily confirmed to us. More convinced than ever before, we shall know in an awe-inspiring way that He is Jehovah indeed and thus we will reverence him more fully than ever before.

67. What will then be the effect of this upon those of us who already have a knowledge of the Sovereign Lord God?

Chapter 14

Hypocritical Religionists
Stunned at the News

WITH stunning impact will the news of Christendom's destruction strike hypocritical religionists who are related to her. They will feel it when the foretold "great tribulation" begins upon her. Yet they may hope that because of her former ability to endure she will survive the tribulation, contrary to Bible prophecy. They may hope desperately that the worst will not come to a thing that has been so sacred to them.

1. How will hypocritical religionists feel or what will they hope when the "great tribulation" strikes Christendom?

[2] Because they have religiously attached God's name to it, they may feel that God and his Son Jesus Christ will never permit Christendom to be destroyed. But how stunned they will be when he does permit it in verification of his prophecy! Just how dumbfounded and stunned they will be the prophet Ezekiel was instructed to pantomime in the seventh century before our Common Era. About two years later, what Ezekiel had pantomimed his fellow exiles imitated in real life, this proving that he had been a true sign or portent. That fulfillment back there became in itself a prophetic event to foreshadow how the hypocritical religionists of our time would be stunned at the report of Christendom's destruction.

[3] Lightning-speed reporting of events by means of radio and television broadcasting with the aid of man-made satellites that are used as deflectors of radio waves is a marvel of our twentieth century. Yet, without the aid of such modern devices, the Creator of the universe and of its natural forces transmitted highly important news to his prophet Ezekiel instantaneously, with lightning speed. By the ordinary means of communication during those days of the camel train and the horse chariot, Ezekiel could never have learned on the very same day of its occurrence what was happening at Jerusalem more than five hundred miles southwest from his city of exile in Babylon, Tel-abib. And yet he did so! By what means? It was not by means of any fire-signal system or by drumbeating, but was as he informs us in these dated words:

[4] "And the word of Jehovah continued to occur to me in the ninth year, in the tenth month, on the tenth day of the month, saying: 'Son of man, write down for yourself the name of the day, this selfsame day. The king of Babylon has thrown himself against Jerusalem on this selfsame day.' "—Ezekiel 24:1, 2.

2. Why do such religionists not expect Christendom to be destroyed, but how will they be affected by her destruction, as pantomimed by the prophet Ezekiel before his fellow exiles?
3, 4. Was it by modern-day radio means of communication, or how did Ezekiel learn on the same day what happened to Jerusalem far away?

[5] Ezekiel did not see on any television screen, by means of direct telecasting, this beginning of the eighteen-month-long siege of Jerusalem by the king of Babylon, Nebuchadnezzar. But, unaided by television, Jehovah saw it directly and immediately reported it to Ezekiel. This was in the ninth year of Ezekiel's exile in Babylon and at the same time the ninth year of the last king of Jerusalem, namely, Zedekiah, whom Nebuchadnezzar himself had installed on the throne. This means the year 609 B.C.E. The tenth month, as counted from the spring month of Nisan according to the Jewish calendar, came to be called Tebeth.

[6] The tenth day of the month Tebeth would correspond with what would ordinarily be toward the end of our month December. Jehovah had already prophetically described to Ezekiel what King Nebuchadnezzar on the march would do to reach his decision to attack Jerusalem. (Ezekiel 21:18-23) Despite its being the time of the northern winter, King Nebuchadnezzar began his assault upon rebellious Jerusalem, as it were, throwing himself against it. This is the same date given for this in 2 Kings 24:20; 25:1 and Jeremiah 52:3, 4. So that day Ezekiel was told to depict what would happen.

[7] Jehovah instructs Ezekiel how to do so, saying: "And compose a proverbial saying concerning the rebellious house, and you must say concerning them, 'This is what the Sovereign Lord Jehovah has said: "Put the widemouthed cooking pot on; put it on, and also pour water into it. Gather pieces in it, every good piece, thigh and shoulder; fill it even with the choicest bones. Let there be a taking of the choicest sheep, and also stack the logs in a circle under it. Boil its pieces, also cook its bones in the midst of it."'"—Ezekiel 24:3-5.

---

5. How was Jehovah able to notify Ezekiel instantaneously, and in what lunar month of what year?
6. So at what season of the northern year did Nebuchadnezzar attack Jerusalem, and how is the date confirmed elsewhere in the Bible?
7. According to Ezekiel 24:3-5, what was Ezekiel told to do with a widemouthed cooking pot?

[8] Years before, according to Ezekiel 11:6-11, the residents of Jerusalem had likened her to a widemouthed cooking pot with themselves safely ensconced within it. Jehovah now uses this same picture. Filling the metallic widemouthed cooking pot with water for boiling would therefore picture what was happening that selfsame day of Tebeth 10, 609 B.C.E., that is to say, the siege of Jerusalem by the king of Babylon. The stacking of the logs underneath and the setting of them afire would comport with this thought. The siege now begun would gradually make it hot like boiling water for those inside Jerusalem. The pieces of flesh put into the pot would picture those inside the city, including the refugees that fled to it from before the advancing armies of Babylon. The good pieces put in would picture those of the better social class of the city, especially the king and his princes. Since the bones make up the framework that supports the fleshly body, the "choicest bones" would picture those that held up the structure of the national organism, namely, the military commanders and their staff of officers. All were to "cook" during the siege.

[9] Was Jerusalem as a symbolic cooking pot worth preserving? Listen! "Therefore this is what the Sovereign Lord Jehovah has said, 'Woe to the city of deeds of bloodshed, the widemouthed cooking pot, the rust of which is in it, and the very rust of which has not gone forth from it! Piece by piece of it, bring it out; no lot must be cast over it. For its very blood has come to be right in the midst of it. Upon the shining, bare surface of a crag she placed it. She did not pour it out upon the earth, in order to cover it over with dust. In order to bring up rage for the executing of vengeance, I have put her blood upon the shining, bare surface of a crag, in order that it may not be covered over.' "—Ezekiel 24:6-8.

---

8. What did the boiling of water in the pot picture, and what did the pieces of the sheep put therein picture?
9. Jerusalem was like what condition of a cooking pot, and how had she treated the blood that was shed in her?

¹⁰ Sometime earlier Jehovah had given a scathing denunciation of Jerusalem, addressing her as a "city that is shedding blood in her midst till her time comes," and detailing the reasons why she has shed so much blood. (Ezekiel 22:3-12) The moral scum and filth within her could not be washed out but clung to her sides, causing a rust to the sides of her as a symbolic cooking pot. She had a low regard for human blood, the blood of her victims, not even pouring it out on the ground and covering it over with dust, as God's law commanded to be done in the case of the blood of a hunted animal. (Leviticus 17:13, 14) No, but, shamelessly, Jerusalem poured out the violently shed blood upon the shining, bare surface of a crag for it to be openly exposed as a testimony to her criminality. This contempt for human blood stirred up Jehovah's rage, inducing him to execute vengeance upon the wanton shedder of blood. As she had done, he would do. He would not let her bloodstained record be covered over, but would expose it to public gaze like blood on a dustless, shining, bare surface of a crag!

¹¹ The gory criminals in Jerusalem must be brought out to justice. Bring them out indiscriminately, without selective lots being cast over them, but, as it were, bring "piece by piece of it" out of the symbolic cooking pot, Jerusalem. Now that the siege of Jerusalem had begun, "woe" was in store for her that would not end until she was destroyed together with all her scum.

DRASTIC ACTION NEEDED TOWARD CHRISTENDOM

¹² The charge of bloodguilt on the part of ancient Jerusalem calls up vividly before our minds the tremendous amount of bloodshed of which her modern-day counterpart, Christendom, is guilty. We can plain-

---

10. To what was the scum on the sides of Jerusalem as a cooking pot due, and how would Jehovah treat her blood similarly to the way that she treated the blood violently shed by her?
11. What was to be done to the gory criminals inside Jerusalem, and what was to be done with her herself?
12. The exposing of Jerusalem's bloodstained record reminds us of the bloodguilt of whom else, and in what will the "siege" of this latter one culminate?

ly see it as if it too were drenching the shining, bare surface of a crag, unable to be covered from men and angels. When the siege of her begins with the start of the "great tribulation," it will spell woe for her that will culminate in her destruction.—Matthew 24:15-22.

¹³ To Christendom applies the "proverbial saying" that was directed to Jerusalem her prototype: "Therefore this is what the Sovereign Lord Jehovah has said, 'Woe to the city of deeds of bloodshed! I myself also shall make the pile great. Make the logs many. Kindle the fire. Boil the flesh thoroughly. And empty out the broth, and let the bones themselves become piping hot. Stand it empty upon its coals in order that it may get hot; and its copper must become heated up, and its uncleanness must be liquefied in the midst of it. Let its rust get consumed. Troubles! It has made one tired, but the great amount of its rust does not go forth from it. Into the fire with its rust!' "—Ezekiel 24:9-12.

¹⁴ Jehovah saw what the gory, scummy city deserved. It must be enveloped in a big blaze as from a great pile of logs. Due to the long-continued cooking at the boiling point her military commanders and officers must get unbearably hot with the increasing intensity of the Babylonian siege, and the other inhabitants, like overcooked flesh, must be reduced to a state like broth with no texture or stability. Out with all of them! Empty out the city completely when it falls to the Babylonian besiegers! Put it like an emptied cooking pot of copper upon the fire of destruction, because of the scum-covered rust that still clings to its sides. Since the filthy rust cannot be washed off, burn it off! Yes, melt down the whole symbolic cooking pot (Jerusalem), to separate the dross from it. Let the fire of the destruction of the bloodguilty city also completely destroy her moral filth, scum and rust. And

13. What "proverbial saying" applies to Christendom, as set out in Ezekiel 24:9-12?
14. Since the scum-covered rust of the symbolic cooking pot, Jerusalem, could not be washed away, what did Jehovah see to be necessary for the city, and for whom else does that go?

that goes for her modern-day counterpart, Christendom, too!

¹⁵ Jehovah herewith addresses himself directly to Jerusalem to explain why he must take such drastic measures toward her: " 'There was loose conduct in your uncleanness. For that reason I had to cleanse you, but you did not become clean from your uncleanness. You will become clean no more until I cause my rage to come to its rest in your case. I myself, Jehovah, have spoken. It must come, and I will act. I shall not neglect, neither shall I feel sorry nor feel regret. According to your ways and according to your dealings they will certainly judge you,' is the utterance of the Sovereign Lord Jehovah."—Ezekiel 24:13, 14.

¹⁶ On that recorded date, Tebeth 10, 609 B.C.E., the Babylonian siege of Jerusalem for the third and last time had begun. This fact proved that the Kingdom of Judah under Jerusalem had refused to be cleansed from her spiritually loose conduct. Her uncleanness was like the scum and filth that created rust on the sides of a copper pot and that could not be scoured away but that had to be destroyed by melting down the cooking pot itself. The symbolic cooking pot was now in the fire, now that this siege by the Babylonians had begun. The persisting uncleanness of Jerusalem would never be cleansed away until Jehovah was obliged to bring his rage to rest by having the bloodguilty Jerusalem destroyed.

¹⁷ Rage, not sympathetic sorrow, was to be expressed to the full, and Jehovah would feel no regret for his extreme measures taken against Jerusalem. He had spoken his mind, and it must not fail in coming true. He would not be negligent in bringing it to pass. His Babylonian executors of divine judgment would mete

---

15. What does Jehovah say directly to Jerusalem regarding the matter of cleansing, and according to what on her part will judgments be executed upon her?
16. What did the beginning of the siege of Jerusalem prove as to her past conduct, and when first would his rage be brought to rest?
17. Since Jehovah had spoken his mind, was regret on his part to be expected, or what?

out to Jerusalem the judgment that she deserved for ungodly ways and deeds. She had to be destroyed, just as her imitator, Christendom, has to be.

[18] "O, have a heart!" a person might be inclined to say to God at this point. Why? Because Jerusalem then contained the magnificent temple that had been built by King Solomon, and so the wrecking of Jerusalem meant the wrecking of the sacred temple that the Jews regarded as a charm against disaster. (Jeremiah 7:1-11) And another thing: The older Jews who had been carried off into exile in Babylon had left behind sons and daughters in Jerusalem and Judah, and, if Jerusalem were destroyed, it would mean death for those sons and daughters. Were not these things precious to these Jews who were involved? Would not the violent taking away of these things be a jarring shock to their sensibilities, stunning them? Would not a corresponding disaster today have the like effect upon those who are sympathetically involved with Christendom? That it would do so, the prophet Ezekiel was called upon to dramatize in a prophetic manner. How he did so he describes in these words:

[19] "And the word of Jehovah continued to occur to me, saying: 'Son of man, here I am taking away from you the thing desirable to your eyes by a blow, and you should not beat your breast, neither should you weep nor should your tears come on. Sigh without words. For the dead ones no mourning should you make. Your headdress bind on yourself, and your sandals you should put upon your feet. And you should not cover over the mustache, and the bread of men you should not eat.' "—Ezekiel 24:15-17.

[20] Why act that way? What was about to happen? Was there to be a death that would affect Ezekiel?

---

18. What material things and human lives were involved with Jerusalem's destruction, and how would violent taking away of such things affect the older survivors?
19. Ezekiel was told to dramatize in what prophetic way the effect of the taking away of desirable things?
20. At Ezekiel's having to act in that way, what question about him arises, and what would the strangeness of his acting thus indicate about some future blow?

Evidently so, since it was something desirable to Ezekiel's eyes that Jehovah would take away by a blow or stroke. Was it to be the wife of this thirty-four-year-old man? Events before midnight would reveal the victim of the blow or stroke. But after it occurred, Ezekiel was to offer no visible or audible sign of grief. He was to put on his headdress, all neatly tied up, and not letting any of it hang down over his face and cover his upper lip. He was not to go barefoot, as King David had long ago done in his grief. (2 Samuel 15:30) After the burial of the one taken away by the blow or stroke, Ezekiel was not to let his sympathizers prepare a consolation meal for him and thus give him something to eat. Why act in this strange, unusual way? It was in order to picture how stunned at a dire calamity a person could become, how expressionless. To produce such an effect the calamity would have to be specially severe, overwhelming.

[21] In order to provide such a prophetic picture Ezekiel had to go through a hard, trying experience and exercise great self-control over his natural human emotions. But he was willing to have this take place if it meant for him to serve as Jehovah's prophetic instrument, and he offered no complaint. How he obediently did what he was told to do and why, he tells us:

[22] "And I proceeded to speak to the people in the morning, and my wife gradually died in the evening. So I did in the morning just as I had been commanded. And the people kept saying to me: 'Will you not tell us what these things have to do with us, that you are doing?' Then I said to them: 'The very word of Jehovah has occurred to me, saying, "Say to the house of Israel: 'This is what the Sovereign Lord Jehovah has said, "Here I am profaning my sanctuary, the pride of your strength, the thing desirable to your eyes and the object of your soul's compassion, and your sons

---

21. Under the circumstances, why would Ezekiel have to exercise great self-control, and why did he offer no complaint?
22. What happened to Ezekiel in the evening, how did he act, and what explanation from Jehovah did he give to the inquirers?

and your daughters whom you people have left behind—by the sword they will fall. And you will have to do just as I have done. Mustaches you will not cover over, and the bread of men you will not eat. And your headdress will be on your heads, and your sandals be upon your feet. You will not beat yourselves nor will you weep, and you will have to rot away in your errors, and you will actually groan over one another. And Ezekiel has become for you a portent. In accord with all that he has done, you will do. When it comes, you will also have to know that I am the Sovereign Lord Jehovah." ' " ' "—Ezekiel 24:18-24.

²³ Years later, in 33 C.E. Jesus Christ foretold and contemplated the destruction that was to come upon the then Jerusalem in the year 70 C.E. with all its horrors. He "wept over it." In tears he said: "If you, even you, had discerned in this day the things having to do with peace—but now they have been hid from your eyes. Because the days will come upon you when your enemies will build around you a fortification with pointed stakes and will encircle you and distress you from every side, and they will dash you and your children within you to the ground, and they will not leave a stone upon a stone in you, because you did not discern the time of your being inspected." (Luke 19:41-44; 21: 20-24) But Jesus Christ as an unmarried man was not called upon to enact a prophetic scene as Ezekiel was commanded to do.

²⁴ Obediently, Ezekiel did not mourn over the death of his wife, "the thing desirable to your eyes." (Ezekiel 24:16) In the year 607 B.C.E. the prophet Jeremiah did mourn and lament over the destruction of Jerusalem and her temple. (Lamentations 1:1 to 5:22) When that calamity actually occurred, Ezekiel himself was not commanded to refrain from doing as Jeremiah

23. How, in 33 C.E., was Jesus Christ emotionally affected when foretelling and contemplating the destruction to come upon the then Jerusalem?
24. How was the prophet Jeremiah affected and moved after experiencing the destruction of Jerusalem, and how would Ezekiel be affected when the news thereof reached him?

did. When the news of the destruction of Jerusalem and her temple reached Ezekiel in Babylon it did not stun and benumb him.

²⁵ It did not require the destruction of Jerusalem, her precious temple and her sons and daughters for Ezekiel to know, as God said, "that I am the Sovereign Lord Jehovah." But as for the people of Israel, who did not know the identity of their God, either in Judah or in Babylon, they did have to be made to know that fact by a stunning blow delivered in the form of the destruction of holy city, temple, children. Never did they bring themselves to believe that Jehovah would profane his own sanctuary by letting pagan, idolatrous Babylonians capture, loot and destroy Solomon's temple that had stood for 420 years. Jehovah did not spare what he described to them as "the pride of your strength, the thing desirable to your eyes and the object of your soul's compassion"—whether that were Jehovah's sanctuary at Jerusalem or their sons and daughters there. In such a stunning way they would have to know that the One who said he would do such a thing and the One who actually did it were one and the same Person, Jehovah. He is!

²⁶ In the approaching "great tribulation" upon Christendom Jehovah's true sanctuary is not what he will profane. "The God that made the world and all the things in it, being, as this One is, Lord of heaven and earth, does not dwell in handmade temples [or, sanctuaries]." (Acts 17:24, *NW; AS*, margin) Jehovah will not profane the antitypical spiritual "temple" in which his High Priest, Jesus Christ, presented to Him the merit of a perfect, human sacrifice in the year 33 C.E., this one appearing in the heavens before the very person of God to do so. (Hebrews 9:24-26) Nor will he profane the temple or sanctuary that He is now building and which is made up of "living stones"; this is

25. Was destruction of Jerusalem and the things therein needed for Ezekiel to know Jehovah, and how about his fellow exiles?
26. In the coming "great tribulation" upon Christendom, what scriptures show whether it is the true "sanctuary" of His that Jehovah will "profane"?

his congregation of faithful anointed followers of his Son Jesus Christ, the chief "living stone." (1 Peter 2:4-6) The apostle Paul when writing to those of this sanctuary class says: "For we are a temple of a living God; just as God said: 'I shall reside among them and walk among them, and I shall be their God, and they will be my people.'" (2 Corinthians 6:16) "In union with him you, too, are being built up together into a place for God to inhabit by spirit." (Ephesians 2:22) The anointed remnant of this sanctuary class make up the modern-day Ezekiel class used by Jehovah.

[27] In view of this it must be the imitation temple class that God will profane, that is, the hypocritical religionists who falsely claim to make up God's spiritual sanctuary.

[28] For decades now since the year 1919 C.E. this anointed remnant of Jehovah's Christian witnesses have been forewarning of the destruction of Christendom according to the prophecies of Ezekiel and other writers of the inspired Bible. More and more they appreciate what this annihilation of Christendom will mean in the way of destruction of human lives and material properties considered sacred by religionists. But this Ezekiel class of Christians does not mourn and lament because of what all this "great tribulation" upon Christendom will mean. They know that it will never mean the destruction of Jehovah's true sanctuary, the spiritual temple in which Jesus Christ presented the merit of his ransom sacrifice back in 33 C.E. Nor will it mean the destruction of the temple of "living stones" that Jehovah is now building. So the actual occurrence of this predicted disaster to Christendom will not stun them. They do not need this to occur for them to "know that I am the Sovereign Lord Jehovah." The hypocritical religionists who ignore Jehovah and trust in things sacred to them are

---

27. What "temple" must it be, then, that Jehovah will profane?
28. At the destruction of Christendom, who are the ones that will be stunned, the anointed Ezekiel class or the hypocritical religionists, and why?

the ones destined to be stunned. They will have to know who Jehovah is.

THE REPORT IN VERIFICATION SURE TO COME!

[29] 'But what if it does not occur?' someone not believing may exclaim. Never fear! The events of the future and the news reports that will come through will prove true the infallible prophecy uttered by Ezekiel. The reassurance was given that the trueness of the prophecy would be confirmed. It was given to Ezekiel, as Jehovah went on to say to him: "And as for you, O son of man, will it not be in the day of my taking away from them their fortress, the beautiful object of their exultation, the thing desirable to their eyes and the longing of their soul, their sons and their daughters, that in that day there will come to you the escaped one for making the ears hear? In that day your mouth will be opened to the escaped one, and you will speak and be mute no longer; and you will certainly become to them a portent, and they will have to know that I am Jehovah."—Ezekiel 24:25-27.

[30] Down to this point Ezekiel had said enough to his people. There was no need for him to add much more in order to make the divine prophecy sound more convincing, to make appear more imposing the certainty of his message. Jehovah had spoken it, and that in itself was enough. So now until the day of the coming of the authentic report of verification Ezekiel would be mute. Not speechless in the full sense, but only speechless as regards further prophesying about the disaster to befall Jerusalem and the Kingdom of Judah. The passing of the time until the coming of the escaped one with the report would be a time of testing.

[31] Jehovah was not going to notify Ezekiel directly

---

29. How would the trueness of Ezekiel's prophecy be confirmed, and how did Jehovah give to Ezekiel the reassurance of this?
30. Why was Ezekiel to be speechless from then on until the escaped one with the report arrived, and speechless to what extent?
31. So, was Jehovah going to notify Ezekiel directly at the time of Jerusalem's downfall, and what were Ezekiel's fellow exiles to be allowed to do?

of the fall of Jerusalem on the day of this disaster as he had notified Ezekiel directly of the beginning of the Babylonian siege on the day that this occurred. Till the escaped one with the report finally arrived, let the Jewish exiles in Babylon think over what Ezekiel had prophesied to them. Let them keep on disbelieving, if they chose. Their unbelief would in due time be blasted to pieces by the arrival of an authentic eyewitness of Jerusalem's downfall.

[32] At that ear-tingling time the hitherto doubters and unbelievers would be stunned into silence, but Ezekiel's muteness would end. He would then be in position to speak from a better background of events. He would have a new, fresh message. His authority as a true inspired prophet of Jehovah would have been established. As a "sign" man or as a "portent" of what was fast impending, he had not proved false. Like the words of Jehovah to him, "you will certainly become to them a portent," Ezekiel will have no reason then to be ashamed of his God before his fellow exiles in Babylon. His role as a prophet and witness of Jehovah will be authenticated, and, as Ezekiel's God said, "they will have to know that I am Jehovah."—Ezekiel 24:27.

[33] Is this not something thrilling for us to contemplate, namely, the fulfillment of this prophetic drama within our generation? It will be definitely indicated when the "great tribulation," like the siege against Jerusalem, begins upon her modern-time counterpart, Christendom. (Ezekiel 24:1-5) After that, the anointed Ezekiel class of today need say no more. What they will have already said concerning the outcome of that "great tribulation" will be enough. No hope can they hold out for the antitypical Jerusalem, Christendom. There is no further opportunity for her, nor for the hypocritical religionists related to her. The "great trib-

---

32. At the arrival of the news by the escapee, how would the hitherto doubters be affected, but what would happen to Ezekiel, and how would his position as prophet and witness be improved?
33. When will the Ezekiel class have said enough concerning the outcome of the "great tribulation," and what about further opportunity for Christendom then?

ulation" must run its full course and take its full toll upon her.

[34] Stunned will those incredulous religionists be when down goes "the beautiful object of their exultation, the thing desirable to their eyes and the longing of their soul, their sons and their daughters"! Reports that will come pouring in from all parts of the earth where Christendom now obtains will stamp as true that the anointed Ezekiel class has a timely "portent" from the Sovereign Lord of the universe. His stated purpose regarding the stunned religionists will then triumph, "They will have to know that I am Jehovah."

34. What will then prove that the Ezekiel class was a timely portent to religionists, and what purpose of Jehovah will triumph?

Chapter 15

The Watchman Lives to Get the Report

OUGHT we not be thankful that there is a Creator who is so interested in our welfare that he has provided a watchman for our safety in these dangerous times? We have reason to be grateful for this divine provision, rather than be irritated because the watchman warns us so promptly and conscientiously. He is not needlessly disturbing our peace and repose.

[2] Scientists, economists, ecologists and historians are shouting out well-founded warnings to this present

1. Because of his great interest in our welfare, what has the Creator provided for us in these troublous times, and how should we feel about this?
2. What worldlings of today do not prove to be His watchman class, why does He have a great account to settle with this system of things, and what does heeding His real watchman mean for us?

system of things about eventual disaster. But these worldlings do not make up the "watchman" class that the Creator of heaven and earth has raised up. Those men or women do not issue warning in the name of the Creator or at His command. Whether we refer to man's natural environment or we refer to moral standards and religious obligations, in all cases the Creator's laws and arrangements are being violated. The account that He has to settle with man's present system of things world wide is great. His settling of accounts in the near future will mean a "great tribulation" of the worst sort that has ever befallen our race. Heeding His real watchman means our salvation.

[3] The Creator's "watchman" for our day was foreshadowed or typed. By whom? By the prophet Ezekiel, during those critical six years that wound up with the first destruction of Jerusalem in 607 B.C.E. Ezekiel was commissioned as a prophet and watchman in the year 613 B.C.E. (Ezekiel 1:1-3; 3:17-21) But now, before the report of Jerusalem's destruction reaches him at his place of exile in Babylon, he is reminded how, as a watchman, he is responsible for the lives of the chosen people of God. After recording the messages that he was called upon to deliver against seven nations who had mistreated God's chosen people. (Ezekiel, chapters twenty-five through thirty-two), the prophet writes:

[4] "And the word of Jehovah proceeded to occur to me, saying: 'Son of man, speak to the sons of your people, and you must say to them, "As regards a land, in case I bring upon it a sword and the people of the land, one and all, actually take a man and set him as their watchman, and he really sees the sword coming upon the land and blows the horn and warns the people, and the hearer actually hears the sound of the horn but he takes no warning at all, and a sword

---

3. How was the Creator's "watchman" foreshadowed or typed, and when?
4. In Ezekiel 33:1-5, what does Jehovah say regarding the placing of a watchman and the case of the heedless hearer of the warning signal of the horn?

comes and takes him away, his own blood will come to be upon his own head. The sound of the horn he heard, but he took no warning. His own blood will come to be upon his own self. And had he himself taken warning, his own soul would have escaped."'"—Ezekiel 33:1-5.

5 Let us here notice that it is Jehovah that brings the "sword" of execution of his judicial decisions upon the land in question. But even if the people of that land set up their own watchman, just the same the resident of the land who fails to heed the watchman's warning and loses his soul or life must shoulder the responsibility for his own death. It is fair to the watchman.

6 "Now as regards the watchman," continues Jehovah, "in case he sees the sword coming and he actually does not blow the horn and the people itself gets no warning at all and a sword comes and takes away from them soul, for its own error it itself must be taken away, but its blood I shall ask back from the hand of the watchman himself."—Ezekiel 33:6.

7 If a people is destroyed at the edge of the executional sword, no injustice was done to it because it did not first get warning. It deserved to be destroyed because of its own error toward God. But this does not excuse the delinquent watchman. He was duty-bound to sound the warning to the people. Modern-day law would call his failure to do so "criminal negligence" on the watchman's part. Certainly, then, Jehovah rightly held him responsible.

8 Jehovah now makes an application of this to Ezekiel, saying: "Now as regards you, O son of man, a watchman is what I have made you to the house of

---

5. According to those words, who is it that brings the sword upon the land, and who shoulders the responsibility for loss of life if a hearer disregards a watchman?
6. What does Jehovah say is the case of a people in danger whose watchman fails to sound warning to them?
7. Although a people deserves to be destroyed, who is held accountable for their death in the case of a delinquent watchman?
8. Who made Ezekiel a watchman and to whom, and how would Ezekiel be dealt with where a wicked man died for failing to get warning, or where he failed to heed Ezekiel's warning?

70 C E

Israel, and at my mouth you must hear the word and give them warning from me. When I say to someone wicked, 'O wicked one, you will positively die!' but you actually do not speak out to warn the wicked one from his way, he himself as a wicked one will die in his own error, but his blood I shall ask back at your own hand. But as regards you, in case you actually warn someone wicked from his way for him to turn back from it but he actually does not turn back from his way, he himself will die in his own error, whereas you yourself will certainly deliver your own soul." (Ezekiel 33:7-9) According to this principle, Jehovah excuses a spiritual watchman, like Ezekiel, for having done his duty.

⁹ "Now," continues Jehovah, "as regards you, O son of man, say to the house of Israel, 'Thus you people have said: "Because our revolts and our sins are upon us and in them we are rotting away, how, then, shall we keep living?"' Say to them, '"As I am alive," is the utterance of the Sovereign Lord Jehovah, "I take delight, not in the death of the wicked one, but in that someone wicked turns back from his way and actually keeps living. Turn back, turn back from your bad ways, for why is it that you should die, O house of Israel?"'" —Ezekiel 33:10, 11.

¹⁰ This divine attitude opens up an opportunity for us today. He is not pleased to have us die in the approaching "great tribulation" in which he executes His judicial decisions upon this wicked system of things. If we turn back from our bad ways and strive to live according to the way marked out in His Word, he will spare us from execution. (Matthew 24:21, 22) That a wicked person's previous record will not be held against him, Jehovah now states:

¹¹ "And as for you, O son of man, say to the sons

---

9. In what is it that Jehovah takes delight, in the death of the wicked one or in the recovery of that one to life?

10. How does this attitude of Jehovah open up an opportunity for us today when the "great tribulation" is impending?

11. How does Jehovah state matters, to show that a person's previous record will not be held against him or, also, in favor of him?

of your people, 'The righteousness of the righteous one will not itself deliver him in the day of his revolt. But as regards the wickedness of the wicked one, he will not be made to stumble [and fall in death] by it in the day of his turning back from his wickedness. Nor will even anyone having righteousness be able to keep living because of it in the day of his sinning. When I say to the righteous one: "You will positively keep living," and he himself actually trusts in his own righteousness and does injustice, all his own righteous acts will not be remembered, but for his injustice that he has done—for this he will die.' "—Ezekiel 33:12, 13.

WHEN ONE'S PAST RECORD DOES NOT COUNT

[12] Regardless of the previous record in life, it is what one actually is at the due time for the execution of divine judgment that counts with God. Hence he goes on to say: "And when I say to the wicked one: 'You will positively die,' and he actually turns back from his sin and carries on justice and righteousness, and the wicked one returns the very thing pledged [by the debtor, at nightfall], pays back the very things taken by robbery, and actually walks in the very statutes of life by not doing injustice, he will positively keep living. He will not die. None of his sins with which he has sinned will be remembered against him. Justice and righteousness are what he has carried on. He will positively keep living."—Ezekiel 33:14-16.

[13] Such treatment of sinners—how gracious it is on Jehovah's part! At his time of executing judgment against an unrighteous nation or organization, He does not let the reformed sinner be put to death, but this spared one is permitted to live on, walking "in the very statutes of life," until his natural death. In Ezekiel's day such walking meant obeying God's law that was given to Israel at Mount Sinai through the media-

---

12. In the case of the wicked one, how does Jehovah state that what one actually is at the time for executing judgment is what counts?
13. Walking "in the very statutes of life" means what, as regards Ezekiel's day and as regards our own day?

tor Moses. But in our day, nineteen centuries after the sacrificial death of Jesus Christ as the "Lamb of God that takes away the sin of the world," a reformed sinner's walking "in the very statutes of life" would mean his accepting the ransom sacrifice of the Lamb Jesus Christ and walking in his footsteps as a true Christian.—John 1:29, 36; 1 Peter 2:21.

[14] That is why it is said concerning the "great crowd" of worshipers that survives the "great tribulation" and enters into God's righteous new system of things: "These are the ones that come out of the great tribulation, and they have washed their robes and made them white in the blood of the Lamb. That is why they are before the throne of God; and they are rendering him sacred service day and night in his temple; and the one seated on the throne [God] will spread his tent over them."—Revelation 7:9-15.

[15] What shall we say of this divine arrangement? That God has misadjusted matters? To say so would be doing like the Israelites of Ezekiel's day. Here is what Jehovah tells Ezekiel about them: "And the sons of your people have said, 'The way of Jehovah is not adjusted right,' but, as for them, it is their way that is not adjusted right." (Ezekiel 33:17) Then Jehovah proceeds to make plain the rightness of his way in dealing with his people in the time for executing judgment by adding:

[16] "When someone righteous turns back from his righteousness and actually does injustice, he must also die for them. And when someone wicked turns back from his wickedness and actually carries on justice and righteousness, it will be on account of them that he himself will keep living."—Ezekiel 33:18, 19.

[17] It is how a person ends up that counts with Jehovah, not what kind of a person, good or bad, that he

14. To correspond with this, what is said about the "great cro
Revelation 7:9-15?
15, 16. What were the Israelites saying about the way of
but what did He say to make plain the rightness of His
17. As regards a righteous person's course, what is it that
Jehovah on judgment day?

was in the past. If Jehovah's day for executing judgment finds that a once righteous person has turned to wickedness and has continued therein, then the penalty for sin must be inflicted upon him.

[18] However, if the arrival of Jehovah's judgment day finds that a once wicked person has repented and turned to what is right in Jehovah's eyes and has continued in this course, he will be spared execution as a reward for repenting, reforming and adhering to righteousness. Jehovah says that he has no pleasure in the death by execution of the wicked. He delights in the repenting and reforming of the wicked ones, because that means that He can spare them and let them keep on living in righteousness to Jehovah's praise. When Jehovah punishes or rewards a person according to what he is on the day for executing judgment according to the divine standards concerning right and wrong, there is nothing maladjusted about that, is there? Hence in the approaching "great tribulation" we cannot expect our past course, if merely self-righteous, to count for us.

[19] Knowing that His way of handling judgment is adjusted right, Jehovah will proceed accordingly. That is why he warned the Israelites of this by saying: "And you people have said, 'The way of Jehovah is not adjusted right.' It will be each one according to his ways that I shall judge you, O house of Israel." (Ezekiel 33:20) Let us therefore not consider God's way to be wrongly adjusted and so hold onto our own wrong thinking. His ways are higher than our ways, and his thoughts than our thoughts. (Isaiah 55:8, 9) According to what our ways result in our being at His time for executing his judicial decisions is the way Jehovah will judge us, each one on an individual basis. O that his decision at that time toward us may be

---

18. In contrast, what is the case with the wicked one, and what is there maladjusted about Jehovah's way of dealing thusly?
19. Like the ancient Israelites, why should we not hold onto our own manner of thinking as to Jehovah's way, and so on what does a desirable decision toward us on judgment day depend?

that we should "keep living"! Let us appreciate now that this all depends upon the deeds of each one of us during what remains of this "year of goodwill on the part of Jehovah."—Isaiah 61:1, 2; 2 Corinthians 6:1, 2.

THE ESCAPEE ARRIVES
WITH THE EYEWITNESS REPORT

[20] The prophet Ezekiel proved to be a faithful vocal watchman toward the house of Israel. Till the tenth day of the tenth lunar month of the year 609 B.C.E., when the Babylonian siege of Jerusalem began, he courageously declared Jehovah's warning to the disaster-threatened Israelites. The destruction of the rebellious city after eighteen months of intensifying siege brought death to an unstated number of besieged Jews. The toll of lives must have been great. But Jehovah was unable to ask back at the hand of Ezekiel the life of a single one of those many slain. Their blood was upon their own heads, because they had refused to pay attention to the warning sounded by watchman Ezekiel. As a result Ezekiel survived to receive finally a report that proved that his warnings as a watchman had not been baseless, unfounded. He tells us:

[21] "At length it occurred in the twelfth year, in the tenth month, on the fifth day of the month of our exile, that there came to me the escaped one from Jerusalem, saying: 'The city has been struck down!' " —Ezekiel 33:21.

[22] Vindicated! Jehovah the Inspirer of the prophecies of Jerusalem's calamity was vindicated! Ezekiel the watchman and proclaimer of those prophecies was vindicated! What a thrilling moment that was when that fugitive from more than five hundred miles away broke the not-unexpected news: "The city has been struck

---

20. Till what date did Ezekiel prove to be a vocal watchman to the house of Israel, and why was it that he survived Jerusalem's destruction and loss of life till the report arrived?
21, 22. When did the report arrive, what effect did it have as regards Jehovah and Ezekiel, and how long had the fugitive been on the way to deliver the report?

down!" It was on the fifth day of the tenth month (Tebeth) of the twelfth year of Ezekiel's exile in Babylon. There are eight Hebrew manuscripts besides the Syriac Version and some manuscripts of the Greek *Septuagint Version* that read "eleventh year" instead of "twelfth year." This would mean that the fugitive from Jerusalem arrived during the latter half of December of the year 607 B.C.E. Since 2 Kings 25:2-4 tells us that Jerusalem was struck down or breached by the Babylonians on the ninth day of the fourth month (Tammuz) of the eleventh year of King Zedekiah's reign but of Ezekiel's exile, this would mean that the fugitive arrived six months after Jerusalem was broken into and captured by the Babylonians. The time would come out the same if, as some do, we count year twelve from the Jewish New Year, Tishri 1, of 607 B.C.E.

[23] What a thrilling moment it will be when, during the coming "great tribulation" on this present system of things, the authentic news comes from all around the earth that the antitypical Jerusalem, Christendom, has fallen at the hands of Jehovah's executional forces! This will be a vindication of the modern-day Ezekiel class, to authenticate that they have not been a false prophet but have been a faithful "watchman" class in sounding out Jehovah's warnings to Christendom. The blood of clergymen and of other adherents of Christendom losing their lives at that time will be upon their own heads. Because these refused to heed the warning given, their blood will not be asked back by Jehovah at the hand of his appointed "watchman," the anointed Ezekiel class. For her own error Christendom will perish. Jehovah will judge her in accord with her own hypocritical, bloodguilty ways.

[24] The ancient prophet Ezekiel was prepared in advance to hear the news that, to an ordinary Jew or

---

23. When the report of the destruction of Christendom world wide comes, what will it authenticate about the anointed Ezekiel class, and who will be held accountable for all the loss of life then?
24, 25. How was Ezekiel prepared in advance to hear the report?

Israelite, would have been heartbreaking. Let us remember that the Jewish day began at eveningtime, at sundown, as we now read what Ezekiel tells us:

²⁵ "Now the very hand of Jehovah had come to be upon me in the evening before the coming of the escaped one, and He proceeded to open my mouth prior to that one's coming to me in the morning, and my mouth was opened and I proved to be speechless no longer."—Ezekiel 33:22.

²⁶ Thus Ezekiel's muteness as regards his prophesying concerning the doomed Jerusalem lasted longer than the eighteen months of Jerusalem's siege. His muteness had begun after he had miraculously been notified by inspiration of Jerusalem's siege on the very day that it began. His muteness did not end by getting a miraculous communication on the day that Jerusalem was "struck down" by the Babylonians. His muteness continued after that event until it would be confirmed by the report of an escaped human eyewitness, whose report would be less questionable by Ezekiel's fellow exiles than an inspired report to the prophet would be. But Jehovah knew that the escapee was near the end of his flight and about to make report, and so on the evening of the day of that one's arrival Jehovah spoke to Ezekiel from the standpoint that Jerusalem had already been destroyed and there were some survivors yet in the land of Judah. To this effect Ezekiel now writes:

²⁷ "And the word of Jehovah began to occur to me, saying: 'Son of man, the inhabitants of these devastated places are saying even concerning the soil of Israel, "Abraham happened to be just one and yet he took possession of the land. And we are many; to us the land has been given as something to possess." Therefore say to them: "This is what the Sovereign

26. To compare with Jerusalem's siege, how long did Ezekiel's muteness last, and why did Jehovah choose to furnish an eyewitness report rather than an inspired report?
27. To those Jews surviving on the land of Judah after the striking down of Jerusalem, what did Jehovah tell Ezekiel to say about the possessing of the land?

Lord Jehovah has said: 'With the blood you keep eating, and your eyes you keep lifting to your dungy idols, and blood you keep pouring out. So should you possess the land? You have depended upon your sword. You have done a detestable thing, and you have defiled each one the wife of his companion. So should you possess the land?' " ' "—Ezekiel 33:23-26.

²⁸ This shows that those Jews who had not been deported by the Babylonians but who were still permitted to stay on the land had not been properly affected by the destruction of Jerusalem. They had not viewed this as an expression of God's condemnation of them and so had not repented of their violations of His law. They still continued to eat animal flesh from which the blood had not been drained according to God's law; they still carried on false worship with detestable idols, idols smeared with dung; they still committed the detestable act of adultery, violating even their neighbor's wife. It mattered not with Jehovah that they were many as compared with their ancestor, the patriarch Abraham, to whom the land had been promised by Jehovah. (Genesis 12:1-7) Because of their not turning away repentantly from their wicked ways, they did not deserve to keep possessing the land. (Jeremiah 42:1 to 44:25) Mere numbers did not count with Jehovah; obedience to his Law did!

DESOLATION OF THE LAND TO BE MADE COMPLETE

²⁹ Jehovah made it plain that those unrepentant, undeported sinners were due to be deprived of using the God-given land, for he now said to Ezekiel: "This is what you should say to them, 'This is what the Sovereign Lord Jehovah has said: "As I am alive, surely the ones who are in the devastated places will fall by the sword itself; and the one who is upon the surface of the field, to the wild beast I shall certainly give him

---

28. Of what were those survivors who had not been deported by the Babylonians still guilty, and what viewpoint did their comments about the land show that they took toward Jerusalem's fall?
29. To what physical state was the land to be reduced, and how would Jehovah bring this about, and for what purpose?

for food; and those who are in the strong places and in the caves will die by the pestilence itself. And I shall actually make the land a desolate waste, even a desolation, and the pride of its strength must be made to cease and the mountains of Israel must be laid desolate, with no one passing through. And they will have to know that I am Jehovah when I make the land a desolate waste, even a desolation, on account of all their detestable things that they have done." ' " —Ezekiel 33:27-29.

[30] Jehovah's decree was not to be set at nought. He had decreed that the land of the Kingdom of Judah should be absolutely desolated of man and domesticated beast, with no one even passing through the desolated land because of fear of its being haunted by demons. It was to lie desolate in this manner for a full period of seventy years, in order that the God-given land might enjoy a sabbath period, to make up for all the sabbath years that the Jews had failed to keep regarding the land. (2 Chronicles 36:17-23; compare Daniel 9:1, 2; Jeremiah 9:11; 26:9; 32:43; 33:10-12; 34:22.) Consequently those defiers of Jehovah's decree had to be ousted, and they were. The utter desolation of the land of Judah did begin in the seventh month of the year of Jerusalem's destruction, about October 4/5 of the year 607 B.C.E. (2 Kings 25:18-26) Any Jewish fugitives round about who desired to repossess the land before the ending of seventy years of utter desolation were prevented from doing so.—Jeremiah 52:24-30.

[31] Correspondingly in our day, the realm, yes, the place that Christendom has occupied in this worldly system of things will be completely desolated without any of her religious institutions remaining therein. Before the so-called pagan, heathen part of Babylon the Great, Christendom will cease to be the dominant part of that world empire of false Babylonish religion. The

---

30. What decree concerning the desolation of the land was not to be set at nought, and when did that divine decree take effect?
31. What, corresponding to that, will befall Christendom, and what will the secular elements of this system of things have to know before their own destruction?

secular elements of today's worldwide system of things will look at the vacuum that she as well as the rest of Babylon the Great has left, but her they will see no more during the brief time before those secular elements are themselves annihilated in the worldwide "great tribulation" in which the whole system comes to a violent end. Christendom never did correctly put God's name before those secular elements. Necessarily, then, in view of what the anointed Ezekiel class have long proclaimed world wide, those secular elements will have to come to the knowledge prescribed for them in the repeatedly stated formula: "They will have to know that I am Jehovah."

ENTRANCED HEARERS, BUT NOT DOERS

[32] As is well known, the modern Ezekiel class, the anointed remnant of Jehovah's Christian witnesses, are a subject of much discussion among the people inside as well as outside of Christendom. But the people in general react toward them just the same as Ezekiel's fellow exiles in Babylon reacted toward him and his prophesying, before the news of Jerusalem's destruction broke upon them with stunning impact. Jehovah observed the exiles and said:

[33] "And as for you, O son of man, the sons of your people are speaking with one another about you beside the walls and in the entrances of the houses, and the one has spoken with the other, each one with his brother, saying, 'Come, please, and hear what the word is that is going forth from Jehovah.' And they will come in to you, like the coming in of people, and sit before you as my people; and they will certainly hear your words but these they will not do, for with their mouth they are expressing lustful desires and after their unjust gain is where their heart is going. And, look! you are to them like a song of sensuous loves, like one with a pretty voice and playing a stringed

32, 33. What observations did Jehovah make on the talk and attitudes of the people respecting Ezekiel, who today meet similar reactions from the people, and when things come true what will the people know?

instrument well. And they will certainly hear your words, but there are none doing them. And when it comes true—look! it must come true—they will also have to know that a prophet himself had proved to be in the midst of them."—Ezekiel 33:30-33.

[34] Whether beside walls casting cooling shade or in the doorways of their homes or elsewhere, people are gossiping and conversing at times after the Ezekiel class and the "great crowd" of their Christian co-workers come around, going from house to house preaching God's Messianic kingdom and the "conclusion of the system of things." (Matthew 24:3-14; Revelation 7:9-17) Many persons, even many who are still related to Christendom, will pass around nice compliments about these Christian witnesses of Jehovah. They may even come to the large public meetings of these witnesses or arrange for a home Bible study to be carried on with them and invite neighbors or relatives to join them in the study. They like the tone and directness of the divine message and respectfully listen to it. But they leave the matter hanging in suspense; they come to no energizing favorable decision toward Jehovah. They merely like to be entertained with a Biblically supported message. Their concern is not to appear outright irreligious, open to the charge of being atheistic communists.

[35] They may be disturbed by the cry of Christendom that Jehovah's Christian witnesses are "false prophets!" They may not be fully convinced that these are true spokesmen for Jehovah the Sovereign Lord. To let themselves come to the conclusion that these were authentic spokesmen would oblige them to do the positive things about it. This would mean for them to stop holding on to lustful desire and going wholeheartedly after unjust gain.

34. How do people today fit the description given by Jehovah, and how do they show they merely want to be entertained by the anointed Ezekiel class and Christian co-workers of these?
35. At what cry on Christendom's part may such persons be disturbed, and what decision with its consequent action do they hold back from making?

³⁶ None of us should want to be like these indecisive, unresponding ones! Better it is to know now, rather than too late, that there is an authentic prophetic class of Christians among us, and to accept and act upon the Bible message, "not as the word of men, but, just as it truthfully is, as the word of God." (1 Thessalonians 2:13) Concerning the message faithfully delivered by the Ezekiel class Jehovah positively states that it "must come true." He asseverates that those who wait undecided until it does "come true" "will also have to know that a prophet himself had proved to be in the midst of them." (Ezekiel 33:33) Such belated knowledge, however, will not mean salvation for them, for it will find their hearts and their ways to be unchanged.

³⁷ What is to be gained by hesitating and doubting to the end that Jehovah can raise up and has raised up a genuine "prophet" within our generation? Certainly it will gain for no one the divine favor and protection needed during the speedily approaching "great tribulation" upon Christendom and the rest of Babylon the Great. If our course is to be that of wisdom and of faith, then, with Bible in hand, we will heed the warning of Jehovah's true watchman and will take refuge where Jehovah indicates in His Word. Then, when Jehovah's prophetic watchman gets the report that Christendom has been stricken down, we, together with the faithful watchman, will continue to live on through the destruction of the whole world empire of false religion and of its secular paramours, with what prospect before us? Ah, with the prospect of enjoying all the unspeakably good things that Jehovah has in store for his worshipers in the righteous new system of pure religion.

---

36. What better course, unlike that of those people, should we take now, and of what value will the knowledge be that is forced upon people when the thing spoken comes true?
37. What will hesitation and doubt down to the end gain for one, and what is the course of wisdom and of faith for us to take because of what prospect?

Chapter 16

A Shepherd-King for All Mankind

KINGS, princes, presidents and governors of the world, not excluding those of Christendom, have not considered themselves as shepherds. To this day such political rulers have not cared to assume duties like those of a shepherd. This has been true from as far back as the Pharaohs of Egypt of the eighteenth century before our Common Era (1728 B.C.E.). Concerning that land it is reported: "Every herder of sheep is a detestable thing to Egypt." (Genesis 46:32-34) To worldly rulers the occupation of shepherd appears too lowly to comport with the dignity of their governmental position. It is an occupation that calls for tenderness and compassion such as worldly rulers are not disposed to display toward the masses who "must be kept under." Also, shepherding is too peaceful an occupation for rulers who are inclined to show belligerency and militancy with the idea of keeping other rulers in their place. So they keep prepared for war.

² What, though, about the very highest one in all the realm of existence, who is also the Sovereign of the Universe? Is he too proud to liken himself to a shepherd? No! So without offense an ancient king, the psalmist David, spoke of Him as a herder of sheep, saying: "Jehovah is my Shepherd." (Psalm 23:1) He acts as shepherd toward all his human creatures. Likewise, he speaks of the rulers of His people as shepherds. In the year 1473 B.C.E. he brought his chosen people

1. Reportedly, from as far back as when have political rulers not liked to consider themselves as shepherds, and why so?
2. Is Jehovah too proud to liken himself to a shepherd, and to what did the psalmist David liken Jehovah, and to what did Jehovah liken Moses' successor Joshua?

into the Promised Land under the leadership of Joshua the son of Nun, who belonged to the tribe of Ephraim and who had been commissioned by the prophet Moses to lead Israel, why? For the loving purpose "that Jehovah's assembly may not become like sheep that have no shepherd."—Numbers 27:15-21.

³ In later years the governmental rulers of Jehovah's people failed to act like unselfish, compassionate Oriental shepherds to their subjects. So Jehovah declared to his prophet Ezekiel what he was determined to do about matters. Ezekiel leads up to a scathing denunciation of these "shepherds" by saying:

⁴ "And the word of Jehovah continued to occur to me, saying: 'Son of man, prophesy against the shepherds of Israel. Prophesy, and you must say to them, to the shepherds, "This is what the Sovereign Lord Jehovah has said." ' "—Ezekiel 34:1, 2.

⁵ This declaration against the governmental shepherds of Israel is recorded as occurring after Jerusalem's destruction. But before her destruction the prophet Jeremiah at Jerusalem was inspired to declare something similar in connection with the second-last king on the royal throne, namely, Coniah (or Jeconiah, or Jehoiachin), in these words: "This is what Jehovah has said, 'Write down this man as childless, as an able-bodied man who will not have any success in his days; for from his offspring not a single one will have any success, sitting upon the throne of David and ruling anymore in Judah.' [1 Chronicles 3:17-19; Matthew 1:11, 12] 'Woe to the shepherds who are destroying and scattering the sheep of my pasturage!' is the utterance of Jehovah.

⁶ "Therefore this is what Jehovah the God of Israel has said against the shepherds who are shepherding my people: 'You yourselves have scattered my sheep; and you kept dispersing them, and you have not turned

3, 4. Like men in what occupation did the later rulers of Israel fail to act, and therefore Jehovah addressed himself to them as being what?
5, 6. Through Jeremiah what did Jehovah say concerning the royal shepherd Coniah (Jehoiachin), what did Jehovah say that the rulers were doing to His sheep, but what would He do for them?

your attention to them.' 'Here I am turning my attention upon you for the badness of your dealings,' is the utterance of Jehovah. 'And I myself shall collect together the remnant of my sheep out of all the lands to which I had dispersed them, and I will bring them back to their pasture ground, and they will certainly be fruitful and become many. And I will raise up over them shepherds who will actually shepherd them; and they will be afraid no more, neither will they be struck with any terror, and none will be missing,' is the utterance of Jehovah.

[7] " 'Look! There are days coming,' is the utterance of Jehovah, 'and I will raise up to David a righteous sprout. And a king will certainly reign and act with discretion and execute justice and righteousness in the land. In his days Judah will be saved, and Israel itself will reside in security. And this is his name with which he will be called, Jehovah Is Our Righteousness.' " —Jeremiah 22:24 to 23:6.

[8] Note, now, how, when giving a similar message to his prophet Ezekiel, Jehovah goes into more detail as to the misconduct of the unfaithful "shepherds of Israel." As we read Jehovah's words of description, we do well to think, not just of the history of the bad kings of Israel, but of their modern counterpart, the professed Christian kings, princes and governors of Christendom.

[9] "This is what the Sovereign Lord Jehovah has said: 'Woe to the shepherds of Israel, who have become feeders of themselves! Is it not the flock that the shepherds ought to feed? The fat is what you eat, and with the wool you clothe your own selves. The plump animal is what you slaughter. The flock itself you do not feed. The sickened ones you have not strengthened, and the ailing one you have not healed, and the broken one

7. In that connection, what did Jehovah purpose to raise up to King David, and what name would Jehovah bestow on what was raised up?
8. As we read Jehovah's words addressed through Ezekiel to the "shepherds of Israel," whom should we have in mind?
9. In Ezekiel 34:2-6, how did Jehovah describe the misconduct of the rulers as "shepherds of Israel," with what result to the sheep?

you have not bandaged, and the dispersed one you have not brought back, and the lost one you have not sought to find, but with harshness you have had them in subjection, even with tyranny. And they were gradually scattered because of there being no shepherd, so that they became food for every wild beast of the field, and they continued to be scattered. My sheep kept straying on all the mountains and on every high hill; and on all the surface of the earth my sheep are scattered, with no one making a search and with no one seeking to find.' "—Ezekiel 34:2-6.

THE PREY OF THE GOVERNMENTAL "SHEPHERDS"

[10] By virtue of their religious claims the church people of Christendom were Jehovah's "sheep." The professed Christian political rulers should therefore have been very careful of how they treated the sheeplike subjects, inasmuch as these were not the property of the political rulers but the property of the God whom they professed to worship. This fact holds true not only respecting the secular authorities of Christendom but also regarding popes, cardinals and archbishops who have held or still hold political office and maintain relations with the political states of this world. For example, since 1929 the popes of Rome have ruled as the absolute sovereign of Vatican City and have maintained diplomatic relations with the political states of this world. The first president of the Republic of Cyprus has been an archbishop of the Greek Orthodox Church. Despite their harsh treatment of the sheeplike people, the political rulers of Christendom have had favor and support from the religious clergy and have been the highly regarded church members of their religious systems.

[11] Notwithstanding their claims to being Christian,

---

10. According to religious claims, whose "sheep" are the church people of Christendom, but who have been their visible governmental "shepherds"?

11. Despite their claiming to be Christian, how have the political rulers of Christendom treated the "sheep," and what must be said about their imitating Jehovah's Fine Shepherd?

the political rulers have made the sheeplike people their prey and have fattened themselves materially off these poor "sheep." How unlike the one whom they claim to follow, namely, Jesus Christ, who said: "I am the door; whoever enters through me will be saved, and he will go in and out and find pasturage. The thief does not come unless it is to steal and slay and destroy. I have come that they might have life and might have it in abundance. I am the fine shepherd; the fine shepherd surrenders his soul in behalf of the sheep"! (John 10:9-11) Imitate this Fine Shepherd and lay down their lives for the sheep? We have not seen the political rulers of Christendom do this. Just because the religious clergy hobnob with the politicians and rank them high among their church members, let no one think that the heavenly Owner of the "sheep," Jehovah, approves of the oppressive course of the political rulers of Christendom. To correct any wrong ideas of ours, He declares:

¹² "Therefore, you shepherds, hear the word of Jehovah, ' "As I am alive," is the utterance of the Sovereign Lord Jehovah, "surely for the reason that my sheep became something for plunder and my sheep continued to be food for every wild beast of the field, because there was no shepherd, and my shepherds did not search for my sheep, but the shepherds kept feeding themselves, and my own sheep they did not feed," ' therefore, you shepherds, hear the word of Jehovah. This is what the Sovereign Lord Jehovah has said, 'Here I am against the shepherds, and I shall certainly ask back my sheep from their hand and make them cease from feeding my sheep, and the shepherds will no longer feed themselves; and I will deliver my sheep out of their mouth, and they will not become food for them.' "—Ezekiel 34:7-10.

¹³ The political "shepherds" of Christendom have

12. What position does the heavenly Owner of the "sheep" take toward those political shepherds, and for what stated reasons?
13. How have the "sheep" of Christendom been sacrificed to various causes, and been scattered and thus fallen prey to "beasts"?

fought among themselves, one professed Christian ruler against another so-called Christian ruler, and have sacrificed their sheeplike people on the altar of nationalism or religious sectarianism. Some political rulers that have been outstanding favorites of the religious clergy have been dictators. The Christian witnesses of Jehovah have experienced violent persecution at the hand of these dictators and extremely nationalistic, totalitarian rulers. Because of the injustices that are not corrected, many of the oppressed people have fled to various newly formed, revolutionary kinds of organizations and have fallen victim to materialistic radicalism and atheistic communism. There is neither political, national nor religious unity in Christendom. Like bewildered sheep without a shepherd, the people are scattered as prey to "beasts."

¹⁴ In the case of ancient Israel of Ezekiel's day, Jehovah delivered his sheep out of the mouth of the self-feeding shepherds in governmental places by having Jerusalem destroyed and the land of Judah desolated. The king and princes had to vacate their governmental office, being captured by the Babylonians and deported. Some were killed as a penalty for their rebellion. In Babylon they were put in prison or subjected to restraints, being stripped of any rulership. (2 Kings 25:18-30; Jeremiah 52:24-34) In modern-day antitype, the destruction of Christendom in the approaching "great tribulation" will absolutely deprive the professed "Christian" political rulers of the religious clergy, for the latter will be put out of religious office by the executional forces of Jehovah. Christendom's clergy will cease to exist. Any worldly politicians surviving Christendom's annihilation will be reserved for execution in the final part of the "great tribulation," namely, in the "war of the great day of God the Almighty" at the world situation called Har–Magedon. —Revelation 16:14-16; 19:11-21.

14. How did Jehovah deliver his "sheep" out of the mouths of the self-feeding shepherds of ancient Israel, and how will he do a similar deliverance in the case of modern Christendom?

¹⁵ Thus the death-dealing removal of all the governmental overseers of the entire worldwide system of things, including the professed Christian rulers of Christendom, will free Jehovah's true "sheep" from the oppression and self-serving operations of the political "shepherds." No more will those unfaithful shepherds feed themselves at the expense of Jehovah's flock of Christian witnesses. No matter how scattered these may find themselves because of the opposition and persecution carried on by political elements, Jehovah knows where his true "sheep" have been dispersed. Like a loving Shepherd, he will search for them and regather them into one fold. His solemn promise as made through his prophet Ezekiel stands good today. The way that he fulfilled this promise toward ancient Israel in the year 537 B.C.E. and thereafter was a prophetic guarantee that he would carry out his promise in the future. Hear, now, His words:

¹⁶ "For this is what the Sovereign Lord Jehovah has said: 'Here I am, I myself, and I will search for my sheep and care for them. According to the care of one feeding his drove in the day of his coming to be in the midst of his sheep that have been spread abroad, that is the way that I shall care for my sheep; and I will deliver them out of all the places to which they have been scattered in the day of clouds and thick gloom. And I will bring them out from the peoples and collect them together from the lands and bring them in onto their soil and feed them on the mountains of Israel, by the stream beds and by all the dwelling places of the land. In a good pasturage I shall feed them, and on Israel's high mountains their abiding place will come to be. There they will lie down in a good abiding place, and on a fat pasturage they will feed upon the mountains of Israel.' "—Ezekiel 34:11-14.

15. Thus Jehovah's true "sheep" will be delivered from the operations of whom, and what prophetic historic guarantee do we have that He will regather his "sheep" into one fold?
16. To that effect, what did Jehovah say in Ezekiel 34:11-14?

THE REGATHERING OF THE SCATTERED "SHEEP"

[17] In ancient times Jehovah began the fulfillment of this prophecy in the year 537 B.C.E., by the restoration of a faithful remnant of Jewish exiles by the good offices of King Cyrus the Persian, the conqueror of Babylon. (2 Chronicles 36:17-23; Ezra 1:1 to 3:6) A larger and final fulfillment of this hope-inspiring prophecy takes place on spiritual Israel, "the Israel of God," to whom the Christian apostle Paul wrote. (Galatians 6:16; 1:1-5) Even now, before the outbreak of the "great tribulation" in which Christendom and all the rest of Babylon the Great will be destroyed, the Heavenly Shepherd Jehovah has demonstrated his ability to gather the scattered remnant of spiritual Israel into a religiously free, spiritually nourishing relationship with Him. (1 Peter 2:25) For them the turbulent times of World War I (of 1914-1918 C.E.) had been a "day of clouds and thick gloom." (Ezekiel 34:12) That day was darkened because of the religious persecution that Christendom (the dominant part of Babylon the Great) heaped on the remnant of spiritual Israel. Thereby the remnant of spiritual Israelites were scattered and came into deep bondage to Babylon the Great.

[18] Babylon the Great, however, failed to maintain her oppressive hold on the true-hearted remnant of spiritual Israelites. In the spring of 1919 Babylon the Great suffered a severe fall from her position of religious power over Jehovah's people, and the shackles of their bondage to her were broken. This was a thing that could have occurred by the power of no one else but Jehovah through his Greater Cyrus, Jesus Christ. (Psalm 126:1-4) As far as their religious rights and privileges from God were concerned, this remnant no longer let themselves become the prey or "food" of

17. Upon whom does the larger and final fulfillment of that prophecy come, and even now before destruction of Babylon the Great, how has Jehovah shown his ability to gather his spiritual "sheep"?
18. When were the shackles of Babylon the Great broken for these "sheep," and thereafter they stepped on the world stage as being what?

the governmental "shepherds" of Christendom. In Christian fearlessness they stepped on the stage of the postwar world as witnesses of Jehovah's Messianic kingdom.—Matthew 24:14.

[19] War-bruised Christendom and all the rest of the world had to take note of the regathered, reunified condition of this Christian remnant of spiritual Israel when they held their first postwar international assembly at Cedar Point, Ohio, U.S.A. Thousands of the once scattered remnant gathered here, and there was a public attendance of 7,000 listeners at the lecture entitled "The Hope for Distressed Humanity," on Sunday, September 7, 1919.

[20] Toward these regathered sheep of spiritual Israel Jehovah has carried out the further declaration of His purpose: " 'I myself shall feed my sheep, and I myself shall make them lie down,' is the utterance of the Sovereign Lord Jehovah. 'The lost one I shall search for, and the dispersed one I shall bring back, and the broken one I shall bandage and the ailing one I shall strengthen, but the fat one and the strong one I shall annihilate. I shall feed that one with judgment.' " —Ezekiel 34:15, 16.

[21] Since that year of liberation, 1919 C.E., Jehovah has made an addition to the original remnant that survived faithfully the "day of clouds and thick gloom" during World War I. Thousands of persons inside and outside Christendom heard the Kingdom message as preached by Jehovah's restored remnant and were filled with the desire to become "disciples" of His Son Jesus Christ. Upon properly understanding Jehovah's requirements for them, they dedicated themselves to him and got baptized in symbol of their dedication, in obedience to Christ's commandment.—Matthew 28:19, 20.

---

19. When in 1919 C.E. and by what event did Christendom and the rest of the world have to take note of the regathered condition of the remnant of spiritual Israelites?
20. What did Jehovah say he would do for the "sheep" lost, scattered, broken and ailing, as in contrast with the strong and fat ones?
21. Since 1919 there was an addition of whom to the original remnant, and in what manner?

²² The evidences that followed in the lives of these dedicated footstep followers of Christ proved that Jehovah had given them spiritual birth to be his spiritual sons and had anointed them with his holy spirit as his ministers. (John 3:3, 5; James 1:18; 1 Peter 1:3-5; Romans 8:15-17) In this way Jehovah made them members of spiritual Israel, "the Israel of God," and they have been enjoying His shepherdlike care and attention in the restored spiritual estate of Jehovah's anointed remnant on earth.

MAINTAINING CONSIDERATE BEHAVIOR AMONG SHEEP

²³ Among these restored "sheep" the Heavenly Shepherd permits no one to misuse his strength with impunity. If anyone takes advantage of his spiritual fatness and strength to the rough treatment and oppression of other "sheep" in the fold, Jehovah will "annihilate" such an unloving, selfish "sheep," cutting such one off from the flock as one who is spiritually dead. Says he: "I shall feed that one with judgment," that is, with the judgment of disfellowshiping from the flock now and literal annihilation in the coming "great tribulation" upon Christendom and all the rest of Babylon the Great.

²⁴ Jehovah maintains the proper dealing of the restored "sheep" in his flock, of the one with the other. There has been enough of crowding, and shoving aside and horning among the religious flocks of Christendom, especially on the part of the haughty, self-important clergymen and those church members who have powerful influence with the clergy. Jehovah desires none of this conduct among his restored flock. He says:

22. How did such become members of spiritual Israel, "the Israel of God"?
23. Among his restored "sheep," what does Jehovah promise to do to anyone that misuses his spiritual fatness and strength?
24. What kind of dealing with one another as carried on among the religious flocks of Christendom does Jehovah not desire among his restored "sheep"?

²⁵ "And as for you my sheep, this is what the Sovereign Lord Jehovah has said: 'Here I am judging between a sheep and a sheep, between the rams and the he-goats. Is it such a little thing for you men that on the very best pasturage you feed but the rest of your pasturages you should trample down with your feet, and that the clear waters you drink but the ones [the waters] left over you should foul by stamping with your very feet? And as for my sheep, on the pasture ground trampled by your feet should they feed and the water befouled by the stamping of your feet should they drink?' Therefore this is what the Sovereign Lord Jehovah has said to them: 'Here I am, I myself, and I shall certainly judge between a plump sheep and a lean sheep, for the reason that with flank and with shoulder you kept pushing and with your horns you kept shoving all the sickened ones until you had scattered them to the outside. And I will save my sheep, and they will no longer become something for plunder; and I will judge between a sheep and a sheep.' "—Ezekiel 34:17-22.

²⁶ In keeping with this prophetic promise Jehovah cleared out from among his restored remnant of spiritual sheep those who are greedy and self-seeking, using their brute strength and their horns of power to enjoy the best of things for themselves to the exclusion of weak or sickened other ones, even spoiling things for others that these might not thrive spiritually. Jehovah has allowed no dividing of his "sheep" into a clergy class and a laity class. As Shepherd Judge between his "sheep," he has enforced the rule laid down through his Son Jesus Christ: "But you, do not you be called Rabbi, for one is your teacher, whereas all you are brothers. Moreover, do not call anyone your [spiritual] father on earth, for one is your Father, the heavenly One. Neither be called 'leaders,' for your

---

25. What will Jehovah do to those "sheep" that mistreat the pasture grounds and waters and that misuse flank and horn?
26. Accordingly, Jehovah has cleared out whom from among his restored "sheep," and what rule laid down by Jesus Christ has He enforced?

Leader is one, the Christ. But the greatest one among you must be your minister."—Matthew 23:8-11.

[27] If anyone tries to be like a horned ram or a horned he-goat and lead away Jehovah's "sheep" after him, Jehovah sees to it that he is expelled. The spiritual food and drink must be made available to all His "sheep," that the whole flock may be spiritually healthy.

THE "ONE SHEPHERD" UNDER ONE GOD

[28] Why is it today that, among Jehovah's restored flock of spiritual Israel, persons like aggressive horned rams and he-goats have been judged according to their deserts and been expelled from the "Israel of God"? It is because Jehovah has put a faithful undershepherd in charge of his flock. In this respect he has not failed regarding his promise in Ezekiel 34:23, 24: "And I will raise up over them one shepherd, and he must feed them, even my servant David. He himself will feed them, and he himself will become their shepherd. And I myself, Jehovah, will become their God, and my servant David a chieftain in the midst of them. I myself, Jehovah, have spoken."

[29] In a correspondency with ancient Israel, Christendom has had men like "shepherd" kings, "shepherd" rulers, in posts of government. For these the clergy have made the claim that such political "shepherds" rule "by the grace of God." Misguided by the clergy's misinterpretation of the Holy Scriptures, many such rulers claimed "the divine right of kings." For instance, King James I, the sponsor of the English Authorized Version of the Bible of 1611, was a stout contender for such "divine right of kings." Quite to his liking, the dedication of this Authorized Version of the Bible

27. How does Jehovah deal with those who try to mislead, and how are all his "sheep" kept spiritually healthy?
28. Because of His fulfilling what promise have such aggressive ones been judged according to their deserts among Jehovah's restored "sheep"?
29. As in ancient Israel, how is it that Christendom has had political rulers like "shepherd" kings?

is addressed as follows: "To the Most High and Mighty Prince James, by the Grace of God, King of Great Britain, France, and Ireland, Defender of the Faith, &c."

[30] True, God has permitted such rulers to govern, but such permission does not mean any "Grace of God" to them or impart "divine right" to them. It is not mere divine permission that allows for a certain "one shepherd" to rule over the restored remnant of spiritual Israel. Jehovah himself directly sets him up over them, for that one has the "legal right."—Ezekiel 21:27.

[31] Who, then, is the "one shepherd" to whom Jehovah gives the royal governmental position because this one has the "legal right" to it? Jehovah calls him "my servant David." (Ezekiel 34:23) This does not mean that Jehovah raises up the original King David from the dead in order to put him in this shepherdlike office. It means a natural descendant of King David, who inherited the royal right from him. Such descendant was the heavenly Son of God, who had his life transferred from heaven to the womb of the Jewish virgin, Mary of Bethlehem, in order that he might be born into the earthly royal line of David, thus to become the "son of David, son of Abraham." (Matthew 1:1 to 2:6; Luke 1:26-38; 2:4 to 3:31; Romans 1:1-4) The fact that the name David means "Beloved" comports well with the declaration that Jehovah made from heaven at the time that Jesus was baptized in water and at the time of his being transfigured on a high mountain: "This is my Son, the beloved." (Matthew 3:13-17; 17:1-5) Jesus likened all mankind to sheep when he said: "I am the fine shepherd, . . . and I surrender my soul in behalf of the sheep."—John 10:14, 15.

---

30. How does the case of those who claim rule by God's "grace" and "divine right of kings" compare with that of the "one shepherd" who rules over spiritual Israel?
31. Who, then, is this "one shepherd" whom Jehovah calls "my servant David," and why are the words "David" and "shepherd" appropriate for that one?

³² That he might resume his shepherding of the "sheep" on earth, Jehovah raised Jesus Christ up from the dead. Hence the Christian apostle Paul, when writing to the Christianized Hebrews, speaks of Jehovah as "the God of peace, who brought up from the dead the great shepherd of the sheep with the blood of an everlasting covenant, our Lord Jesus." (Hebrews 13: 20) Resurrected back to spirit life such as he originally had, Jesus Christ is now a heavenly Shepherd. In view of this there could be only the "one shepherd" that Jehovah could raise up over the remnant of spiritual Israel, namely, this resurrected Jesus the Messiah.

³³ When did Jehovah do so? In the year 1914 C.E., when the "appointed times of the [Gentile] nations" ended, about October 4/5 of that war-shattered year. Concerning those Gentile nations the prophecy is made concerning his kingdom that he "is to shepherd all the nations with an iron rod." (Revelation 12:5) That means the breaking to pieces of all those ungodly nations as though being a potter's vessel. (Psalm 2:8, 9) But the remnant of spiritual Israel he does not shepherd with such a rod or scepter.

³⁴ "He himself will feed them," says Jehovah, "and he himself will become their shepherd. And I myself, Jehovah, will become their God, and my servant David a chieftain in the midst of them. I myself, Jehovah, have spoken." (Ezekiel 34:23, 24) During the first world war (1914-1918 C.E.) the "shepherd" kings of Christendom and their patriotic subjects persecuted the anointed remnant of spiritual Israel. After World War I Jehovah's "servant David," or Jesus Christ, took over the shepherd's care of them.

³⁵ Like the ancient Persian conqueror of Babylon,

32. According to Hebrews 13:20, why is there only the "one shepherd" whom Jehovah could raise up over spiritual Israel's remnant?
33. When did Jehovah raise up this "one shepherd" over the remnant of spiritual Israel, and how does he deal with the nations?
34. How did the "shepherd" kings of Christendom treat the anointed remnant during World War I, and when did Jehovah's "servant David" take over the care of them?
35. How did he act toward the remnant of spiritual Israel like ancient Cyrus the Persian, how did he feed them and serve as their "chieftain," and whom did they acknowledge as their God?

respecting whom Jehovah said: "Cyrus, 'He is my shepherd,'" Jesus Christ delivered the remnant of spiritual Israel from Babylon the Great and her political associates from the year 1919 onward. With spiritual food he has fed them till now. He has become their chieftain in whose footsteps they follow as sheep. His God, Jehovah, has become their God. In appreciation of this, the anointed remnant, in the year 1931, embraced the Scripturally based name, "Jehovah's witnesses."—Isaiah 43:10-12, *AS; NW*.

"OTHER SHEEP, WHICH ARE NOT OF THIS FOLD"

[36] Shortly after they began identifying themselves as the Christian witnesses of Jehovah, the attention of the anointed remnant was specially drawn to Jesus' words, in John 10:16: "And I have other sheep, which are not of this fold; those also I must bring, and they will listen to my voice, and they will become one flock, one shepherd." The "other sheep" mean all the others of the world of mankind for whom the Fine Shepherd surrendered his soul or laid down his life as a ransom sacrifice.

[37] In the spring of the year 1935 it was revealed to the anointed remnant that a numberless "great crowd" of these "other sheep" was to be taken out from this system of things before the outbreak of the "great tribulation" upon Christendom. These began being baptized as "disciples" of Jesus Christ. But thereafter Jehovah revealed by his Word and dealings that He was not begetting them to a heavenly future but was reserving them for life in the coming Paradise earth along with all the rest of the "other sheep." (Matthew 28:19, 20; Revelation 7:9-17) Nevertheless, He kept them in association with the anointed remnant that thus there might be "one flock."

---

36. After they embraced that name, to what "sheep" was the attention of the anointed remnant specially drawn, and who are those "sheep"?
37. What revelation concerning the "other sheep" was given in 1935, and for what future did Jehovah indicate that he was reserving these baptized disciples of Christ?

[38] Thus in companionship and cooperation with the remnant of spiritual Israel, the "great crowd" enjoys the peace and protection that Jehovah has promised to his restored remnant, saying:

[39] "And I will conclude with them a covenant of peace, and I shall certainly cause the injurious wild beast to cease out of the land, and they will actually dwell in the wilderness in security and sleep in the forests. And I will make them and the surroundings of my hill a blessing, and I will cause the pouring rain to descend in its time. Pouring rains of blessing there will prove to be. And the tree of the field must give its fruitage, and the land itself will give its yield, and they will actually prove to be on their soil in security. And they will have to know that I am Jehovah when I break the bars of their yoke and I have delivered them out of the hand of those who had been using them as slaves. And they will no longer become something to plunder for the nations; and as regards the wild beast of the earth, it will not devour them, and they will actually dwell in security, with no one to make them tremble."—Ezekiel 34:25-28.

[40] What a beautiful prophecy this is of the peace and security that prevail within the ranks and congregations of the anointed remnant of spiritual Israel, now joined by the "great crowd" of baptized sheeplike ones who are being gathered out of nations, tribes, peoples and tongues! According to Jehovah's "covenant" for Christian peace, he has driven out and kept out all ferocious beastlike personalities dangerous to sheeplike Christians. By his holy spirit operating upon the true baptized disciples of Christ he has transformed their personalities into a peaceful, harmless sheeplikeness. They lovingly seek to protect one another spiritually as well as materially amidst this hostile world. The effect of this has been as predicted: They have come

to know that the God who has broken the bars of their religious yoke of bondage and delivered them from their Babylonish enslavers is the one "whose name is Jehovah." (Psalm 83:18) Little wonder, then, that they take delight in being his active, vocal witnesses.

A PARADISAIC "PLANTING FOR A NAME"

[41] Christendom will be uprooted and destroyed in the coming "great tribulation," but the organization of Jehovah's Christian witnesses is planted in the earth to remain through the present turbulent times and through the "great tribulation" in which the present worldwide system of things ends. This is the meaning of Jehovah's words, when he says concerning restored spiritual Israel: "And I will raise up for them a planting for a name, and they will no more become those taken away by famine in the land, and they will no longer bear the humiliation by the nations. 'And they will have to know that I, Jehovah their God, am with them and that they are my people, the house of Israel,' is the utterance of the Sovereign Lord Jehovah." —Ezekiel 34:29, 30.

[42] In fulfillment of this divine promise, the modern-day remnant of spiritual Israel have been brought into a spiritual Paradise. (2 Corinthians 12:4) The "planting" that Jehovah has raised up for these restored ones has remained to this day and is producing more abundantly than ever previously since the year 1919. Under Jehovah's blessings, like pouring rains, their earthly estate has brought forth superabundantly the "fruits" of the kingdom of God. (Matthew 21:43) This productive plantation has become "for them a planting for a name," a renowned or famous plantation. Jehovah's written Word, the Holy Bible, he has opened up to their understanding, and not only are they sharing

---

41. In harmony with Ezekiel 34:29, 30, for how long is the organization of Jehovah's Christian witnesses planted in the earth, in contrast with Christendom?
42. The "planting" that Jehovah has raised up for them has become what in a spiritual sense, and how has the overflow of spiritual food been made available to the nations?

the resulting spiritual food among themselves but, by means of millions on millions of pieces of printed literature, they are making this overflow of spiritual food available to all the nations possible in many languages.

[43] This has resulted in their gaining a name earth wide as distributors of Bible literature. Opposed nations cannot halt or diminish this worldwide export of spiritual food by spiritual Israelites and thereby humiliate them by calling them famine-stricken.

[44] Never again will the worldly nations be able to repeat what they did during World War I in banning and censoring the circulation of Jehovah's kingdom message world wide so as to bring about the death of the remnant of spiritual Israel by spiritual famine. Whether by underground movement or by open above-ground distribution in broad daylight, the printed message of life issues forth in larger and larger volume, penetrating to the far corners of the earth to feed persons who are conscious of their spiritual need as regards the one living and true God. (Matthew 5:3) Due to their being blessed with such spiritual prosperity and overabundance of spiritual food, they have been made to know that Jehovah, the God whose name they bear, is with them and that they are his people, the spiritual "house of Israel," even though they are a small remnant in comparison with populous Christendom.

[45] Who, then, of all the many religious people of the world are today the spiritual "sheep" of the Divine Shepherd, Jehovah, and under His "one shepherd," Jesus Christ the Greater David? In speech straightforwardly addressed to the remnant of spiritual Israel, the Supreme Shepherd says: " 'And as regards you

---

43. How has this gained a name for these spiritual Israelites, and how have nations been prevented from humiliating them as being famine-stricken?

44. Why will the nations be unable to repeat what they did during World War I to attempt the spiritual death of Jehovah's remnant, and thus what have these spiritual Israelites been made to know?

45. As respects all the many religious people of the world, what question arises, and how does the Supreme Shepherd answer this?

my sheep, the sheep of my pasturing, you are earthling men. I am your God,' is the utterance of the Sovereign Lord Jehovah."—Ezekiel 34:31.

[46] The anointed remnant of spiritual Israel, restored to God's favor since 1919, are manifestly living in the "year of goodwill on the part of Jehovah." (Isaiah 61:1, 2) By making them "the sheep of my pasturing" he is treating them as His "men of goodwill," concerning whom the angelic "multitude of the heavenly army" said at the time of Jesus' birth in David's city, Bethlehem: "Glory in the heights above to God, and upon earth peace among men of goodwill."—Luke 2:10-14.

[47] The "great crowd" that comes out of all nations, tribes and peoples discern that Jehovah has made choice of the remnant of spiritual Israelites and they likewise put themselves under his Shepherd-King Jesus Christ, as his "other sheep." Despite their not being spiritual Israelites but coming from all earthly nations, tribes, peoples and tongues, they listen to the voice of the Fine Shepherd, Jesus Christ, and sheeplike they follow him as the "one shepherd" whom Jehovah has raised up over spiritual Israel. Why do they follow along with the remnant of spiritual Israel as "one flock" under "one shepherd"? It is because they know for a fact that Jesus Christ is Jehovah's Shepherd-King for all mankind.—John 10:16; Revelation 7:9-17.

---

46. In what favorable period are these designated "sheep" living, and what kind of "earthling men" are they in connection with Jehovah? 47. Under whose shepherding does the "great crowd" of "other sheep" place itself, and why do they follow along as "one flock" with the remnant of spiritual Israel?

Chapter 17

A "Garden of Eden" for the Sake of His Name

IN THE twentieth century before our Common Era, at least a portion of the land of Palestine looked like the garden of Eden in which the Creator placed the first man, Adam.

² Genesis 13:10 tells us: "So Lot raised his eyes and saw the whole District of the Jordan, that all of it was a well-watered region before Jehovah brought Sodom and Gomorrah to ruin, like the garden of Jehovah." (Genesis 2:7-15) Four hundred years later the Promised Land of Palestine was still beautiful, like a "decoration" on our earth. Jehovah spoke of it as "a land that I had spied out for them [the Israelites], one flowing with milk and honey. It was the decoration of all the lands." (Ezekiel 20:5, 6) That included what became the territory of the Kingdom of Judah, of which Jerusalem was the capital. The Babylonian conquest of the land of Judah in 607 B.C.E. resulted in the land's being left desolate, without human inhabitant and domestic animal. It became like a jungle. (Micah 3:12; Jeremiah 26:17, 18) Would it ever again be transformed into a land like the garden of Eden?

³ Shortly after Jewish exiles in Babylon had learned from a fugitive firsthand that Jerusalem had been struck

1, 2. In the twentieth century B.C.E. what portion of the land of Palestine was like the "garden of Jehovah," and how did the land of the Kingdom of Judah become like a jungle?
3, 4. After Jerusalem's destruction, what heartwarming message concerning the land did Jehovah give to Ezekiel, and when did the enemies speak about the spiritual estate of His anointed remnant, as in Ezekiel 36:1, 2?

down by the Babylonians, Jehovah gave the heartwarming assurance that the now desolated land of Judah would not always lie thus without man or domestic animal. He would lift the reproach off his name and would magnify his name by what he would miraculously do for that land. To his faithful prophet Ezekiel he said: "And as for you, O son of man, prophesy concerning the mountains of Israel, and you must say, 'O mountains of Israel, hear the word of Jehovah. This is what the Sovereign Lord Jehovah has said: "For the reason that the enemy has said against you, 'Aha! Even the high places of old time —as a possession it has become ours!' " ' "—Ezekiel 36:1, 2.

⁴ That is the way the worldly enemies talked against the spiritual estate of the anointed remnant of spiritual Israel after this estate had been desolated by religious persecution and suppression during World War I. Christendom was then ready to take over the whole religious field during the postwar period, to the exclusion of the downtrodden remnant of spiritual Israelites. But Jehovah had other thoughts and said prophetically through Ezekiel:

⁵ "Therefore prophesy, and you must say, 'This is what the Sovereign Lord Jehovah has said: "For the reason, even for the reason that there has been a lying desolate and a snapping at you from all sides, in order for you to become a possession to the remaining ones of the nations and you continue being talked about with the tongue and there is a bad report among people, therefore, O mountains of Israel, hear the word of the Sovereign Lord Jehovah! This is what the Sovereign Lord Jehovah has said to the mountains and to the hills, to the stream beds and to the valleys and to the devastated places that were laid desolate and to the abandoned cities that have come to be for plunder and for ridicule to the remaining ones of the

5. Into what condition had the various features of the land of Israel come, and what was the attitude of the remaining nations toward the land?

nations that are round about; therefore this is what the Sovereign Lord Jehovah has said,

⁶ " ' " 'Certainly in the fire of my zeal I will speak against the remaining ones of the nations and against Edom, all of it, those who have given my land to themselves as a possession with the rejoicing of all the heart, with scorn in the soul, for the sake of its pasture ground and for the plunder.' " ' "—Ezekiel 36:3-5.

⁷ By repeated reference to himself Jehovah leaves no room for question as to who is speaking. The enemy nations right around the desolated land of Judah had their own selfish purpose regarding the vacant territory, but He, Jehovah, had another and different purpose. Those nations showed their hatred of Jehovah by coveting the desolated land of His exiled people, but he had decreed that the land should keep a sabbath of being unoccupied and unworked for seventy years. (2 Chronicles 36:19-21; Daniel 9:2) Those self-seeking nations had to be blocked in carrying out their greedy efforts against Jehovah's will. This obliged Jehovah to speak, not just with words but more fully with deeds, "against the remaining ones of the nations and against Edom, all of it," in the fire of his zeal for his name and his cause. This would fulfill, for instance, what he had said in the previous chapter against Edom and its mountainous region of Seir:

⁸ "Indefinitely lasting desolate wastes are what I shall make you, and your own cities will not be inhabited; and you people will have to know that I am Jehovah. . . . A desolate waste is what you will become, O mountainous region of Seir, even all Edom, all of it; and they will have to know that I am Jehovah."—Ezekiel 35:9, 15.

⁹ The land of Jehovah's exiled people was to lie desolate with no Edomites and no other enemy nationali-

---

6. How did Jehovah say that he would address himself to such nations?
7, 8. What was Jehovah's will concerning the land, how would he have to speak in order to block the greedy efforts of the nations against his will, and so what would the land of Edom become?
9. Must the land of Israel lie desolate as long as the land of Edom, and what has the land of Israel borne that obliges Jehovah to speak?

ties plundering its abandoned cities and using its pasture ground. Yes, "desolate" the land must lie, but not forever as the land of Edom was decreed to lie. "Therefore," said Jehovah to his prophet Ezekiel, "prophesy concerning the soil of Israel, and you must say to the mountains and to the hills, to the stream beds and to the valleys, 'This is what the Sovereign Lord Jehovah has said: "Look! I myself in my zeal and in my rage must speak, for the reason that humiliation by nations is what you have borne." ' "—Ezekiel 36:6.

[10] Jehovah was enraged at the way the enemy nations were humiliating the "soil of Israel" because he had permitted it to be desolated in the punishment of the Israelites because of their bloodguiltiness and idolatry. To no less degree was Jehovah displeased at the close of World War I in 1918 C.E. because of the way that the enemy religionists, particularly those of Christendom, were talking about the religious estate of Jehovah's dedicated people (spiritual Israel). They had desolated that estate by persecution and high-handed action during the hysterical days of mankind's first world war. True, there was some faultiness on the record back there of his remnant of spiritual Israelites, but still their religious estate ought to be respected. Why? Because it was connected with His holy name and his name ought to be respected, not misrepresented. How, then, would he speak in his zeal and rage in postwar times? Would there be any beautification again of the spiritual estate of the spiritual Israelites who were devoted to His name? Listen:

[11] "Therefore this is what the Sovereign Lord Jehovah has said, 'I myself have raised my hand in an oath that the nations that you have round about —they themselves will bear their own humiliation. And you yourselves, O mountains of Israel, will give forth

10. By the end of World War I, why was Jehovah displeased at the way enemy religionists (particularly those of Christendom) had acted, and why should the spiritual estate of his spiritual Israel have been respected?
11. In Ezekiel 36:7-12, what did Jehovah say to the mountains of Israel as to whether they would be beautified again?

your very own boughs and bear your own fruitage for my people Israel, for they have drawn near to the point of coming in. For here I am in favor of you, and I shall certainly turn toward you, and you will actually be cultivated and sown with seed. And I will multiply upon you humankind, the whole house of Israel, all of it, and the cities must become inhabited, and the devastated places themselves will be rebuilt. Yes, I will multiply upon you humankind and animalkind, and they will certainly multiply and become fruitful, and I shall actually cause you to be inhabited as in your former condition and I will do more good than in your initial state; and you will have to know that I am Jehovah. And upon you I will cause humankind to walk, even my people Israel, and they must take possession of you, and you must become a hereditary possession to them, and you will not bereave them again of any more children.' "—Ezekiel 36:7-12.

GREATER BEAUTIFICATION OF
THE SPIRITUAL ESTATE

¹² When Jehovah raises his hand in an oath and swears to anything that he purposes to do, it is impossible for it to fail of coming true. (Hebrews 6: 17, 18) The solid facts of history prove that Jehovah's sworn words were fulfilled upon the land of Judah after its lying desolate without man and domestic animal ended in 537 B.C.E. (Ezra 1:1 to 3:7) But as for Edom, before the desolation of the land of Judah ended, the prophecy of Jeremiah 25:15-21 went into fulfillment upon this age-old enemy of Israel, when the king of Babylon subjugated the land of Edom in 602-601 B.C.E. Later, according to the movement of the tides of history, the Edomites became a displaced people and, after the second destruction of Jerusalem in 70 C.E., the Edomites ceased to exist as a people. Other enemy nations that had rejoiced at the desolating of Judah

---

12. What kind of guarantee is Jehovah's swearing with an oath to his statement of purpose, and what fulfillment of prophecy was there in 537 B.C.E., but what humiliation came upon enemy nations?

bore their own respective humiliation at the hand of the king of Babylon. (Jeremiah 25:21-24) A divine retribution!

[13] In the modern outworking of Ezekiel's prophecy, Christendom with its hundreds of religious sects underwent a great humiliation in 1919 C.E. How so? Because the humiliating things that she had predicted and hoped for against the persecuted remnant of spiritual Israelites failed to be realized. The spiritual estate of these spiritual Israelites did not continue desolate, but in that year it began to become alive with them as they fearlessly renewed their worldwide work of witnessing to Jehovah's kingdom.—Matthew 24:14.

[14] Because of the increased threat of world domination by atheistic communism, Christendom was recommended by democratic politicians as a powerful religious buffer against the menacing tide of international communism. At length, according to the *Britannica Book of the Year* 1968 church membership of Christendom swelled up to a maximum number of 977,383,000 Roman Catholics, Eastern Orthodox church members and Protestants. But the very next year Christendom reportedly experienced a decline, noticeably so! According to the *Britannica Book of the Year* 1969 (page 647) Christendom's membership dropped to 924,-274,000. This is a drop back to less than the total of 933,055,000 as estimated for the year 1963.* The following two years (1970 and 1971) no recovery of the loss was reported, no new figures being given. Indicative of what is actually taking place, however, the New York *Times,* under date of May 21, 1970, under the bold headlines "Catholics Report Drop in U.S. Rolls, First This Century," stated the following:

* See *Britannica Book of the Year* 1964, page 728, column 1.

13. As regards her predictions and hopes concerning the remnant of spiritual Israelites, how did Christendom undergo a great humiliation in 1919 C.E.?
14. In view of what threat was there a swell in Christendom's membership, but what happened to her membership according to the 1969 report, and what did American Roman Catholics report in 1970?

The Roman Catholic Church in the United States experienced its first decline in membership in this century, according to figures released in the latest edition of The Official Catholic Directory.

The new total of members of the Church is 47,872,089 a decrease of 1,149 below the figure of a year ago, according to the 1970 edition of the statistical compilation issued by P. J. Keney & Sons of New York.

. . .

As for the seminaries, the total enrollments there were down to 17,317, a drop of 2,256, and there were a total of 118 of the diocesan seminaries, 19 fewer than in the preceding year. . . .

In the meantime the world population has exploded to more than 3,552,000,000.

¹⁵ How, though, about the symbolic "mountains" of the spiritual estate of the "Israel of God" since the end of World War I in 1918? By the population thereof do such "mountains" now have reason to know that Jehovah is in favor of them and that the One who swore to his good word of promise with an oath is really Jehovah? Let these symbolic "mountains of Israel" recall their own recent history.

¹⁶ At the time that the government of Canada banned the book *The Finished Mystery* in February of 1918 and then this Bible commentary was withdrawn from circulation in March of 1918 because of the United States government's censorship, there were 7,000 members of the anointed remnant that were actively engaged in circulating this book and other Watch Tower Society publications by personally going from house to house. (See *The Watch Tower* as of September 15, 1919, page 281, paragraph 3; and March 1, 1918, page 78.) Shortly thereafter there was a desolating of the public activities of the remnant of spiritual Israel on the "mountains of Israel." But in the following year (1919) the desolated condition was brought to a halt,

15. What question, though, is asked about the population on the symbolic "mountains" of the spiritual estate of the "Israel of God"?
16. How was desolation brought upon the public activities of the remnant of spiritual Israel in 1918, but what occurred in the following year?

and those "mountains" began to be repeopled with a courageous revived remnant of spiritual Israelites.

¹⁷ From then onward there was a steady increase in the active spiritual Israelites upon those mountains of their spiritual estate, enjoying the rich fruitage with which Jehovah blessed their restored relationship with Him. In the year 1928 there were 44,080 of the remnant who were reporting an active part in the proclamation of the good news of Jehovah's Messianic kingdom. By that time they knew that the Divine One who was doing such wonderful things for them in spite of worldwide opposition was Jehovah. After the question was raised in the *Watch Tower* issue of January 1, 1926, page 3, "Who will honor Jehovah?" they responded: "We will do so." This decision they backed up with vigorous action. They appreciated that the time had come for Jehovah to "make an indefinitely lasting name for his own self." (Isaiah 63:12; 2 Samuel 7:23) Realizing more keenly than ever that he was taking out of all nations a "people for his name," the anointed remnant saw good to identify themselves before all the world by the name drawn from the Holy Scriptures, Jehovah's witnesses.—Isaiah 43:10; 44:8.

¹⁸ By the year 1935 the "great crowd" of the Fine Shepherd's "other sheep" began to get associated with the anointed remnant of spiritual Israelites and thus became active upon the symbolic "mountains of Israel." Consequently the number active in the preaching of the good news of God's kingdom rose to 59,047 in 1938, this including a number of those "other sheep." (John 10:16; Revelation 7:9-17) Even the worldwide persecutions during World War II did not bereave the symbolic "mountains of Israel" of its population or even reduce it, for at the close of World War II in 1945 there were 127,478 world wide who were announcing

17. From then onward, what took place upon the "mountains" of the spiritual estate of spiritual Israel, and how have the spiritual Israelites shown that they know the Doer of this to be Jehovah?
18. In 1935 who began to become active with the anointed remnant of the symbolic "mountains of Israel," and today how have those "mountains" more reason than ever before to "know that I am Jehovah"?

Jehovah's established Messianic kingdom. In the years since then the growth each year of the population on those symbolic "mountains of Israel" has been steady, until in February of this year 1971 there were 1,502,-180 who reported a share in the worldwide witness to God's name and kingdom. It has been truly from Jehovah that humankind has been multiplied upon those "mountains of Israel," and today, more than ever, they have reason to know "that I am Jehovah."

[19] So since 1919 the remnant of spiritual Israel has taken possession of those "mountains of Israel," and these have become a "hereditary possession to them." (Ezekiel 36:12) They have shared the Kingdom fruitage and privileges of this spiritual estate with the increasing "great crowd" of sheeplike ones whom the reigning King, Jesus Christ, is now separating from the goatlike people of all the nations. (Matthew 25:31-46) When the name, Jehovah's witnesses, was first embraced by the anointed remnant in the year 1931, the question arose in the mind of many worldly observers: "Will the name stick?" Likewise, another question called for an answer: "Will the spiritual estate pictured by the 'mountains of Israel' prove to be too difficult a responsibility and hardship for the anointed remnant of spiritual Israelites to occupy and hold? Especially so in the postwar period with its atheistic communism, Fascism and Nazism, dictators, militant 'Catholic Action,' nationalism, Brain Age intellectualism, irreligiousness and lowered moral standards."

[20] Would the pressures from such worldly things in this age of anarchy and violence cause the restored spiritual Israelites to disappear from their newly occupied spiritual estate, as if they were devoured, swallowed up by invading aggressors or by a famine in

19. As regards the symbolic "mountains of Israel" becoming a "hereditary possession" of restored spiritual Israel, what question arose as to occupancy thereof as well as to their identifying name?
20, 21. Because of the pressures of such worldly things, what question arose as to how the "mountains" would deal with their occupants, and what assurance did Jehovah give in addressing those "mountains"?

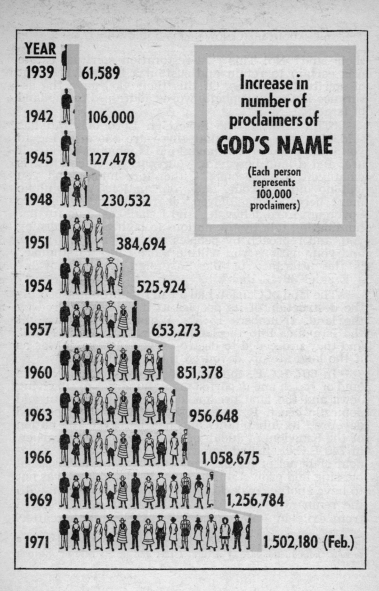

YEAR	
1939	61,589
1942	106,000
1945	127,478
1948	230,532
1951	384,694
1954	525,924
1957	653,273
1960	851,378
1963	956,648
1966	1,058,675
1969	1,256,784
1971	1,502,180 (Feb.)

Increase in number of proclaimers of **GOD'S NAME**

(Each person represents 100,000 proclaimers)

their land? No! This post-restoration spiritual estate was certain to retain and sustain a faithful remnant of spiritual Israelites. Of this their God gave the assurance in these prophetic words addressed to the land of Israel:

21 "This is what the Sovereign Lord Jehovah has said, 'For the reason that there are those saying to you: "A devourer of humankind is what you yourself are, and a land bereaving your nations of children is what you have become," ' 'therefore humankind you will no more devour, and your nations you will no more bereave of children,' is the utterance of the Sovereign Lord Jehovah. 'And I shall cause no further humiliating talk by the nations to be heard concerning you, and reproach by peoples you will bear no more, and your nations you will no more cause to stumble,' is the utterance of the Sovereign Lord Jehovah." —Ezekiel 36:13-15.

22 The land of Canaan had a bad reputation respecting the destruction of its peoples as if being devoured by the land. (Numbers 13:32) When Jehovah brought the Israelites into the land of Canaan in 1473 B.C.E. and they proceeded to destroy seven nations, it was as if the land ate up, devoured those inhabitants.

23 In 607 B.C.E. the king of Babylon conquered the land of Judah and deported many hundreds of surviving Jews and the land became desolate without man and domestic beast. It again appeared as if the land had devoured its inhabitants and had bereaved the nation of the Kingdom of Judah of its children just as earlier, in 740 B.C.E., it had bereaved the nation of the Kingdom of Israel of its children. But by Jehovah's special blessing and protection the once desolated land was not to have another experience like this in connection with the remnant of faithful Israelites that were restored from exile in Babylon in 537 B.C.E. and thereafter.

22, 23. How had the land of Canaan gained a bad reputation as a devourer of its inhabitants, and how did Jehovah remove that "reproach" both in the case of natural Israel and in the case of spiritual Israel?

So too it has been with the spiritual estate to which a remnant were restored in the postwar year of 1919 C.E. They are still there, alive, fruitful, multiplying.

HAVING COMPASSION ON HIS HOLY NAME

²⁴ Was it because of their own worthiness or merit that all such divine goodness came upon the typical remnant in 537 B.C.E. and afterward and upon the antitypical remnant in 1919 C.E. and afterward? No! Why not? Because they had made their former God-given estate unclean by bloodshed and idolatry. Hence Jehovah explains:

²⁵ "And the word of Jehovah continued to occur to me, saying: 'Son of man, the house of Israel were dwelling upon their soil, and they kept making it unclean with their way and with their dealings. Like the uncleanness of menstruation their way has become before me. And I proceeded to pour out my rage upon them on account of the blood that they had poured out upon the land, which land they had made unclean with their dungy idols. And I proceeded to scatter them among the nations, so that they were dispersed among the lands. According to their way and according to their dealings I judged them. So they came in to the nations where they came in, and people proceeded to profane my holy name in saying with reference to them, "These are the people of Jehovah, and from his land they have gone out." And I shall have compassion on my holy name, which the house of Israel have profaned among the nations where they have come in.' "—Ezekiel 36:16-21.

²⁶ Because the Israelites had gone out from Jehovah's land as exiles, it appeared that Jehovah, their professed God, was not able to protect them against their enemies. This brought reproach upon his holy name.

24, 25. Was it because of their own worthiness or merit that such divine goodness came upon Jehovah's remnant, and how does He explain the matter in Ezekiel 36:16-21?

26. Israel's going as exiles out of their own land gave what appearance to Jehovah, so affecting his name in what way, and why did he have to show self-respect also in the case of His modern-day remnant?

It caused the Gentile nations to speak profanely of his name. Similarly when the anointed remnant of spiritual Israelites were brought into bondage to Babylon the Great and her political and military paramours during World War I, it made it seem as if they as members of the International Bible Students Association were not genuine Christians. It seemed as if the true God was not on their side and was not protecting them. This brought reproach upon the name of the God of the Bible to whom they were truly dedicated as baptized disciples of Christ. Hence Jehovah was obliged to show self-respect by having compassion on his own name. It was a holy name and did not deserve to be profaned by worldlings. Because he had a devoted remnant who were connected with his name, then whatever he did in compassion on his name, would call for compassion on that remnant.

²⁷ That his own holy name and its reputation was the main thing to be taken into account, God made plain to Ezekiel, saying:

²⁸ "Therefore say to the house of Israel, 'This is what the Sovereign Lord Jehovah has said: "Not for your sakes am I doing it, O house of Israel, but for my holy name, which you have profaned among the nations where you have come in."' 'And I shall certainly sanctify my great name, which was being profaned among the nations, which you profaned in the midst of them; and the nations will have to know that I am Jehovah,' is the utterance of the Sovereign Lord Jehovah, 'when I am sanctified among you before their eyes. And I will take you out of the nations and collect you together out of all the lands and bring you in upon your soil. And I will sprinkle upon you clean water, and you will become clean; from all your impurities and from all your dungy idols I shall cleanse you. And I will give you a new heart, and a new spirit I shall put inside you, and I will take away the heart

---

27, 28. For the sake of whom or what was Jehovah bringing the Israelites back onto their own soil, and what relationship would then exist between Him and them?

of stone from your flesh and give you a heart of flesh. And my spirit I shall put inside you, and I will act so that in my regulations you will walk, and my judicial decisions you will keep and actually carry out. And you will certainly dwell in the land that I gave to your forefathers, and you must become my people and I myself shall become your God.' "—Ezekiel 36:22-28.

29 Not for any worthiness on their part, but for the sake of his own holy name Jehovah restored the anointed remnant of spiritual Israel to their privileged estate in 1919 C.E., soon after World War I ended. This surprised the nations of Christendom and of heathendom. It became evident to them that the Lord God was acting in favor of them after all. And when they plainly made public that the name of their God is Jehovah (as on page 14 of *The Harp of God*, published in 1921),* then the nations had no excuse for not knowing who the liberator and restorer of the remnant of spiritual Israelites was. Then Jehovah's declaration of purpose that applies to nations who profaned God's name because of what happened to the spiritual Israelites went into effect:

30 " 'And the nations will have to know that I am Jehovah,' is the utterance of the Sovereign Lord Jehovah, 'when I am sanctified among you before their eyes.' "—Ezekiel 36:23, NW; AS.

31 Evidently because the divine name has become so prominently connected with Jehovah's Christian witnesses, translators in Christendom who are bringing out new, modern versions of the Holy Bible omit the name Jehovah, almost or altogether, and substitute for

* *The Harp of God* reached a printing of 5,819,037 copies, in 22 languages. It is now out of print and out of stock.

29. For the sake of what did Jehovah restore his anointed remnant in 1919, and how did it become apparent that He was their liberator and restorer?
30. What divine purpose of international importance then went into effect?
31. Despite what procedure on the part of modern Bible translators has the divine name become more widely known?

it the word "GOD" or "the LORD." Nonetheless, the name of Jehovah becomes more widely known because He has sanctified it among his remnant of spiritual Israelites before the eyes of the Gentile nations inside and outside Christendom.

[32] The nations are being shown that Jehovah has produced a dedicated people who regard His name as so holy, so sacred, so worthy of reverence, that they seek to keep it from reproach due to any misconduct on their part; rather, they seek to do all things for the glory of His name. So they choose to obey Him as Ruler rather than men when there is any conflict between God's law and laws framed by God-ignoring men. (Acts 5:29) When the nations harass and persecute the people whom Jehovah has taken out for his name, these nations find that they have an embarrassing problem on their hands. They find that when they use their political power to frame "trouble by decree," frame "mischief by a law" against the people bearing Jehovah's name, this legal subterfuge does not work out in the end and Jehovah makes it public that he has no alliance or fellowship with such troublemakers. (Psalm 94:20, *NW; AV;* Zechariah 12:2-4) No nation can unrighteously tamper with His faithful witnesses without having eventually to reckon with Jehovah.

[33] As the impurities of menstruation are washed away with clean water, so Jehovah has cleansed his restored remnant from religious uncleanness by his cleansing agencies, like sprinkling clean water upon them. Since he has cleansed them from the "dungy idols" of this worldly system of things, how consistent it is for them to refuse to idolize political, military or religious dignitaries or to make idolatrous gestures and attitudes toward images, statues or emblems! He has taken away from them any stoniness of heart and given them a "heart of flesh" that has love and affection to move

---

32. How have Jehovah's dedicated people endeavored to sanctify his name among the nations, and what have nations that tamper with his faithful people found out?
33. How has Jehovah cleansed his restored remnant, even from "dungy idols," and what kind of "heart" has he given them?

them to keep his judicial decision and to walk in his regulations.

[34] He has put a "new spirit," that is, "my spirit," inside them, so that they produce the fruitage of His spirit such as "love, joy, peace, long-suffering, kindness, goodness, faith, mildness, self-control," against which things there is no divine law. (Galatians 5:22, 23) As baptized followers of his Son Jesus Christ they have indeed become Jehovah's people, and he has become their God to whom their exclusive devotion is given.—Ezekiel 36:25-28.

[35] In order to correct any misimpression that the nations got about Him because of his disciplining his people, Jehovah has thus abundantly blessed his restored remnant since 1919. It has been just as he prophetically promised through his prophet Ezekiel: " 'And I will save you from all your impurities and call to the grain and make it abound, and I shall put upon you no famine. And I shall certainly make the fruitage of the tree abound, and the produce of the field, in order that you may no more receive among the nations the reproach of famine. And you will be bound to remember your bad ways and your dealings that were not good, and you will be bound to feel a loathing at your own person on account of your errors and on account of your detestable things. Not for your sakes am I doing this,' is the utterance of the Sovereign Lord Jehovah, 'let it be known to you. Be ashamed and feel humiliation because of your ways, O house of Israel.' "—Ezekiel 36:29-32.

[36] Because of such divine goodness to them in their restored spiritual estate, the members of the anointed remnant feel a loathing of themselves when they look back at what they were in the past, taking note of

---

34. What does the "new spirit" that he has given to them produce, and to what extent has he become their God?
35. Jehovah promised to bless his restored people in what way, and why would their feelings show that it was not for their sakes that He did this?
36. Because of such undeserved goodness to them, how do they feel respecting the things they did in the past, and for God's letting what be known to them are they grateful?

their errors and bad dealings that were not glorifying
to God's name. It makes them ashamed, it makes them
feel humiliated, just to think about it. This attitude
takes away from them any inclination to engage in spiritual and immoral impurities once again, willingly. Thus,
because of the effect that Jehovah's undeserved kindness has upon them in their restored estate, he saves
them from all their impurities. They keenly appreciate
that it was not for any past goodness of theirs, not
for their sakes, that, figuratively speaking, he called
for the life-sustaining grain to sprout up from the
ground and produce so abundantly, so that worldly nations cannot reproach them for having any famine
of spiritual food and provisions. They are thankful for
God's letting it be known to them that for the sake
of his holy name he has done all this for them. So in
all humility they sanctify the name of Jehovah in their
lives.

"LIKE THE GARDEN OF EDEN" WITH A POPULATION

[37] Because of such divine compassion in behalf of
Jehovah's name, the spiritual estate of the restored
remnant has become a spiritual Paradise. Informed
observers who noted the transformation have acknowl-
edged this. It is just as the name-respecting God has
foretold, saying:

[38] "This is what the Sovereign Lord Jehovah has
said, 'In the day of my cleansing you from all your
errors I will also cause the cities to be inhabited, and
the devastated places must be rebuilt. And the desolated land itself will be cultivated, whereas it had
become a desolate waste before the eyes of every
passerby. And people will certainly say: "That land
yonder which was laid desolate has become like the
garden of Eden, and the cities that were a waste and
that were laid desolate and that were torn down are
fortified; they have become inhabited." And the nations that will be left remaining round about you will

---

37, 38. Consequently, what has the spiritual estate of the restored
remnant now become, and how did Jehovah foretell this to Ezekiel?

have to know that I myself, Jehovah, have built the things torn down, I have planted what has been laid desolate. I myself, Jehovah, have spoken and I have done it.' "—Ezekiel 36:33-36.

³⁹ Regarding the start of the ancient fulfillment of that bright prophecy, it is written, in Ezra 3:1, 2: "When the seventh month [Tishri] arrived [at the close of the seventy years of desolation in 537 B.C.E.] the sons of Israel were in their cities. And the people began to gather themselves as one man to Jerusalem. And Jeshua the son of Jehozadak and his brothers the priests and [Governor] Zerubbabel the son of Shealtiel and his brothers proceeded to rise up and build the altar of the God of Israel, to offer up burnt sacrifices upon it, according to what is written in the law of Moses the man of the true God." The Israelites that returned from Babylon then numbered 42,360, along with whom there came 7,337 slaves and some 200 to 245 professional singers. This amounted to almost 50,-000 persons.—Ezra 2:64, 65; Nehemiah 7:66, 67.

⁴⁰ Likewise in the year 1919 of our Common Era, the release in March of eight prominent officials and agents of the Watch Tower Bible & Tract Society from the federal penitentiary at Atlanta, Georgia, U.S.A., occurred as a symbol of the release of the International Bible Students from Babylonish bondage and oppression. The very next month, on Sunday night, April 13, many thousands of these dedicated Bible Students gratefully gathered together in their congregations around the world to celebrate the Lord's Supper, that being the anniversary of Jesus' instituting of this memorial of his death. Early reports from congregations that had an attendance of thirty or more in just eight European cities and 164 other cities in North and South America showed a total attendance of 17,-961. Later additional reports were not published. (See

39. What does Ezra 3:1, 2 tell us about the start of the ancient fulfillment of that prophecy?
40. What, corresponding with that first postexile gathering in Jerusalem, took place in 1919 C.E. concerning Jehovah's restored people?

The Watch Tower under date of May 15, 1919, page 151.) Later that year, on September 1-8, the first postwar general convention of the International Bible Students Association was held in Cedar Point, Ohio, U.S.A., attended by some 6,000 Bible Students. The public attendance was 7,000 on Sunday, September 7, 1919.

[41] The congregations of the restored remnant of spiritual Israelites were like the cities of ancient Israel. They became "fortified" especially by the better organization of them for actively carrying out Jesus' prophecy of Matthew 24:14, to preach the good news of God's established kingdom in all the inhabited earth for a witness to all the nations. They became more fully fortified in the year 1938 when the centralized theocratic rule, rather than the local congregational rule, of organization was applied to all the congregations around the globe. The number of these fortified congregations and their inhabitants increased.

[42] Jehovah himself was manifestly the One who did this, forasmuch as the nations of Christendom and of the world were in opposition to it or not cooperative with it. He was the One that blessed the spiritual estate of his restored remnant so that it became very fruitful and productive. To amplify the presenting of the "fruits" of God's kingdom to all the inhabited earth, printing plants were established by the Watch Tower Bible & Tract Society and enlarged in many parts of the earth for the production of Bible literature by the millions of copies in many languages, for the restored remnant to distribute free to the people or at a surprisingly small nominal contribution. The terrible havoc wrought by World War II of 1939-1945 did not decrease this.—Matthew 21:43.

[43] Not only did the offering of the "fruits" of the

---

41. How did the figurative "cities" that had been desolated become "fortified" and "inhabited"?
42. Why was it manifestly Jehovah that did this, and how was the presenting of the "fruits" of God's kingdom amplified?
43. Besides the "fruits" of God's kingdom, in what other way did the congregation of Jehovah's people become fruitful, and what were honest observers obliged to exclaim about their spiritual estate?

Kingdom increase by the expanding of the Kingdom preaching world wide, but the spirituality of the congregations grew also. Especially so after World War II, despite the now increased tempo in the demoralization of human society inside Christendom as well as outside. Among the congregations the "fruitage of the spirit" of God became more luxuriant with "love, joy, peace, long-suffering, kindness, goodness, faith, mildness, self-control." (Galatians 5:22, 23) This has become manifest not only in the local congregations of Jehovah's witnesses but also in the more public gatherings, in circuit, district, national and international assemblies throughout the earth. In contrast with the dilapidated religious condition of Christendom, honest observers of the spiritual prosperity of the spiritual estate of Jehovah's witnesses have been obliged to exclaim: "That land yonder which was laid desolate has become like the garden of Eden." (Ezekiel 36:35) To whom is this due?

[44] The real credit for this goes, not to the anointed remnant and the "great crowd" of Christ's "other sheep," but to Jehovah. Long ago he had spoken of it prophetically. In our time He has done it. For the sake of his much-maligned Name he has transformed the once desolated spiritual estate of his anointed remnant into a spiritual Paradise, a "garden of Eden," which, like the original garden of Eden in Adam's day, is the planting of Jehovah. (Genesis 2:7-9) Let the nations of the world take note of that fact.

[45] Back there in the days of the prophet Ezekiel in exile in Babylon this Paradisaic transformation of the desolated homeland was something yet to be sought and searched for, with decades of exile for them yet to undergo in Babylon. This state of affairs at that time is what God commented upon to his prophet Eze-

---

44. To whom was this transformation due, and who should take note of that fact?
45. Through Ezekiel, what did Jehovah promise to do about the uninhabited cities of Judah, and what were the exiled Israelites then to do about this?

kiel, saying: "This is what the Sovereign Lord Jehovah has said, 'This is what I shall yet let myself be searched for by the house of Israel to do for them: I shall multiply them like a flock with men. Like a flock of holy persons, like the flock of Jerusalem in her festal seasons, thus the cities that had been a waste will become full of a flock of men; and people will have to know that I am Jehovah.' "—Ezekiel 36:37, 38.

⁴⁶ Back there, over two thousand five hundred years ago, that repeopling of the devastated cities of the land of Judah needed to be searched for from Jehovah by those exiled Jews who repented and who desired the fulfillment of Jehovah's merciful promises, especially for the sanctifying and vindicating of his holy name. A number of those exiled Jews did survive and return to their homeland to see the realization of Jehovah's promise to repopulate their beloved homeland. (Ezra 3:12) Today, in this twentieth century, we are decades removed from the liberation year of 1919. For the anointed remnant it is no longer a matter of searching for Jehovah to repopulate with holy persons the spiritual estate of the "Israel of God." This is now an accomplished fact, and the end of the fulfillment of the prophecy is not yet.—Galatians 6:16.

⁴⁷ On the six great continents above the Antarctic region and on the islands of the seven seas the number of congregations of Jehovah's Christian witnesses has increased, in order to enjoy as widely as possible the spiritual estate, the spiritual Paradise, of the Christian Israel of God. In doing better or more good for the spiritual estate of his Christian witnesses than at its beginnings or in its "initial state," Jehovah has filled it with a vast "flock of men." (Ezekiel 36:11) As the twelve tribes of Israel used to flock to Jerusalem and its

46. As regards the prophecy of the repeopling of the cities of the land of Judah, how does the situation of the anointed remnant today contrast with that of the exiled Jews?
47. How extensively have the congregations of Jehovah's Christian witnesses increased, and how, as regards a "flock of holy persons," is it manifest that He has done better for their spiritual estate than at its beginning?

temple during the three "festal seasons" of the year (at Passover, at Pentecost, and at the festival of booths), so Jehovah's Christian witnesses have enjoyed flocking together, not only to their local Kingdom Halls, but, in an amazing manner, to their regular circuit, district, national and international assemblies.

⁴⁸ For instance, during the district assemblies designated as for "Men of Goodwill," in the year 1970, the attendances surpassed expectations. At these district assemblies on all six continents the talk for the general public was mainly on the subject "Saving the Human Race—in the Kingdom Way."* The attendances at these from June into December totaled over a million.

⁴⁹ Back in the year 33 C.E., at the festal season of Pentecost, at the beginning of the Christian congregation, the apostle Peter said to a flock of Jews who were interested in everlasting salvation: "And everyone who calls on the name of Jehovah will be saved." (Acts 2:21; quoted from Joel 2:32) Jehovah's Christian witnesses of today still believe in that unchangeable way of salvation.

⁵⁰ For that reason they not only flock together, but also make known the name of Jehovah as the divine Author of salvation through his Son Jesus Christ. (Romans 10:10-14) Otherwise, from just the flocking of His dedicated people it would not become known by the people that, as He said, "I am Jehovah." But because the increasing flock of Jehovah's Christian witnesses proclaim his name everywhere as the one name to call upon for salvation through Jesus Christ, more and more people are seeking the life-giving association

---

* In Freetown, Liberia, Lagos, Nigeria, and in Nairobi, Kenya, Africa, the public talk was entitled "Restoration of All Things of Which God Spoke."

48. How is the case of the "Men of Goodwill" District Assemblies from June to December, 1970, an example of such flocking?
49. In what way of salvation, as stated by Peter to Jews on the day of Pentecost, do Jehovah's Christian witnesses still believe?
50. How does God's name become known through this flocking together of Jehovah's Christian witnesses, and what may be said about the people seeking life-giving association with them?

with these witnesses. At the annual celebration of the Lord's Supper on March 22, 1970, what was the attendance world wide? The total of reports received showed it to be 3,226,168. (Page 43 of *1971 Yearbook of Jehovah's Witnesses*) This was for over 26,000 congregations of Jehovah's witnesses.

[51] At the time of their celebrating that annual memorial of the sacrificial death of the Lord Jesus Christ, "the Lamb of God that takes away the sin of the world," there was just an average of 1,384,782 witnesses of Jehovah who were regularly proclaiming the good news of Jehovah's Messianic kingdom in more than two hundred lands. From the difference between that number of active proclaimers and the worldwide attendance at the Lord's Supper, it is evident that nearly two million persons were then experiencing what the accredited Doer of all these marvelous things foretold, namely, "people will have to know that I am Jehovah." (Ezekiel 36:38) Beyond all contradiction this Jehovah has transformed the once desolated spiritual estate of his anointed witnesses, the present remnant of spiritual Israel, into a spiritual "garden of Eden," and this He has done for the sake of his own worthy name.—Ezekiel 36:22.

---

51. From a comparison of the published number of Kingdom proclaimers and the number of attenders at the Lord's Supper, what is evident regarding Jehovah's declared purpose, and why?

Chapter 18

Resurrection to Unity
in a "Garden of Eden"

THE resurrection of a dead nation to life on its own estate precedes the resurrection of the thousands of millions of the human dead to life on a Paradise earth.

[2] Who can perform such a miraculous reviving of a nation? There is One who can do so, the One who used the ancient prophet Elijah and his successor Elisha to raise the dead to life. (1 Kings 17:8-24; 2 Kings 4:11-37; 8:4, 5; Hebrews 11:35) That was in the tenth century before our Common Era, and so hundreds of years before the city of Jerusalem was destroyed by the Babylonians in 607 B.C.E. To the Divine Being who cured her of barrenness, Hannah the mother of the prophet Samuel said under inspiration: "Jehovah is a Killer and a Preserver of life, a Bringer down to Sheol, and He brings up." (1 Samuel 2:1, 6) Centuries prior to Hannah, her forefather Abraham believed in Jehovah's power to make dead things live, and concerning this faith of his we read: "This was in the sight of the One in whom he had faith, even of God, who makes the dead alive and calls the things that are not as though they were." (Romans 4:17) He can resurrect a nation as easily as one man.

---

1. Resurrection to life of a dead nation to its estate precedes what other resurrection?
2. In relation to the one who can miraculously revive a nation, what did Elijah and Elisha do, what did Hannah say, and what did Abraham believe?

[3] When, after the destruction of Jerusalem, the surviving Jews were dragged off to Babylon for an exile of seventy years, they were practically a dead nation. Because of their not putting faith in the prophecies of God's Word, their hopes of living again as a united nation on their God-given homeland were dead, for the majority of exiled Jews. The land of Babylon appeared to be the burial place of their nation. Babylon may have thought so too. But Jehovah, who had foretold the repeopling of the mountains and hills and valleys of the then desolated land of Israel, had in mind a miracle. The prophet Ezekiel had a vision of it, and he amazes us as he tells us about it in these words:

[4] "The hand of Jehovah proved to be upon me, so that he brought me forth in the spirit of Jehovah and set me down in the midst of the valley plain, and it was full of bones. And he had me pass along by them all round about, and, look! there were very many on the surface of the valley plain and, look! they were very dry. And he began to say to me: 'Son of man, can these bones come to life?' To that I said: 'Sovereign Lord Jehovah, you yourself well know.' And he went on to say to me: 'Prophesy over these bones, and you must say to them, "O you dry bones, hear the word of Jehovah." ' "—Ezekiel 37:1-4.

[5] A person of today might think, What good would it do to prophesy over a valley plain full of scattered dry bones? How could they respond to prophesying by a mere man?

[6] But let us not jump to conclusions in this modern scientific age. It is the word of Jehovah that is to be spoken in prophesying, and his word has superhuman, supernatural power. Six thousand years ago he spoke

3. In what state were the hopes of the Jewish exiles, what did the land of Babylon appear to be for their nation, and what, though, did Jehovah have in mind?
4. In vision, where did Jehovah set Ezekiel down, and what did he ask Ezekiel about what he saw there?
5. At such a command, what might a person today think?
6. But whose word was Ezekiel to speak in prophesying, and what dynamic power had that word long previously shown?

for the creation of all forms of life on our earth, and he can speak for the re-creation of life on a desolated land. (Genesis 1:11-25) Hear now his dynamic words:

⁷ "This is what the Sovereign Lord Jehovah has said to these bones: 'Here I am bringing into you breath, and you must come to life. And I will put upon you sinews and cause to come upon you flesh, and I will overlay upon you skin and put in you breath, and you must come to life; and you will have to know that I am Jehovah.'"—Ezekiel 37:5, 6.

⁸ This makes us wonder how the Creator went about it when he created a wife for the first man in the garden of Eden, concerning which we read: "Hence Jehovah God had a deep sleep fall upon the man and, while he was sleeping, he took one of his ribs and then closed up the flesh over its place. And Jehovah God proceeded to build the rib that he had taken from the man into a woman and to bring her to the man." (Genesis 2:21, 22) But even for a fully formed body to live it must have breath from Jehovah breathed into it. The account of man's creation stresses that essential, saying: "Jehovah God proceeded to form the man out of dust from the ground and to blow into his nostrils the breath of life, and the man came to be a living soul. Further, Jehovah God planted a garden in Eden, toward the east, and there he put the man whom he had formed." (Genesis 2:7, 8) So, too, when this same Creator put breath into those bodies that he had built up from the valley plain full of dry bones, they came to life.

⁹ When those dry bones became reclothed with sinew, flesh and skin and got the breath of life, they were bound to know something. They knew that they had not created or re-created themselves. They experienced

7. Through Ezekiel, what did Jehovah say to those dry bones?
8. Such clothing of bones with bodies and breathing into them to make them live reminds us of what steps in the creation of the first man and woman?
9. When those dry bones were reclothed and life was restored, what did they come to know?

what their Creator and Reviver had foretold: "And you will have to know that I am Jehovah."—Ezekiel 37:6.

¹⁰ Jehovah is the Almighty God because he can do what to us humans in this twentieth century is impossible. So may we not think that we are looking at an impossible vision, as Ezekiel now tells us what followed his obeying Almighty God in faith: "And I prophesied just as I had been commanded. And a sound began to occur as soon as I prophesied, and here there was a rattling, and bones began to approach, bone to its bone. And I saw, and, look! upon them sinews themselves and flesh itself came up and skin began to be overlaid upon them above. But as regards breath, there was none in them." (Ezekiel 37:7, 8) Scientists today know how to put human skeletons together, but they cannot put sinews and flesh upon those reconstructed bones and then vital organs inside. But Jehovah here pictures himself as being able to do *the impossible!*

¹¹ "And," says Ezekiel, "he went on saying to me: 'Prophesy to the wind. Prophesy, O son of man, and you must say to the wind, "This is what the Sovereign Lord Jehovah has said: 'From the four winds come in, O wind, and blow upon these killed people, that they may come to life.' " ' "—Ezekiel 37:9.

¹² It was no pollution-laden wind that Ezekiel called to blow upon those reconstructed human bodies and to start their lungs functioning, in order that they might live. Jehovah waited upon Ezekiel's prophesying before he reactivated those miraculously formed bodies, for we read: "And I prophesied just as he had commanded me, and the breath proceeded to come into them, and they began to live and stand upon their feet, a very, very great military force."—Ezekiel 37:10.

---

10. When Ezekiel prophesied at God's command, what happened to those dry bones, and what did Jehovah do that scientists cannot do?
11. What was Ezekiel told to say in prophesying to the wind?
12. When Ezekiel thus prophesied to the wind, what happened?

THOSE WHOM THE REVIVIFIED ONES PICTURED

[13] Inasmuch as all those animated bodies are spoken of as a "military force" or army, it denotes that these were no weaklings; they were able-bodied persons qualified for military service. But whom did all those "killed people" whom Ezekiel saw revitalized in the vision picture? Ezekiel tells us God's own explanation by saying:

[14] "And he went on to say to me: 'Son of man, as regards these bones, they are the whole house of Israel. Here they are saying, "Our bones have become dry, and our hope has perished. We have been severed off to ourselves." Therefore prophesy, and you must say to them, "This is what the Sovereign Lord Jehovah has said: 'Here I am opening your burial places, and I will bring you up out of your burial places, O my people, and bring you in upon the soil of Israel. And you will have to know that I am Jehovah when I open your burial places and when I bring you up out of your burial places, O my people.' And I will put my spirit in you, and you must come to life, and I will settle you upon your soil; and you will have to know that I myself, Jehovah, have spoken and I have done it," is the utterance of Jehovah.' "—Ezekiel 37:11-14.

[15] Thus the exiled Jews, then inclined to hopelessness, were to become reanimated with new hope based upon the unbreakable word of Jehovah. As Jehovah's mouthpiece, Ezekiel by his prophesying was to have a part in the enlivening of those depressed Israelites with hope of restoration to their beloved homeland, hundreds of miles away. But Jehovah was the One who by putting his holy spirit in the repentant Israelites would really reorganize them and make them alive with eagerness and willingness to be restored to their own

13. What is indicated by the designating of those revivified bodies a "very great military force"?
14. Whom did Jehovah identify those "killed people" as being, and what did he say that he would do for them?
15. What was Ezekiel's part toward reanimating those hopeless Jews, but what was Jehovah's part toward getting them back to the "soil of Israel"?

soil, at Jehovah's due time. He was the One that would miraculously open the way for them to leave their "burial places" in the land of Babylon and go back to the "soil of Israel."

¹⁶ The "whole house of Israel" was to share in this opportunity for repatriation. Since this meant all the tribes of Israel, including those ten tribes that established the Northern Kingdom of Israel, this takes away the basis for the claim of the British Israelite religionists who think those "ten tribes" were lost in the Assyrian territories to which they were deported and that these British Israelites are really those tribes who have come to light again.

¹⁷ Jehovah had spoken this by his prophets, including Ezekiel. Did the Israelites later have to know that Jehovah had actually done it, true to his spoken word? Recorded history answers Yes! It was the foretold Cyrus the Persian whom He used to bring about the surprise fall of Babylon to the Medes and Persians one night in the autumn of 539 B.C.E. In the second year after that, namely, in 537 B.C.E., King Cyrus the Conqueror issued his decree freeing the Israelites to leave their exile in Babylon and return to Jerusalem to rebuild the temple of their God. Now let us notice to whom Cyrus gave the responsibility for this, in this account:

"To fulfill Jehovah's word by the mouth of Jeremiah, until the land had paid off its sabbaths. All the days of lying desolated it kept sabbath, to fulfill seventy years.

"And in the first year of Cyrus the king of Persia, that Jehovah's word by the mouth of Jeremiah might be accomplished, Jehovah roused the spirit of Cyrus the king of Persia, so that he caused a cry to pass through all his kingdom, and also in writing, saying: 'This is what Cyrus the king of Persia has said, "All the kingdoms of the earth Jehovah the God of the heavens has given me, and he himself has commissioned me to build

16. How many were to share in that opportunity for repatriation, and how does this prove the claim of British Israelites to be baseless?
17. Did those Israelites later have reason to know that what Jehovah had spoken he had done, and in his decree in behalf of them to whom did King Cyrus give the responsibility for action?

him a house in Jerusalem, which is in Judah. Whoever there is among you of all his people, Jehovah his God be with him. So let him go up." ' "

Those words of 2 Chronicles 36:21-23 do not say why he should go up. But the words of Ezra 1:1-4 fill out Cyrus' decree, saying:

"So let him go up to Jerusalem, which is in Judah, and rebuild the house of Jehovah the God of Israel—he is the true God—which was in Jerusalem. As for anyone that is left from all the places where he is residing as an alien, let the men of his place assist him with silver and with gold and with goods and with domestic animals along with the voluntary offering for the house of the true God, which was in Jerusalem."

[18] When Cyrus the Great, the king of Persia, thus associated Jehovah with this unexpected, unusual event, how could the Israelites fail to know that it was Jehovah who was opening their burial places in Babylon and bringing them out alive for further activity in his service and worship in their desolated homeland! Assisted by sympathetic Israelites who could not then conveniently leave Babylon, 42,360 Israelties responded to Jehovah's outpoured spirit and became alive to the opportunity to repeople the hills, mountains and valleys of the soil of Israel, rebuild Jerusalem and its temple and restore Jehovah's worship there, to the glory of his name internationally. More than 7,500 non-Israelite slaves and professional singers accepted the privilege to go with them for the united service of Jehovah. (Ezra 2:64-67) This was indeed like a "very, very great military force."—Ezekiel 37:10.

[19] The historic fulfillment of Ezekiel's vision of the valley plain full of dry bones was as prophetic as the vision itself. It has had its further fulfillment in our twentieth century. This fulfillment is pointed forward to as being due to occur, in the last Bible book that

18. From the wording of Cyrus' decree, what did the Israelites know concerning their God, and how many responded to this opportunity to repeople the desolated homeland?
19. Besides the vision itself, what else in connection therewith was prophetic, and how was this pictured in the Bible's last book?

was written about 96 C.E., or more than seven centuries after Ezekiel's vision. Let us note how the reviving of the spiritual Israelites is pictured therein:

"And when they have finished their witnessing, the wild beast that ascends out of the abyss [the third head of this seven-headed beast picturing the Babylonian World Power] will make war with them and conquer them and kill them. And their corpses will be on the broad way of the great city which is in a spiritual sense called Sodom and Egypt, where their Lord was also impaled. And those of the peoples and tribes and tongues and nations will look at their corpses for three and a half days, and they do not let their corpses be laid in a tomb. And those dwelling on the earth rejoice over them and enjoy themselves, and they will send gifts to one another, because these two prophets tormented those dwelling on the earth.

"And after the three and a half days spirit of life from God entered into them, and they stood upon their feet, and great fear fell upon those beholding them. And they heard a loud voice out of heaven say to them: 'Come on up here.' And they went up into heaven in the cloud, and their enemies beheld them."—Revelation 11:7-12.

[20] In the modern outworking of this prophetic picture the remnant of Christian spiritual Israelites were killed, as far as their prophetic and witnessing work freely and publicly was concerned, at the climax of the international persecution against them in the last year of World War I. They came into a spiritual condition just like that of the dry bones seen by Ezekiel in the valley plain, in Babylon. (Genesis 11:2-9) Their continuing in this condition was not as long as the seventy years of exile of the ancient Israelites in Babylon, but was pictured as being for three and a half days, long enough for rigor mortis to take hold of a corpse. So it was that, as early as in the spring of the following year (1919 C.E.), "spirit of life from God" entered and resurrected them to vigorous public activity again in preaching "this good news of the kingdom"

20. How was this Revelation picture fulfilled, and in what period of time, and with what ascension of the "two witnesses" as it were to heaven?

internationally. (Matthew 24:14) The 'going up to heaven in the cloud' certainly indicated that they were religiously separated from the "great city which is in a spiritual sense called Sodom and Egypt," and which is antitypical Jerusalem or Christendom, the predominant religious member of Babylon the Great. They left that world empire of false religion.

[21] The liberated remnant of spiritual Israelites came to know very definitely that it was Jehovah who opened their "burial places" in Babylon the Great and brought them out spiritually alive in order to restore them to their proper spiritual estate on this war-torn earth. In the case of their ancient prototypes, the restored Israelites had to work hard at cultivating the long-desolated soil of Israel to the state that would cause observing people to say: "That land yonder which was laid desolate has become like the garden of Eden." (Ezekiel 36:35) Just so, too, the restored remnant of spiritual Israelites had to work hard at cultivating the "fruitage of the spirit" and producing the "fruits" of God's kingdom in order to have their postwar estate "become like the garden of Eden," a spiritual Paradise. (Galatians 5:22, 23; Matthew 21:43) This called for united effort on their part. That there would be such internal organizational unity Jehovah instructed Ezekiel to picture by a fine illustration, as follows:

[22] "And the word of Jehovah continued to occur to me, saying: 'And as for you, O son of man, take for yourself a stick and write upon it, "For Judah and for the sons of Israel his partners." And take another stick and write upon it, "For Joseph, the stick of Ephraim, and all the house of Israel his partners." And cause them to approach each other into one stick for yourself,

---

21. Whom did the remnant of spiritual Israel come to recognize as the one who brought them out of their graves in Babylon the Great, and how did they have to imitate the ancient Israelites to bring their estate to a spiritual Paradise?
22. What illustration was Ezekiel told to enact to show the unifying of the Israelite remnant, and what explanation thereof did Jehovah give?

and they will actually become just one in your hand. And when the sons of your people begin to say to you, "Will you not tell us what these things mean to you?" speak to them, "This is what the Sovereign Lord Jehovah has said: 'Here I am taking the stick of Joseph, which is in the hand of Ephraim, and the tribes of Israel his partners, and I will put them upon it, that is, the stick of Judah, and I shall actually make them one stick, and they must become one in my hand.' And the sticks upon which you write must prove to be in your hand before their eyes.'' ''—Ezekiel 37:15-20.

RESTORING INTERNAL ORGANIZATIONAL UNITY

²³ The tribe of Ephraim descended from Joseph the son of Jacob (Israel). The ten tribes that revolted from the royal house of David after the death of King Solomon included this tribe of Ephraim, as its most powerful tribe. The first king of the new ten-tribe Kingdom of Israel was of this tribe, namely, "Jeroboam the son of Nebat an Ephraimite." (1 Kings 11:26 to 12:25) Fittingly, then, one stick was written upon by Ezekiel to stand for exiles of that fallen kingdom. The tribe of Judah along with the tribe of Benjamin and the priests and Levites remained loyal to the royal family of David. Appropriately the other stick was written on by Ezekiel to stand for the exiles of this recently fallen Kingdom of Judah. Prophetically the two sticks were brought together in Ezekiel's hand, either being merely held together in his hand or miraculously merging together. What did it foretell?

²⁴ What Jehovah had in mind by this he tells Ezekiel, saying: "And speak to them, 'This is what the Sovereign Lord Jehovah has said: "Here I am taking the sons of Israel from among the nations to which they have gone, and I will collect them together from round about and bring them onto their soil. And I shall ac-

---

23. Why were the markings on the two sticks appropriate, in accord with history?
24. How did Jehovah explain the meaning of the bringing together of the sticks in Ezekiel's hand?

tually make them one nation in the land, on the mountains of Israel, and one king is what all of them will come to have as king, and they will no longer continue to be two nations, nor will they be divided any longer into two kingdoms. And they will no longer defile themselves with their dungy idols and with their disgusting things and with all their transgressions; and I shall certainly save them from all their dwelling places in which they have sinned, and I will cleanse them, and they must become my people, and I myself shall become their God." ' "—Ezekiel 37:21-23.

[25] Hence there were no "lost ten tribes of Israel" that remained behind in the territories of fallen Babylon. Members of all the original twelve tribes of Israel returned to the soil of Israel after King Cyrus' decree of liberation of 537 B.C.E. Consequently, in the year 2 B.C.E., when the forty-day-old baby Jesus was brought into the rebuilt temple at Jerusalem, there was a member of the once rebellious tribe of Asher there, and God was pleased to use even her as a prophetess. Who was she? Anna, the daughter of Phanuel. (Luke 2:36-38) The one about whom Anna prophesied then, namely, Jesus, was the one who was to become the "one king" whom all the reunited twelve tribes of Israel were to have over them.

[26] Quite rightly, then, on the day of Pentecost, thirty-three and a half years later, the Christian apostle Simon Peter said to a crowd of thousands of Israelites at Jerusalem, concerning the resurrected Jesus who had ascended to heaven: "Therefore let all the house of Israel know for a certainty that God made him both Lord and Christ, this Jesus whom you impaled." (Acts 2:36) Through him they could be reconciled to Jehovah as their God.

[27] At the end of the "appointed times of the nations"

---

25. What evidence cropped up in 2 B.C.E. to show that there were no "lost ten tribes of Israel," and who was there identified as being the future "one king" over all Israel?
26. On the day of Pentecost, who did the apostle Peter say should know that God had made Jesus "both Lord and Christ"?
27. When did Jehovah install this one as king with the "legal right"?

in the year 1914 C.E., Jehovah installed Jesus Christ as king in the heavens, to reign as David's descendant who had the "legal right" to the royal crown.—Ezekiel 21:25-27; Luke 21:24.

[28] The anointed remnant of spiritual Israel had to unite under him as their "one king" by Jehovah's appointment. During World War I, after the death of the first president of the Watch Tower Bible & Tract Society on October 31, 1916, efforts were made by certain ambitious ones among the International Bible Students Association to break up the unity of the remnant into several religious sects. But the faithful members of the remnant resisted the various pressures toward disunity and sectarianism such as prevails in Christendom. Then in the liberation year of 1919 the faithful survivors of World War I reunited with the one objective, namely, to be loyal to Jehovah's reigning King, Jesus Christ, and to preach world wide "this good news of the kingdom." Jehovah forgave their transgressions and cleansed them of the "dungy idols" of worldly nationalism and other religiously disgusting things.

[29] Before Jesus Christ suffered his sacrificial death, he prayed with his faithful apostles in behalf of this unity among all true spiritual Israelites, saying: "I make request, not concerning these only, but also concerning those putting faith in me through their word; in order that they may all be one, just as you, Father, are in union with me and I am in union with you, that they also may be in union with us, in order that the world may believe that you sent me forth. Also, I have given them the glory that you have given me, in order that they may be one just as we are one." (John 17:20-22) What Jesus thus prayed for has now been achieved among spiritual Israel.

---

28. What efforts were made to break up the unity of the remnant of spiritual Israel, and in 1919 C.E. under whom did they unite as their "one king" appointed by Jehovah?
29. Before his death, how did Jesus pray with his apostles for the unity of spiritual Israel, and has this now been achieved?

³⁰ Not only that, but since 1935 C.E. the "great crowd" of those "other sheep" mentioned by Jesus have overcome racial, national, tribal and language bars and distinctions and, like the more than 7,500 non-Israelites that left Babylon with the homeward-bound remnant, they have united with the anointed remnant of spiritual Israel to serve Jehovah's "one king," Jesus Christ. Today all of them, the remnant and the "other sheep," have become "one flock" under the "one shepherd."—Revelation 7:9-17; Ezra 2:64, 65; John 10:11-16.

³¹ That this unified condition under the "one king" and the "one shepherd" would result in peace inside the spiritual "garden of Eden" since the year 1919 C.E., Jehovah foretold, as he went on to say to his prophet Ezekiel: "And my servant David will be king over them, and one shepherd is what they will all come to have; and in my judicial decisions they will walk, and my statutes they will keep, and they will certainly carry them out. And they will actually dwell upon the land that I gave to my servant, to Jacob, in which your forefathers dwelt, and they will actually dwell upon it, they and their sons and their sons' sons to time indefinite, and David my servant will be their chieftain to time indefinite.

³² "And I will conclude with them a covenant of peace; an indefinitely lasting covenant is what there will come to be with them. And I will place them and multiply them and place my sanctuary in the midst of them to time indefinite. And my tabernacle will actually prove to be over them, and I shall certainly become their God, and they themselves will become my people. And the nations will have to know that I, Jehovah, am sanctifying Israel when my sanctuary

---

30. Since 1935 C.E., who have united with the anointed remnant under the "one king," and what have they all become together?
31. Whom did Jehovah say that he would give to be king over his restored people, and where were they to dwell?
32. What kind of covenant was Jehovah to conclude with his restored people, and by placing what among them were the nations to know that he was sanctifying his restored people?

comes to be in the midst of them to time indefinite."
—Ezekiel 37:24-28.

³³ Jehovah has given his reigning King Jesus Christ
as a "covenant" or solemn promissory guarantee for
the peace of all his obedient subjects. By His spirit,
which produces the fruitage of love, joy, peace, long-
suffering, kindness, goodness, faith, mildness and self-
control, Jehovah has removed all beastly viciousness
of personality from his restored people. His sanctuary,
as picturing pure Christian worship, is among these
staunch adherents to his written Word, the Holy Bible.
His tabernacle of divine protection and family relationship is over them. It is very manifest to all honest
observers that those dedicated, baptized subjects of
the reigning King have become the people of Jehovah,
for they have really abandoned all worldly forms of
idolatry and have made Jehovah the only God whom
they worship.—Isaiah 42:6; 49:8; Hosea 2:18-20;
Micah 4:1-5.

³⁴ Although these devoted subjects of Jehovah's
reigning King are no part of this unpeaceful world,
yet they are physically still in it. (John 17:14-16;
15:19) For that reason the worldly nations of today
are observing something; they are coming to know
something about these Christian witnesses of Jehovah.
What? That their God is a living God superior to all
the nations of mankind and that he must be taber-
nacling or dwelling in the midst of them inasmuch as
he does for them what His Bible foretold. Yes, and that
He is noticeably sanctifying them, making them holy,
clean, morally and religiously different from the rest
of mankind. The only One who could do this is the
living and true God, and he is the One who calls himself Jehovah.—Psalm 83:18.

---

33. How has the peace of Jehovah's covenant been brought about
among his restored people, what is the evidence that his sanctuary
was placed among them, and in what way is his tabernacle over them?
34. Because Jehovah's tabernacle proves to be in the midst of these
subjects of His reigning King, what are the nations coming to know
about these Christian witnesses of Jehovah?

Chapter 19

Defeat Awaits
Attack by Nations under Gog

THE nations of this twentieth century do not know
who "Gog of the land of Magog" is—not yet.
They do not expect to be brought under his control
and be led to their destruction. Even to the nations
of Christendom that have the Holy Bible, just who
Gog is has long been obscure, also where his land of
Magog is.* This is true also of the natural, circumcised
Jews, who expect Gog's attack to be made upon them
sometime in the indefinite future. The very last book
listed in the inspired Christian Scriptures makes use
of the names of Gog and Magog and foretells an attack
under devilish supernatural influence—but a thousand
years from now. (Revelation 20:7, 8) However, who
the Gog is with whom we today are vitally concerned
becomes free from obscurity as we consider what the
whole Bible, from Genesis to Revelation (Apocalypse),
has to say about his role within our generation.

² Putting us on our guard, Jehovah introduces this
today-living Gog to us through his prophet Ezekiel
during his exile in the land of Babylon. After foretelling the restoring of a faithful remnant of exiled
Jews to their homeland in the Middle East, Jehovah

---

* *Webster's New International Dictionary of the English Language,*
Second Edition (1943), says on Gog: "Ruler of Magog. Ezekiel xxxviii.
2." But see the article "The Attack by Gog of Magog," beginning on
page 581 of the issue of October 1, 1953, of *The Watchtower.*

1. What is the present-day case concerning the identity of Gog of
Magog, but by what procedure does his identity become free from
obscurity for us?
2. Through whom does Jehovah introduce this Gog of Magog to us,
and after foretelling what restoration?

inspired Ezekiel to write on what was then far future:

³ "And the word of Jehovah continued to occur to me, saying: 'Son of man, set your face against Gog of the land of Magog, the head chieftain of Meshech and Tubal, and prophesy against him. And you must say, "This is what the Sovereign Lord Jehovah has said: 'Here I am against you, O Gog, you head chieftain of Meshech and Tubal. And I shall certainly turn you around and put hooks in your jaws and bring you forth with all your military force, horses and horsemen, all of them clothed in perfect taste, a numerous congregation, with large shield and buckler, all of them handling swords; Persia, Ethiopia and Put with them, all of them with buckler and helmet; Gomer and all its bands, the house of Togarmah, of the remotest parts of the north, and all its bands, many peoples with you.' " ' "—Ezekiel 38:1-6.

⁴ Why is not Babylon mentioned among those confederates of Gog of the land of Magog? Because the setting for Gog's attack is after the liberation of the Jews to return to their homeland to rebuild Jehovah's temple at Jerusalem, and this liberation took place after the fall of Babylon to King Cyrus the Persian in 539 B.C.E. Thus Babylon had ceased to be acting as the third world power of Bible history and was subject to Persia. Yet when Gog attacks, Persia accepts the leadership of this Gog of Magog, taking a secondary position. The question is, When? History of the world records that the Persian Empire fell before the Macedonian conqueror, Alexander the Great, in 331 B.C.E., but not to Gog.

⁵ In turn, the Grecian Empire fell to the Roman Empire finally in 30 B.C.E., but not to Gog. More modernly, the Roman Empire fell before the Seventh World

3. Ezekiel was told to address this Gog in what manner, and how did Jehovah say that he would bring that one forth?
4. What is the reason why Babylon is not mentioned among Gog's confederates, and when did Persia lose its leading world position, and to whom?
5. In the successive falls of the successive world powers, which of them fell to Gog, and what question arises concerning the Eighth World Power?

Power of Britain and America in 1763 C.E., but not to Gog. And in 1919 C.E. this Anglo-American Dual World Power maneuvered the bringing forth of the Eighth World Power, namely, the League of Nations, which League was succeeded by the United Nations in 1945 C.E. Its 127 members include Ethiopia and Iran (formerly Persia). In the near future is the United Nations to be under Gog's leadership? Is the Anglo-American Dual World Power also to come thereunder?

⁶ Back in the year 63 B.C.E., on the anniversary of the day that Nebuchadnezzar captured Jerusalem in 607 B.C.E.,* the Roman soldiers under General Pompey broke into the Jerusalem of the restored Jews. The city became tributary to Rome. In the year 66 C.E. the Jews revolted against Imperial Rome, the Sixth World Power of Bible history. When, in the year 70 C.E., the Roman armies fought their way south through the Province of Judea and attacked Jerusalem, this was no attack upon the restored Jews by Gog of Magog. Why not? Because the attack was not defeated, but the Romans under General Titus captured and destroyed Jerusalem and carried away the surviving Jews into slavery. Three years later the Romans completed their conquest of the Province of Judea by capturing its last stronghold at the southeastern corner of the province, namely, the fortress of Masada, halfway down the west shore of the Dead Sea.—Matthew 24:15-22; Mark 13:14-20.

⁷ No Gog of Magog having put in appearance then, what next? What Jesus Christ predicted. He foretold the destruction of Jerusalem that occurred in 70 C.E. and said that Jerusalem would thereafter continue to be trampled on by the Gentile nations until the "times of the Gentiles," or "the appointed times of the na-

---

* M'Clintock and Strong's *Cyclopædia*, Vol. V, p. 602, col. 1.

---

6. When the Roman armies subjected Jerusalem and Judea by the year 63 C.E., why was this not the predicted attack by Gog of Magog? 7. According to Jesus' prediction, what time period continued on after Jerusalem's destruction in 70 C.E., but the problems arising from Jerusalem's capture by the Israelis in 1967 have resulted in what?

tions," should be fulfilled. (Luke 21:20-24) Inasmuch as those Gentile Times, which began at Jerusalem's desolation by the Babylonians in 607 B.C.E., were to run for 2,520 years, they were fulfilled around October 4/5 of the year 1914 C.E. But only thirty-four years later, in 1948 C.E., the Republic of Israel was established, and on May 11, 1949, it joined the United Nations. First in 1967, by the six-day war of June 5-10, the Israelis took over possession of all of Jerusalem, along with all territory adjacent to the west bank of the Jordan River. The problems that thereby arose divided the two giant political powers, Communist Russia to Israel's north and democratic America to its west.

⁸ It was on the festal day of Pentecost (Sivan 6th) of the year 33 C.E. that the peaceful "Israel of God," spiritual Israel, was founded, it being represented by the Christian congregation with its twelve apostles of Jesus Christ. (Galatians 6:16; Acts 2:1-43) To this day the natural circumcised Jews, inside and outside the Republic of Israel, have nothing to do with the Christian "Israel of God," spiritual Israel. So the Jews have not come out before all the world as the Christian witnesses of Jehovah, in marked contrast to the present-day anointed remnant of spiritual Israel. In connection with which "Israel," then, will the Sovereign Lord of the universe oblige all the nations to "know that I am Jehovah"? Upon which "Israel" is Jehovah's prophecy by Ezekiel concerning the attack by Gog of Magog due to be fulfilled? It is upon the restored remnant of the spiritual "Israel of God."

THE MODERN-DAY GOG IDENTIFIED

⁹ It is against the remnant of spiritual Israel that Jehovah leads Gog of Magog as if by hooks in his jaws. This indicates that Jehovah has taken Gog of Magog

8. When was the congregation of spiritual Israel founded, and so upon which Israel, the natural or the spiritual, is the attack by Gog of Magog to be fulfilled?
9. Who, then, is this Gog of Magog, and why?

captive and leads him around at will. Inasmuch as the anointed remnant of the spiritual Israelites are spread all around the earth, this Gog could not be any particular nation or the chieftain of any such nation. This "head chieftain," as Gog is called, is the one who is in control of all the nations of this world, inside and outside the membership of the United Nations. Jesus Christ called him "the ruler of this world." (John 12:31; 14:30; 16:11) Also, in Revelation 12:9 he further identifies him as "the great dragon," "the original serpent, the one called Devil and Satan, who is misleading the entire inhabited earth." In the presence of Jesus Christ when on earth, the Devil as a Tempter laid claim to "all the kingdoms of the inhabited earth," and Jesus did not deny it.—Luke 4:5-7.

¹⁰ When is it that Jehovah puts symbolic "hooks" in the jaws of this modern-day Gog, to lead him as a captive to his own destruction? It is after the end of the Gentile Times in 1914 C.E. and after Satan the Devil and his demon angels have been cast out of heaven and down to our earth. The birth of God's Messianic kingdom took place in heaven at the close of the Gentile Times in 1914, as described in Revelation 12:1-5. Then "war broke out in heaven" between the forces of the newborn kingdom and the forces of Satan the Devil. Satan was defeated and was ousted from all access to the holy heavens and was restrained with his demons at the earth. (Revelation 12:7-9) At that victory for the Messianic kingdom of God a loud voice in heaven was heard crying out:

¹¹ "Now have come to pass the salvation and the power and the kingdom of our God and the authority of his Christ, because the accuser of our brothers has been hurled down, who accuses them day and night before our God! And they conquered him because of the blood of the Lamb and because of the word of their witnessing, and they did not love their souls even

10, 11. When is it that Jehovah puts symbolic "hooks" in Gog's jaws to lead him, and what did the loud voice in heaven say after the war in heaven ended?

in the face of death. On this account be glad, you heavens and you who reside in them! Woe for the earth and for the sea, because the Devil has come down to you, having great anger, knowing he has a short period of time."—Revelation 12:10-12.

¹² Accordingly, the actual Gog of Magog who fulfills Ezekiel's prophecy is Satan the Devil after his ouster from heaven, and the land of Magog is his location at the earth in which he is confined, with no freedom or power to leave it and reenter heaven. It is like the "remotest parts of the north," which are isolated and obscure and sparsely inhabited.—Ezekiel 38:6.

¹³ What was this Gog of Magog to do after his ouster from heaven that followed the Kingdom's birth in 1914? Revelation 12:13-17 tells us: "Now when the dragon saw that it was hurled down to the earth, it persecuted the woman [Jehovah's heavenly organization] that gave birth to the male child [God's Messianic kingdom]. . . . And the dragon grew wrathful at the woman, and went off to wage war with the remaining ones of her seed, who observe the commandments of God and have the work of bearing witness to Jesus."

¹⁴ From this prophetic vision nothing could be plainer than that the hostile attitude of Gog of Magog is against the remnant of spiritual Israelites, because these "observe the commandents of God and have the work of bearing witness to Jesus" as the King installed in the heavenly throne in 1914 C.E. Whereas this modern-day Gog of Magog was taken captive, to have "hooks" put in his jaws, the faithful remnant of spiritual Israelites were liberated from Babylon the Great in the year 1919 to reoccupy their rightful spiritual estate on earth. This estate is what Jehovah has

---

12. Consequently, who is the actual Gog, and what is the land of Magog?

13. After his ouster from heaven, what would this modern-day Gog do, according to Revelation 12:13-17?

14. The hostile attitude of this Gog of Magog is against which Israel, and what has Jehovah done to the estate that they now occupy?

caused to become "like the garden of Eden," spiritually speaking.—Ezekiel 36:35.

THE CHALLENGE TO ATTACK

15 We are reminded of an ancient challenge to enemies to make war on Jehovah's people, at Joel 3:9-17*, as we read Jehovah's call to the captive Gog of Magog to ready himself for assault on the remnant of spiritual Israelites and those dedicated sheeplike "aliens" who have associated themselves with the remnant in their spiritual Paradise: "Be ready, and let there be preparation on your part, you with all your congregation, those congregated alongside you, and you must become their guard." (Ezekiel 38:7) Thus Jehovah tells Gog of Magog to be the commander-in-chief or "guard" of all the nations and peoples whom he musters for the coming attack upon Jehovah's Christian witnesses. These preparations are, not for a Third World War with nuclear bombs and rocketry, but for framing effective measures to exterminate the spiritual "Israel of God" from the face of the earth.

16 That it would be a long time after Jehovah gave the prophecy to Ezekiel before it would be fulfilled, His next words to Gog now show: "After many days you will be given attention. In the final part of the years you will come to the land of people brought back from the sword, collected together out of many peoples, onto the mountains of Israel, that have proved to be a constantly devastated place; even a land that has been brought forth from the peoples, where they have dwelt in security, all of them. And you will be bound to come up. Like a storm you will come in. Like clouds to cover the land you will become, you

* See Chapter Two, page 33, paragraph 31.

15. With what words does Jehovah call upon Gog to ready himself for attacking, and for what kind of war does this mean making preparations?
16. How long after Ezekiel's getting the prophecy about Gog would it be fulfilled, and against what land was Gog to come?

and all your bands and many peoples with you."
—Ezekiel 38:8, 9.

[17] Since the "time of the end" for this wicked system of things began at the fulfillment of the Gentile Times in 1914 C.E., we today who are living more than half a century after that date are doubtlessly living "in the final part of the years." Gog of Magog, also, must know that the "short period of time" that was to be allowed to him after his ouster from heaven has not much longer to run.

[18] Shortly, now, Jehovah must give Gog attention and turn him around and lead him and his highly militarized forces to their own undoing. By a ruse on the part of Jehovah the outwitted Gog of Magog is maneuvered into coming against the spiritual estate of the spiritual "Israel of God." The remnant of spiritual Israelites that were preserved from the "sword" of World War I and its persecutions have been dwelling there. They have been liberated and collected together out of the "many peoples" that make up Babylon the Great, the world empire of false religion. In their God-given estate they have been peacefully living "in security" under Jehovah's protection since 1919 C.E., in Christian neutrality toward worldly wars.

[19] It is not mentioned here that the one whom Jehovah calls "David my servant" is reigning as a King-Shepherd over them. But that is to be understood, since Jehovah promised that, when He brought them back from Babylon to their proper estate, they would have this Messianic descendant of David as their King and Shepherd. (Ezekiel 34:23, 24; 37:22-25) In the case of ancient Israel, when the Jewish remnant left Babylon and returned to the land of Judah they did not

17. Why must we today be living in the "final part of the years" as mentioned in that prophecy?
18. How have the people that are to be attacked been brought back from the "sword," out of what peoples have they been collected, and how have they dwelt in their God-given estate?
19. Did the one spoken of as "David my servant" reign over the Jews restored to their homeland in 537 B.C.E., and in this respect what must be said about the restored remnant of spiritual Israel today?

there have a descendant of the royal line of David rule as king over them. But in the case of the remnant of spiritual Israel, they have had the Messianic descendant of King David, namely, Jesus Christ, ruling as King over them from the "heavenly Jerusalem" since the Gentile Times ended in 1914 C.E. He has been their Governmental Shepherd to keep them "in security" spiritually.

²⁰ Gog of Magog would like to invade and get up as high among the restored people of Jehovah as he can, even "onto the mountains of Israel," indeed onto "Mount Zion," the seat of government, to assure himself of success. So he comes with the vast "congregation" of war-minded persons that he can muster, many "bands and many peoples." "Like clouds to cover the land" with their shadow, so the multitudes of Gog's army of aggression will swarm over the earth, bedarkening the ground with their presence. This is a warning to the remnant of spiritual Israel and their dedicated sheeplike associates. They should not be surprised that they will have the whole world of mankind under Satan the Devil against them. Not amazed should they be even if military dictatorship world wide came.

²¹ To His people, who are the target of the coming attack, Jehovah reveals what are the motives of the heart of Gog of Magog in that he says to him: "This is what the Sovereign Lord Jehovah has said, 'And it must occur in that day that things will come up into your heart, and you will certainly think up an injurious scheme; and you must say: "I shall go up against the land of open rural country. I shall come in upon those having no disturbance, dwelling in security, all of them dwelling without wall, and they do not have even bar and doors." It will be to get a big spoil and to do much plundering, in order to turn your hand back upon devastated places reinhabited and upon a people

---

20. How high up would Gog like to get onto the estate of Jehovah's people, and how will his war-minded congregation be like clouds to cover the land?
21. What are the heart motives of Gog behind his attack, and how is the state of those he attacks described?

gathered together out of the nations, one that is accumulating wealth and property, those who are dwelling in the center of the earth.' "—Ezekiel 38:10-12.

THE PURPOSE OF GOG'S ATTACK

²² The remnant of spiritual Israel and their dedicated fellow residents trust in the protection of their God Jehovah. For that reason they do not arm themselves with lethal weapons and join in the extreme military preparations of the nations during this age of violence and international anarchy. They seem to be so lacking in political influence, so unfortified and open to invasion, that Gog is lured on to attack them. But how could Gog "get a big spoil" and "do much plundering" among these spiritual Israelites and their companions? Are they not in general poor people, not having much of the goods of this world? (James 2:5; 1 Corinthians 1:27-29) Their spirituality is not what Gog and his hordes desire, although they would like to destroy it, for in it lies the invincible strength of the spiritual Israelites. But these unarmed, harmless Christian witnesses of Jehovah wield an influence for Jehovah's Messianic kingdom. They are continually seeking first the interests of that kingdom and persist in preaching it world wide, and are successfully gathering people of all races and nationalities to the side of that kingdom. They have Kingdom interests!

²³ Ah, those Kingdom interests! They are things not in line with the schemes of Satan's nations for world domination. They are what Gog and his hordes would like to spoil and plunder. This ambitious objective of Gog to put out of the way all who do not support world domination by nations under him is discerned by worldly peoples. Jehovah points this fact out by saying with respect to Gog when on the march: "Sheba and Dedan and the merchants of Tarshish and all its maned

---

22. How is it manifest that the remnant of spiritual Israel trust in Jehovah for protection, and why does the question arise as to one's being able to plunder them?
23. How are those "Kingdom interests" something to be plundered, and who on earth are they who discern the objective of Gog's attack?

young lions—they will say to you: 'Is it to get a big spoil that you are coming in? Is it to do much plundering that you have congregated your congregation, in order to carry off silver and gold, to take wealth and property, to get a very great spoil?'" (Ezekiel 38:13) The materialistically minded people, like ancient Sheba, Dedan and merchants of Tarshish, and the bold, fearless leaders among them, like "maned young lions," recognize the selfish objective of Gog. It is to rob those spiritual Israelites of the interests and "fruits" of God's Messianic kingdom and thus bring these upholders of Jehovah's universal sovereignty to ruin.

²⁴ The faithful remnant of spiritual Israel in their spiritual estate figuratively dwell "in the center [*Hebrew*, navel] of the earth." (Ezekiel 38:12) They take a Christian neutral stand toward all the political and military conflicts of the nations all around them. They are the focal point, the prime target, of Gog's hostility. Down to the last they remain the loyal ambassadors and envoys of the established Kingdom of God by Jesus Christ. (2 Corinthians 5:20) When all other things religious round about them go down in destruction, they will remain standing as the only unconquered living practicers of God's true religion.

²⁵ In the approaching "great tribulation" Christendom will be destroyed as the antitypical unfaithful Jerusalem, yes, all of Babylon the Great will be destroyed by the armed forces of the Eighth World Power. (Luke 21:20; Matthew 24:15-22) But the faithful remnant of spiritual Israel and their dedicated companions will survive this. (Revelation 17:1-11, 15-18) Here, then, will be where Gog of Magog will step into the picture in fulfillment of Ezekiel's prophecy. The remnant of spiritual Israel are the last religious stronghold to overcome and plunder. It is the "center" of his earthly problem.

---

24. Figuratively speaking, in what way are the remnant of spiritual Israel dwelling in the center or navel of the earth?
25. After what destruction will Gog go into action against the remnant of spiritual Israel, and why?

²⁶ Almighty God, the Sovereign Lord, has kept Gog of Magog in reserve for this very situation. Just as in the case of Pharaoh at the time of the exodus of Israel from Egypt in Moses' day, so Jehovah has allowed Satan the Devil, who now takes on the role of Gog of Magog, to remain alive till now for a certain purpose. What purpose? To show his irresistible power over this Gog of Magog and thus to sanctify himself as Most Holy in connection with this longtime enemy. (Exodus 9:16; Romans 9:16) Jehovah emphasized this unalterable purpose of His as he next said to Ezekiel:

²⁷ "Therefore prophesy, O son of man, and you must say to Gog, 'This is what the Sovereign Lord Jehovah has said: "Will it not be in that day when my people Israel are dwelling in security that you will know it? And you will certainly come from your place, from the remotest parts of the north, you and many peoples with you, all of them riding on horses, a great congregation, even a numerous military force. And you will be bound to come up against my people Israel, like clouds to cover the land. In the final part of the days it will occur, and I shall certainly bring you against my land, for the purpose that the nations may know me when I sanctify myself in you before their eyes, O Gog." ' "—Ezekiel 38:14-16.

²⁸ The coming "great tribulation" will affect this entire worldwide system of things. After Christendom and the rest of Babylon the Great have been destroyed in it and the faithful remnant of spiritual Israel still remain alive in their spiritual estate because of Jehovah's protection, Gog of Magog will indeed know that these spiritual Israelites are "dwelling in security." These spiritually prosperous people, who alone on earth stand for Jehovah's Messianic kingdom, will truly be

---

26. As with Pharaoh of ancient Egypt, in what way has Jehovah kept Gog in reserve for this very situation?
27. How does Jehovah, in further words to Gog, emphasize this unalterable purpose of His?
28. Why will Gog then know that the spiritual Israelites "dwell in security," and why will this serve as a lure to Gog?

a prize for Gog and the earthly nations under him to capture and display as a trophy of war against Jehovah. This prize should be so easy to grab. Why? Because those spiritual Israelites are, to all outward appearances, so defenseless, so helpless, and so few in comparison with Gog's vast military force, sweeping in as if on horses, a dense numerous army "like clouds to cover the land." Thus, as by means of a lure, Jehovah pulls on the hooks in the jaws of the captive Gog of Magog and maneuvers him to "bring you [Gog] against my land."

²⁹ As Gog's attack is to occur "in the final part of the days," it must be in the final part of this "time of the end," in the final part of the "great tribulation" when the spiritual Israelites are still found to be "dwelling in security" after the antireligious forces destroy Christendom and all the remainder of Babylon the Great. Jehovah's judgment having in that way been executed upon all of Babylon the Great, the militarized nations under Gog will remain as the last part of this system of things that is to be put out of existence. Those nations, then being without the long-prevalent, traditional religions, will put God out of their minds and consider Jehovah as if he did not exist. Hence Jehovah will have to make them know him as a real, existing God. How will he do this? Before their eyes he will sanctify himself in this encounter with their invisible "head chieftain," Gog of Magog. In that way he will demonstrate that He is not to be profaned as unholy.

³⁰ Jehovah is "the One telling from the beginning the finale, and from long ago the things that have not been done." (Isaiah 46:10) Therefore Jehovah is not left unprepared for the coming attack by Gog of Magog; He shows this by not leaving his dedicated witnesses

29. What does the phrase "in the final part of the days" indicate as to the time of Gog's attack, and in this matter the nations will have what attitude because of being then without the traditional religions?
30. How had Jehovah previously shown his foreknowledge of Gog's attack, and so what did he do for His people?

on earth unprepared for this final attack by the enemy forces under Satan the Devil. In evidence of this he said, in further address to Gog of Magog: "This is what the Sovereign Lord Jehovah has said, 'Are you the same one of whom I spoke in the former days by the hand of my servants the prophets of Israel, who were prophesying in those days—years—as to bringing you in upon them?' "—Ezekiel 38:17.

MUSTERING THE EARTHLY HORDES UNDER GOG

[31] In addition to having spoken about Gog of Magog by means of his prophets in former days and years, Jehovah fittingly brings this identically same individual to mind again by means of Ezekiel. Knowing how Satan the Devil, who takes on the role of Gog of Magog, got started and what are his motives, Jehovah knows what the finale of Satan's course will be as Gog of Magog. He knows that it means at last a showdown fight between him and Satan the Devil alias Gog. He keeps his remnant of spiritual Israel from thinking that the ancient prophecy concerning Gog has nothing to do with them as Christians. He does this by foretelling the final maneuvers of Satan or Gog in the book listed as the very last one in the Bible, Revelation or Apocalypse. There, in connection with the next to the last plague, we read, in Revelation 16:12-16:

[32] "And the sixth one poured out his bowl upon the great river Euphrates [where the prototype of Babylon the Great was located], and its water was dried up, that the way might be prepared for the kings from the rising of the sun.

[33] "And I saw three unclean inspired expressions that looked like frogs come out of the mouth of the dragon and out of the mouth of the wild beast and out of the mouth of the false prophet. They are, in fact, expressions inspired by demons and perform signs, and they

---

31. What has Jehovah kept the anointed remnant of spiritual Israel from thinking as to Gog's attack, and how?
32, 33. With what descriptions does Jehovah foretell, in Revelation 16:12-16, the final maneuvers of Satan the Devil?

go forth to the kings of the entire inhabited earth, to gather them together to the war of the great day of God the Almighty. . . . And they gathered them together to the place that is called in Hebrew Har–Magedon."

[34] That symbolic dragon is identified as Satan the Devil, now ousted from heaven and playing the role of Gog of Magog. (Revelation 12:3, 4, 7-12) The symbolic wild beast is Satan's entire political system world wide, to which this dragon gave "its power and its throne and great authority." (Revelation 13:1, 2) The symbolic false prophet is a part of that worldwide political system and is pictured as the two-horned wild beast that engineers the creating of a political "image" of the first wild beast, for worship by the peoples. So the "false prophet" proves to be the Dual World Power of Britain and America, and the political "image" is today the United Nations as an international organization for world peace and security. So then, since the worldwide political organization, including the Anglo-American Dual World Power, gets its power, throne and authority from the dragon, Satan the Devil, he invisibly controls the whole political system.

[35] The froglike 'inspired expression' that comes out of the dragon's mouth goes forth to the "kings of the entire inhabited earth," which kings therefore make up the entire world-embracing political system under Satan the Devil alias Gog. To where does that 'inspired expression,' as backed up by "inspired expressions" from the "wild beast" and the "false prophet," lead all those political kings of earth? To war against "God the Almighty." The "great day" for that war is when the symbolic "dragon," or Gog of Magog, makes his attack upon the spiritual "Israel of God." Revelation 16:16 calls the "place" of the war, not "the land of Israel," but Har–Magedon; however, the Hebrew

34. Whom do the dragon, the wild beast and the false prophet picture, and how is it that Satan controls the worldwide political system?
35. To what does the inspired expression out of the dragon's mouth gather earth's kings, and when does the "great day" come for the "war" against God the Almighty?

name Har–Magedon apparently denotes a world situation connected with that land.—Compare Joel 3:9-17.

[36] The aggressive movement of Gog and his international hordes is not just against the land of Jehovah's restored people but also against their King, whom Jehovah calls "my servant David." (Ezekiel 34:23, 24; 37:22-25) He is the enthroned Jesus Christ, Jehovah's Beloved One, the Messianic Descendant of King David. Inevitably, then, a war against Jehovah and his restored remnant of spiritual Israel means also war against Jehovah's Messianic King, now installed as King in the heavens over the restored remnant of spiritual Israel. Revelation, chapter seventeen, portrays prophetically the order of events: before the political "image" that is now the United Nations (the Eighth World Power) "goes off into destruction," member nations of it destroy the great religious "harlot," Babylon the Great. All the political rulers are pictured by the ten horns of this beastly "image," and regarding these Revelation 17:12-14 predicts:

[37] "And the ten horns that you saw mean ten kings, who have not yet received a kingdom, but they do receive authority as kings one hour with the wild beast [the Eighth World Power]. These have one thought, and so they give their power and authority to the wild beast. These will battle with the Lamb [the once-sacrificed Jesus Christ], but, because he is Lord of lords and King of kings, the Lamb will conquer them. Also, those called and chosen and faithful with him will do so."—Compare Revelation 19:11-21.

HOW JEHOVAH DEFEATS GOG'S ATTACK

[38] Really, though, Jesus Christ fights, not primarily for his own heavenly throne, but for the vindication

---

36. War against Jehovah and his remnant of spiritual Israel means war also against whom else, and after what destruction does the war proceed against that one?

37. In Revelation 17:12-14, how is the war of those political rulers pictured, and what is the outcome thereof?

38. For what does Jesus Christ fight, and so failure to mention whom in Ezekiel's account nicely fits in with this?

of Jehovah's universal Sovereignty and for the glorification of Jehovah's name. Nicely, then, in order that the glory may go to whom it primarily belongs, there is no mention made to Gog of the reigning king, "David my servant," as Jehovah himself foretells what he will do when He is provoked to war by the God-defying attack made by Gog of Magog. He says:

[39] " 'And it must occur in that day, in the day when Gog comes in upon the soil of Israel,' is the utterance of the Sovereign Lord Jehovah, 'that my rage will come up into my nose. And in my ardor, in the fire of my fury, I shall have to speak. Surely in that day a great quaking will occur in the soil of Israel. And because of me the fish of the sea and the flying creatures of the heavens and the wild beasts of the field and all the creeping things that are creeping on the ground and all mankind that are upon the surface of the ground will be bound to shiver, and the mountains will actually be thrown down and the steep ways will have to fall, and to the earth even every wall will fall.' " —Ezekiel 38:18-20.

[40] The unjustified attack of Gog and his militarized hordes is made on a spiritually prosperous people who have a God-given right to a place on earth and full freedom for the worship of the living and true God. This fact provokes the Sovereign Lord Jehovah to a feeling of outrage, hot indignation. In rebuke to such devilish conduct he will speak with expressions that bespeak control by Him as Creator over the earth and all the forces of earth's environment.

[41] The quaking of the earth would be in that section of the land where Gog and his attack forces had penetrated. In the case of actual attack by Gog in the future, his predatory hordes will be all around the globe where Jehovah's Christian witnesses are peace-

39. In that day when he is provoked to speak in anger, what does Jehovah say will happen in the "land of Israel"?
40. What is it that provokes Jehovah to hot indignation, and the expressions that he then makes will bespeak what kind of control?
41. Where would the foretold earthquake have to occur, and what will indicate that Jehovah is causing it?

fully worshiping their God. For all of Gog's hordes to feel it, the quaking of the earth would have to be global. For it to affect mountains, toppling them, it would have to be very bad, the worst in human history. Just how this universally terrifying earthquake will take place we confidently wait to see. The fact that it coincides with Gog's invasion, just as divinely foretold, proves that Jehovah is causing it in his rage and fury!

⁴² Gog desperately resorts to the "sword" of warfare against Jehovah's restored remnant of spiritual Israel and the "great crowd" of their fellow worshipers, and so Jehovah meets him with like for like. Jehovah's peace-keeping witnesses on earth do not take up the "sword" against Gog's hordes, but Jehovah does. This is His fight! And now at last the nations of this scientifically advanced world will see Him fight—no mistaking of it! And how He can fight! Listen, as He describes his war tactics and operations:

⁴³ " 'And I will call forth against him throughout all my mountainous region a sword,' is the utterance of the Sovereign Lord Jehovah. 'Against his own brother the sword of each one will come to be. And I will bring myself into judgment with him, with pestilence and with blood; and a flooding downpour and hailstones, fire and sulphur I shall rain down upon him and upon his bands and upon the many peoples that will be with him. And I shall certainly magnify myself and sanctify myself and make myself known before the eyes of many nations; and they will have to know that I am Jehovah.' "—Ezekiel 38:21-23.

⁴⁴ At that point the battlefield of Har–Magedon is reached. The "war of the great day of God the Almighty" is on! (Revelation 16:14, 16; 19:11-16, 20, 21)

---

42. To what weapon does Gog resort, how does Jehovah meet him, and why do not Jehovah's witnesses take any action?
43. How will Jehovah deal with the swords of Gog's hordes, with what natural forces will he bring himself into judgment with Gog, and thus what will he do in his own behalf?
44. Jehovah will thus outdo what modern means of warfare by all the militarized nations?

As weapons of warfare Jehovah wields the forces of creation, flooding cloudbursts of rain, hailstones of undeclared size, downpours of streaking fire and sulphur—all of which will release more destructive energy than all the atomic and nuclear energy that the nations hold in reserve in the oversupply of bombs that they have stockpiled for World War III. All their scientific devices for germ warfare and chemical warfare will be surpassed by the raging pestilence with which he can plague them, a pestilence that could kill off 185,000 in a single night in a given locality. (2 Kings 19:35, 36) The blood of Jehovah's Christian witnesses they are anxious to spill, but it will be their own blood that they will drink by the violent loss of their own lives.

[45] Panic—world panic outside the ranks of Jehovah's Christian witnesses! Gog's hordes will be thrown into confusion. Instead of keeping united to strike down Jehovah's worshipers as their victims, they will turn their swords against their own ranks, brother warrior against brother warrior, not religionist against religionist, but radical against radical, Communist against Communist, anarchist against anarchist, nihilist against nihilist. Those whom this suicidal warfare among themselves does not kill off, Jehovah will execute as if going into a judicial court against them with all his supernatural means of wiping all opponents of His universal sovereignty out of existence. He must be vindicated at Court.

[46] Almighty God thus becomes very much alive to all the nations and peoples under Gog's woeful control. The God of the global flood in Noah's day again goes into action on a global scale on this his "day of judgment and of destruction of the ungodly men." (2 Peter 2:5; 3:6, 7, 10-12) The "great tribulation" upon this worldwide system of things reaches its culmination, and the last vestiges of this ungodly system of things

---

45. Where will panic occur, how will it affect those seized by it, and what will Jehovah judicially do?
46. So the "great tribulation" comes to its culmination in what way and on what scale?

are destroyed as the entire human society of God-ignoring people is annihilated.

[47] Before the eyes of all the nations under Gog of Magog Jehovah will thus magnify himself, displaying himself as the Greatest in all the realm of the living. He will sanctify himself, proving that He is holy and not in sympathy with any part of this unholy system of things. He will make himself known otherwise than just on the pages of the Holy Bible. The stubborn-minded nations under Gog will be forced to see that such a world catastrophe could come from only the One who foretold it and warned of doing it. Facing destruction at His hand, they will, just before they go down into it, know what He said, "know that I am Jehovah."

47. In what sense will Jehovah sanctify himself before the eyes of all the nations, and before their destruction what will they know?

Chapter 20

Land of Magog No More to Threaten Mankind

THE unseen base of operations from which Gog launches his attack upon the spiritual "Israel of God" is the "land of Magog." This "land" must come in for attention after Gog's militant forces on earth have been crushed in defeat. Thus the unseen inhabitants of the "land of Magog" must witness first the disastrous defeat of the devilish campaign against the spiritually prosperous worshipers of Jehovah. The na-

1. After the defeat of Gog's attack on Jehovah's worshipers, what "land" must come in for attention, and what might persons who could get sucked in with that attack well do now?

tions and peoples whom Gog allies with himself in the campaign gain, not glory, but only undying shame, out of this impious campaign. All persons who might yet get sucked into that coming campaign against Jehovah's Christian witnesses would now do well to consider what He says by Ezekiel to the Gog by whom they might get recruited:

[2] "And as regards you, O son of man, prophesy against Gog, and you must say, 'This is what the Sovereign Lord Jehovah has said: "Here I am against you, O Gog, you head chieftain of Meshech and Tubal. And I will turn you around and lead you on and cause you to come up from the remotest parts of the north and bring you in upon the mountains of Israel. And I will strike your bow out of your left hand, and your arrows I shall cause to fall out of your own right hand. On the mountains of Israel you will fall, you and all your bands and the peoples that will be with you. To birds of prey, birds of every sort of wing, and the wild beasts of the field I will give you for food." ' " —Ezekiel 39:1-4.

[3] Jehovah has good reason to be against Gog of Magog because of that one's hostile attitude against Jehovah's faithful worshipers coupled with his constant readiness to despoil such worshipers. Gog deserves destruction, and at the due time Jehovah seeks an overt act on Gog's part, an act that will be glaringly manifest to heaven and earth, that all may agree that Jehovah has just cause for destroying Gog. Jehovah catches him right on the spot, engaged in his outrageous depredations, and knocks his means of warfare out of his power. No decent burial with military honors is promised for the slain hordes under Gog as their "head chieftain." For carrion birds and beasts they will lie exposed for food. With reference to their inglorious outcome we

2. From where would Jehovah cause Gog to come, what would He do to Gog's weapons, and what would He do with Gog's fallen peoples?
3. Why has Jehovah good reason to be against Gog, for what that will openly justify him in taking action on Gog does He wait, and how will his slain hordes be disposed of?

read further: " 'Upon the surface of the field you will fall, for I myself have spoken,' is the utterance of the Sovereign Lord Jehovah." (Ezekiel 39:5) Gog's fallen hordes will never return home in triumph!

⁴ What, though, about the location where this vicious God-defying attack on Jehovah's restored people was conceived, up there in "the remotest parts of the north"? This is the invisible realm of Satan the Devil and his demons at the earth since their being ousted from heaven after being defeated in the war in heaven. This debased location at the earth is a menace, a continuous threat to mankind and a source of woe to earth and sea, and it must be done away with. Jehovah will wipe out this threat to the peace and security of earth's inhabitants, for he goes on to say:

⁵ "And I will send fire upon Magog and upon those who are inhabiting the islands in security; and people will have to know that I am Jehovah. And my holy name I shall make known in the midst of my people Israel, and I shall no more let my holy name be profaned; and the nations will have to know that I am Jehovah, the Holy One in Israel."—Ezekiel 39:6, 7.

⁶ No place will be too isolated, for instance, islands, so as not to feel the execution of Jehovah's judgments for having any part or any sympathy with the antichristian attack by Gog of the land of Magog. No, not even the most remote location, "the land of Magog" itself. How will Jehovah consume this locality by sending "fire upon Magog"? By ridding this invisible place of restraint at the earth of its occupants, namely, of Satan the Devil and the demons over which he is the "head chieftain." This riddance follows the "war of the great day of God the Almighty" at Har–Magedon,

4. Where is the "land of Magog," and what does it constitute for earth's inhabitants?
5. How does Jehovah say that he will wipe out that threat to earth's peace and security?
6. Will any place be too remote to feel the execution of Jehovah's judgments, and how will he consume the land of Magog by sending "fire on Magog"?

foretold in Revelation 16:14, 16; 19:11-21, and is described in Revelation 20:1-3, as follows: "And I saw an angel coming down out of heaven with the key of the abyss and a great chain in his hand. And he seized the dragon, the original serpent, who is the Devil and Satan, and bound him for a thousand years. And he hurled him [away from his place of detention at the earth] into the abyss and shut it and sealed it over him, that he might not mislead the nations anymore until the thousand years were ended. After these things he must be let loose for a little while."

⁷ This wiping out finally of the symbolic "land of Magog" will mean a sweeping victory for Jehovah, and those persons who will not have taken their stand for His Messianic kingdom will be made to realize that they are on the side that is resisting and fighting against the Sovereign Lord of the universe. By having His judicial decisions executed upon them such people "will have to know that I am Jehovah," as he has declared. No more will they be in position to profane Jehovah's name by asserting that He is too weak to protect his people from worldly attack and to defend his earthly interests with success. By his preserving and delivering his Christian witnesses during the final assault by Gog of Magog, Jehovah will as never before make his name known in the midst of spiritual Israel that has suffered international reproach. As the last relics of this ungodly system of things go down into destruction the effect is bound to be just as He has decreed: "The nations will have to know that I am Jehovah, the Holy One in Israel."—Ezekiel 39:7.

⁸ That will be an unforgettable "great day" for this Holy One of Israel when he defeats the innumerable hordes that make up the earthly attack forces of Gog, their "guard" and "head chieftain."

---

7. Why will the people no longer be in position to profane Jehovah's name regarding spiritual Israel, and in what knowledge will his taking action result?
8. When Gog's forces are defeated, for whom will it be a "great day"?

DISPOSAL OF WAR EQUIPMENT AND DEAD BODIES

⁹ Some idea of the vast war equipment that these hordes of people will have can be gained from how long it will take for the combustible parts of them to be disposed of. The long time needed for this Jehovah sets out in his next words: " 'Look! It must come and it must be brought to be,' is the utterance of the Sovereign Lord Jehovah. 'This is the day of which I have spoken. And the inhabitants of the cities of Israel will certainly go forth and burn and build fires with the armor and bucklers and large shields,—with the bows and with the arrows and with the handstaves and with the lances; and with them they will have to light fires seven years. And they will not carry sticks of wood from the field, nor will they gather firewood out of the forests, for with the armor they will light fires.' " (Ezekiel 39:8-10) After Jehovah's victory his people will adapt the materials of any remaining war relics of the nations to useful purposes.

¹⁰ The innumerable hordes under Gog of Magog attacked the spiritual estate of Jehovah's Christian witnesses with the intent to despoil them, but it proves to be just the opposite: " 'And they will certainly make spoil of those who had been making spoil of them, and plunder those who had been plundering them,' is the utterance of the Sovereign Lord Jehovah."—Ezekiel 39:10.

¹¹ As it were, the attack forces under Gog of Magog dig their own graves by attacking the God-given estate of Jehovah's Christian witnesses on earth. But how will comparatively few survivors of the "war of the great day of God the Almighty" at Har–Magedon be able to bury "those slain by Jehovah" who will lie "in that

9. How does Jehovah indicate the vast quantity of war equipment used by Gog's hordes on earth, and how will Jehovah's people use the war relics?

10. With what intent do Gog's hordes attack the God-given spiritual estate, but how do matters turn out?

11, 12. What questions arise as to disposal of the bodies of "those slain by Jehovah," and what arrangement does Jehovah say that he will make regarding Gog's crowd?

day from one end of the earth clear to the other end of the earth"? (Jeremiah 25:33) And after those "birds of every sort of wing" and the "wild beasts of the field" satisfy themselves with feeding on the cadavers of Gog's hordes, what will there be left to bury? But if there is anything left to bury, Jehovah will allow for it to the eternal shame of those losing their lives in Gog's attack. We read:

[12] " 'And it must occur in that day that I shall give to Gog a place there, a burial place in Israel, the valley of those passing through on the east of the sea, and it will be stopping up those passing through. And there they will have to bury Gog and all his crowd, and they will be certain to call it the Valley of Gog's Crowd. And those of the house of Israel will have to bury them for the purpose of cleansing the land, for seven months. And all the people of the land will have to do the burying, and it will certainly become for them a matter of fame in the day that I glorify myself,' is the utterance of the Sovereign Lord Jehovah."—Ezekiel 39:11-13.

[13] This is not to be understood as meaning that his Christian witnesses whom Jehovah preserves through the "great tribulation" upon this system of things will be gravediggers and corpse buriers for the opening seven months of the righteous new system of things upon this earth. Its taking so many months to bury Gog's crowd is merely a picture to portray the vastness of the crowd of ungodly people who will perish in the destruction of this system of things, as well as the fewness of those whom Jehovah preserves alive on earth. Furthermore, as corpses were unclean in Israel, the burying of the corpses of Gog's crowd results in cleansing the land and signifies that this earth will be purified from all defilement by the ungodly servants of Satan the Devil alias Gog. Nothing of them will be left to defile the "new earth."—2 Peter 3:13.

13. What is indicated by the fact that it takes so long to bury Gog's crowd, and to what state will such burials bring this earth?

¹⁴ All memory of those God-defying participants in Gog's attack will be as nauseating as the stink arising from the putrefying carcasses of Gog's crowd—a stench so strong as to stop persons from going any farther and passing by. The Valley of Gog's Crowd is pictured as being to the east of the Dead Sea, near where the enemy land of Moab used to be. (Ezekiel 25:8-11) It would become no shrine so that surviving friends and relatives of the slain would visit this cemetery on a Memorial Day to do honor to the memory of the heroic war dead. No hope of a resurrection is memorialized for the participants in Gog's attack, cursed ungodly persons whom Jehovah executes on his day of judgment. (Matthew 25:31-33, 41-46) They have earned eternal infamy for themselves. Jehovah's miraculous preserving of his Christian witnesses in the face of such a worldwide attack by overwhelmingly superior numbers will be eternally famous. By destroying their attackers, Gog's crowd, Jehovah will glorify himself for all time.

¹⁵ The "new earth" of human society under Jehovah's Messianic kingdom of the heavens in the hands of "David my servant" must be perfectly clean of all traces of Gog's crowd. To make a vivid picture of this, the "utterance of the Sovereign Lord Jehovah" goes on to say respecting the survivors of Gog's attack: "And there will be men for continual employment whom they will divide off, passing along through the land, burying, with those passing through, those left remaining on the surface of the earth, in order to cleanse it. To the end of seven months they will keep making search. And those passing through must pass along through the land, and should one actually see the bone of a man he must also build beside it a marker, until those who do the burying will have buried it in the Valley of

14. What will be the case of the memory of those participants in Gog's attack, and how will Jehovah's preserving of his attacked Christian witnesses affect himself?
15. How is the bringing of the "new earth" to a clean state portrayed by the operations of the "men for continual employment" who are divided off?

Gog's Crowd. And the name of the city will also be Hamonah. And they will have to cleanse the land." —Ezekiel 39:14-16.

¹⁶ In the Hebrew language the name Valley of Gog's Crowd is Gei-Hamon-Gog, and the city Hamonah (meaning "Crowd") would be established by the Valley of Gog's Crowd, to mark the burial place. Of course, the city Hamonah ("Crowd") would not be inhabited by any member of Gog's crowd of attackers. Also, the city's name being just Hamonah ("Crowd") would not honorably memorialize Gog's name.

¹⁷ The city would be inhabited by the miraculously delivered survivors of Gog's infamous attack. This reminds us of Proverbs 2:21, 22: "The upright are the ones that will reside in the earth, and the blameless are the ones that will be left over in it. As regards the wicked, they will be cut off from the very earth; and as for the treacherous, they will be torn away from it." Gog's attack taking place earth wide wherever the Christian witnesses of Jehovah are active, no literal city named Hamonah near the scene of their defeat could be reasonably erected. But the "new earth" organization of the surviving witnesses of Jehovah will be an organization of the living in stark contrast to dead hordes of Gog's crowd.

SACRIFICIAL FEAST FOR BIRDS AND BEASTS

¹⁸ Among Gog's crowd should be many hunters who have gunned down birds and wild animals wantonly for sheer sport or for greedy commercialism, like Nimrod of Babylon. (Genesis 10:8-10) There is likely a thought of retribution contained in Jehovah's further words to his prophet Ezekiel: "And as regards you, O son of man, this is what the Sovereign Lord Jehovah has said, 'Say to the birds of every sort of wing and to all the wild beasts of the field: "Collect yourselves togeth-

16, 17. What does the city's name Hamonah mean, by whom will it be inhabited, and why could it not picture a literal city by that name? 18, 19. To what "great sacrifice" does Jehovah invite all sorts of birds and wild beasts, and why is there a sense of retribution contained therein?

376 "THE NATIONS SHALL KNOW THAT I AM JEHOVAH" Ezekiel 39:17-20

er and come. Gather yourselves together all around to my sacrifice, which I am sacrificing for you, a great sacrifice on the mountains of Israel. And you will certainly eat flesh and drink blood. The flesh of mighty ones you will eat, and the blood of the chieftains of the earth you will drink, rams, young male sheep, and he-goats, young bulls, the fatlings of Bashan all of them. And you will be certain to eat fat to satisfaction and to drink blood to drunkenness, from my sacrifice that I will sacrifice for you." '

[19] " 'And you must get satisfied at my table on horses and charioteers, mighty persons and all sorts of warriors,' is the utterance of the Sovereign Lord Jehovah."—Ezekiel 39:17-20.

[20] Gog's crowd is thus said to include "chieftains of the earth" who are likened to rams, he-goats, young bulls, that fattened on the fine pasture grounds of Bashan to the northeast of the Sea of Galilee; cavalrymen on horses, charioteers, "mighty persons and all sorts of warriors." Suchlike ones in our modern day must fall by the edge of Jehovah's "sword" of execution in the "war of the great day of God the Almighty" at Har–Magedon. The description of that war as set out in Revelation 19:17-21 speaks of kings, military commanders, horses and their riders, freemen and slaves, small ones and great, all of whom are to be slain, lie unburied and be feasted upon by scavenger birds.

[21] This feast for the birds of every sort and for the wild beasts is called a "sacrifice" by Jehovah, for sacrifices made to him in pre-Christian times called for the slaughter of animal and bird victims. Their blood has to flow. In Revelation 19:17 it is called "the great evening meal of God." The offering of communion sacrifices or peace offerings to Jehovah used to be

---

20. By the naming of those to be feasted upon by all whom Jehovah invites to his "great sacrifice," Gog's crowd includes whom, and whom does Revelation 19:17-21 also mention?
21. Why was the feast as provided for the birds and wild beasts called by Jehovah a "sacrifice," and what will thus being feasted upon spell for the executed ones of Gog's crowd?

the occasion for feasting on part of the victim's flesh by the offerer and his kinsmen. In the sacrificial feast that Jehovah spreads for the birds and wild beasts by his glorious victory over Gog's crowd, Jehovah places no bar upon them against drinking the blood of the slain humans, a thing forbidden to human creatures from Noah's day onward. (Genesis 9:1-4) This spells great reproach for the executed ones of Gog's crowd. When, for instance, the scavenger dogs of Jezreel devoured the carcass of wicked Queen Jezebel, they left only some bones to be buried. (2 Kings 9:30-37) How much, then, will the birds and wild beasts leave of the carcasses of Gog's crowd to be buried in the Valley of Gog's Crowd? Bones?

²² The fact that Jehovah leaves the bodies of those slain at the defeat of Gog's attack lying exposed on the ground for birds and wild beasts to gorge themselves upon symbolizes that they will not be laid in respected memorial tombs in hope of a resurrection for them. The unburied dead, "those slain by Jehovah," will be so enormously many that even the carrion birds and scavenging wild beasts could never take care of their consumption. The burial of even what remains after these lower creatures have their fill would be stupendous. Doubtless the Almighty God will use some highly scientific means, whether including antimatter or not, to dispose of the surplus of decaying bodies in a speedy and sanitary way. This remains for the survivors of the "war of the great day" to see and witness. We remember that Noah and his seven fellow survivors of the global Deluge were not burdened with burying the human victims of that world catastrophe after they came out of the ark and renewed Jehovah's worship on earth.—Genesis 8:18-22.

²³ 'How horrible all this!' Should that be our reaction

22. Jehovah's letting the slain lie exposed on the ground to be consumed by scavengers indicates what concerning their future, and how might Jehovah dispose of the surplus of dead bodies?
23. How might some react at the thought of such an end to Gog's attack, and yet what is to be expected concerning this prophecy?

of mind toward this prophecy of the disastrous defeat of Gog's dastardly attack upon the only remaining peaceful worshipers of Jehovah on earth at the end of this violent system of things? Not rightly so! No matter how terrible it may seem to people who as a community took part in gory world wars Nos. I and II, Jehovah has spoken it prophetically, and that means it will be sure to come to pass.

²⁴ Since we must face it in the oncoming future, we do well to consider whether our present line of action will in due time put us within the rank of Gog's crowd in defiance of Jehovah. Let us not overlook the everlasting benefit that will come to the race of mankind by the annihilation of Gog's crowd and the doing away with of the threat-filled "land of Magog." Especially, let us take into account the everlasting vindication that it will bring to Jehovah's universal sovereignty and sacred name. This thing of supreme importance he calls to our consciousness, saying:

²⁵ "And I will set my glory among the nations; and all the nations will have to see my judgment that I have executed and my hand that I have placed among them. And those of the house of Israel will have to know that I am Jehovah, their God from that day forward. And the nations will have to know that it was because of their error that they, the house of Israel, went into exile, on account of the fact that they behaved unfaithfully toward me, so that I concealed my face from them and gave them into the hand of their adversaries, and they kept falling, all of them, by the sword. According to their uncleanness and according to their transgressions I did with them, and I kept concealing my face from them."—Ezekiel 39:21-24.

---

24. Hence, what should we consider with regard to our present course of action, and what are the benefits and the thing of supreme importance that we should not overlook in this connection?
25. How will the nations have their misunderstanding corrected as to why Jehovah let the house of Israel go through such hard experiences?

CORRECTING WRONG CONCLUSIONS
DRAWN BY NATIONS

²⁶ Consequently, what Jehovah does to the embattled Gog's crowd will be no disgrace to Him. His protective power over his restored people will then become glorious, and the nations under Gog will be made to see it. He will show them his "hand," and it will be all-powerful; and they will feel it when he places it down among them. The nations formed wrong conclusions because Jehovah's Christian witnesses appeared to have no divine protection when they were persecuted during World War I and came under temporary bondage to Babylon the Great. They mistook this to mean that the God of these witnesses was no God or that he was too weak to protect and deliver his witnesses from the hands of the nations who worshiped gods different from Jehovah. The nations did not appreciate that Jehovah was merely disciplining his people for their shortcomings and lack of faith, their error, uncleanness and transgressions even if of an unwitting kind. Hence he concealed his face of favor and approval from them and let the "hand of their adversaries" take hold of them and mistreat them.

²⁷ The nations do not need to wait until Jehovah performs his magnificent deliverance of his people from Gog's attack. Before then they have had proof that he had turned his face of favor toward his repentant people and was showing supernatural power toward them. Because of the wrong conclusions drawn by the nations concerning Jehovah's disciplining of his people, then in exile in Babylon, he stated his purpose to the prophet Ezekiel as follows:

²⁸ "Therefore this is what the Sovereign Lord Jehovah has said, 'Now is when I shall bring back cap-

---

26. How will Jehovah make his protective power glorious, to whom will He show his hand, and what wrong conclusions as to why His people suffered mistreatment by the nations will be corrected?
27. Have the nations had to wait till Gog's attack to see that Jehovah has turned his face toward his people?
28. How did Jehovah then say that he would show jealousy for his name and sanctify himself with respect to the "house of Israel" even before Gog's attack?

tive ones of Jacob and actually have mercy upon all the house of Israel; and I will show exclusive devotion for my holy name. And they will have borne their humiliation and all their unfaithfulness with which they have acted toward me, when they dwell on their soil in security, with no one to make them tremble. When I bring them back from the peoples and I actually collect them together out of the lands of their enemies, I will also sanctify myself among them before the eyes of many nations.' "—Ezekiel 39:25-27.

²⁹ As with ancient Israel in the year 537 B.C.E., so Jehovah showed that he had jealousy or exclusive devotion for his holy name in the year 1919 C.E. How? In that first postwar year of this "time of the end" he liberated them from their bondage to Babylon the Great and her political and military paramours. After that the holiness of Jehovah became plainer and plainer to the restored remnant of spiritual Israel, so that they appreciated that this called for greater religious and moral cleanness on their part and more clear-cut separation of them from this unholy world. Inasmuch as Jehovah caused this by the greater unfolding of his Holy Bible to them and the operation of his holy spirit upon them, he sanctified himself among these obedient spiritual Israelites while the eyes of the many nations among whom they preached the good news of God's kingdom looked on. To such nations it should then have become manifest that the God of these spiritual Israelites was at work among them in a holy way.

³⁰ Even now, before his wondrous vindication of his universal sovereignty upon the attacking hordes of Gog occurs, the nations should have come to know that Jehovah, the God of the remnant of spiritual Israel, is a living God, a God who is jealous for his name and who stands for no compromise and defilement with

29. How did Jehovah show jealousy for his name in 1919 C.E., and how did he make it manifest before the eyes of the nations that he was sanctifying himself among the remnant of spiritual Israel?
30. Who on earth should already know that Jehovah stands for no compromise or defilement with this world, and how did He say to Ezekiel that he would bring about this knowledge?

this unclean world. Jehovah's Christian witnesses have come to know this already, just as their God foretold through Ezekiel, saying: " 'And they will have to know that I am Jehovah, their God, when I send them in exile to the nations and actually bring them together upon their soil, so that I shall leave none of them remaining there any longer. And I shall no longer conceal my face from them, because I will pour out my spirit upon the house of Israel,' is the utterance of the Sovereign Lord Jehovah."—Ezekiel 39:28, 29.

[31] Today, more than half a century after their liberation from Babylon the Great in 1919 C.E., the anointed remnant of spiritual Israel appreciate the freedom that they enjoy in their spiritual estate to which Jehovah has restored them. They rejoice to overflowing at the condition like that of the "garden of Eden" to which their spiritual estate has been rehabilitated. They jubilate in that the one whom Jehovah calls "my servant David" is their heavenly Shepherd-King. As he instructed them to do, they have prayed for more of the spirit of Jehovah their God, and this prayer has been abundantly answered. He has poured out his spirit upon these spiritual Israelites. This is notably evident from the "fruitage" of Jehovah's spirit, namely, the qualities of a godly personality like that of Jesus Christ. (Luke 11:13; Galatians 5:22, 23; Ephesians 4:20-24) Because he has thus dealt so mercifully and lovingly just as he foretold by His prophets, they know that he is Jehovah their God. They have now been gathered in worldwide Christian unity, bound together by love, that fruit of God's spirit which is "a perfect bond of union."—Colossians 3:14.

[32] Accepting the message of God's Messianic kingdom that these spiritual Israelites proclaim under God's spirit, a "great crowd" of sheeplike seekers of the true

31. How is it evident that he no longer conceals his face from spiritual Israel, and what shows that he has poured out his spirit upon them?
32. Who have accepted the message of God's kingdom preached by the spiritual Israelites, where do they now reside, and to whose victory do they joyfully look forward?

God have come out of all nations and taken up residence with them in their spiritual Paradise. There they are worshiping the same God, Jehovah, under His Shepherd-King, Jesus Christ. (Revelation 7:9-17; Matthew 25:31-40, 46; John 10:16) Forewarned, they await together the coming attack by Gog of Magog and his international hordes. Full of faith, they joyfully look forward to Jehovah's resounding victory over that wicked enemy Gog for the vindication of Jehovah's sovereignty and of his holy name.

Chapter 21

Life in Security
under Messiah's Reign

LIFE in security on earth under a righteous government! Such a desirable thing will be more certain for mankind than ever previously after the attack by Gog and his greedy hordes has been smashed and the "land of Magog" has been wiped out. The people who became the target of Gog's unprovoked attack were already "dwelling in security" under divine protection in their God-given estate on earth before Gog's attack was launched. O how much more fully they will dwell in security in all respects after Jehovah vindicates his universal sovereignty and restores his full control over earth by gloriously triumphing over Gog of Magog! (Ezekiel 38:11, 14) This will signify that there will be complete freedom everywhere on earth to worship the victorious God who makes all nations to know that he is Jehovah!

---

1. Who already "dwell in security" under divine protection, but after what event will security be enjoyed much more fully in all respects?

² It is expressly God's purpose and arrangement for the pure and undefiled worship of him to be carried on by the survivors of Gog's attack. Jehovah graphically portrayed this in the vision that he gave to his prophet Ezekiel some years after the prophecy concerning Gog's unjustified effort to eradicate the worship of Jehovah from the earth. It was an extensive vision that took the last nine chapters of Ezekiel's prophecy to describe. Historical data in its introduction authenticate it:

³ "In the twenty-fifth year of our exile, in the start of the year, on the tenth day of the month, in the fourteenth year after the city had been struck down, on this very same day the hand of Jehovah proved to be upon me, so that he brought me to that place. In the visions of God he brought me to the land of Israel and gradually set me down upon a very high mountain, on which there was something like the structure of a city to the south.

⁴ "And he proceeded to bring me there, and, look! there was a man. His appearance was like the appearance of copper, and there was a flax cord in his hand, and a measuring reed, and he was standing in the gate. And the man began to speak to me: 'Son of man, see with your eyes, and with your ears hear, and set your heart upon all that I am showing you, because for the purpose of my showing you, you have been brought here. Tell everything that you are seeing to the house of Israel.' "—Ezekiel 40:1-4.

⁵ The twenty-fifth year of King Jehoiachin's and Ezekiel's exile in Babylon being the fourteenth year after the city of Jerusalem was broken down by the Babylonians in 607 B.C.E., the date of Ezekiel's temple

2. It is Jehovah's purpose for what to be carried on by the survivors of Gog's attack, and in what vision is this portrayed?
3. How did Ezekiel authenticate this vision at the start, and in it where did Jehovah's spirit set him down?
4. What was the appearance of the one whom Ezekiel there saw, what did he have, where was he standing, and what did he say to Ezekiel?
5. What is the B.C.E. date for that twenty-fifth year of Ezekiel's exile in Babylon, and on what day of what lunar month did he have the vision?

vision would be Nisan 10, 593 B.C.E., if the "start of the year" is taken to designate the month Nisan, the first month of the sacred year. But if the secular year were meant, then the date would be Tishri 10, which was the day of atonement, on which in a Jubilee Year the trumpet was blown to proclaim liberty throughout all the land.—Leviticus 25:8-13.

⁶ In that year of 593 B.C.E., the land of Judah still had fifty-six years to lie desolate (till 537 B.C.E.). But when in his vision Ezekiel is transported back to that land he sees already built a new temple for Jehovah's worship on Mount Moriah, this temple being of such proportions as to be "something like the structure of a city to the south." The mountain's being described as being a "very high mountain" locates its fulfillment in the era when "the mountain of the house of Jehovah will become firmly established above the top of the mountains, and it will certainly be lifted up above the hills."—Isaiah 2:2.

⁷ The man in the vision who served as Ezekiel's guide evidently shone like burnished copper and had in his hand means of making measurements about the temple. He pictured Jehovah's angel who was to take Ezekiel on a tour through the temple and make explanations. Evidently Ezekiel first saw him standing in the east gate, from which the inspection tour began.—Ezekiel 40:3, 6.

⁸ Ezekiel did not construct this temple in his imagination, but in the vision Jehovah as the heavenly Designer presented it as already put up, ready for inspection and measurement. It pictures the "true tent, which Jehovah put up, and not man." So this visionary temple had the "typical representations of the things in the heavens." In the spring of 33 C.E. the resur-

6. In what condition was the land of Judah then lying, and yet what does Ezekiel see on Mount Moriah, and its being called a "very high mountain" locates matters as in what era?
7. Whom did the glorious man whom Ezekiel saw represent, and what service was he to render to Ezekiel?
8. Who was the Designer of that temple, and what did this visionary temple really represent?

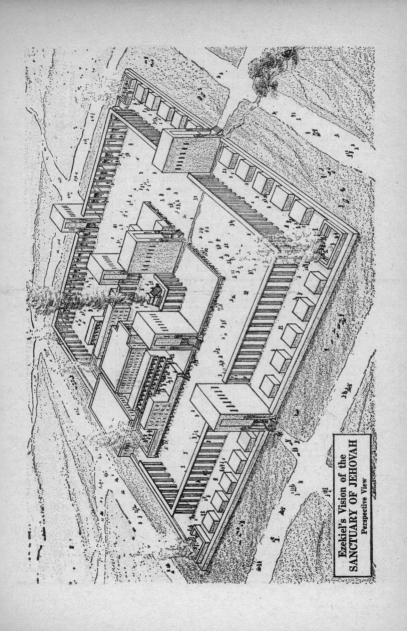

Ezekiel's Vision of the
SANCTUARY OF JEHOVAH
Perspective View

rected Jesus Christ entered into the Most Holy of that "true temple," namely, "into heaven itself, now to appear before the person of God for us." (Hebrews 8:2; 9:23, 24) There he presented the merit of his perfect human sacrifice that he had offered on earth upon Jehovah's altar arrangement. (Hebrews 13:10-12, 20) Such a temple Ezekiel saw pictured.

[9] In the course of this detailed inspection the prophet Ezekiel sees, as it were, the inauguration or sanctification of this sacred structure when Jehovah takes up residence in the sanctuary of it. In Ezekiel 43:1-7 he describes it. Referring first to his angelic guide, Ezekiel goes on to tell us:

"Then he made me go to the gate, the gate that is facing toward the east. And, look! the glory of the God of Israel was coming from the direction of the east, and his voice was like the voice of vast waters; and the earth itself shone because of his glory. And it was like the appearance of the vision that I had seen, like the vision that I saw when I came to bring the city to ruin [in a prophetic way]; and there were appearances like the appearance that I saw by the river Chebar, and I went falling upon my face.

"And the glory of Jehovah itself came into the House by way of the gate the front of which was toward the east. And a spirit proceeded to raise me up and bring me into the inner courtyard, and, look! the House had become full of the glory of Jehovah. And I began to hear someone speaking to me out of the House, and the man himself had come to be standing beside me. And He went on to say to me:

"'Son of man, this is the place of my throne and the place of the soles of my feet, where I shall reside in the midst of the sons of Israel to time indefinite; and no more will they, the house of Israel, defile my holy name.'"

[10] This temple vision, given to Ezekiel fifty-six years before the exiled Jews were permitted to quit Babylon and return to Jerusalem and rebuild there the altar of sacrifice to Jehovah, was a divine guarantee that His

---

9. By what act is that temple inaugurated, and how does Ezekiel describe the vision of it?
10. Of what was that visionary temple a guarantee, both in the case of natural Israel and in the case of spiritual Israel?

worship would be renewed in the desolated land. (Ezra 1:1 to 3:6) It is also a prophetic guarantee to the restored remnant of spiritual Israel. Of what? That Jehovah's pure worship will be carried forward without further disturbance after Jehovah defeats the threatening attack by Satan the Devil alias Gog of Magog and his ungodly hordes.

[11] Then the provisions for everlasting life in security on earth will be made available to the worshipers of Jehovah with real physical and environmental benefits to them as never before. The spiritual paradise from which Gog of Magog tries to oust them and their sheeplike fellow worshipers will then have its physical counterpart. In what way? In a worldwide Paradise-like "garden of Eden." This was forevisioned in what Ezekiel further saw after the inspection of the temple was finished. He writes:

[12] "And gradually he brought me back to the entrance of the House, and, look! there was water going forth from under the threshold of the House eastward, for the front of the House was east. And the water was going down from under, from the right-hand side of the House, south of the altar."—Ezekiel 47:1.

THE DEEPENING STREAM OF LIFE-GIVING WATER

[13] This water from the temple of Jehovah's restored worship proves to be life-giving water, "water of life." It issues from the original Life-Giver, Jehovah, who has taken up his permanent residence in his heavenly temple, where he thrones above the cherubs and where he receives the blood value of the sacrifice of atonement in behalf of condemned, dying mankind. We notice that the life-giving water flows past the altar of sacrifice in the inner courtyard, instead of westward

---

11. Then the spiritual paradise of Jehovah's worshipers will have its counterpart in what way, and to whom and where was this foreshadowed?
12. What did Ezekiel see proceeding forth from the House, and in what direction?
13. What kind of "water" is that, what is its source, and what does its flowing past the altar of sacrifice indicate as being taken under recognition?

388   "THE NATIONS SHALL KNOW THAT I AM JEHOVAH"   Ezekiel 47:1, 2

through the rear of the House right next to the Most Holy. This fact emphasizes that the Life-Giver, Jehovah, sends forth this "water of life" with full recognition of the ransom sacrifice of his Son and High Priest, Jesus Christ. That is why the Christian apostle John wrote:

"If we are walking in the light as he himself is in the light, we do have a sharing with one another, and the blood of Jesus his Son cleanses us from all sin."

"And this is the witness given, that God gave us everlasting life, and this life is in his Son. He that has the Son has this life; he that does not have the Son of God does not have this life."—1 John 1:7; 5:11, 12.

[14] This agrees with what is said to be the source of a similar river of water of life, described in the last chapter of the Bible. Telling of the attractive features of the heavenly New Jerusalem that descends from God out of heaven, John writes:

"And I did not see a temple in it, for Jehovah God the Almighty is its temple, also the Lamb [Jesus Christ] is."

"And he showed me a river of water of life, clear as crystal, flowing out from the throne of God and of the Lamb down the middle of its broad way."—Revelation 21:1, 2, 22; 22:1, 2.

Thus the symbolic river of God's provisions for the everlasting life of mankind flows out from Jehovah the King of the universe and through his reigning King Jesus Christ, "the Lamb of God that takes away the sin of the world."—John 1:29, 36; 3:35, 36.

[15] In Ezekiel's vision this water that issues forth from the temple in which Jehovah has taken up residence is directed to where life is needed. Telling how Jehovah's angel guides him further on his observation tour, Ezekiel writes: "And he gradually brought me forth by the way of the north gate and took me around

14. That stream of water of life agrees with what similar river mentioned in the last chapter of the Bible, and how does the writer John describe it and its source?
15. To where was the stream of water of life directed, and why was Ezekiel taken in a roundabout way for an outside view of the stream?

by the way outside to the outer gate that is facing toward the east, and, look! water was trickling from the right-hand side." (Ezekiel 47:2) Ezekiel had to be led in this roundabout way because the outer eastern gate had been sanctified by the passing of Jehovah's glory through it into the temple and was therefore shut. (Ezekiel 44:1-3; compare 10:19; 11:22, 23.) So Ezekiel was brought to the northern side of the water that was trickling forth from the temple south of its eastern outer gate.

¹⁶ Now Jehovah's angel, appearing as the coppery-colored man, uses his measuring line made of flax. Says Ezekiel: "When the man went forth eastward with a measuring line in his hand, he also proceeded to measure a thousand in cubits and to make me pass through the water, water up to the ankles."—Ezekiel 47:3.

¹⁷ A thousand cubits eastward from the temple the trickle of water had become a stream ankle deep. This would allow for more worshipers coming to the temple to drink of this life-giving water.

¹⁸ In behalf of gaining eternal life those on earth who survive the dastardly attack by Gog of Magog will drink of this water of life, accepting all the provisions for life that Jehovah affords through his once-sacrificed Messiah, Jesus the Lamb of God. These survivors of the "great tribulation" with which the present system of things ends will be comparatively few as against the great mass of mankind who are destroyed in that calamitous end of this system of things. Life-giving water in quantity of an ankle-deep stream of water would be sufficient for them. Like Noah and his family who survived the global deluge, these survivors will give a righteous start to human society. They will

---

16. What measurement did the copper-colored man now make, and what did he have Ezekiel do?
17. For what would this greater depth of water allow?
18. As pictured in Ezekiel's vision, how great a quantity of symbolic "water of life" will the survivors of Gog's attack need, and what will they then give to human society under the heavenly kingdom of God's Messiah?

furnish the foundation of the "new earth," that is, to human society as organized under the heavenly kingdom of Jehovah's Messiah, Jesus Christ.—2 Peter 2:5; 3:5-13.

[19] However, the life-giving benefits of the ransom sacrifice of Jesus Christ and of his Messianic kingdom will not be limited to those relatively few survivors of the fiery destruction of the "heavens and the earth that are now." Not alone for them did the Messiah Jesus die. He is "the Lamb of God that takes away the sin of the world." (John 1:29, 36) "We behold Jesus, who has been made a little lower than angels, crowned with glory and honor for having suffered death, that he by God's undeserved kindness might taste death for every man." (Hebrews 2:9) "He is a propitiatory sacrifice for our sins, yet not for ours only but also for the whole world's." (1 John 2:2) "For there is one God, and one mediator between God and men, a man, Christ Jesus, who gave himself a corresponding ransom for all."—1 Timothy 2:5, 6.

[20] On the basis of this, Jesus Christ said: "The hour is coming in which all those in the memorial tombs will hear his voice and come out." (John 5:28, 29) Ah, yes, as the apostle Paul said: "There is going to be a resurrection [of the dead] of both the righteous and the unrighteous."—Acts 24:15.

[21] There will be enough "water of life" made available for all those resurrected out of death for whom the Messiah Jesus died. Accordingly the stream of water that Ezekiel saw God's angel measure did not stop at ankle depth. "And he continued measuring a thousand [cubits] and then made me pass through the water, water up to the knees." (Ezekiel 47:4) Reasonably, all the ransomed dead humans will not be restored to

19. What scriptures are there to show whether the benefits of Christ's ransom sacrifice will be limited to the survivors of the end of this system of things or not?
20. On the basis of that ransom sacrifice, what did Jesus say, and also the apostle Paul, regarding the dead?
21. By the next measurement of God's angel, how deep did the stream of water of life become, and what does this suggest regarding the resurrection of the dead?

life on earth at one time, which would create an earthly population explosion too great for the survivors of Gog's attack to take care of with the necessary provisions. The dead will be resurrected in controlled numbers to life on earth under Messiah's reign so that, for the time being, the symbolic stream of "water of life" knee deep will be ample for them.

[22] In course of time during the thousand-year reign of the Messiah Jesus more of the ransomed dead humans will be resurrected. (Revelation 20:4-6, 11-15) Ample supplies of the "water of life" that flows out from the presence of Jehovah in his heavenly temple will be provided for these additional resurrected ones. The symbolic stream continues on and gets deeper with more volume of water, for Ezekiel 47:4 goes on to say: "And he continued measuring a thousand [cubits] and now made me pass through—water up to the hips." How well the angel's measuring in lengths of a thousand cubits reminds us of the number of the years of the Messiah's reign—a thousand years! In the course of those years, as more subjects of Messiah's kingdom come to be on earth they will be able to take care of more persons resurrected in larger numbers at one time.

[23] Before the thousand years of Messiah's reign are ended the common earthly grave of mankind (Ha′des) and the sea of watery graves for many humans must be emptied of those held in them in death. (Revelation 20:13, 14) The symbolic "water of life" must be extended to the very last one of the ransomed dead of mankind. Symbolic water only hip deep will not suffice for this. So an ample volume of water must be provided for the full and complete number of the ransomed dead resurrected to life on earth. This is what Ezekiel saw pictured in his vision, concerning which he further

22. By the third measurement of God's angel, how deep did the stream of water of life become, and what further does this suggest regarding the resurrection to life on earth?
23. By the final measurement of God's angel, how deep did the stream of water of life become, and what does this suggest regarding application of the ransom benefits to the dead?

writes: "And he continued measuring a thousand [cubits]. It was a torrent that I was not able to pass through, for the water had got high, water permitting swimming, a torrent that could not be passed through." —Ezekiel 47:5.

PERFECT HEALTH IN AN EARTHLY PARADISE!

[24] How comforting it is to have envisioned to us that all the ransomed dead of mankind will have the precious opportunity to take advantage of the Messiah's millennial reign and of God's provision for everlasting life through it! And what a grand place our earth will then be in which to gain life unending in a Paradise with perfect human health and happiness! (Luke 23: 42, 43) This is now pictured in the further unfolding vision as Ezekiel tells us:

[25] "At that he said to me: 'Have you seen this, O son of man?' Then he had me walk and had me return to the bank of the torrent. When I returned, why, look! on the bank of the torrent there were very many trees, on this side and on that side. And he went on to say to me: 'This water is going forth to the eastern region and must go down through the Arabah. And it must come to the sea. It being brought forth into the sea itself, its water is also actually healed. And it must occur that every living soul that swarms, in every place to which the double-size torrent comes, will get life. And it must occur that there will be very many fish, because there is where this water will certainly come, and the seawater will be healed, and everything will be alive where the torrent comes.' "—Ezekiel 47:6-9.

[26] The banks of this torrent of the "water of life" become beautiful as life manifests itself in very many trees that line both banks. The water torrent does not

---

24. Of what will all the ransomed dead be thus able to take advantage, and for the enjoyment of what will the earth then be a fine place?
25. As suggestive of the foregoing, what is Ezekiel now shown and what is he told?
26. Thus how have the banks of that torrent become beautiful, and to what body of water does that torrent flow and how, and with what effect there?

stop four thousand measured cubits from the eastern wall front of Jehovah's temple but continues on eastward to the Arabah. That is to say, to the trench or rift valley through which the Jordan River descends southward to the Dead Sea, the lowest surface body of water on earth. Its waters are so salty that no aquatic life can exist in it. It is indeed a salty sea that is dead. But now suddenly "very many fish" appear in it. What has happened?

²⁷ The torrent of water from Jehovah's temple, now double-size, has reached the Arabah and run down it (not joining the Jordan River) and entered the Dead Sea. A miracle has occurred! The Dead Sea waters have been healed—sweetened. It begins to swarm with fish. Water of life, indeed, has issued from the temple of Jehovah's worship.

²⁸ Live evidence appears that at last there are fish in the once dead Salt Sea. The prophet Ezekiel reports the evidence, saying: "And it must occur that fishers will actually stand alongside it from En-gedi even up to En-eglaim. There will come to be a drying yard for dragnets. In their kinds their fish will prove to be, like the fish of the Great Sea, very many."—Ezekiel 47:10.

²⁹ Today En-gedi ("Spring of the Kid") is about midway down the west shore of the Dead Sea. En-eglaim ("Spring of Two Calves") is today understood to be at Ain Feshka, where there is a freshwater spring that empties into the Dead Sea, about eighteen miles north of En-gedi. This would mean that for eighteen miles there would be fishers casting in their dragnets and hauling in fish of all kinds from the Dead Sea. The variety of fish caught would correspond with the variety found in the Great Sea or Mediterranean Sea. These fishers do not picture the disciples to whom Jesus Christ when on earth said: "Come after me,

---

27. So what has happened to the waters of the Dead Sea?
28. What live evidence is now pointed out to show that at last there are fish in that Salt Sea?
29. Where are En-gedi and En-eglaim located, and whom do the fishers between those two places not picture?

and I will make you fishers of men." (Matthew 4:19; Luke 5:10) During the thousand-year reign of the Messiah Jesus there will be no catching of men like fish to become disciples of Jesus.

[30] So the appearance of those fishers along the Dead Sea from En-gedi up to En-eglaim is merely a pictorial device to prove that there are actually live fish in those waters once brackish but now healed, sweetened. Messiah's kingdom accomplishes a miracle!

[31] In the vision the salty Dead Sea pictures the element or surrounding conditions in which mankind has had to exist for the past six thousand years. It has been death-dealing, because all mankind has inherited imperfection and sin from our rebellious first parents, Adam and Eve, and consequently death, the penalty for sin. (Romans 5:12) Imperfect mankind has also been ruining the natural environment in which it exists. (Revelation 11:18) Thus that condemnation to death, due to inherited sinfulness and imperfection, has judicially hung over mankind since the birth of Cain, Adam and Eve's first child, down till now. —Genesis 4:1-8.

[32] Added to that bad handicap is the terrible fact that the invisible rulership of the vast majority of mankind has been exercised by Satan the Devil. "The whole world is lying in the power of the wicked one." (1 John 5:19) Since the ouster of that wicked one from heaven during the time of World War I, he has taken on the role of Gog of Magog.—Job 1:6, 7; John 12:31; 2 Corinthians 4:4; Revelation 12:3, 4, 7-13; Ezekiel 38:1 to 39:15.

[33] In view of this, how will the life-giving "water" of God's provisions heal or sweeten the element or surrounding conditions in which mankind has long existed? The invisible environment surrounding all

30. So those fishers are used as a pictorial device to prove what?
31. What do the salty waters of the Dead Sea picture?
32. Added to that natural handicap, what bad rulership has mankind come under?
33. What invisible environment needs to be removed from around mankind, and will it be?

mankind contains Satan the Devil and his demons. Ever since they were defeated in the recent war in heaven and were hurled down to our earth, the invisible vicinity of this earth has been the location of their restrained state. It has become a symbolic "land of Magog" for a newly arrived Gog, the debased Satan the Devil. This woe-causing, death-dealing environment must be removed from around mankind. It will be, for Jehovah says: "I will send fire upon Magog." —Ezekiel 39:6.

[34] By means of his mighty angel, Jesus Christ, Jehovah will destroy Magog in that Satan the Devil and his demons who have been detained in this area of restraint at the earth will be removed therefrom. The reigning Messiah, Jesus, will bind Satan and his demons as with chains and will hurl them into the "abyss" far from the vicinity of the earth. There these polluters of mankind's environment will be confined for the thousand years of Messiah's reign, that they might no longer mislead mankind in the ways of death. Then over all mankind there will reign the "new heavens," composed of the Messiah Jesus and his congregation of glorified spiritual Israelites. Also, by applying to redeemed mankind the lifesaving benefits of his ransom sacrifice, he will lift off them the condemnation to death due to inherited sin and imperfection. —Revelation 20:1-6; 21:1-5.

[35] Thus relief will come by the "water" of life-giving provisions that issues forth from Jehovah's presence at his heavenly temple. Redeemed mankind will be rewarded for obedience to the Messianic kingdom and will come alive in the healed element or set of circumstances. They will be like those fish that miraculously began swarming in the waters of the Dead Sea, not unclean sea creatures, but clean fish that can be netted by fishers and eaten according to Jehovah's law. The

---

34. By whom and how will this invisible environment be removed from mankind, and how will mankind's natural death-dealing condition be taken away?
35. For what on their part will redeemed mankind be rewarded, and like what in the Dead Sea will they become?

"sea" in which they swarm will no more deserve to be called the Dead Sea. It is a sea of life!

36 Anything not reached by that "water of life" from Jehovah through the Messiah Jesus will not be healed and will not have life within it. This is called attention to in the vision by these words of Jehovah's angel: "There are its swampy places and its marshy places, and they will not be healed. To salt they will certainly be given." (Ezekiel 47:11) Such unhealed places would be sources of salt for use in seasoning food. Of course, too, in a figurative way, if anyone on earth willfully refuses Jehovah's healing "water" of life's provisions through the reigning Messiah Jesus, he will not gain everlasting life. Just as it is written concerning resurrected humans under Jehovah's Messianic kingdom: "This means the second death, the lake of fire. Furthermore, whoever was not found written in the book of life was hurled into the lake of fire."—Revelation 20:14, 15.

37 Jehovah's healing, life-giving provisions through the Messiah Jesus will include an Edenic paradise, extended earth wide, with all the means for sustaining human life in perfection. This our enraptured eyes see as Jehovah's angel turns our attention from the sea to the "double-size torrent" of water, saying: "And alongside the torrent there will come up, along its bank on this side and on that side, all sorts of trees for food. Their leafage will not wither, nor will their fruitage be consumed. In their months they will bear new fruit, because the water for them—it is coming forth from the very sanctuary. And their fruitage must prove to be for food and their leafage for healing."—Ezekiel 47:12.

38 How beautifully corresponding with this is the

---

36. What resulted to adjacent places not reached by the water that streamed from Jehovah's temple, and what is pictured by that?
37. What earthly estate is included in Jehovah's life-giving provisions through Messiah, and how is our attention called to this by what was shown to Ezekiel in vision?
38. In correspondency with this, what features of John's vision concerning God's governmental arrangement for mankind are there, and when also are these fulfilled?

vision given over six hundred years later to the Christian apostle John concerning the heavenly New Jerusalem! Among the excellent features of this divine governmental arrangement for mankind John records these: "And the broad way of the city was pure gold, as transparent glass. And he showed me a river of water of life, clear as crystal, flowing out from the throne of God and of the Lamb down the middle of its broad way. And on this side of the river and on that side there were trees of life producing twelve crops of fruit, yielding their fruits each month. And the leaves of the trees were for the curing of the nations." (Revelation 21:21; 22:1, 2) This vision, too, is fulfilled during the thousand-year reign of the Messiah Jesus with his Bride, his congregation of faithful spiritual Israelites.—Revelation 21:2.

[39] In this latter vision the "river of water of life" is seen proceeding from the "throne of God and of the Lamb," this picturing that Jehovah and his Messiah Jesus are reigning with everlasting benefit to redeemed mankind. In the vision to Ezekiel the torrent of water for the trees 'comes forth from the sanctuary' into which the "glory of Jehovah" has entered. As this torrent of healing, life-giving water flows down to mankind throughout the thousand-year reign of Messiah, it will be accompanied by a growth of plants for beauty and food, like the paradisaic Garden of Eden with its vegetation and trees for beauty and for food. (Genesis 1:29, 30; 2:7-16) Neither blight nor drought will afflict that restored Paradise of Pleasure for obedient mankind, so as to cause its leafage to wither or its fruitage to be consumed by pests. As if by means of fruit trees producing a fresh crop every month, there will be no shortage of food all year round.

[40] Obedient mankind will enjoy continuous perfect health, for the "leafage" of those fruitful trees will

---

39. In John's vision, what is pictured in that the river of water of life proceeds out of the throne of God and of his Lamb, and how is an unfailing supply of food for redeemed mankind pictured?
40. How is the guarantee for continuous perfect health of mankind pictured?

never wither but always serve for healing. What a joy life on earth will be then!

⁴¹ All these bounties in profusion in the near future await those rendering the pure and undefiled form of worship to Jehovah, for, let us not overlook, the healing, life-giving "water" of divine provisions "is coming forth from the very sanctuary," the holy place of Jehovah's worship. (Ezekiel 47:12) For all his undeserved kindness to redeemed mankind, man's in-born inclination to render worship will gratefully express itself in adoring the only One worthy of being worshiped, Jehovah, at His sanctuary. (Matthew 4:10; Psalm 95:6, 7) With boundless joy the approved worshipers of the Sovereign Lord Jehovah will hear the comforting proclamation:

⁴² "Look! The tent of God is with mankind, and he will reside with them, and they will be his peoples. And God himself will be with them. And he will wipe out every tear from their eyes, and death will be no more, neither will mourning nor outcry nor pain be anymore. The former things have passed away." —Revelation 21:3, 4.

41, 42. How is it pictured that all these life provisions await those who render the right form of worship, and what comforting proclamation will the approved worshipers hear as to things then past?

Chapter 22

Human Happiness in Paradise under Divine Government

"THE happy God"—that is what Jehovah is called. (1 Timothy 1:11) His loving purpose is to make all his human creatures eternally happy. In the twenty-fifth year of the exile of his prophet Ezekiel, he set out the boundaries of the territory that his chosen people were to occupy. This He did by means of His angel after he had inspired Ezekiel to prophesy concerning the downfall of the devilish Gog of Magog. This closing part of the vision given to Ezekiel evidently hints at how Jehovah through his Messiah Jesus will locate the members of redeemed humankind all over the earth in His new order. The whole earth, in a Paradise state, is the assigned home of mankind, just as it is written under divine inspiration in Psalm 115:16: "As regards the heavens, to Jehovah the heavens belong, but the earth he has given to the sons of men." He will locate individuals on earth where He, as earth's Creator and Owner, chooses to place them.

² As an illustration of this, in Ezekiel's vision, Jehovah himself designated the place of each one of the twelve tribes of Israel, with its boundaries marked. Assigned to the north of an administrative strip of land were seven tribes with their respective land portions running parallel to one another from east to the

---

1. What is the purpose of the "happy God" concerning his human creatures, and where will the redeemed members thereof be located?
2. How was Jehovah's locating of members of redeemed mankind according to His designation illustrated in Ezekiel's vision in connection with the twelve tribes of Israel?

Mediterranean Sea on the west, each one of equal width from north to south, namely, Dan at the top, then Asher, Naphtali, Manasseh, Ephraim, Reuben and Judah. South of the administrative strip of land were the land portions of the remaining five tribes, running parallelwise from east to west, namely, first Benjamin, then Simeon, Issachar, Zebulun, and Gad at the bottom. (Ezekiel 47:13 to 48:8, 23-29) As regards the tribe of Levi, it was given no such land portion as its inheritance, for it had been selected out of the twelve original tribes of Israel to serve Jehovah at his sanctuary. So the members of this tribe were located around Jehovah's sanctuary in the administrative strip.

[3] The administrative strip ran from the eastern border at the Jordan River and the Dead Sea to the Western or Mediterranean Sea. It was to have around the neighborhood of Mount Moriah a special donation of land, a "contribution that you people should contribute." It was to be 25,000 cubits square, or about 42,500 feet (8 miles) square. This, in fact, was the width from north to south of the administrative strip. At the center of this square "contribution" of land was where Jehovah's sanctuary was to be located, or four miles from each side. (Ezekiel 48:8) This square "contribution" was to be divided into three sections, running from east to west, each section being thus 25,000 cubits long.

[4] The top or northern section was to be ten thousand cubits wide from north to south. This was assigned to the nonpriestly Levites. None of this assignment of land was to be sold or exchanged, "for it is something holy to Jehovah." (Ezekiel 48:13, 14) This holy strip of land did not contain Jehovah's sanctuary.

[5] Immediately south of this Levitical strip of land was the section reserved for the priests. It too was to be ten

3. In the administrative strip of land, where was the special "contribution" of land to be located, and in this, where was the sanctuary of Jehovah to be situated?
4. The nonpriestly Levites were assigned to what strip of land, and its being holy to Jehovah did not allow for what?
5. The priests were assigned to what strip of land, what building did it contain, and what was it called as to its sanctity?

thousand cubits wide from north to south, or about 3.22 miles. (Ezekiel 48:9-12) This priestly section did contain Jehovah's sanctuary or temple. It was a "holy contribution for the priests," and was called "something most holy, on the boundary of the Levites."

[6] The third or bottom section of the square "contribution" of land was to be therefore only five thousand cubits wide from north to south, or 1.61 miles. In the center of this section was to be the city. As Ezekiel 48:15 says, "it is something profane for the city, for a dwelling place and for pasture ground. And the city must come to be in the midst of it." The city wall was to be 4,500 cubits square. Thus it had a perimeter of 18,000 cubits, and was about one mile and a half square. All around the city there was a strip of pasture ground two hundred and fifty cubits wide, or about one twelfth of a mile. This made the whole city area 1.61 miles square, or 5,000 cubits square, so that its northern side bordered on the holy section of the priests. —Ezekiel 48:15-17.

[7] As the "profane" section for the city was 25,000 cubits long from east to west, this meant that on each side of this 5,000-cubit-square city there was an area 10,000 cubits long. This open land must be cultivated; its produce must be for food for all those working in the city. It was an intertribal staff of city workers. Persons from all twelve non-Levite tribes of Israel served in the city and so had a common interest in it. —Ezekiel 48:18, 19.

VISIBLE REPRESENTATIVES OF
HEAVENLY GOVERNMENT

[8] Who was the visible head of the city government? It was the "chieftain" or *Nasi*, who had a special

---

6. What were the dimensions of the third or bottom strip of the special "contribution" of land, and what were the features of the land area for the city?
7. Where was the food produced for those working in the city, and from whom was this staff of city workers taken?
8. Who was the visible head of this city government, and where was his domain located?

territory or domain assigned to him. Where? In the administrative strip of land, where the 25,000-cubit-square "contribution" of land lay. What was left of this administrative strip on the east side and on the west side of this land "contribution" was the domain of the "chieftain." The part to the west ran from the western boundary of the land "contribution" all the way to the Mediterranean Sea. The part to the east ran from the eastern boundary of the land "contribution" eastward to the Jordan River and the Dead Sea or Eastern Sea. (Ezekiel 47:18) The tribe of Judah bordered his domain on the north, and the tribe of Benjamin bordered his domain on the south.—Ezekiel 48:20-22.

⁹ The 4,500-cubit-square city in the midst of the "profane" section of the land "contribution" had twelve outlets through its walls, three on each side of the city. These gates were named after the twelve original tribes of Israel. On the north, from right to left, were the gates named for the tribes of Reuben, Judah and Levi. In the east wall were the gates for Joseph (who represented Manasseh and Ephraim), Benjamin and Dan. In the south wall were the gates for Simeon, Issachar and Zebulun. In the western wall were the gates for Gad, Asher and Naphtali. (Ezekiel 48:30-34) The city's having twelve gates named after the tribes of Israel is reflected in the heavenly New Jerusalem, the congregational Bride of Christ, concerning which we read:

"It had a great and lofty wall and had twelve gates, and at the gates twelve angels, and names were inscribed which are those of the twelve tribes of the sons of Israel. On the east were three gates, and on the north three gates, and on the south three gates, and on the west three gates. The wall of the city also had twelve foundation stones, and on them the twelve names of the twelve apostles of the Lamb. Also, the twelve gates were twelve pearls; each one of the gates was made of one pearl. And the broad way of the city was pure gold, as transparent glass."—Revelation 21:12-14, 21.

9. How many and where were the outlets through the city wall, how were they named, and how are those gates reflected in those of the heavenly New Jerusalem?

Out of this heavenly city and down its broad way proceeded the crystal-clear "river of water of life." —Revelation 22:1, 2.

¹⁰ In the case of ancient Israel Jehovah's temple as built by Solomon was inside the city of Jerusalem. But in Ezekiel's vision the city is separate from the holy temple, even though both city and temple are in the special "contribution" of land. This separateness is emphasized by the fact that the city is said to be in "something profane for the city, for a dwelling place and for pasture ground." (Ezekiel 48:15) The priests and Levites did not live or work in the city. So in the fulfillment of the vision under Messiah's thousand-year reign, the city with its pasture ground would not picture the heavenly New Jerusalem, which is the Messiah's faithful congregation of spiritual Israelites or his Bride. (Revelation 21:1, 2, 9-21) It pictures an earthly, visible seat of administration over the affairs of redeemed mankind.

¹¹ Inasmuch as Jehovah took all the males of the tribe of Levi in exchange for the firstborn sons of Israel that had been spared from death on that Passover night in Egypt, the Levites and the Levitical priests picture what Hebrews 12:23 calls "the congregation of the firstborn who have been enrolled in the heavens." The high priest of those priests and Levites typifies, of course, the one named in Hebrews 3:1. That verse is addressed to this congregation of the firstborn ones and says: "Consequently, holy brothers, partakers of the heavenly calling, consider the apostle and high priest whom we confess—Jesus." The congregation of the firstborn ones supplies his underpriests. To these 1 Peter 2:5, 9 says: "You yourselves also as living stones are being built up a spiritual house for the purpose of a holy priesthood . . . But you are 'a

---

10. How did the relationship of the visionary city and temple differ from that of Jerusalem and Solomon's temple, and what therefore did the city of Ezekiel's vision picture?

11. Whom do the Levites picture as a whole, and whom do the priests together with their high priest picture, for service where?

chosen race, a royal priesthood, a holy nation, a people for special possession, that you should declare abroad the excellencies' of the one that called you out of darkness into his wonderful light." These are the ones that, after their resurrection from the dead to spiritual life in heaven, serve Jehovah in his sanctuary.

¹² The "chieftain" or *Nasi,* who has his domain on the east and west sides of the 25,000-cubit-square "contribution" of land, is not spoken of as being the one whom Jehovah calls "my servant David," whom He raises up as a royal Shepherd over Jehovah's flock. (Ezekiel 34:23, 24; 37:24, 25) Thus he is not used in an individual sense to picture the heavenly Messiah Jesus, concerning whom Jehovah foretold: "I myself, Jehovah, will become their God, and my servant David a chieftain in the midst of them." (Ezekiel 34:24; 37:25) In the temple vision the "chieftain" or *Nasi* takes on a collective meaning and stands for those whom the heavenly Messiah Jesus appoints as his visible representatives in the "new earth." These would include those whom Psalm 45:16 mentions. That verse is addressed to the King Jesus Christ and refers to his earthly children, saying: "In place of your [earthly] forefathers, they will come to be your sons, whom you will appoint as princes [*sarim*] in all the earth." These and all other appointed "princes" will give mankind a just administration and will keep them in security, for this is guaranteed in Isaiah chapter 32, in these grand words:

"Look! A king will reign for righteousness itself; and as respects princes, they will rule as princes for justice itself. And each one must prove to be like a hiding place from the wind and a place of concealment from the rainstorm, like streams of water in a waterless country, like the shadow of a heavy crag in an exhausted land.

"And in the wilderness justice will certainly reside, and in the orchard righteousness itself will dwell. And the work of the true righteousness must become peace;

---

12. What is indicated in the fact that the "chieftain" or *Nasi* is not spoken of as "my servant David," and the title is used to apply how, and by this arrangement what kind of administration will be given to redeemed mankind?

and the service of the true righteousness, quietness and security to time indefinite. And my people must dwell in a peaceful abiding place and in residences of full confidence and in undisturbed resting-places."—Isaiah 32:1, 2, 16-18.

¹³ From all parts of the land and from all the ranks of ransomed mankind there will voluntarily come those who will actively cooperate with the "chieftain" class. Where? As it were, at the "city," which is the visible official seat of the "chieftain" class for administering the affairs of all mankind. In this way these volunteers show a Christlike spirit toward them as true representatives of the reigning Messiah Jesus. The seat of administration will be open to access from all sides by persons who want to approach with any vital matter, just as the foursquare city of Ezekiel's vision had twelve gates, three on each side, open to all twelve tribes of Israel.

¹⁴ Through such visible princely representatives on earth the Messiah Jesus and his glorified congregation, enthroned with him in the invisible heavens, will sit "judging the twelve tribes of Israel," all redeemed mankind.—Matthew 19:28; Luke 22:29, 30.

¹⁵ This citylike seat of administration under Messiah's reign will be pervaded with Jehovah's spirit. The fruitage of his spirit will abound there to his glory, namely, "love, joy, peace, long-suffering, kindness, goodness, faith, mildness, self-control." (Galatians 5:22, 23) This fruitful spirit of Jehovah will operate there to guide in all judicial matters of mankind. It will aid in the uplift of all obedient mankind to perfection of heart, mind, and body in the earth's reestablished Paradise. Jehovah, enthroned in his heavenly sanctuary, will approve of this symbolic city and shower his favor upon it. His divine presence will be there by

13. From where will those who cooperate with the "chieftain" class come, and how open to access by persons with vital matters will the seat of administration be, as pictured in Ezekiel's vision?
14. Through such visible representatives, who will act as judges and toward whom?
15. With what will that seat of administration be pervaded, how will Jehovah's presence be there, and what will its new name be?

directing his loving, beneficent attention to it. Therefore, in assurance of this, the prophecy that He inspired in Ezekiel closes with giving to this symbolic foursquare city a new name, saying: "Round about there [the perimeter] will be eighteen thousand cubits; and the name of the city from that day on will be Jehovah Himself Is There." (*NW; Yg; AS*) "And the city's name for ever after shall be Jehovah-shammah." —Ezekiel 48:35, *NEB*.

¹⁶ When the future earthly seat of worldwide administration bears such a glorious name as Jehovah-shammah, how could any of the redeemed ones of mankind anywhere throughout this Paradise earth fail to know what is the name of the one living and true God? Only for a little while longer now will this earth, with its religious confusion and darkness, continue to be tne only place in all the realm of intelligent creation where God the Creator is unknown by name to countless numbers of persons or else his name is ignored or even profaned by self-centered persons. For, look! a new day is dawning, the long-looked-for day! Already the early rays of its aurora are brightening the faces of God-fearing persons who see the prophecies of the Holy Bible coming true. Soon now, when the sun of that incoming day rises and ascends to its zenith overhead, not a place on earth will be left in darkness and not know God's matchless name and fame. That will be the day for the fulfillment of the divine words:

"The earth will be filled with the knowing of the glory of Jehovah as the waters themselves cover over the sea."—Habakkuk 2:14.

¹⁷ Awake, therefore, O people of all races and nationalities! Arise now from your slumbering to a lifesaving knowledge of Jehovah in this fleeting time of oppor-

---

16. What is the earthly situation today as regards the knowledge or acknowledgment of the divine name, but what will it be in the day that is already dawning?
17. Therefore, to what knowledge should all peoples arise in this opportune time, and why?

tunity! Read his inspired Word and call upon His name for salvation through Jesus Christ. In this peaceful way, with eternal blessing to yourselves, spare yourselves from being forced to acknowledge His name against your will, for that would mean your endless destruction. Embrace the hope now of finding yourselves among the everlastingly happy survivors at the time when the Sovereign Lord God fulfills his own repeatedly declared prophecy, "The nations shall know that I am Jehovah."—Ezekiel 36:23; 39:7, *AS.*

NOTE: For a map illustrating the foregoing division of the land, see the rear endsheet of this book on the right-hand page.

Subject Index

A

Accusation against Christendom, 257-261
"Age of violence," 129-131
Ahab, victory over Syria, 29, 30
Amalekites, enemies, 24, 25

B

Babylon, acts presumptuous, 128
not confederate of Gog, 350
Babylon and other nations, had to know Jehovah, 31-35
Babylon the Great, destroyed, 180, 364
punishment, 254-257
Ben-hadad, Samarian siege, 28-30

C

"Chain," meaning, "Make," 137
Chariot, follows prophet, 88, 89
in Ezekiel's vision pictorial, 48-51
moves to post, 209, 210
Chariot wheels, described, 41-46
Cherubs, carved, on Ark, 38
Ezekiel's vision, 38-51
position and activity, 184-187
Christendom, after her destruction, what? 235, 236
calamity coming upon, 103, 104
detestable religious system gets just deserts, 124-127
drastic action needed, 268-275
drinks cup of prototype, 252-257
future of, 252-256
has had "shepherd" kings, 304
infected with demonism, 159-162
judged, 261-264
membership dropped, 317, 318
members worship sun, 156-159
modern fulfillment, 122-127
not "Israel of God," 68, 69
political rulers and demonism, 224
religious leaders charge, 133-136
restored? 206-209
sects fornicators, 258-261
to know destruction comes from Jehovah, 199-202
to know Jehovah, 120-122
why days numbered, 92, 93
worse than heathen, 104-106
Christendom and Christianity, distinguished, 202
Christendom's destruction, not that of Christianity, 202-206
Christendom's end near, 122-127
"Coals of fire," symbolic, 187-191

Conditions during siege, 106-111
Congregations of restored remnant, "inhabited," 330-334
Convention, Cedar Point, Ohio, 1919 C.E., 64, 330
Columbus, Ohio, 1924 C.E., 83-85
Washington, D.C., 1935 C.E., 178

D

Dates, 1514-1513 B.C.E., Pharaoh ruler of Egypt, 16
1513 B.C.E., mediator, 86
1473 B.C.E., Israelites in Promised Land, 115, 322
997 B.C.E., calf worship, 28
997 B.C.E., start of "error" of house of Israel, 99
997 B.C.E., start of Kingdom of Israel, 98, 99
997 B.C.E., tribes split, 69
844 B.C.E., Ninevites spared, 77
740 B.C.E., Kingdom of Israel destroyed, 30, 98
642 B.C.E., Josiah abolished sun worship, 155
617 B.C.E., Ezekiel taken to Babylon, 36, 95
617 B.C.E., Israelites taken to Babylon, 203
617 B.C.E., Jerusalem under siege, 94
613 B.C.E., Ezekiel prophet, 67
613 B.C.E., Ezekiel watchman, 73
613 B.C.E., Ezekiel's vision, 36, 37, 52, 54, 93, 116, 123
607 B.C.E., desolation of Jerusalem and Judah, 32, 57
607 B.C.E., 40-year period of bearing "error" ended, 103
607 B.C.E., Gentile Times began, 57, 352
607 B.C.E., Jerusalem destroyed, 57, 101, 137
607 B.C.E., Jerusalem trampled on, 231
607 B.C.E., Judah desolated, 115
593 B.C.E., temple vision, 384
591 B.C.E., Ezekiel completed book, 34, 52
539 B.C.E., fall of Babylon, 340
537 B.C.E., exiles freed, 340
537 B.C.E., Jews restored, 32, 34
33 C.E., organization of Christian congregation, 52
70 C.E., second destruction of Jerusalem, 233, 316, 351

408

1529 C.E., Protestant movement established, 69
1914 C.E., an era ended, 57
1914 C.E., Gentile Times ended, 57, 58, 73, 105, 352
1914 C.E., modern Ezekiel, 58
1914 C.E., World War I, 34
1916 C.E., Russell's death, 346
1917 C.E., "The Finished Mystery" published, 62
1918 C.E., Federal Council of Churches declare for League, 60
1918 C.E., World War I ended, 63, 73, 315
1919 C.E., League of Nations brought forth, 351
1919 C.E., natural Jews seek homeland, 67
1919 C.E., officers of Society released from prison, 63
1919 C.E., ordination, appointment, commission, 67
1919 C.E., remnant revived, 82
1919 C.E., "The Golden Age," 83
1920 C.E., "The Finished Mystery" released from ban, 65
1924 C.E., "Watch Tower" on "God's Organization," 51
1929 C.E., book "Prophecy" on "God's Organization," 51, 52
1931 C.E., remnant identified by name, 66, 172
1931 C.E., "Vindication" book published, 52, 171
1934 C.E., "marking" begins, 177
1945 C.E., United Nations succeeds League, 73, 351
1945 C.E., World War II ends, 156
1948 C.E., Republic of Israel established, 352
Dead Sea, picture, 393, 394
"Decoration of one's ornament," meaning, 134-136
Dedication, "other sheep" make and symbolize, 178-180
Demon interference to be thwarted, 223-228
Demonism, Christendom, 159-162
political rulers rely on, 224
Desolation complete, 288-290
Disposal of war equipment and dead bodies, 372-375
Divine purpose in God's execution work, 136-140
Down with "high one," 229-232
Dragon, symbolic, identified, 363
Dry bones restored, 337, 338

E

Elijah and Elisha, used by Jehovah to raise the dead, 335
Escapee arrives with the eye-witness report, 285-288
Ezekiel, as watchman, 74-76
calls attention to name, 33-35
carried into exile, 36, 37
first vision, 35-38
modern-day counterpart, 57-66
pantomimed siege, 105-111
prophet, 56, 74-76, 105, 210
second vision, 38-41
"sign man," 93-96
speaks despite attempted restraints, 90-92
taken into exile, 95
vision of bones prophetic, 341-344
watchman to house of Israel, how, 86-88
wife dies, 272, 273
Ezekiel delivers own soul as watchman, 85-88
Ezekiel goes 'in rage,' 81-85
Ezekiel sent to own people, 76-81
Ezekiel's message 'stunning,' meaning, 81
Ezekiel's prophecy, true, 276-278
Ezekiel's temple, picture, 384
Ezekiel's visionary city and temple, compared, 403

F

False prophet, identified, 363
False shepherds, 294-296
Famine, pestilence, 111-113
Famine, pestilence and sword, destruction of Judah, 120-122
Fearlessness, Ezekiel, 69-72
of modern-day "Ezekiel," 70-72
Feast for birds, beasts, 375-378
"Finished Mystery, The," 318
Foreheads marked, symbolic, 171
whose, how, 165, 166
Foreheads smashed, 167-171
40 days bearing error, 99-104
40-year period of bearing the "error" of Judah, ends, 101-103
"Four living creatures," 38-51

G

"Garden of Eden," 328-334
"Garland," crown, 126-128
"Genocide," threat, 9
"Glory of Jehovah," action required after vision, 89-92
described, 46-51
effect of vision on Ezekiel, 53, 54

position described, 193, 194
God's sanctuary, defiled, 259, 260
Gog, actual, identified, 354
Babylon not confederate of, 352
burial, 373-375
comes with "congregation," 357
defeated, 364-368
introduced, 349, 350
knows "short period of time," 356
no respected burial, 377
uses "sword" of warfare, 366
who included in crowd, 376-378
Gog, modern, identified, 352-354
Gog's attack, purpose, 358-362
Gog's hordes mustered, 362-364
"Golden Age, The," 64, 83-85
"Great crowd," aid modern-day 'man with the inkhorn,' 179, 180
association with remnant, 319-323
united with remnant, 347
"Great multitude," 178
"Great tribulation," Babylon the Great destroyed in, 180
reaches culmination, 367, 368

H

"Happy God," purpose, 399
Har-Magedon, 363, 364, 366, 367
"Harp of God, The," 325
Hearers entranced, 290-292
Heavenly government, 401-407
"He comes who has the legal right," 232-235
Historic forecast, 243-246
"Holy contribution," 401
"House of Israel," 339-344
How the rule of penalties works upon Christendom, 252-257

I

Idol worshipers have to know who God is, 117-119
"Indictment," resolution, 83-85
International Bible Students, officials released, 329
Israel and Syria, know, 28-30
Israelites, immoral, 117-119
obligated to witness, 22-25

J

Jehovah, appearance, 143, 144
challenges Gog to attack, 355-358
compassion on name, 323-328
corrects conclusions, 379-382
decision from temple, 184-187
defeats Gog's attack, 364-368
displeased at "soil of Israel," 315
distinguished by miracles, 12-17

distinguished by qualities, 25-27
justified in destroying, 169
known as Deliverer, 11-17
known as "God Almighty," 10
known as Protector, 24, 25
puts "hooks" in jaws, 353, 354
removed reproach, 322, 323
Rider of chariot, 46-51
served notice on nations, 16, 17
Shepherd, 293
"speedy witness," 183-187
vindicated at Magog, 378
weapons of warfare, 367
Jehovah's sanctuary, 400, 401
Jehovah's "sword," 216-219
rejects royal scepter, 220, 221
to encircle the Israelites, 222
Jeremiah, describes siege, 96
Jerusalem, report of fall, 285-288
why siege permitted, 96, 97
Jesus Christ, as "covenant," 348
"David my servant," 356, 357
"Lord and Christ," 345, 346
Jews, not witnesses, 352

K

"Killer," identified, 224-228
Kingdom interests, Gog would like to plunder, 358-362
Kingdom of Israel, 97-99
revolted, became nation, 69
ten-tribe, calamity suffered, 30
Kingdom of Judah, 289, 312
formation, 97
identified as "high one," 230-232
revolted, became nation, 69
to disappear, 221-223
"Know that I am Jehovah," declaration made 62 times, 32, 53

L

Land of Israel, desolated, 314, 315
"Land of Magog," destroyed, 371
inhabitants of, witness Devil's defeat, 368, 369
location, 370, 371
League of Nations, 65
Christendom's watchman, 73
favored by churches, 60
ratified in 1919, 65
Levites, picture, 403
Life-giving provisions, 396-398
Life-giving water, 387-392

M

Maintaining considerate behavior among "sheep," 302-304
Man in "linen," mission, 164-166
prophetic figure, 171

reported to Jehovah, 186
Man doing marking, 180, 181
"Man with the writer's inkhorn,"
  subject of talk in 1931 C.E., 172
"Mark," symbolic, 174-180
Marked ones, identified, 173, 174
Marker of foreheads, 164, 165
Marking foreheads, 176-180
Marking reported, 180, 181
Material riches, 131-136
"Men of goodwill," 311
"Men of Goodwill" District Assemblies, 333
Micah, prophet, reports, 132, 133
Modern-day counterpart, Ezekiel, 57-66
Modern-day discerning of heavenly organization, 51-54
Modern-day "Ezekiel," 62-66
commissioned, 66-69
fearlessness required, 70-72
forewarned, 90-92
not to mourn Christendom, 275
vindicated, 286
Modern-day Gog, symbolic
  "hooks" in jaws, 353, 354
Modern-day marker, 171-173
Modern science and human philosophy, worship of, 156-159
Moses, acts and speaks, 13-17
"Most Holy," profaned, 134-136
"Mountains of Israel," symbolic, become "possession," 320
Mustering Gog's hordes, 362-364

N

Name, attitude of nations toward greatest, 7, 8
Jehovah jealous for his, 380
Jehovah's, proclamation, 25-27
Jehovah's, reproached, 323, 324
Jehovah restored remnant for his, 325-328
"Jehovah's witnesses" identifies remnant, 172, 173
meaning of Jehovah's, 34
number of occurrences, 53
number of occurrences of Jehovah in Hebrew Scriptures, 53
of city in Ezekiel's vision, 406
vindication of God's, 7, 8
Nebuchadnezzar, resorted to demonism, 225, 226
Nimrod, prototype, 153
Ninevites, Jesus' prophecy, 79
repented, and spared, 77
No basis for exulting over false premises, 219-221

O

Officers of Watch Tower Society, imprisoned, 63
Oholah and Oholibah, meaning of names, 240
symbolic, 238-241
"Oholah" sets bad historical example, 241-243
Oholibah, symbolic, 243-246
symbolic, treatment of Babylonians, 247-252
"One shepherd," 304-307
Organization, pictured, 48-51
Organizational unity of remnant, internal, restored, 343-348
"Other sheep," identified, 177-180
marking, symbolic, 174-180
"not of this fold," 307-309

P

Paradisaic "planting," 309-311
Paradise, spiritual, 328-334
Penalties, rule of, works, 252-257
Pharaoh, forced to know Jehovah through plagues, 16-21
reaction to demand, 15-20
Places not reached by water, picture, 396
Plagues, first (river into blood), felt by Israelites, 16, 17
second (frogs), 17
third (gnats), all over Egypt, 17
fourth (gadflies), 18
fifth (pestilence), 18, 19
Priests together with high priest, picture, 403, 404
Prophecy, Ezekiel's, confirmed as true, 276-278
Pure worship, survives, 122
survivors carry on, 383

Q

Quaking of earth, global, 365, 366

R

Record, past, not count, 282-285
Redeemed ones, rewarded, 395
Regathering of "sheep," 300-302
Religious issue, 9-11
Remnant, accepted commission to deliver message, 76-81
cleansed, 326-328
endured as watchman, 90-92
enjoy "garden" condition, 381, 382
obligations, 88
restored, 329-334
sanctify Jehovah's name, 326-328
sent to Christendom, 78-81

Remnant in bitterness, 82-85
Remnant of spiritual Israel, bring spiritual paradise, 343
desolating of activities, 318
dwelling in center of earth, 359
"great crowd" active, 319-323
growth, 318-323
"Report," effects on exiles, 218
Rider of chariot, 46-51
"Righteous men," 261-264
"River of water of life" from throne, picture, 397, 398
"Rod," for divine use, 127-131
violence brings own punishment by, 129-131

S

Scroll, Jehovah's message, 76
Seat of administration, for ones with vital matters, 405, 406
Seventy older men, Jehovah a speedy witness against, 183-187
worship false gods, 147-149
"Sheep," delivered, 298, 299
maintaining behavior, 302-304
regathering, 300-302
sheeplike ones as prey, 296-299
Siege of Jerusalem, food and health conditions, 105-111
pantomined by Ezekiel, 105-111
"Six men," identified, 163
killers, 166-168, 183
Slighted lovers react, 247-252
"Soil of Israel," picture, 216
prophecy against, 215, 216
religionists desolate, 315
"Sovereign Lord Jehovah," 215
times in Ezekiel's prophecy, 34
Spiritual Israel, 316-323
growth of "mountains," 318-323
Spiritual paradise, 387
Stream of life-giving water, ankle deep, 389, 390
deepening, 387-392
hip deep, 391
knee deep, 390, 391
swimming deep, 392
Sun worship, 154-159
Survivors of siege of Jerusalem, instructions to, 109-111
Sweetness of roll eaten by Ezekiel, meaning, 75, 76
"Sword" of aggressive warfare, against idol worshipers, 117-119
"Sword of Jehovah," 215-219
Symbolic sun worship, 156-159
"Symbol of jealousy," 145, 146
Syria, made to know, 28-30

T

Tammuz, identified, 150-153
Telling to others the series of visions, 210-212
Temple, Jehovah's name, 27
Temple vision, a guarantee, 386
Ten tribes, not lost, 340, 345
Thing not "continue," 221-223
390 days of bearing error, 97-99
meaning for Jerusalem, 105-111
"Thrusting out the shoot," 155
Translators, in Christendom omit name Jehovah, 325, 326
True religion, not affected by Christendom's end, 207-209
True worship, protection, 18-21
Twenty-five men, princes, 194-199
2,520 years, 57

U

United Nations, watchman, 73

V

Valley of Gog's Crowd, 374, 375
Visible representatives of heavenly government, 401-407
Vision of dry bones, fulfillment in 20th century, 341-344
Vision of Ezekiel, purpose, 74-76
Visions, telling others, 210-212

W

War equipment, disposal, 372-375
Watchman, accountable, 180, 181
typed for our day, 279-282
"Water of life," result to places not reached by, 396
Wheelwork and cherubs involved, described, 191-194
Where smashing begins, 167-171
Wicked one, spared if, 284, 285
Widemouthed cooking pot, city likened to, 195-199
siege pictured, 266-268
symbolic, 200
Wild beast, identified, 363
Witnesses, Israelites were, 22-25
Worship, true, protection, 18-21
Worshiping a sun, 154-159
Worship of creatures, 146-149
Worship of Tammuz, 150-153
World Powers, First (Egypt), 8
Second (Assyria), 30

Y

'You will die,' meaning, 87

Z

Zedekiah, rebel, 95, 96, 227, 228

The Mysterious Book of Revelation Explained!

Most mysteries are fiction. But the Bible book of Revelation tells of mysteries that deal with events of real life in our own day. It reveals that we are rapidly approaching the thrilling climax of God's purpose for our time, affecting every person on earth.

This fascinating Bible book centers around the greatest mystery of all time——the "Mystery of God"!

Would you like to know the meaning of Revelation's mysteries? This knowledge is available. You may now have a verse-by-verse explanation of all twenty-two chapters of Revelation. You can learn what the "Mystery of God" means to you. Read the following books:

"Then Is Finished the Mystery of God"
(Explaining Revelation chapters 1-13)

"Babylon the Great Has Fallen!" God's Kingdom Rules!
(Explaining Revelation chapters 14-22)

Obtain these two eye-opening hardbound volumes that explain the entire book of Revelation. Send only $1.25.

To order, see addresses on the last page.

Is the Bible Really the Word of God?

Have you ever been asked the question, "How can we be sure that the Bible is not just an ordinary book written by wise men of the past?" What answer could you offer? Equip yourself with many convincing proofs of the Bible's divine origin. Read the book **Is the Bible Really the Word of God?** Among its faith-building chapters are "Genesis Account of Creation—Fact or Fiction?" "Was There an Earth-wide Flood?" "The Bible and Ancient History—Do They Agree?" Hardbound, 192 pages, only 25c.

Did Man Get Here by Evolution or by Creation?

What about the teaching of evolution? Can you accept it and believe the Bible too? Why not read the book **Did Man Get Here by Evolution or by Creation?** It offers a reliable answer. Here are a few of its chapters: "Does Life Come from Nonliving Matter?" "Do Mutations Result in New Life Forms?" "Are Apelike Men Our Ancestors?" Pocket-size, 192 pages, generously illustrated, thoroughly documented, just 25c a copy.

The Truth That Leads to Eternal Life

What does the Bible itself actually teach? What hope does it offer us for the future? The book **The Truth That Leads to Eternal Life** tells you what the Bible is all about. It does so in a simple and reasonable manner. Next to the Bible itself it is the most widely distributed book in the Western world. It is only 25c.

Listening to the Great Teacher

How can you teach the Bible and its principles to your children? It is not easy to teach them to be kind, loving, unselfish, honest, peaceable, forgiving, morally upright and obedient. But now parents can have help in doing so from a new kind of book—**Listening to the Great Teacher.** It is designed for parents and children to read together. Delightfully illustrated, large print, easily understood, 192 pages, pocket-size, pink cover, 46 fascinating chapters. Only 25c.

To order, use the nearest address on the last page.

Enjoy Reading the Bible

Why not increase your enjoyment in reading the Bible? You can do this by obtaining the **New World Translation of the Holy Scriptures**. Its everyday language helps you to grasp information more readily. You can obtain this excellent translation in any of the following editions:

● **REGULAR:** Bound in green vinyl, with Appendix, concordance, 1,472 pages; size 7 ¼″ x 4 7/8″ x 1 ⅛″. Available in English, Spanish, Portuguese, Italian and Dutch. Only $1.

● **DELUXE:** Flexible black or maroon cover, pages gold-edged. Same features as regular edition. English only; $3.

● **LARGE-PRINT:** To make your reading of the Holy Scriptures more enjoyable, you may wish to have a Bible with larger type. This edition (revised 1971) has 1,376 pages. It measures 7 ½″ x 9 ½″ x 1 ½″. English only. Yours for $5.

The Kingdom Interlinear Translation of the Greek Scriptures

It is fascinating when you can discern the flavor of the original language in which the Christian Scriptures were written and to see what each expression means. This is possible because of this unique word-for-word translation of the Greek text. The left-hand column contains the original Greek text. Between the lines of the Greek text is found a word-for-word English translation. In the right-hand column appears the modern-language rendering of the **New World Translation**. This 1,184-page volume will be sent for $2.

Aid to Bible Understanding

Your enjoyment in reading and studying the Bible can be enhanced greatly by learning the background of people and places mentioned in the Bible. You can find this information in the 1,700-page volume **Aid to Bible Understanding**. This work has endeavored to consider every person, place, plant and creature mentioned in the Bible. Alphabetically arranged; published by the Watchtower Society in 1971. Charts and illustrations. $7 a copy.

To order, see addresses on the last page.

CHIEF OFFICE AND OFFICIAL ADDRESS OF
Watch Tower Bible & Tract Society of Pennsylvania
Watchtower Bible and Tract Society of New York, Inc.
International Bible Students Association
124 Columbia Heights, Brooklyn, New York 11201, U.S.A.

ADDRESSES OF BRANCH OFFICES:

ALASKA 99502: 2552 East 48th Ave., Anchorage. ARGENTINA: Calle Honduras 5646-48, Buenos Aires 14. AUSTRALIA: 11 Beresford Road, Strathfield, N.S.W. 2135. AUSTRIA: Gallgasse 44, A-1130 Vienna. BAHAMAS: Box N-1247, Nassau, N.P. BARBADOS, W.I.: Fontabelle Rd., Bridgetown. BELGIUM: rue d'Argile 60, B-1950 Kraainem. BOLIVIA: Casilla No. 1440, La Paz. BRAZIL: Rua Guaíra, 216, Bosque da Saúde, São Paulo 8, SP. BRITISH HONDURAS: Box 257, Belize. BURMA: P.O. Box 62, Rangoon. CANADA: 150 Bridgeland Ave., Toronto 390, Ontario. CENTRAL AFRICAN REPUBLIC: B.P. 662, Bangui. CEYLON: 7 Alfred House Rd., Colombo 3. CHILE: Casilla 261-V, Correo 21, Santiago. COLOMBIA: Apartado Aéreo 2587, Barranquilla. CONGO, REPUBLIC OF THE: B.P. 634, Kinshasa, Limete. CONGO REPUBLIC: B.P. 2.114, Brazzaville. COSTA RICA: Apartado 10043, San José. CUBA: Avenida 15 Núm. 4608, Almendares, Marianao, Havana. CYPRUS: P.O. Box 1590, Nicosia. DAHOMEY: B.P. 874, Cotonou. DENMARK: Kongevejen 207, 2830 Virum. DOMINICAN REPUBLIC: Avenida Francia 33, Santo Domingo. ECUADOR: Casilla 4512, Guayaquil. EL SALVADOR: Apartado 401, San Salvador. ENGLAND: Watch Tower House, The Ridgeway, London N.W. 7. FIJI: Box 23, Suva. FINLAND: Kuismatie 58, Tikkurila. FRANCE: 81, rue du Point du Jour, 92 - Boulogne-Billancourt. GERMANY (WESTERN): Postfach 13025, 62 Wiesbaden-Dotzheim. GHANA: Box 760, Accra. GREECE: No. 4 Kartali St., Athens 611. GUADELOUPE: B.P. 239, Pointe-à-Pitre. GUATEMALA: 11 Avenida 5-67, Guatemala 1. GUYANA: 50 Brickdam, Georgetown 1. HAITI: Post Box 185, Port-au-Prince. HAWAII 96814: 1228 Pensacola St., Honolulu. HONDURAS: Apartado 147, Tegucigalpa. HONG KONG: 312 Prince Edward Rd., Second Floor, Kowloon. ICELAND: P.O. Box 251, Reykjavik. INDIA: South Avenue, Santa Cruz, Bombay 54. INDONESIA: Djalan Batutjeper 25, Djakarta. IRELAND: 86 Lindsay Rd., Glasnevin, Dublin 9. ISRAEL: P.O. Box 44520, Haifa. ITALY: Via Monte Maloia 32, 00141 Rome. JAMAICA, W.I.: 41 Trafalgar Rd., Kingston 10. JAPAN: 5-5-8 Mita Minato-Ku, Tokyo, 108. KENYA: Box 7788, Nairobi. KOREA: Box 7 Sodaemun P.O., Seoul, 120. LEEWARD ISLANDS, W.I.: Box 119, St. Johns, Antigua. LIBERIA: P.O. Box 171, Monrovia. LUXEMBOURG: 15, rue de l'Egalite, Luxembourg-Bonnevoie, G.D. MAURITIUS: 106A Prince of Wales St., Rose Hill. MEXICO: Calzada Melchor Ocampo 71, Mexico 4, D.F. NETHERLANDS: Voorburgstraat 250, Amsterdam 17. NETHERLANDS ANTILLES: Oosterbeekstraat 11, Willemstad, Curaçao. NEWFOUNDLAND, CANADA: 239 Pennywell Rd., St. John's. NEW ZEALAND: 621 New North Rd., Auckland 3. NICARAGUA: Apartado 183, Managua, D.N. NIGERIA: P.O. Box 194, Yaba, Colony. NORWAY: Inkognitogaten 28 B., Oslo 2. OKINAWA, RYUKYU IS.: Higashi P.O. Box 2004, 91 Asato, Naha City. PAKISTAN: 8-E Habibullah Rd., Lahore. PANAMA: Apartado 1386, Panama 1. PAPUA: Box 113, Port Moresby. PARAGUAY: Casilla de Correo 482, Asunción. PERU: Gervasio Santillana 370, Miraflores, Lima. PHILIPPINE REPUBLIC: 186 Roosevelt Ave., San Francisco del Monte, Quezon City D-503. PUERTO RICO 00927: Calle Onix 23, Urb. Bucaré, Río Piedras. RHODESIA: P.O. Box 1462, Salisbury. SENEGAL: B.P. 3107, Dakar. SIERRA LEONE: Box 136, Freetown. SINGAPORE: 11 Jalan Sejarah, Singapore 11. SOUTH AFRICA: Private Bag 2, P.O. Elandsfontein, Transvaal. SURINAM: Wicherstraat 8-10, Box 49, Paramaribo. SWEDEN: Box 8, S-175 00 Jakobsberg. SWITZERLAND: Ulmenweg 45, Postfach, 3601 Thun. TAIWAN (REPUBLIC OF CHINA): 5 Lane 99, Yun-Ho St., Taipei, Taiwan 106. THAILAND: 69/1 Soi 2, Sukhumwit Rd., Bangkok 11. TOGO REPUBLIC: B.P. 1237, Lomé. TRINIDAD, W.I.: 21 Taylor St., Woodbrook, Port of Spain. UNITED STATES OF AMERICA: 117 Adams St., Brooklyn, N.Y. 11201. URUGUAY: Francisco Bauzá 3372, Montevideo. VENEZUELA: Avda. Honduras, Quinta Luz, Urb. Las Acacias, Caracas, D.F. ZAMBIA: Box 1598, Kitwe.

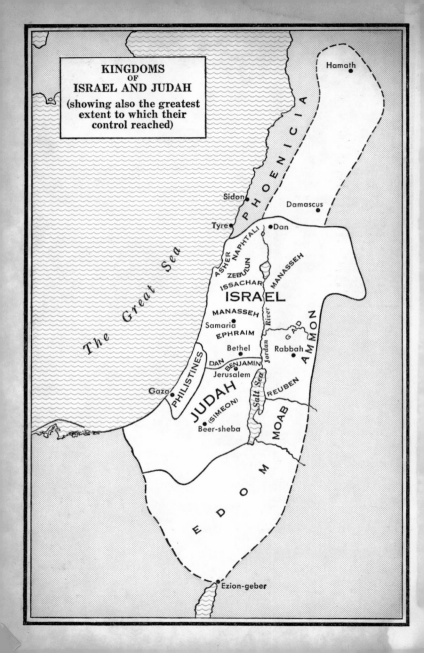

KINGDOMS
OF
ISRAEL AND JUDAH

(showing also the greatest
extent to which their
control reached)